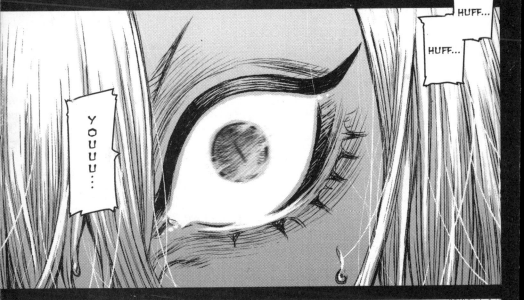

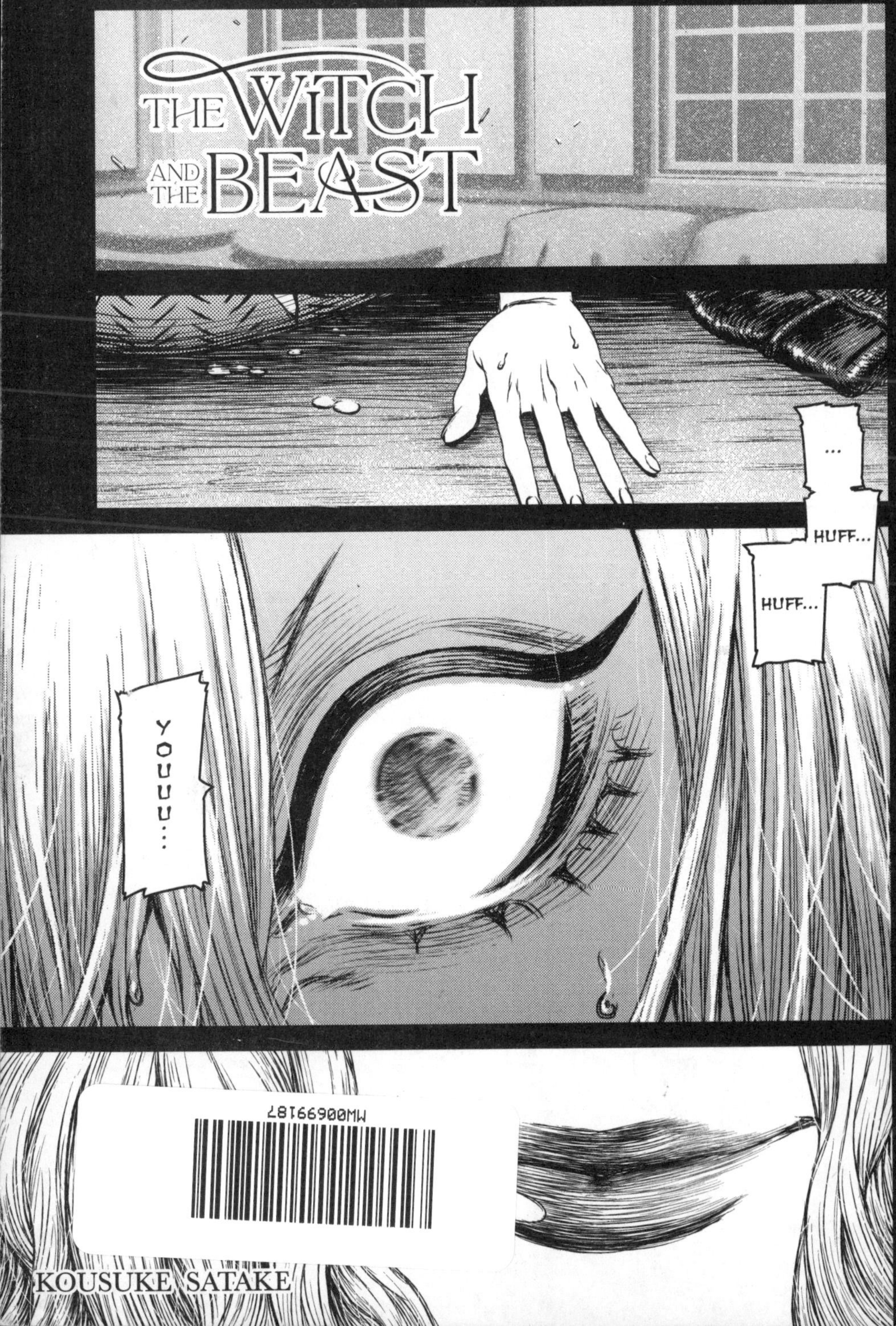

...

HUFF...

HUFF...

YOUUU...

KOUSUKE SATAKE

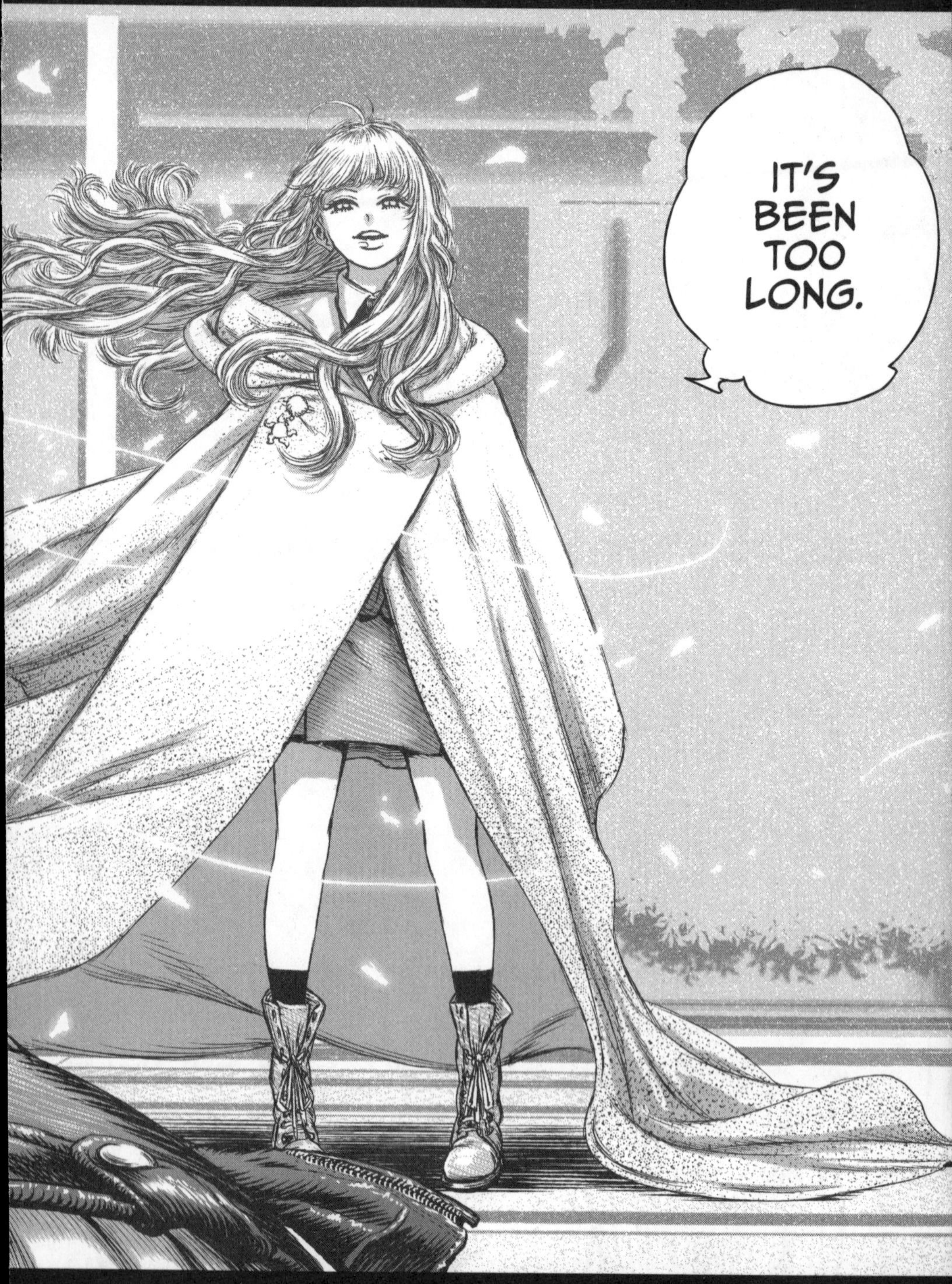
IT'S BEEN TOO LONG.

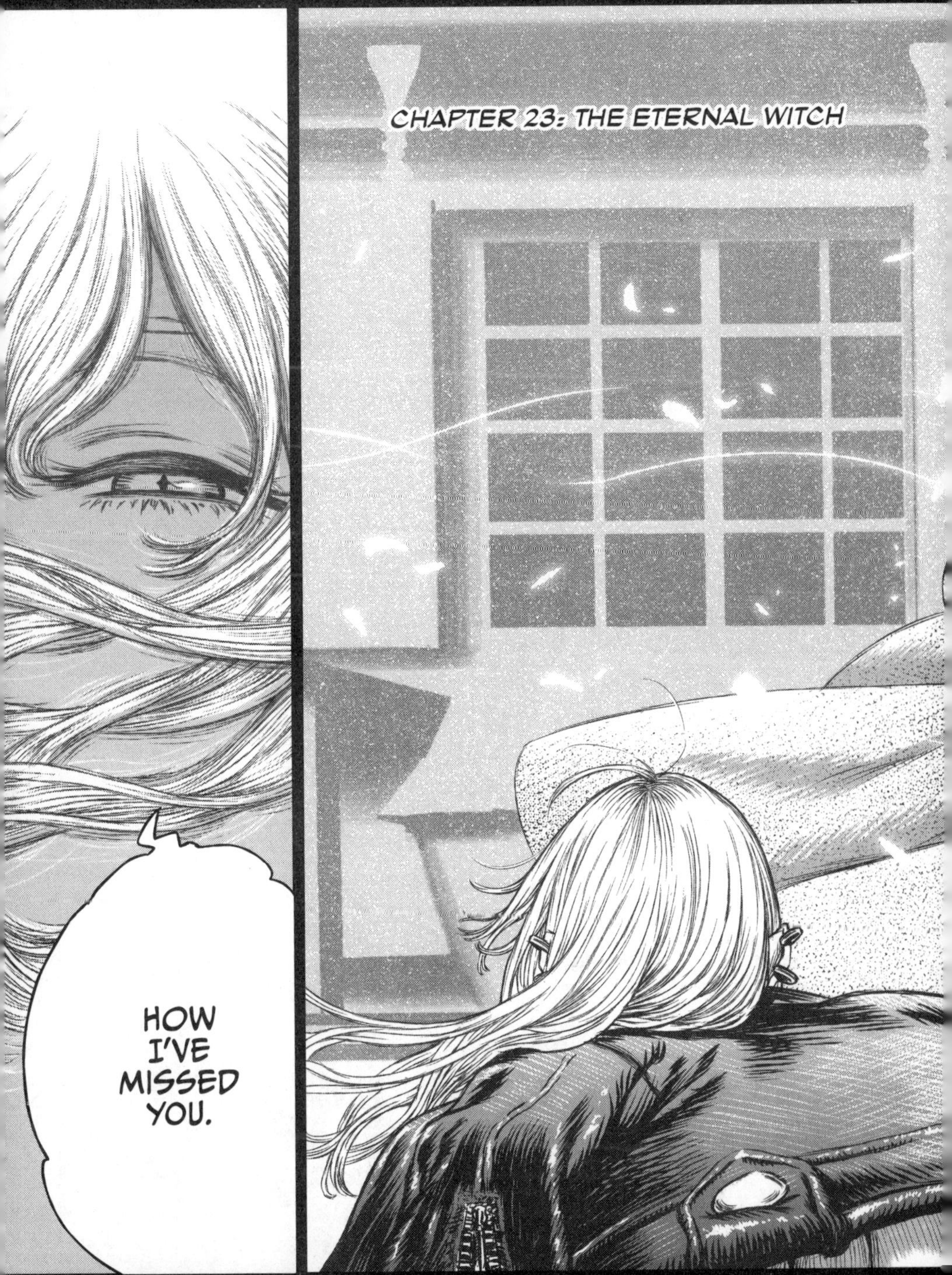
CHAPTER 23: THE ETERNAL WITCH
HOW I'VE MISSED YOU.

...

...

IF YOU'RE ABLE TO MAINTAIN YOUR SANITY HERE...

...THEN THAT *CLOAK* MUST BE NO DIFFERENT FROM MINE.

AND HERE I THOUGHT IT WAS THE ONLY ONE OF ITS KIND...

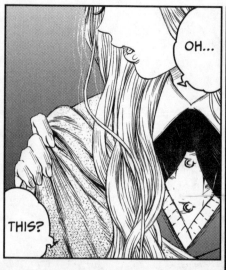

OH...

THIS?

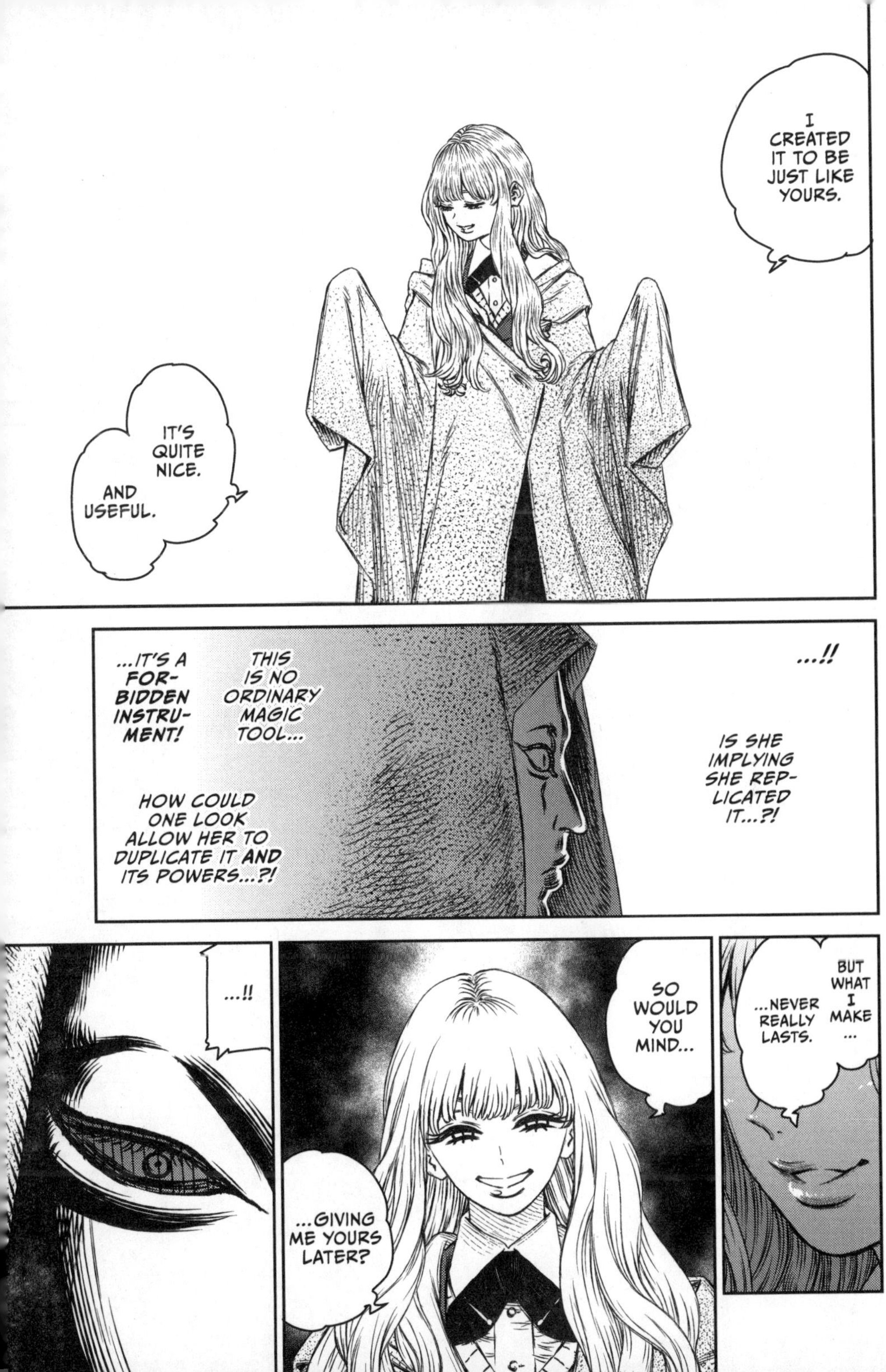
I CREATED IT TO BE JUST LIKE YOURS.
IT'S QUITE NICE.
AND USEFUL.
...!!
IS SHE IMPLYING SHE REPLICATED IT...?!
THIS IS NO ORDINARY MAGIC TOOL...
...IT'S A FORBIDDEN INSTRUMENT!
HOW COULD ONE LOOK ALLOW HER TO DUPLICATE IT AND ITS POWERS...?!
BUT WHAT I MAKE...
...NEVER REALLY LASTS.
SO WOULD YOU MIND...
...GIVING ME YOURS LATER?
...!!

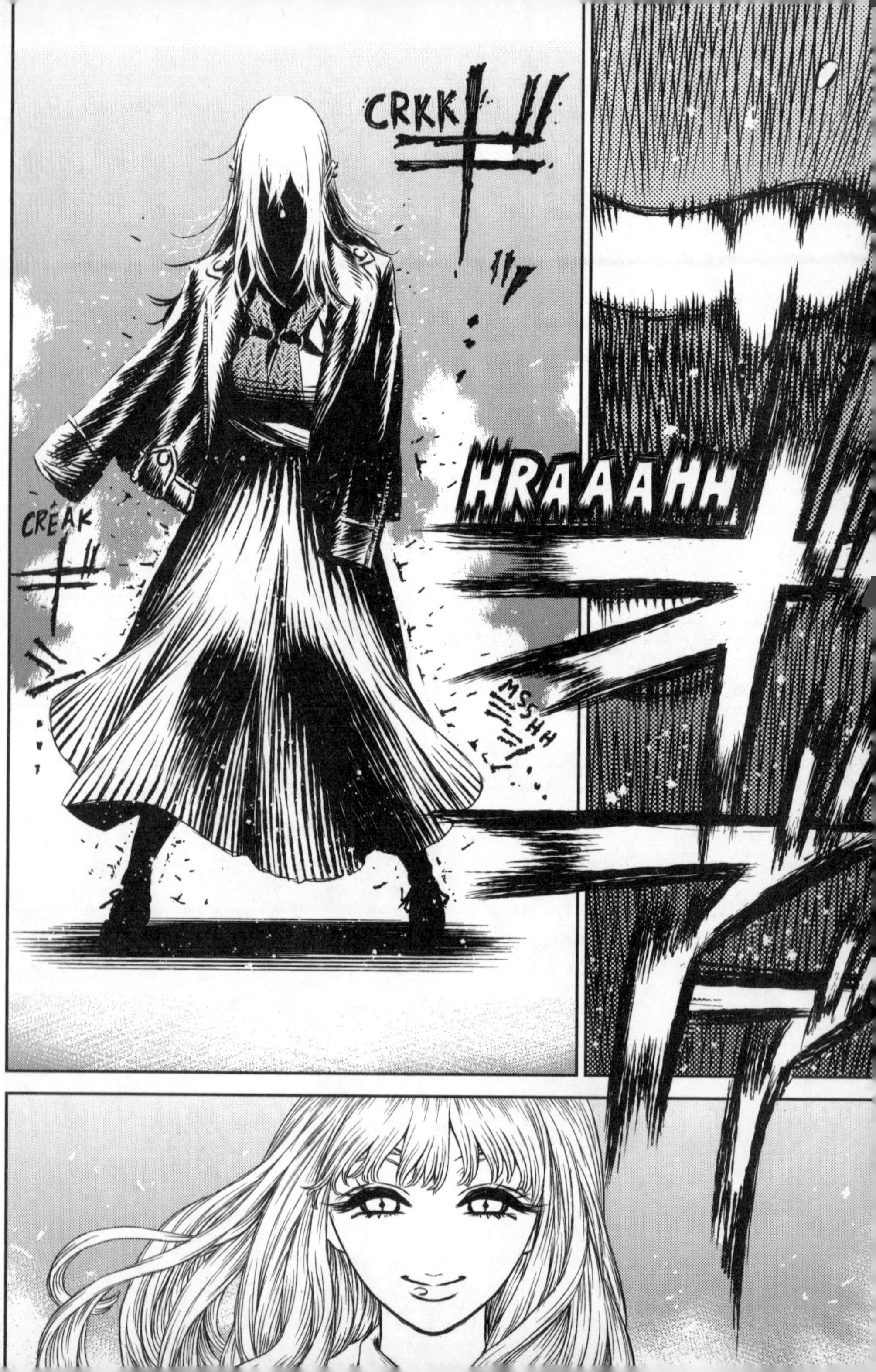
HRAAAHH
CRKK
CREAK
MSSHH

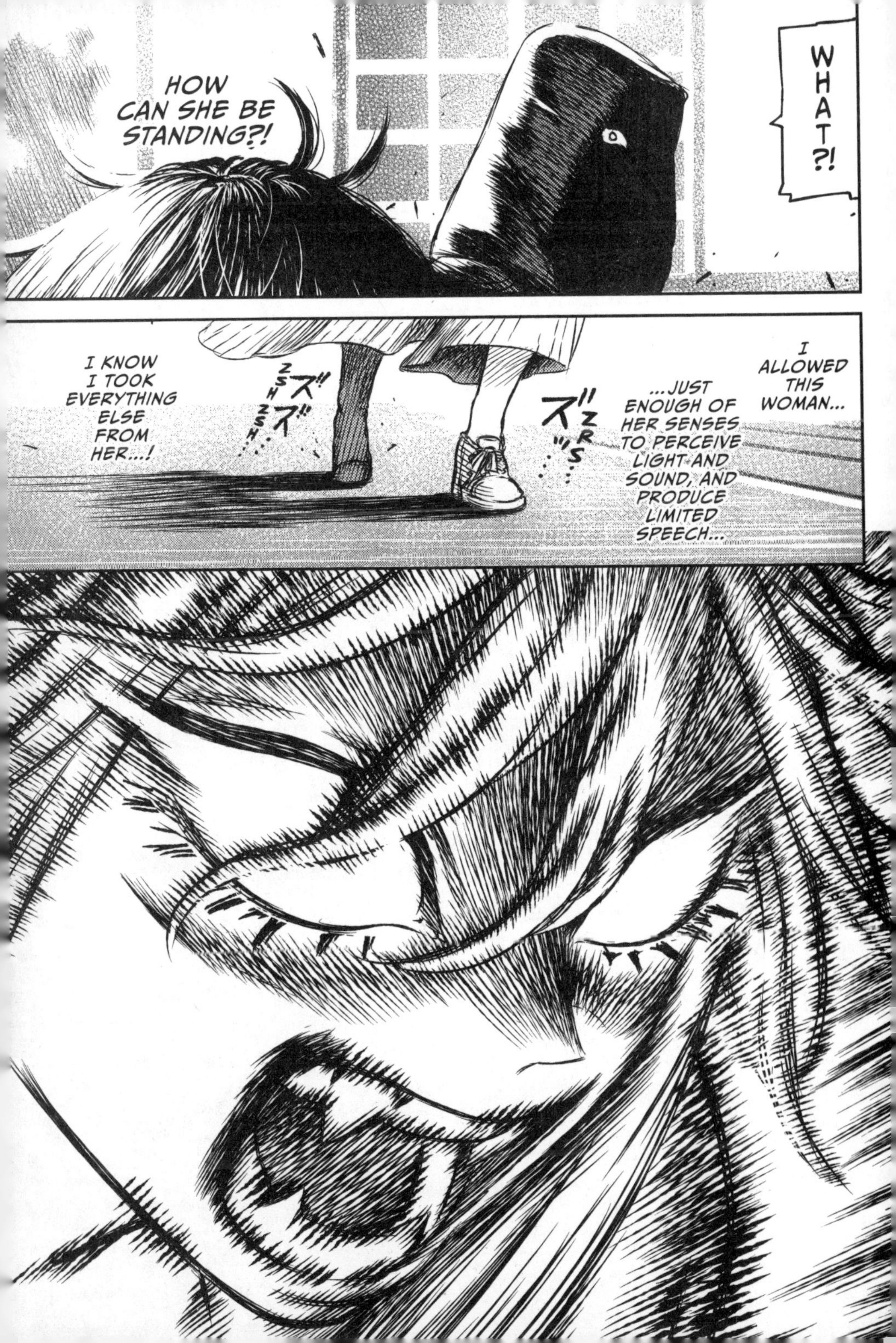
WHAT?!
HOW CAN SHE BE STANDING?!
I ALLOWED THIS WOMAN...
...JUST ENOUGH OF HER SENSES TO PERCEIVE LIGHT AND SOUND, AND PRODUCE LIMITED SPEECH...
ズ" ZRS
ズ"ズ" ZSH ZSH
I KNOW I TOOK EVERYTHING ELSE FROM HER...!

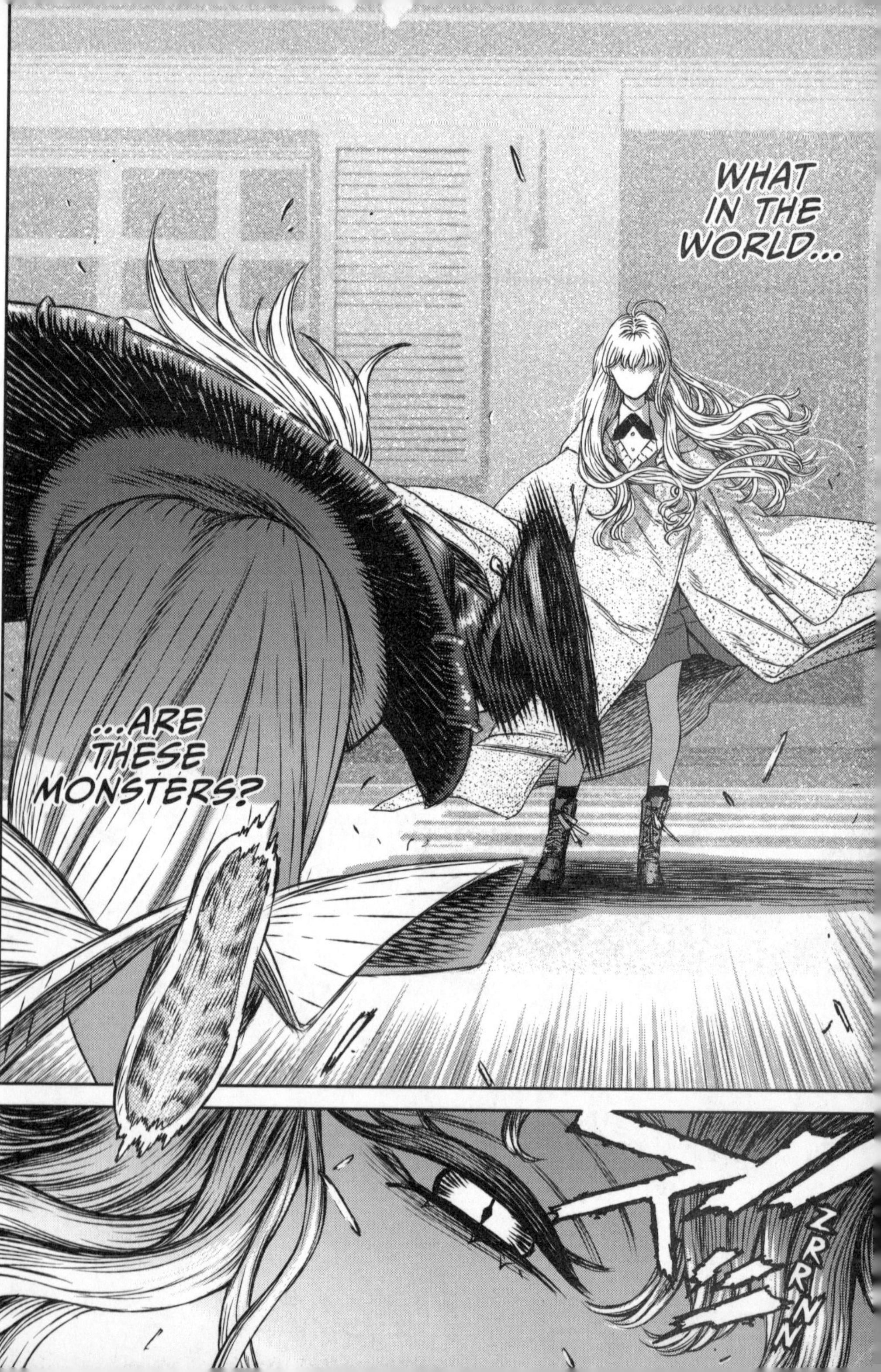
WHAT IN THE WORLD...
...ARE THESE MONSTERS?
ZRRINN

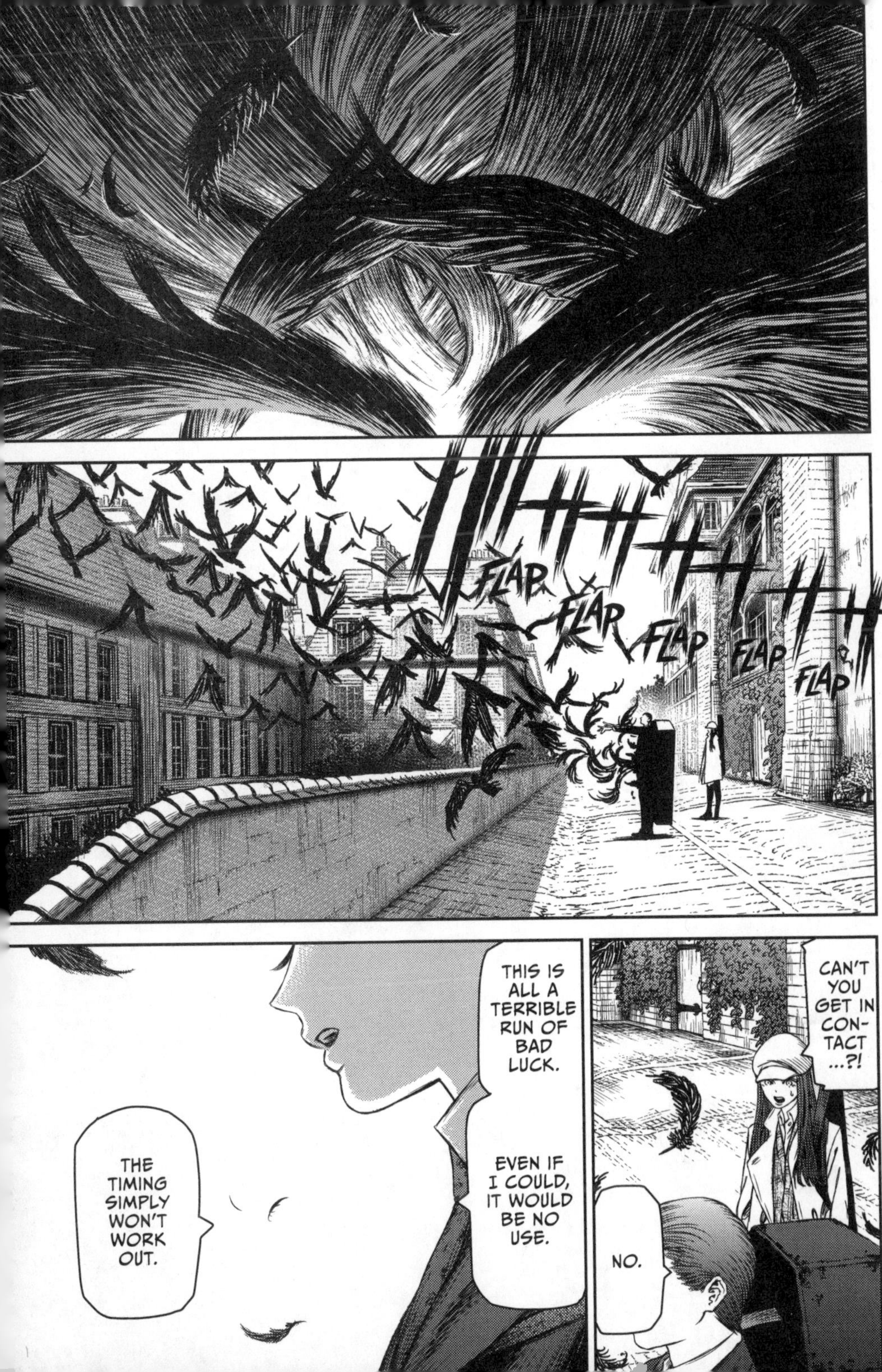
FLAP
FLAP
FLAP
FLAP
FLAP
CAN'T YOU GET IN CON-TACT ...?!
NO.
THIS IS ALL A TERRIBLE RUN OF BAD LUCK.
EVEN IF I COULD, IT WOULD BE NO USE.
THE TIMING SIMPLY WON'T WORK OUT.

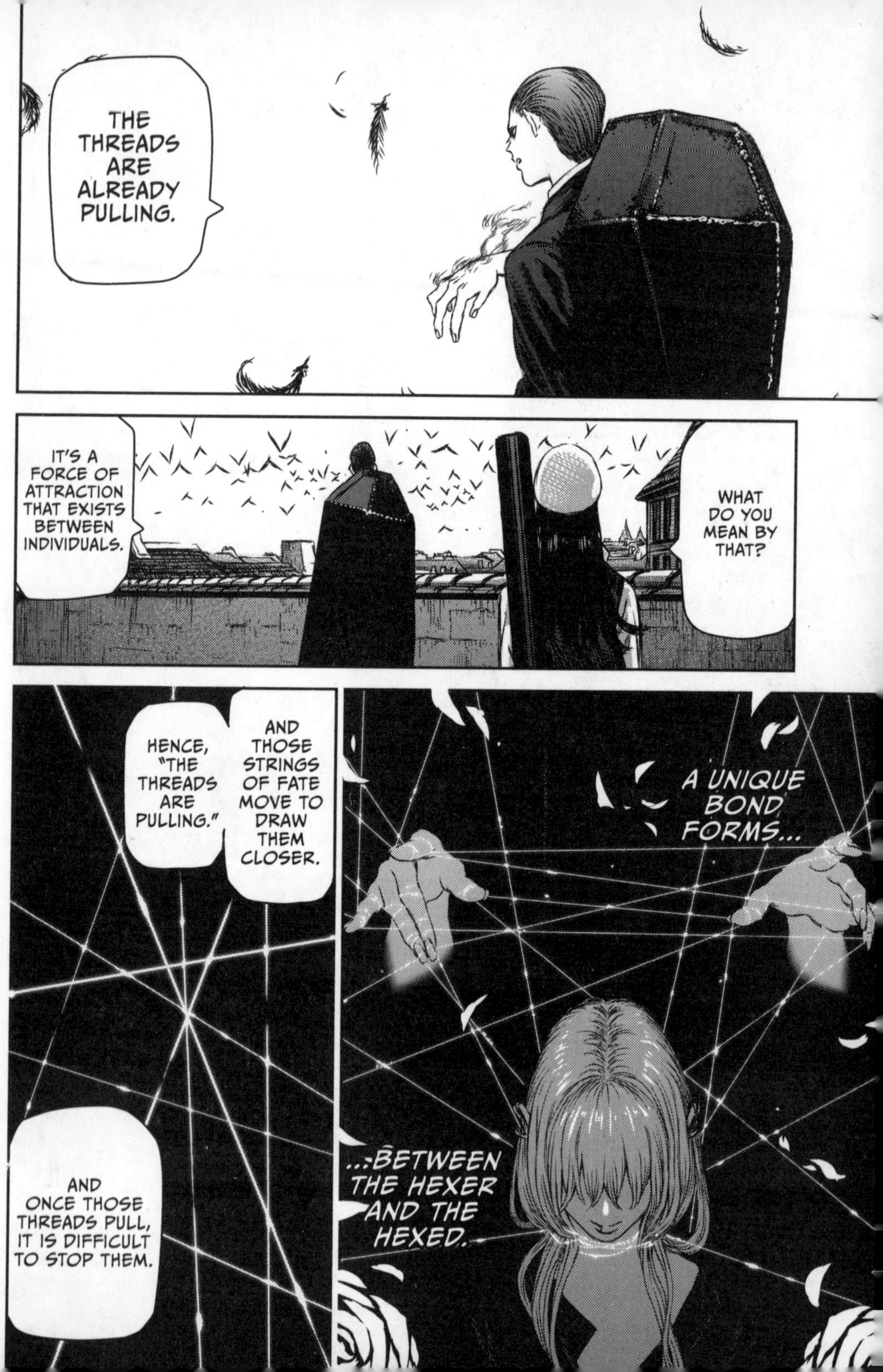
THE THREADS ARE ALREADY PULLING.
WHAT DO YOU MEAN BY THAT?
IT'S A FORCE OF ATTRACTION THAT EXISTS BETWEEN INDIVIDUALS.
A UNIQUE BOND FORMS...
...BETWEEN THE HEXER AND THE HEXED.
AND THOSE STRINGS OF FATE MOVE TO DRAW THEM CLOSER.
HENCE, "THE THREADS ARE PULLING."
AND ONCE THOSE THREADS PULL, IT IS DIFFICULT TO STOP THEM.

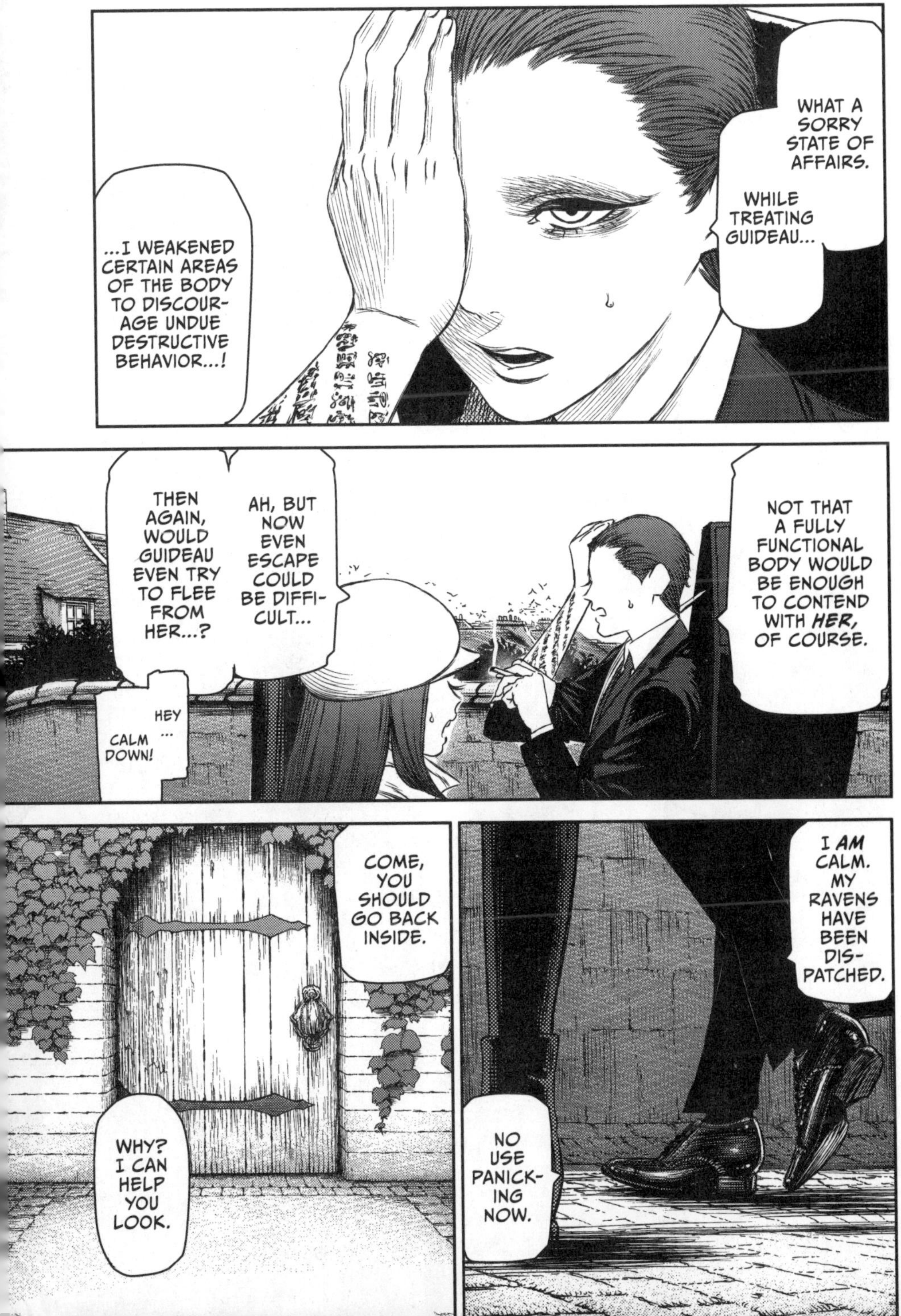
WHAT A SORRY STATE OF AFFAIRS.
WHILE TREATING GUIDEAU...
...I WEAKENED CERTAIN AREAS OF THE BODY TO DISCOURAGE UNDUE DESTRUCTIVE BEHAVIOR...!
NOT THAT A FULLY FUNCTIONAL BODY WOULD BE ENOUGH TO CONTEND WITH *HER*, OF COURSE.
AH, BUT NOW EVEN ESCAPE COULD BE DIFFICULT...
THEN AGAIN, WOULD GUIDEAU EVEN TRY TO FLEE FROM HER...?
HEY... CALM DOWN!
I *AM* CALM. MY RAVENS HAVE BEEN DISPATCHED.
NO USE PANICKING NOW.
COME, YOU SHOULD GO BACK INSIDE.
WHY? I CAN HELP YOU LOOK.

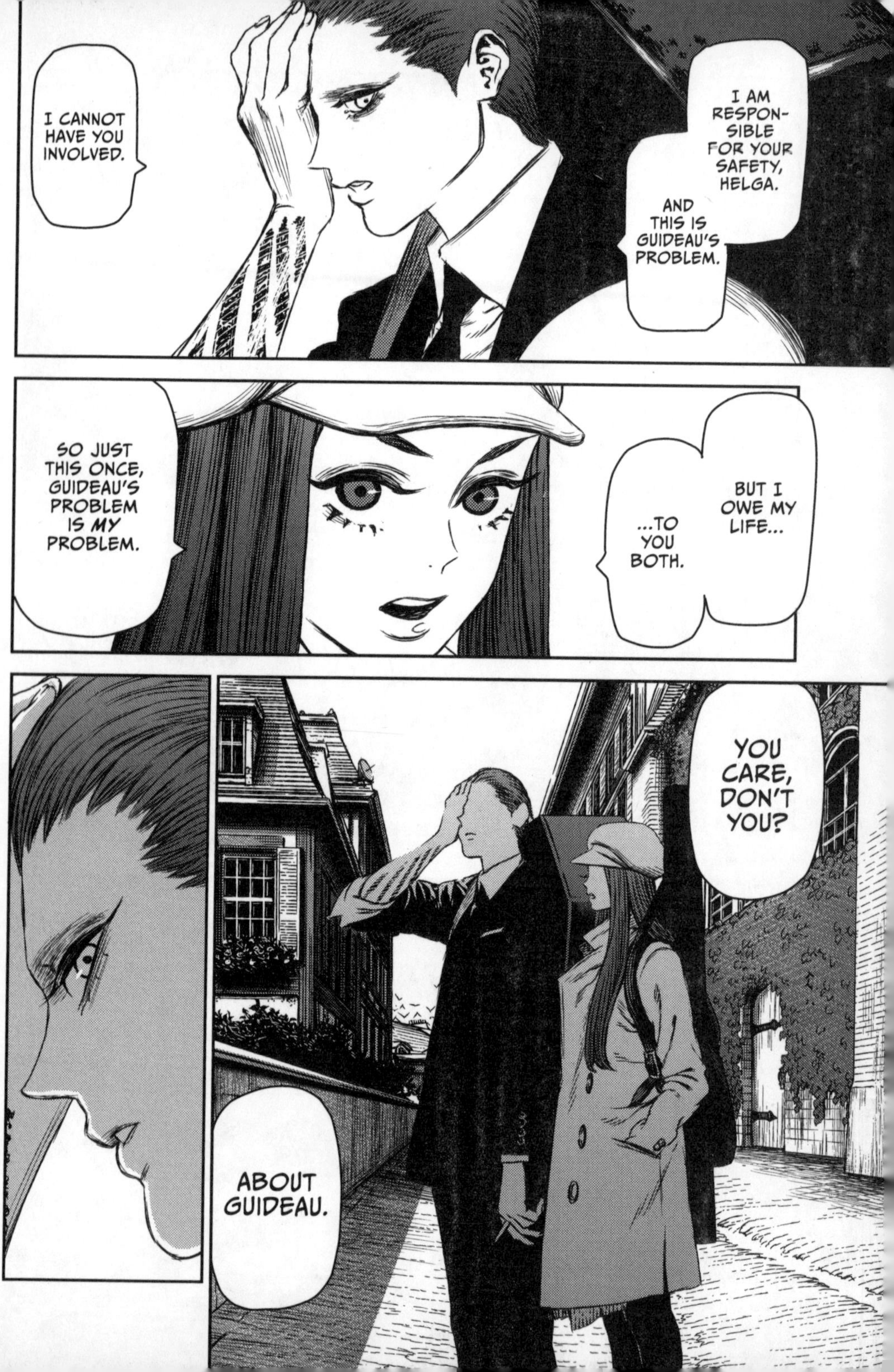
I AM RESPON-SIBLE FOR YOUR SAFETY, HELGA.
AND THIS IS GUIDEAU'S PROBLEM.
I CANNOT HAVE YOU INVOLVED.
BUT I OWE MY LIFE...
...TO YOU BOTH.
SO JUST THIS ONCE, GUIDEAU'S PROBLEM IS *MY* PROBLEM.
YOU CARE, DON'T YOU?
ABOUT GUIDEAU.

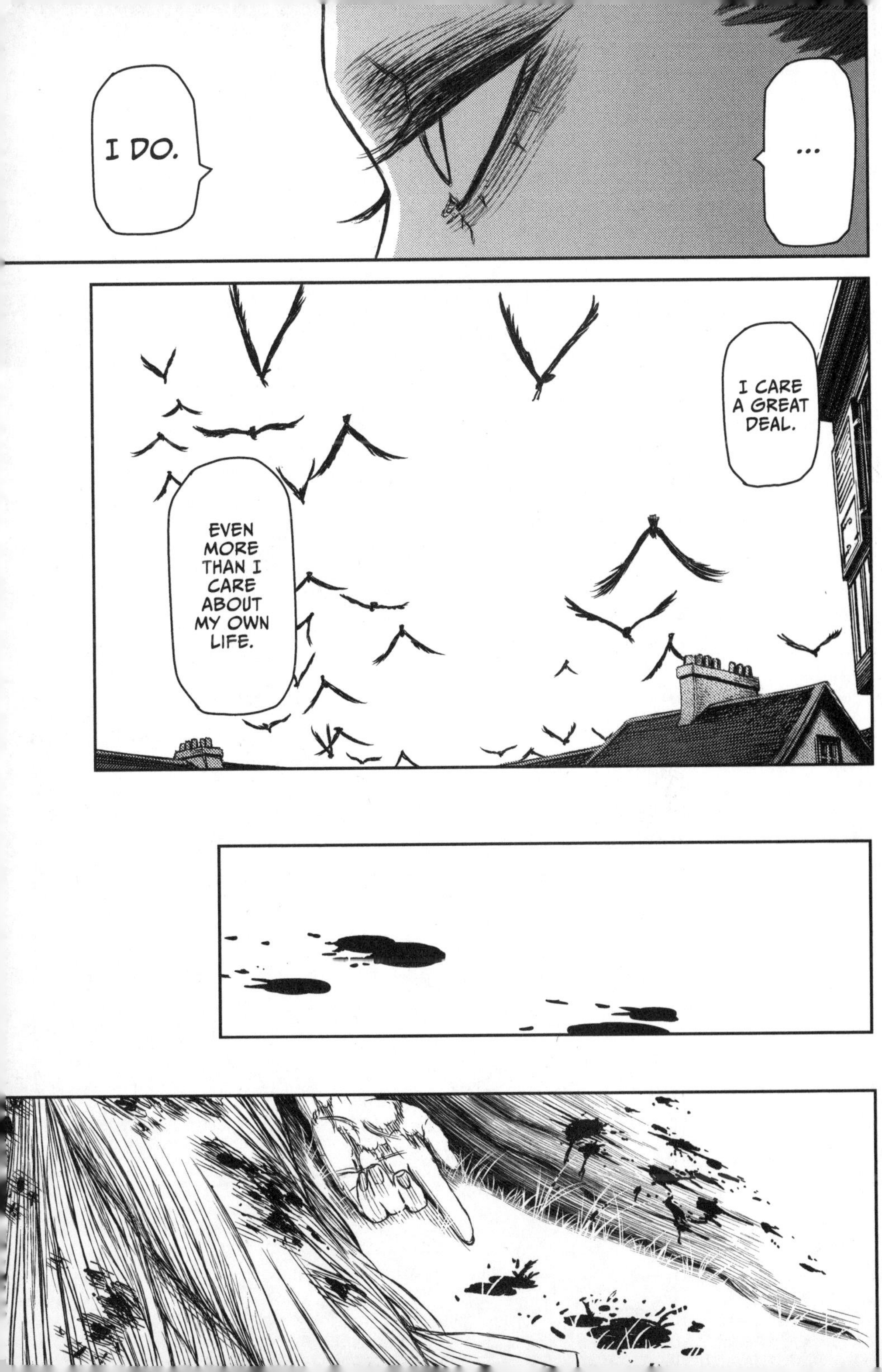
...
I DO.
I CARE A GREAT DEAL.
EVEN MORE THAN I CARE ABOUT MY OWN LIFE.

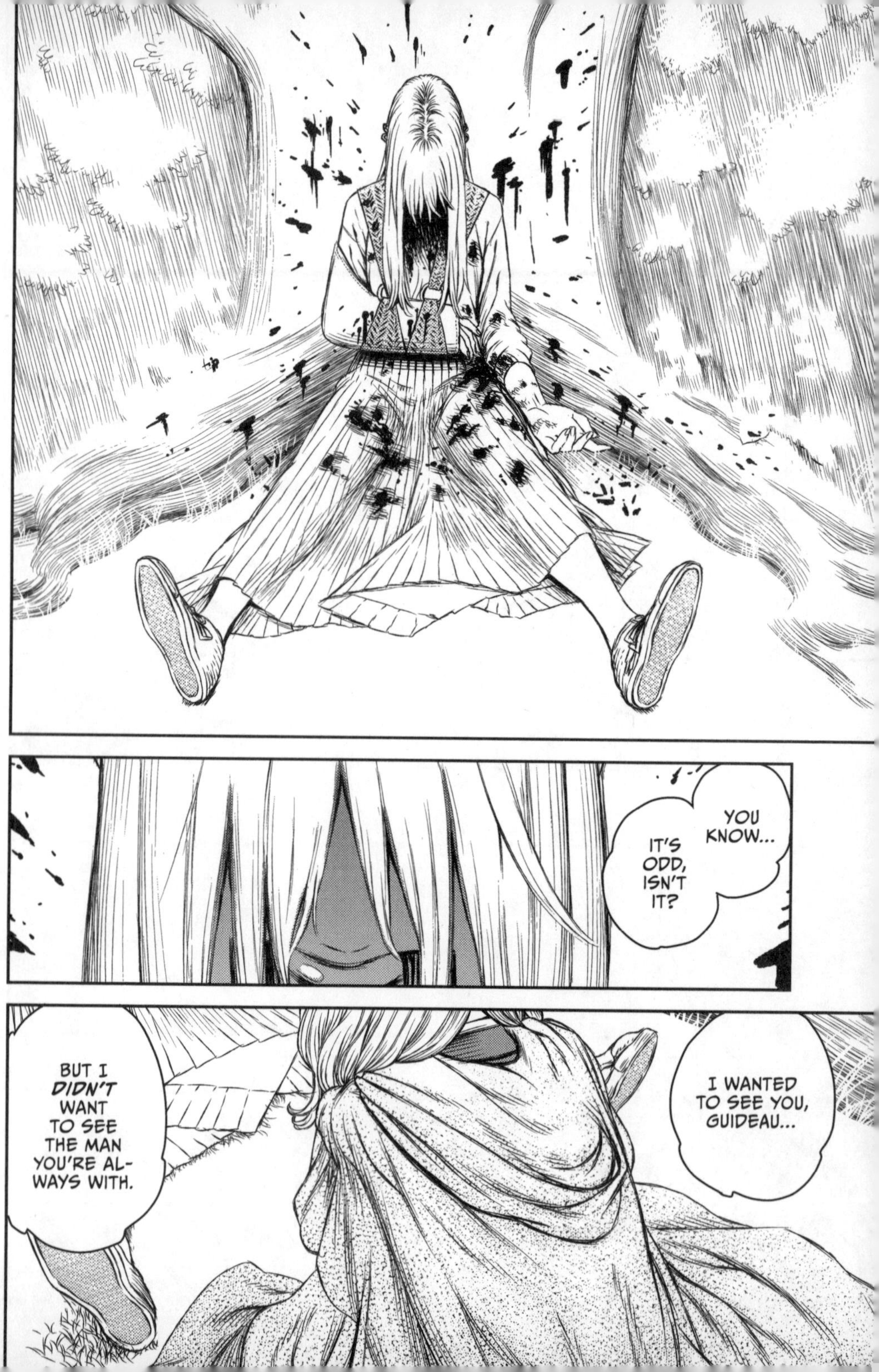
YOU KNOW...
IT'S ODD, ISN'T IT?
I WANTED TO SEE YOU, GUIDEAU...
BUT I *DIDN'T* WANT TO SEE THE MAN YOU'RE AL-WAYS WITH.

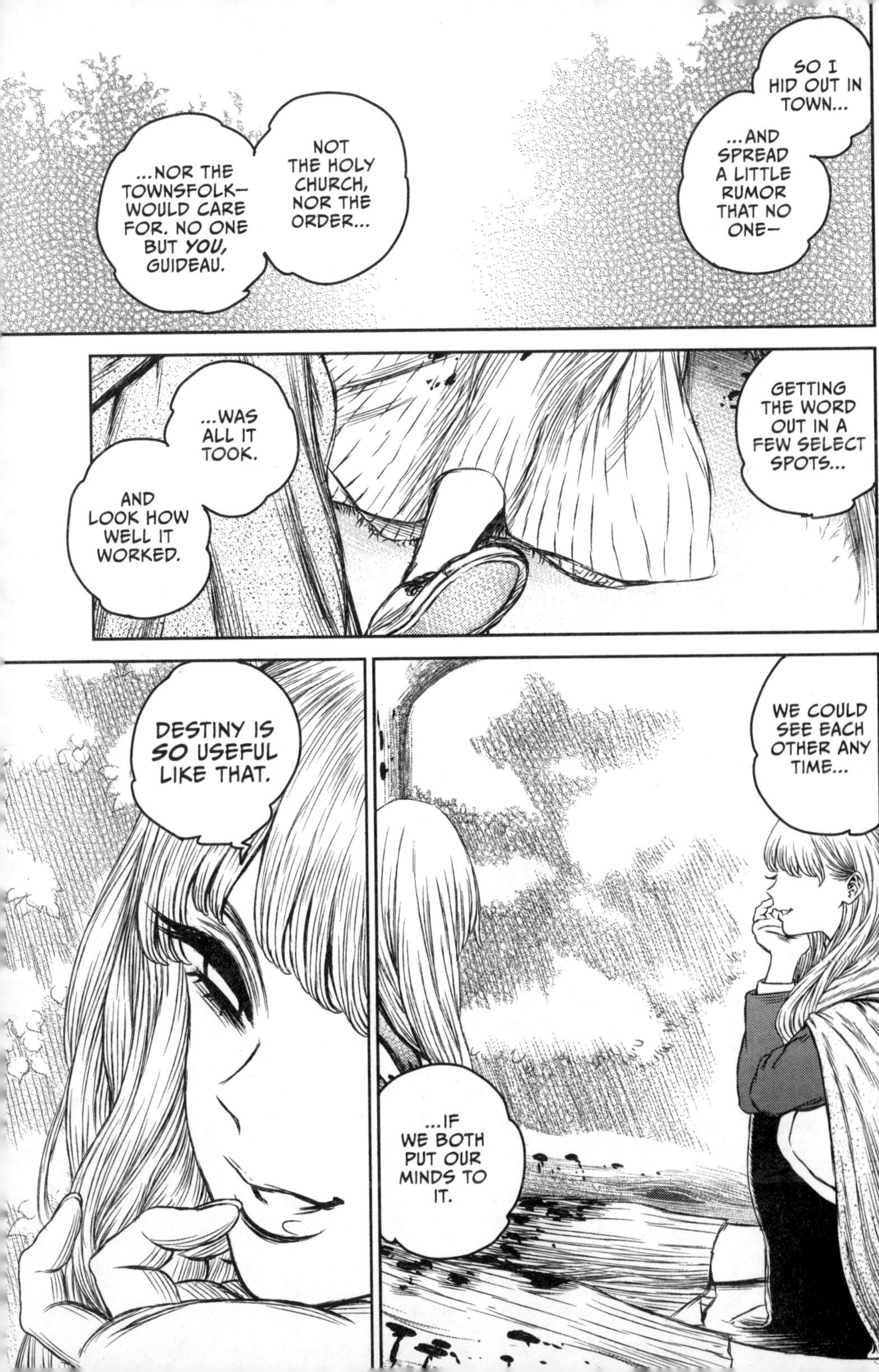
SO I HID OUT IN TOWN...
...AND SPREAD A LITTLE RUMOR THAT NO ONE—
NOT THE HOLY CHURCH, NOR THE ORDER...
...NOR THE TOWNSFOLK—WOULD CARE FOR. NO ONE BUT *YOU*, GUIDEAU.
GETTING THE WORD OUT IN A FEW SELECT SPOTS...
...WAS ALL IT TOOK.
AND LOOK HOW WELL IT WORKED.
WE COULD SEE EACH OTHER ANY TIME...
...IF WE BOTH PUT OUR MINDS TO IT.
DESTINY IS *SO* USEFUL LIKE THAT.

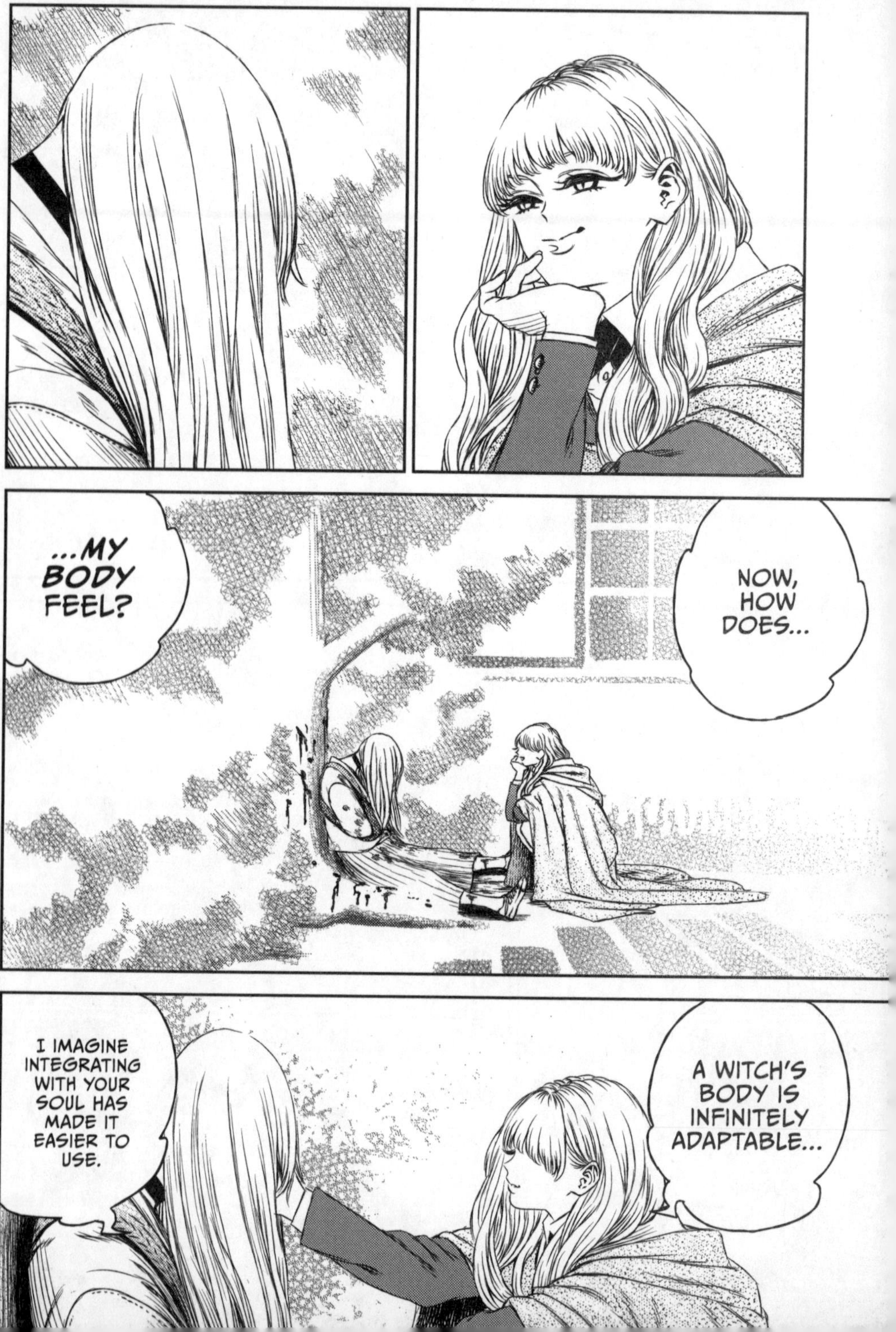
NOW, HOW DOES...
...MY BODY FEEL?
A WITCH'S BODY IS INFINITELY ADAPTABLE...
I IMAGINE INTEGRATING WITH YOUR SOUL HAS MADE IT EASIER TO USE.

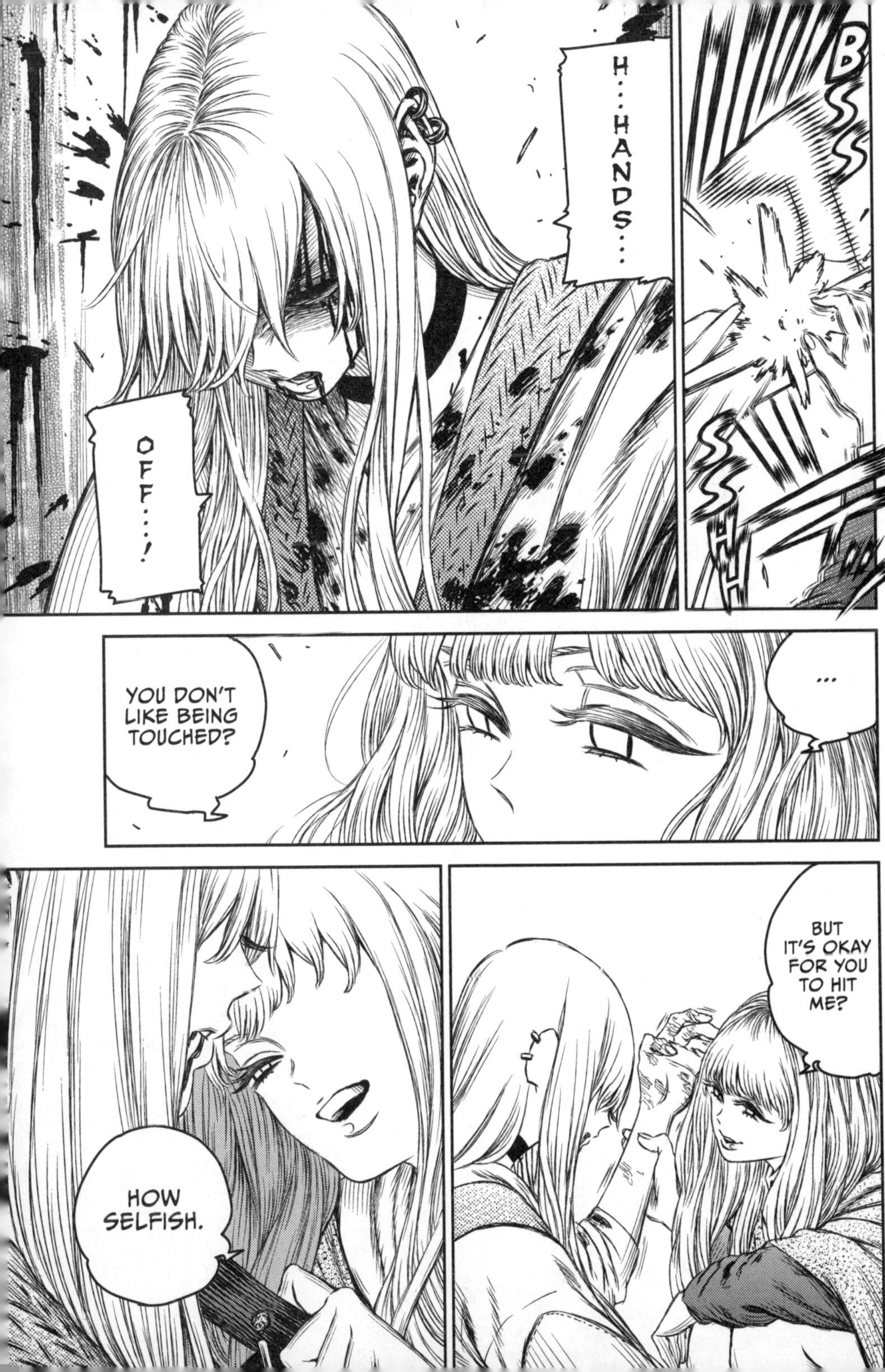
BSSS
SSHH
H...HANDS...
OFF...!
...
YOU DON'T LIKE BEING TOUCHED?
BUT IT'S OKAY FOR YOU TO HIT ME?
HOW SELFISH.

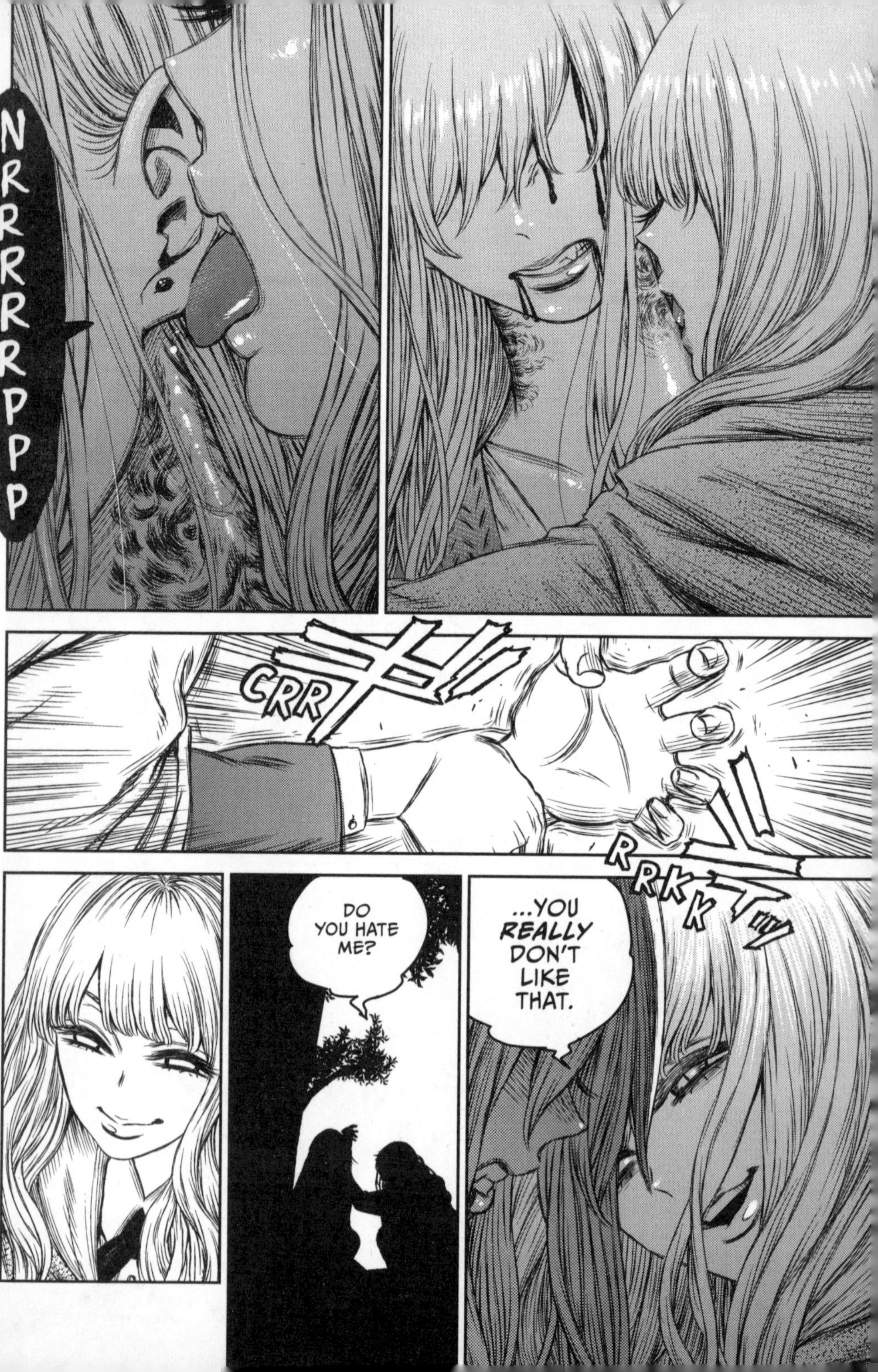
NRRRRRPPP
CRR
RRKK
...YOU REALLY DON'T LIKE THAT.
DO YOU HATE ME?

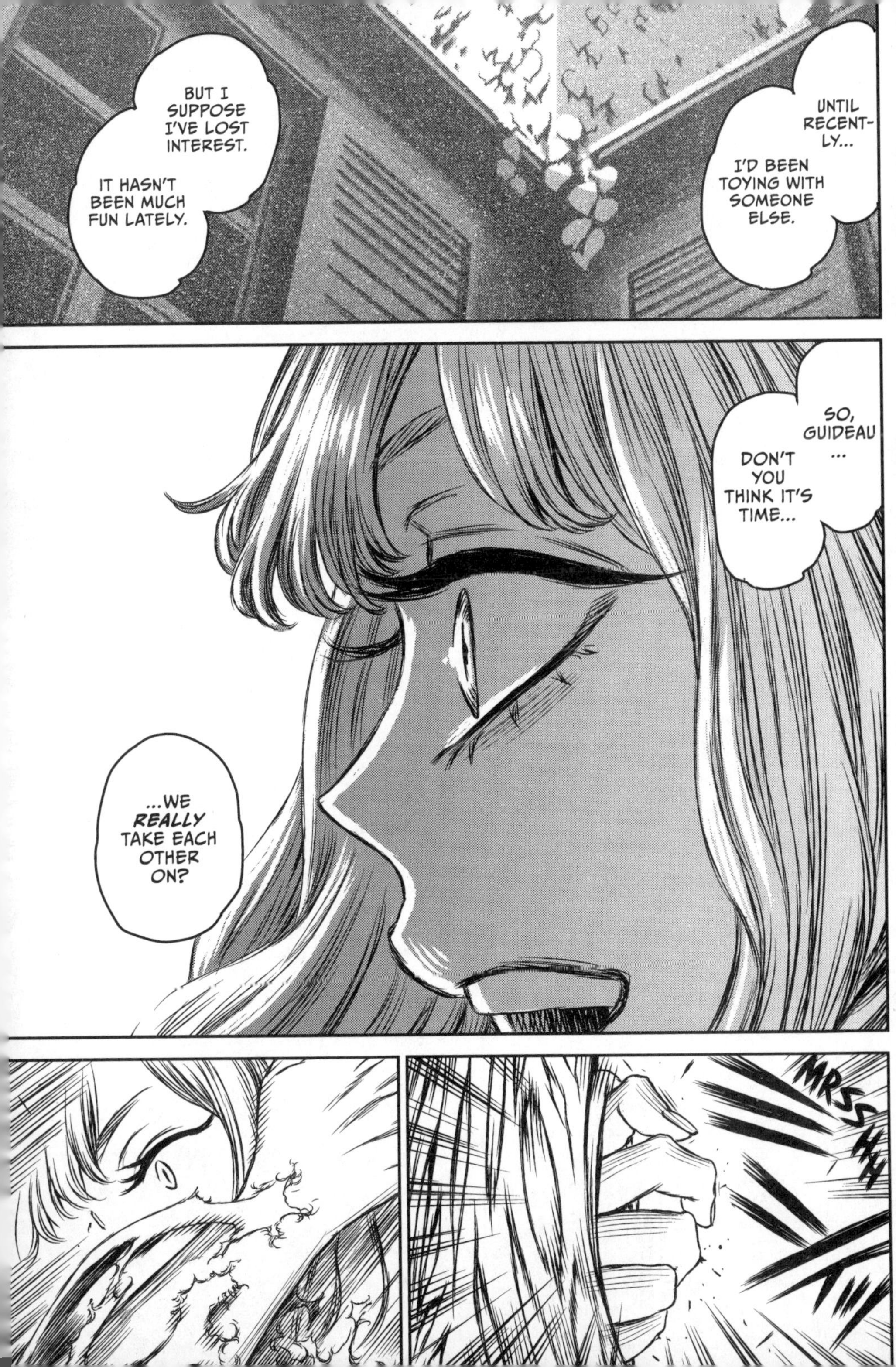
UNTIL RECENTLY... I'D BEEN TOYING WITH SOMEONE ELSE.
BUT I SUPPOSE I'VE LOST INTEREST. IT HASN'T BEEN MUCH FUN LATELY.
SO, GUIDEAU... DON'T YOU THINK IT'S TIME...
...WE *REALLY* TAKE EACH OTHER ON?
MRSSHH

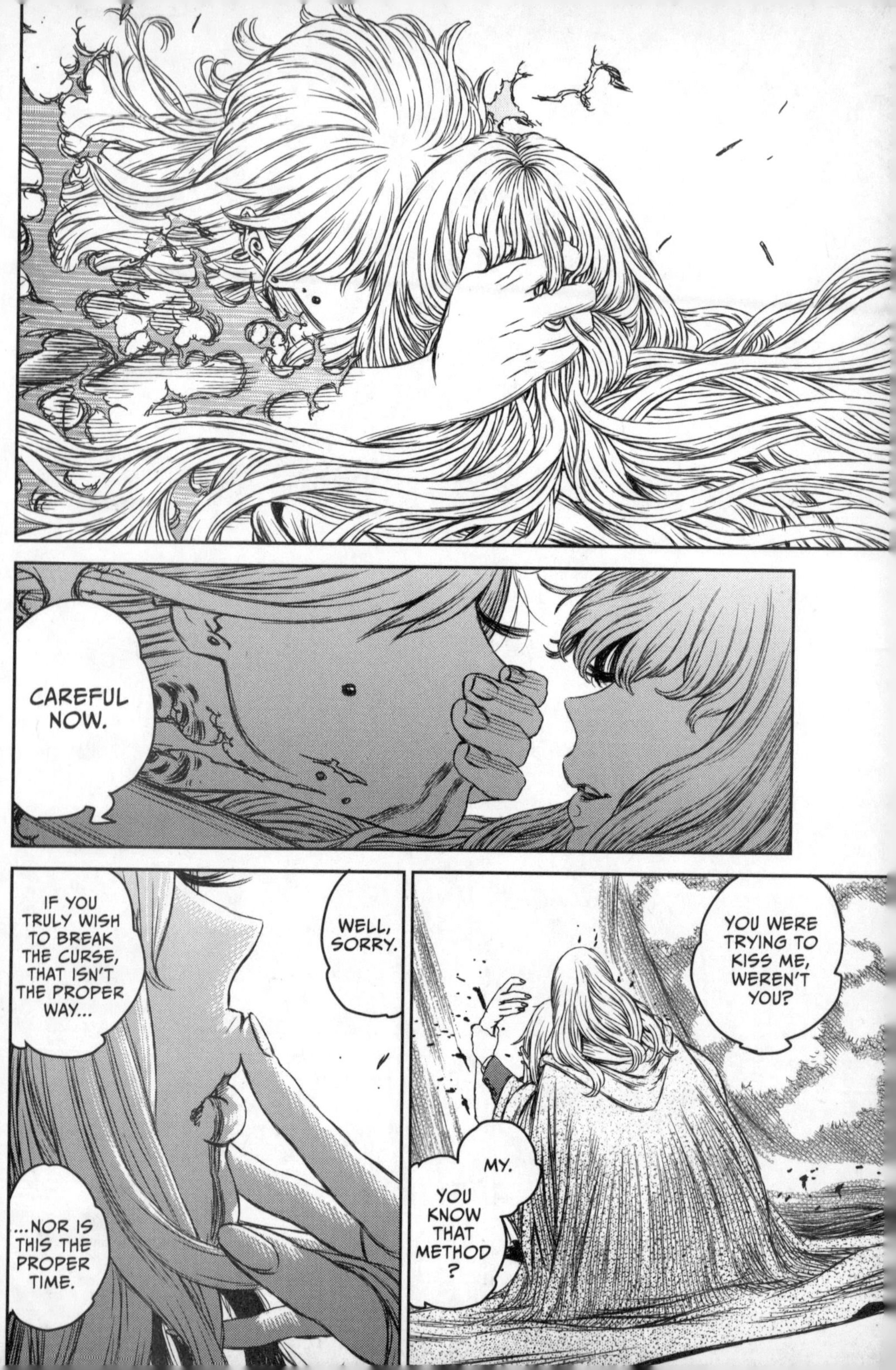
CAREFUL NOW.
YOU WERE TRYING TO KISS ME, WEREN'T YOU?
MY. YOU KNOW THAT METHOD?
WELL, SORRY.
IF YOU TRULY WISH TO BREAK THE CURSE, THAT ISN'T THE PROPER WAY...
...NOR IS THIS THE PROPER TIME.

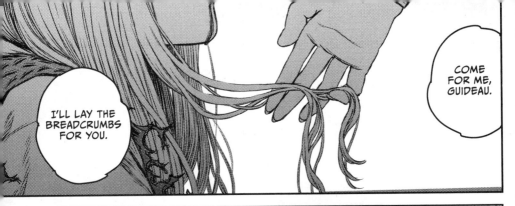

COME FOR ME, GUIDEAU.
I'LL LAY THE BREADCRUMBS FOR YOU.
IF YOU CAN FOLLOW THEM ALL TO ME...
...THEN I'LL DO MY PART AS WELL.
I'VE FORGOTTEN HOW MANY DECADES IT'S BEEN...
...BUT LET'S CONTINUE WHAT WE BEGAN THAT DAY.

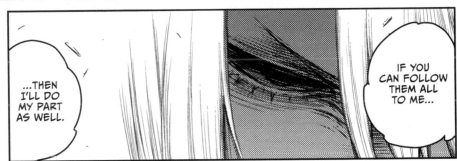

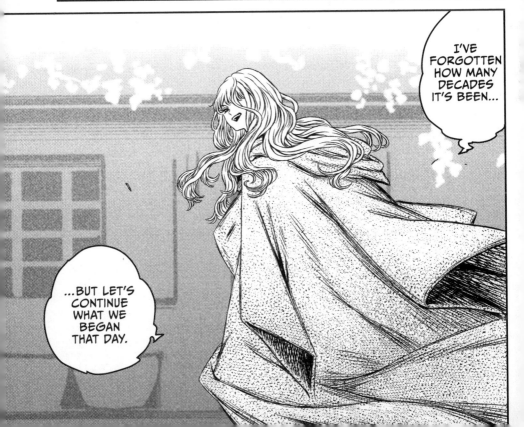

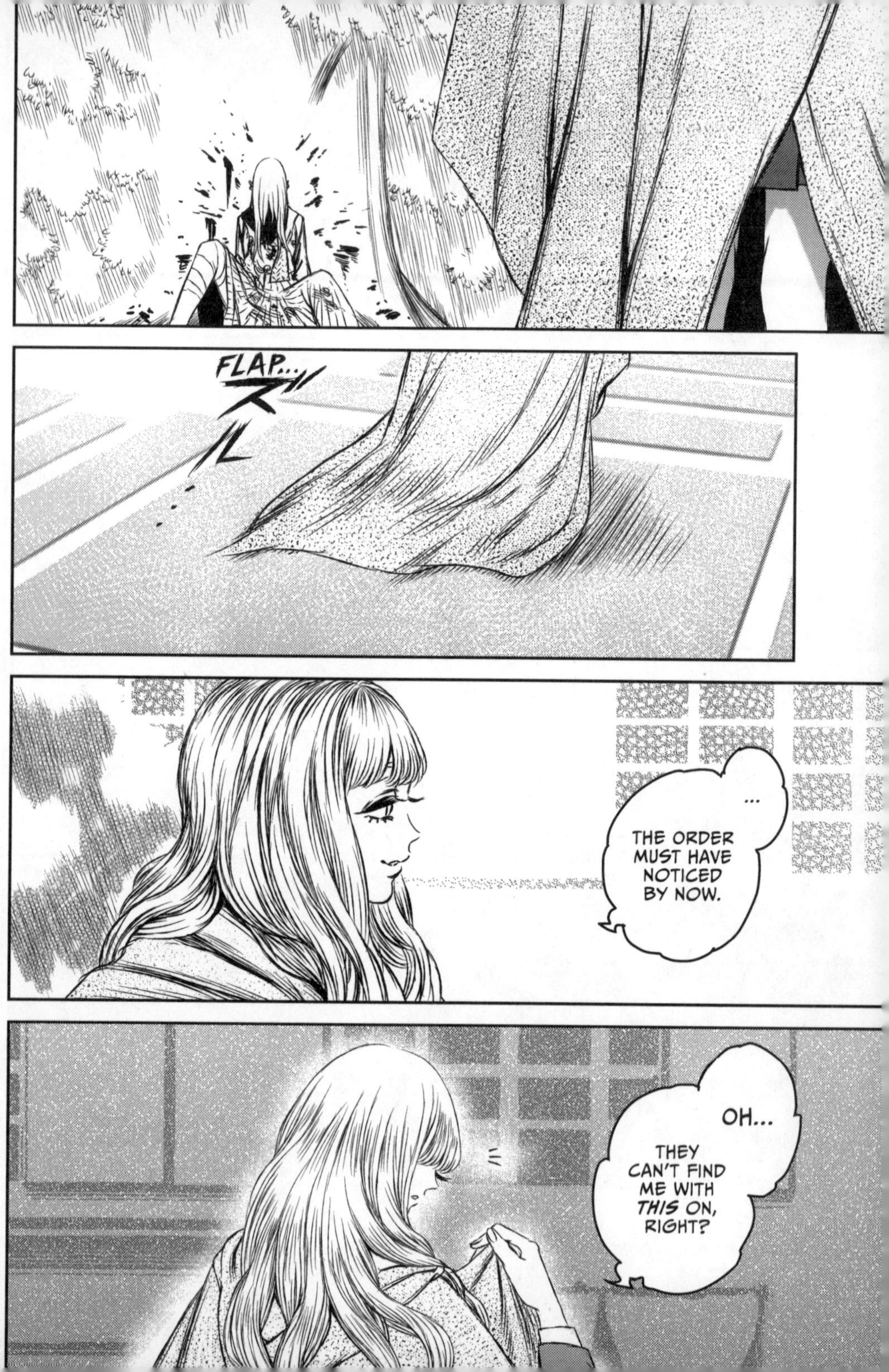
FLAP...
ズル
...
THE ORDER MUST HAVE NOTICED BY NOW.
OH...
THEY CAN'T FIND ME WITH *THIS* ON, RIGHT?

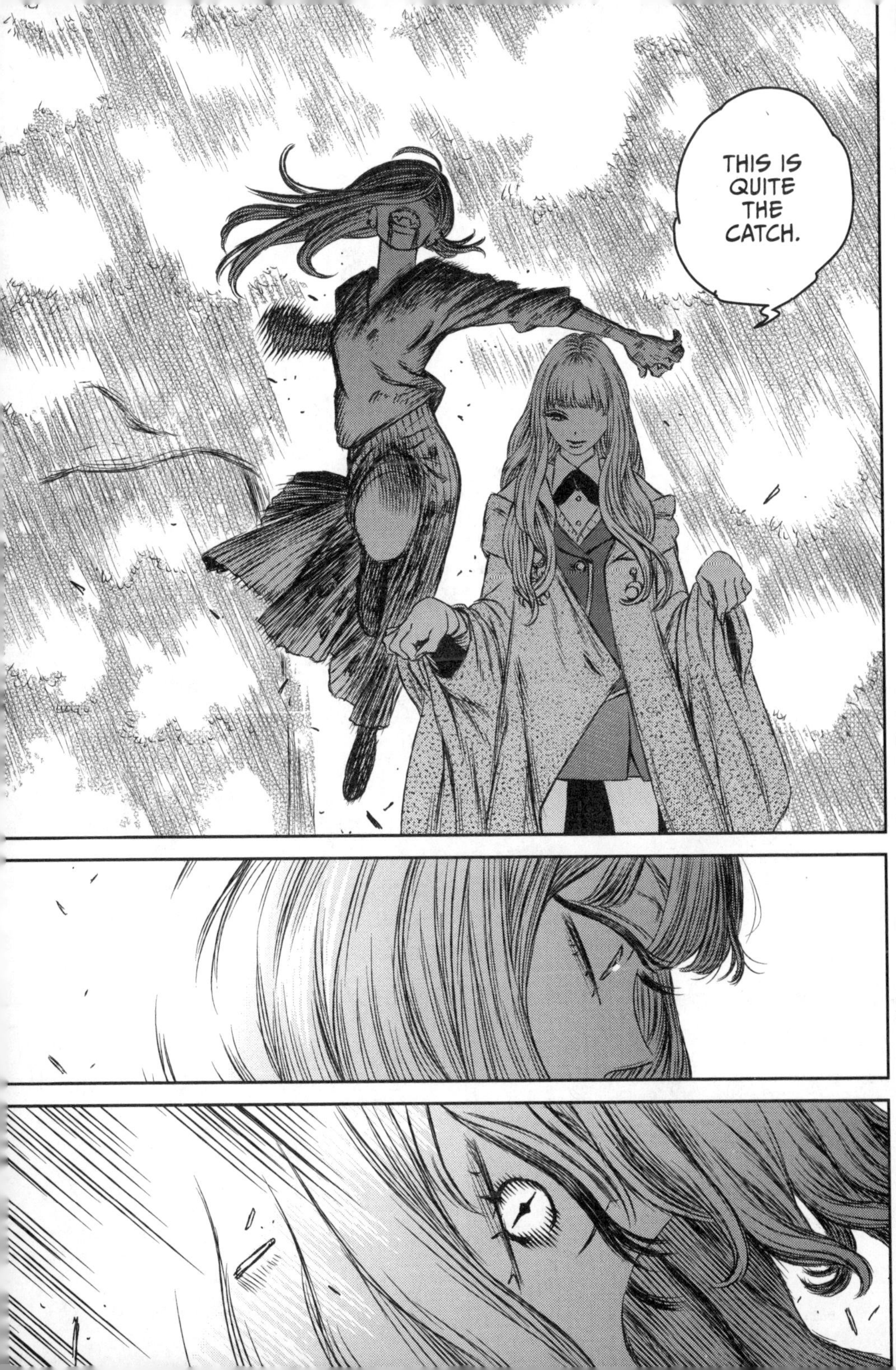
THIS IS QUITE THE CATCH.

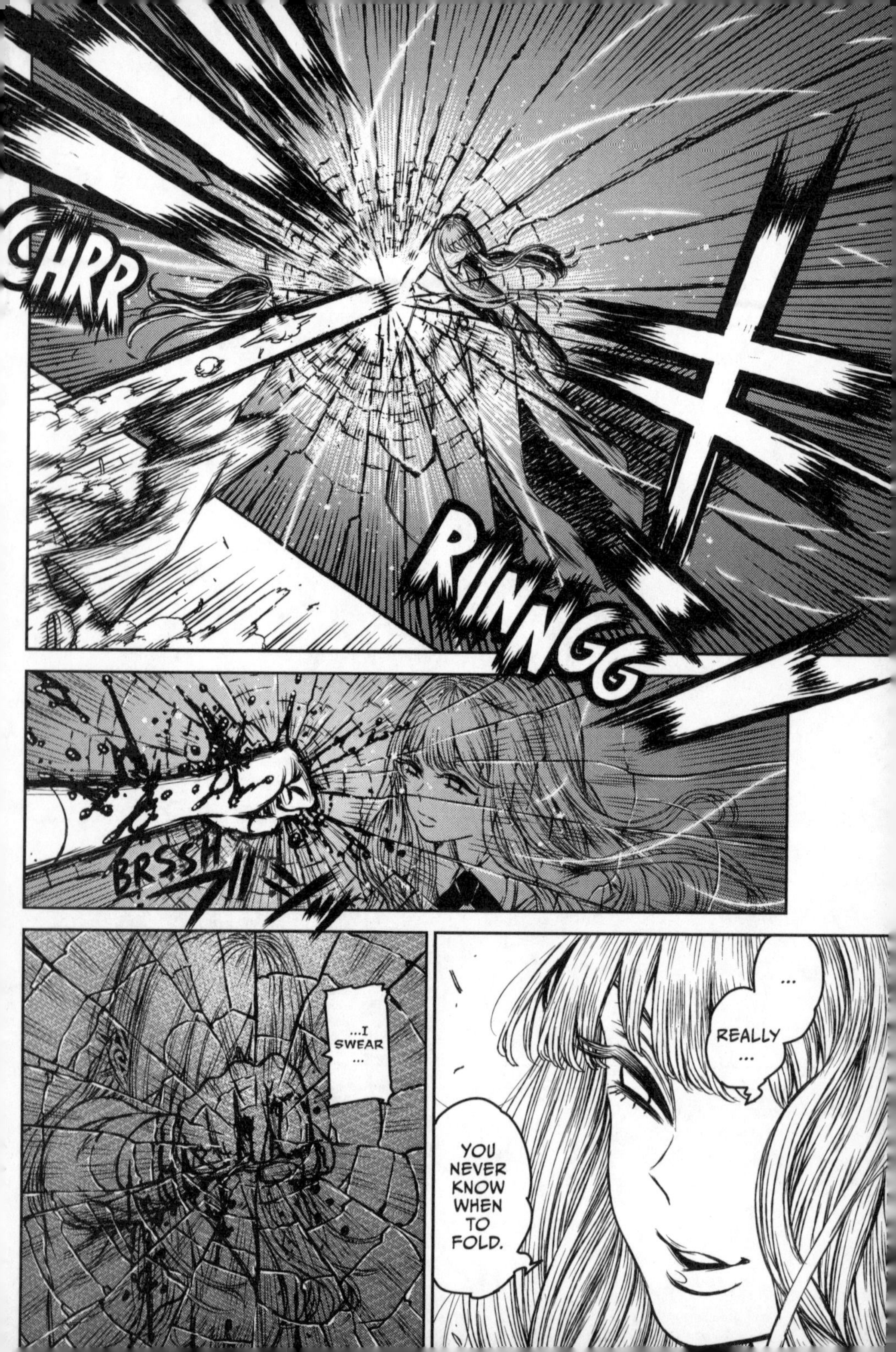
CHRR
RINNGG
BRSSH
...REALLY...
YOU NEVER KNOW WHEN TO FOLD.
...I SWEAR...

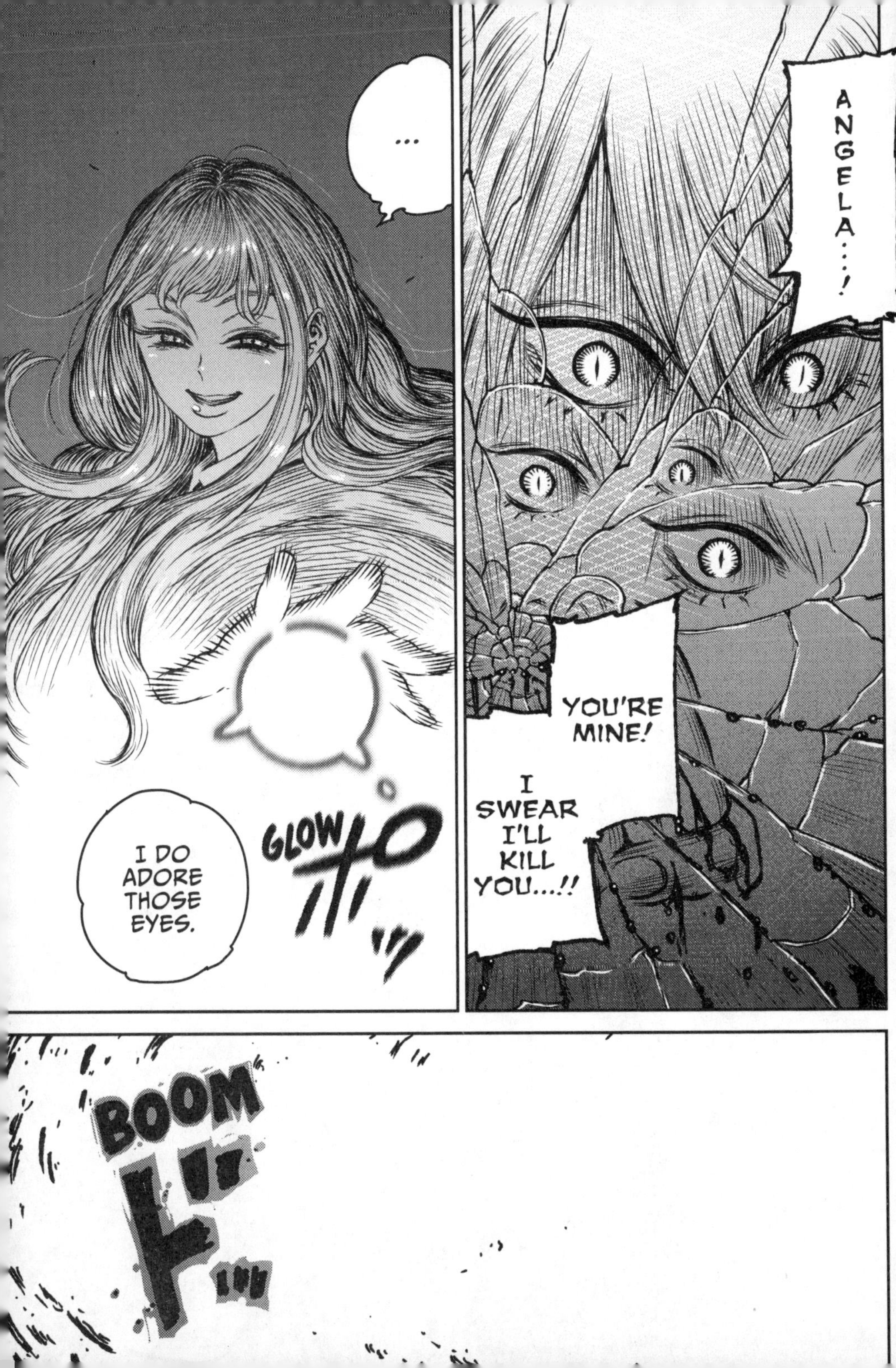

ANGELA...!
YOU'RE MINE!
I SWEAR I'LL KILL YOU...!!
...
GLOW
I DO ADORE THOSE EYES.
BOOM

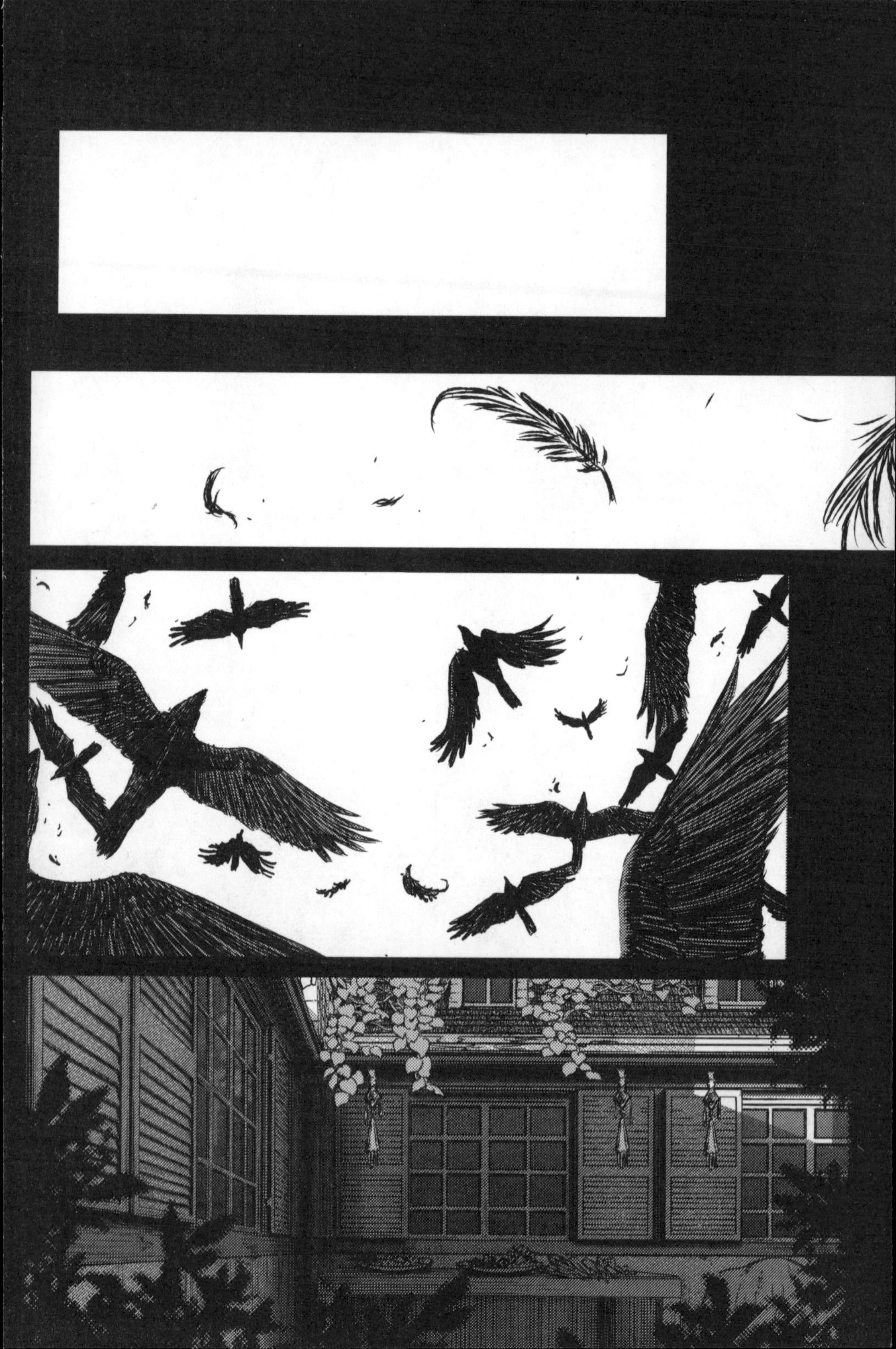

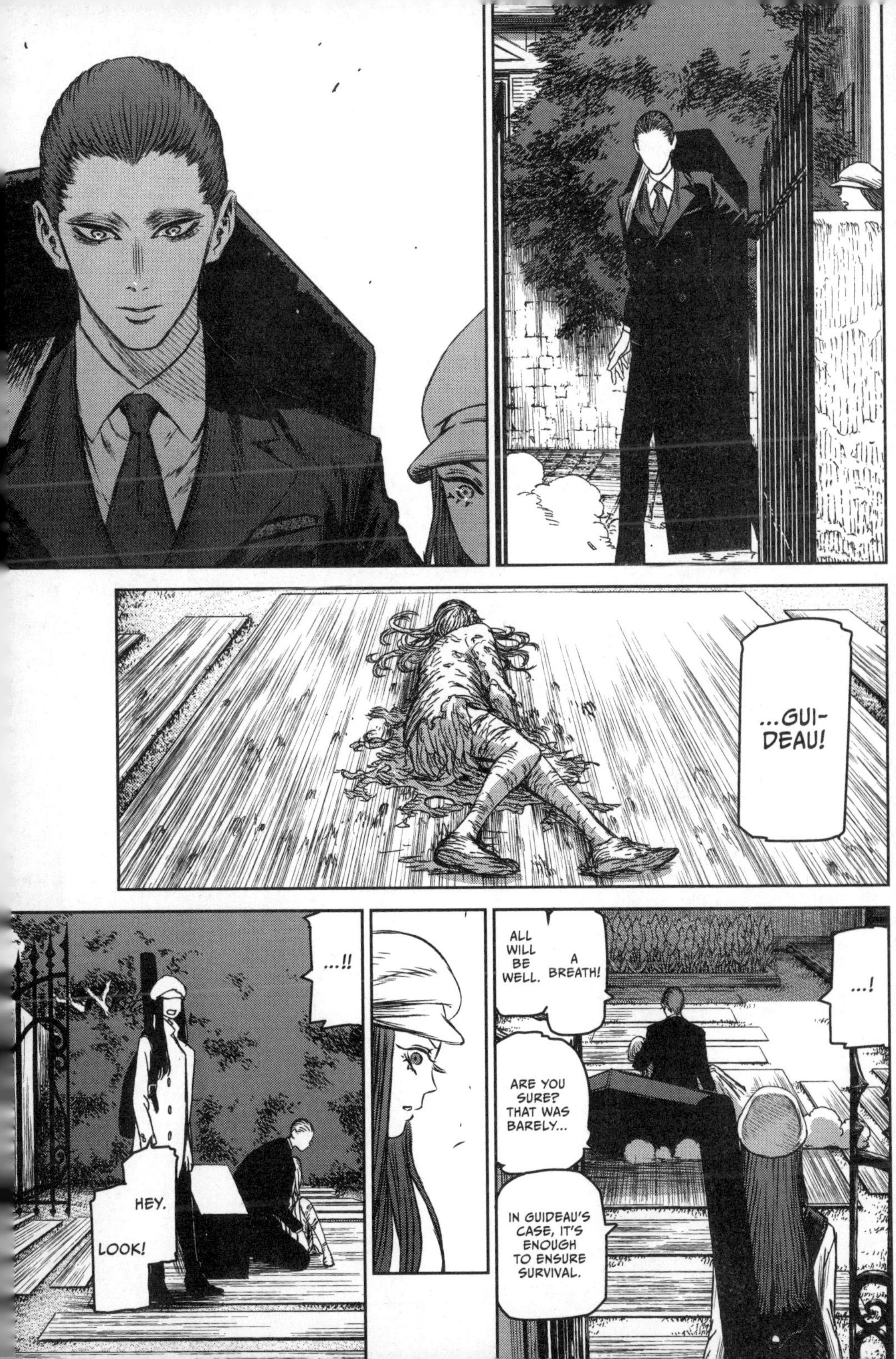

...GUI-DEAU!
...!
A BREATH! ALL WILL BE WELL.
ARE YOU SURE? THAT WAS BARELY...
IN GUIDEAU'S CASE, IT'S ENOUGH TO ENSURE SURVIVAL.
...!!
HEY.
LOOK!

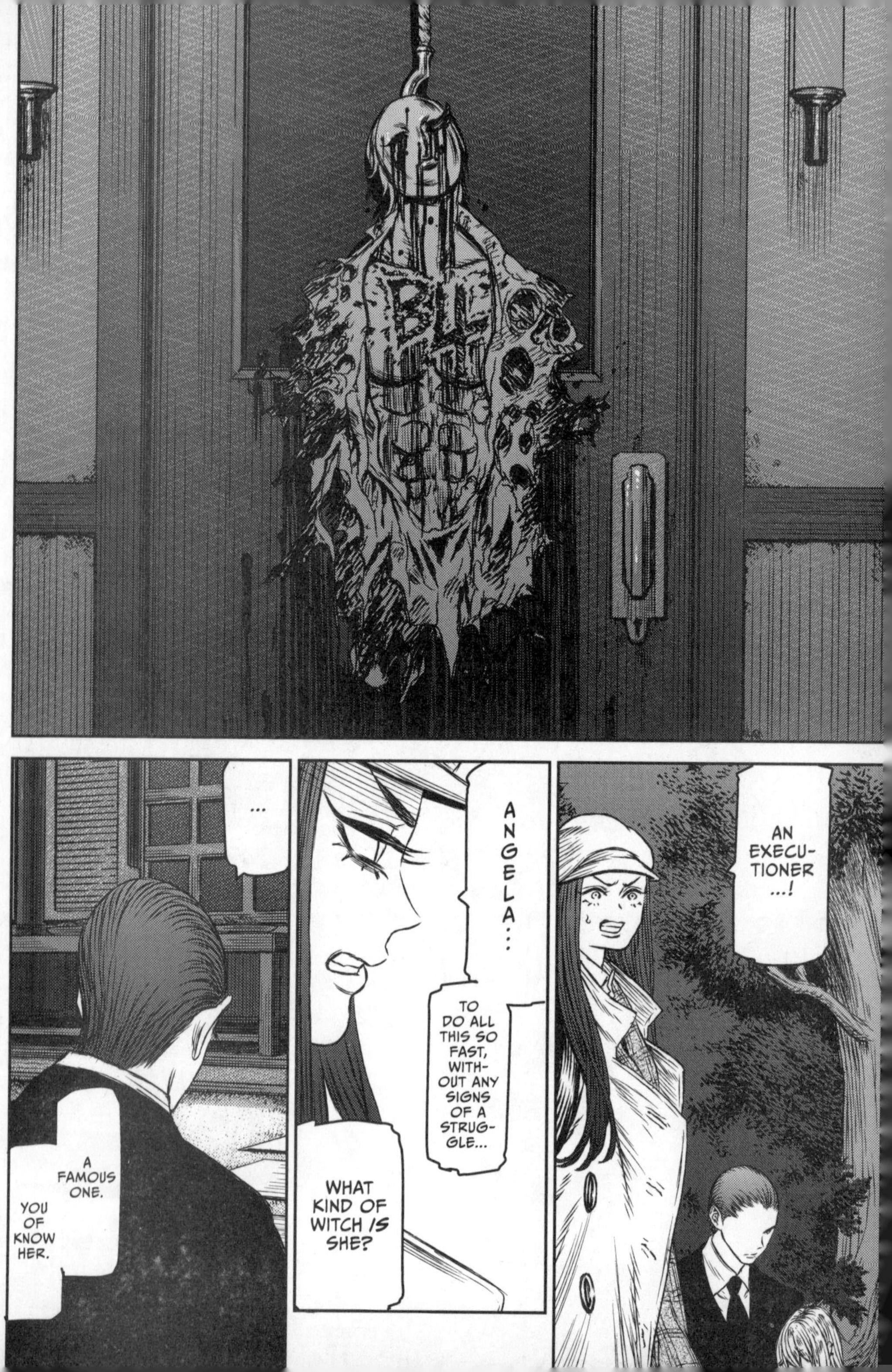
AN EXECU-TIONER ...!
ANGELA...
TO DO ALL THIS SO FAST, WITH-OUT ANY SIGNS OF A STRUG-GLE...
WHAT KIND OF WITCH *IS* SHE?
...
A FAMOUS ONE.
YOU OF KNOW HER.

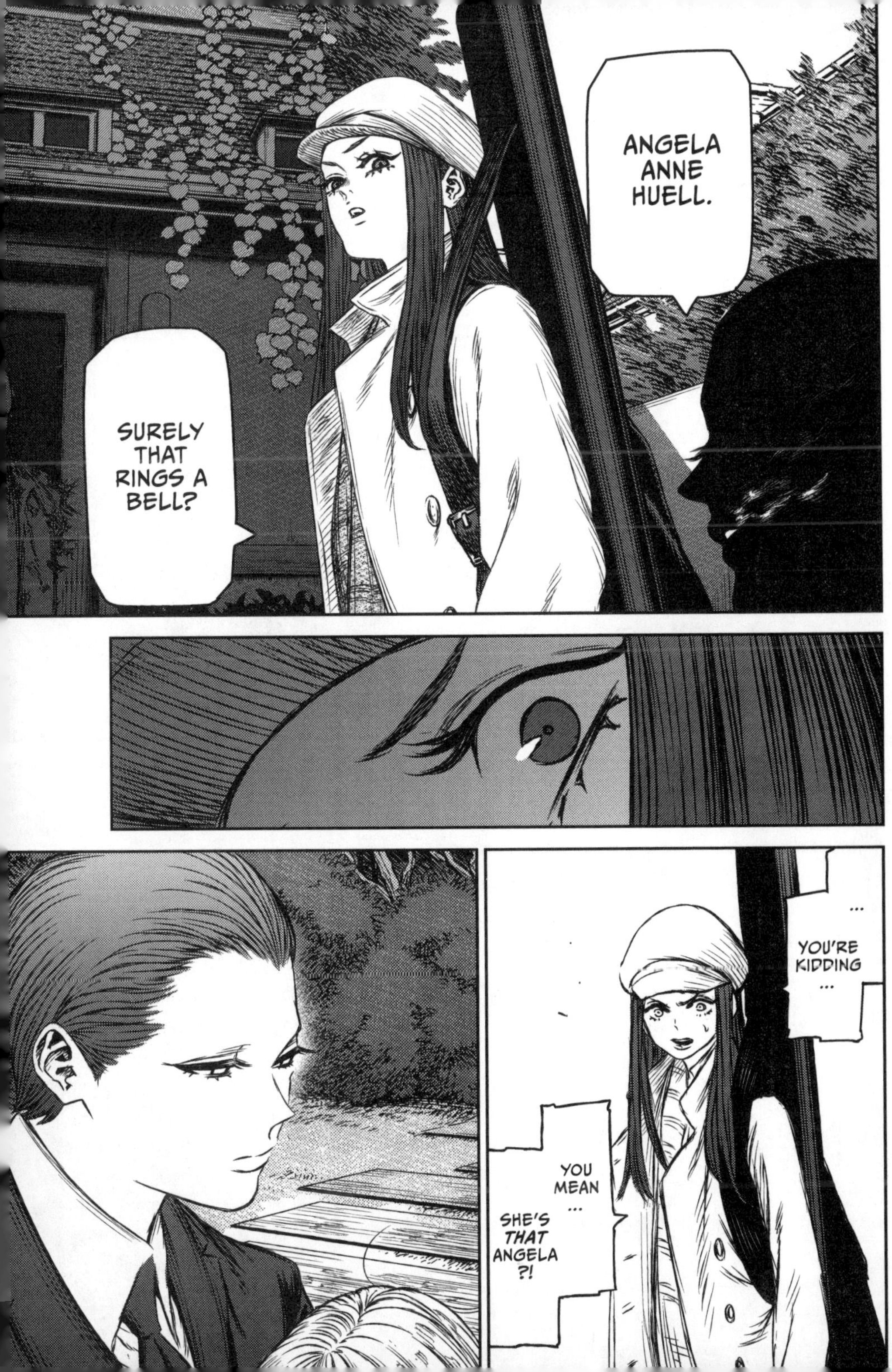

ANGELA ANNE HUELL.
SURELY THAT RINGS A BELL?
... YOU'RE KIDDING ...
YOU MEAN ... SHE'S *THAT* ANGELA ?!

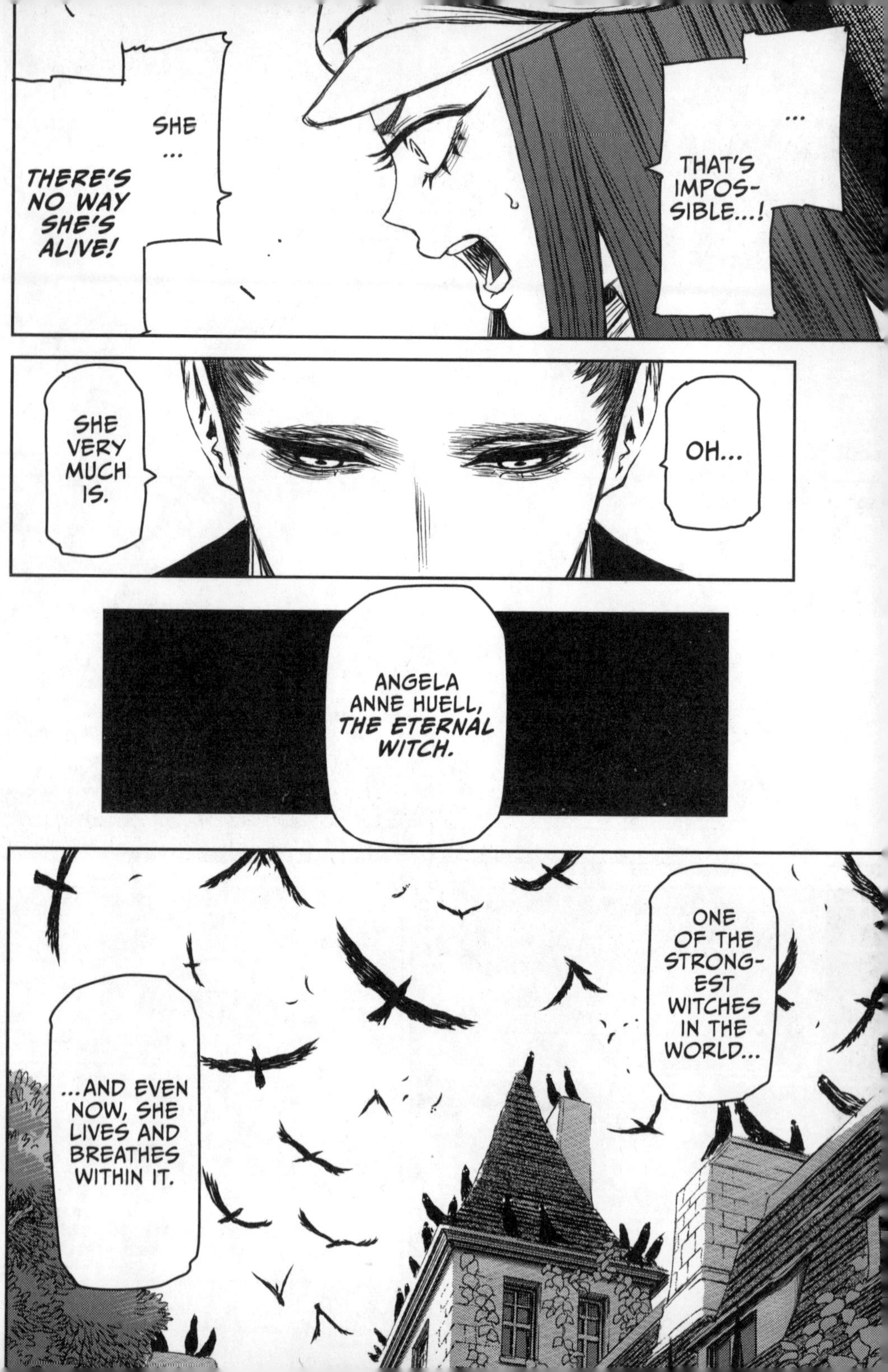
...
THAT'S IMPOSSIBLE...!
SHE ...
THERE'S NO WAY SHE'S ALIVE!
OH...
SHE VERY MUCH IS.
ANGELA ANNE HUELL, THE ETERNAL WITCH.
ONE OF THE STRONGEST WITCHES IN THE WORLD...
...AND EVEN NOW, SHE LIVES AND BREATHES WITHIN IT.

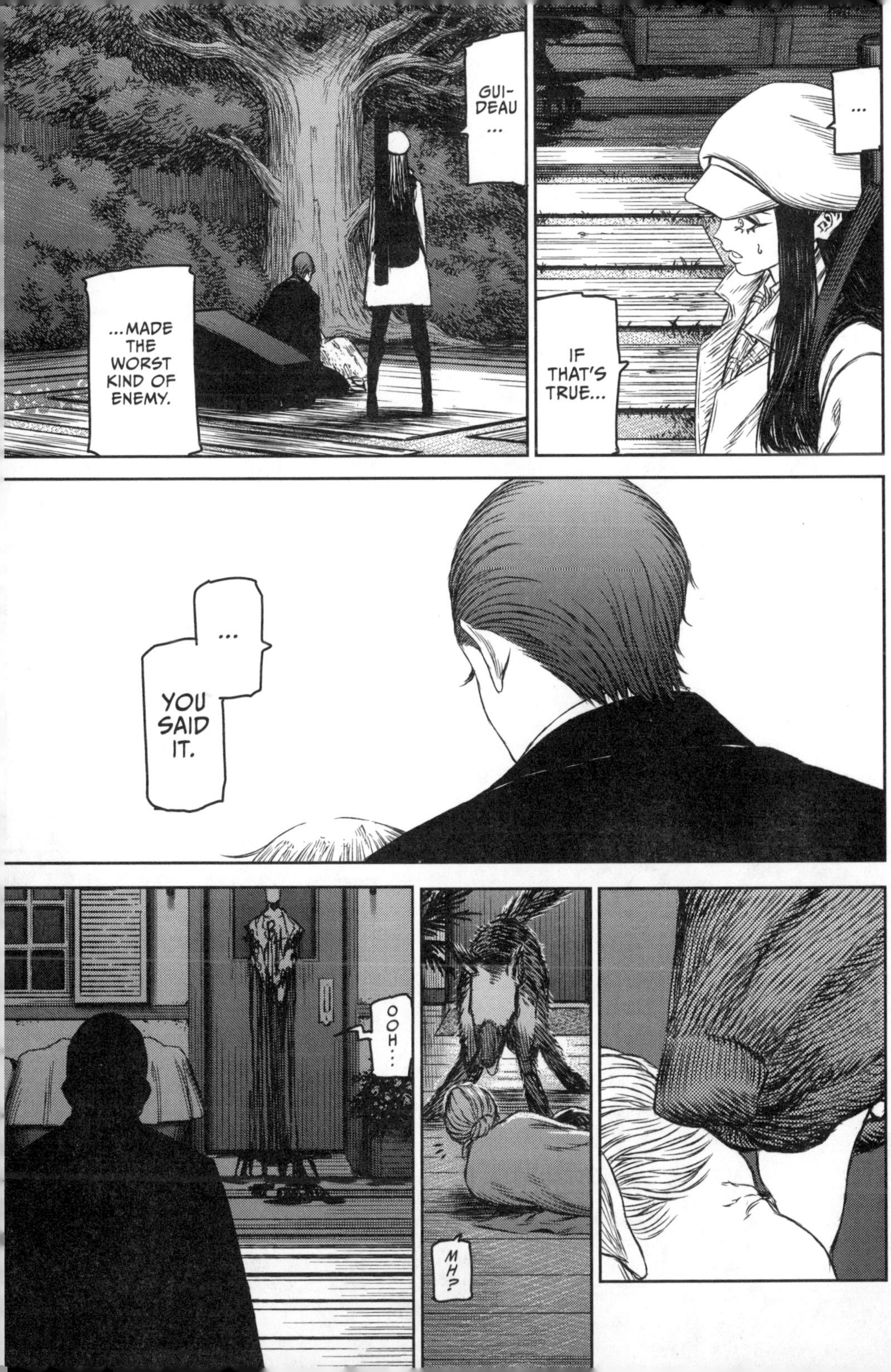
...
IF THAT'S TRUE...
GUI-DEAU ...
...MADE THE WORST KIND OF ENEMY.
...
YOU SAID IT.
MH?
OOH...

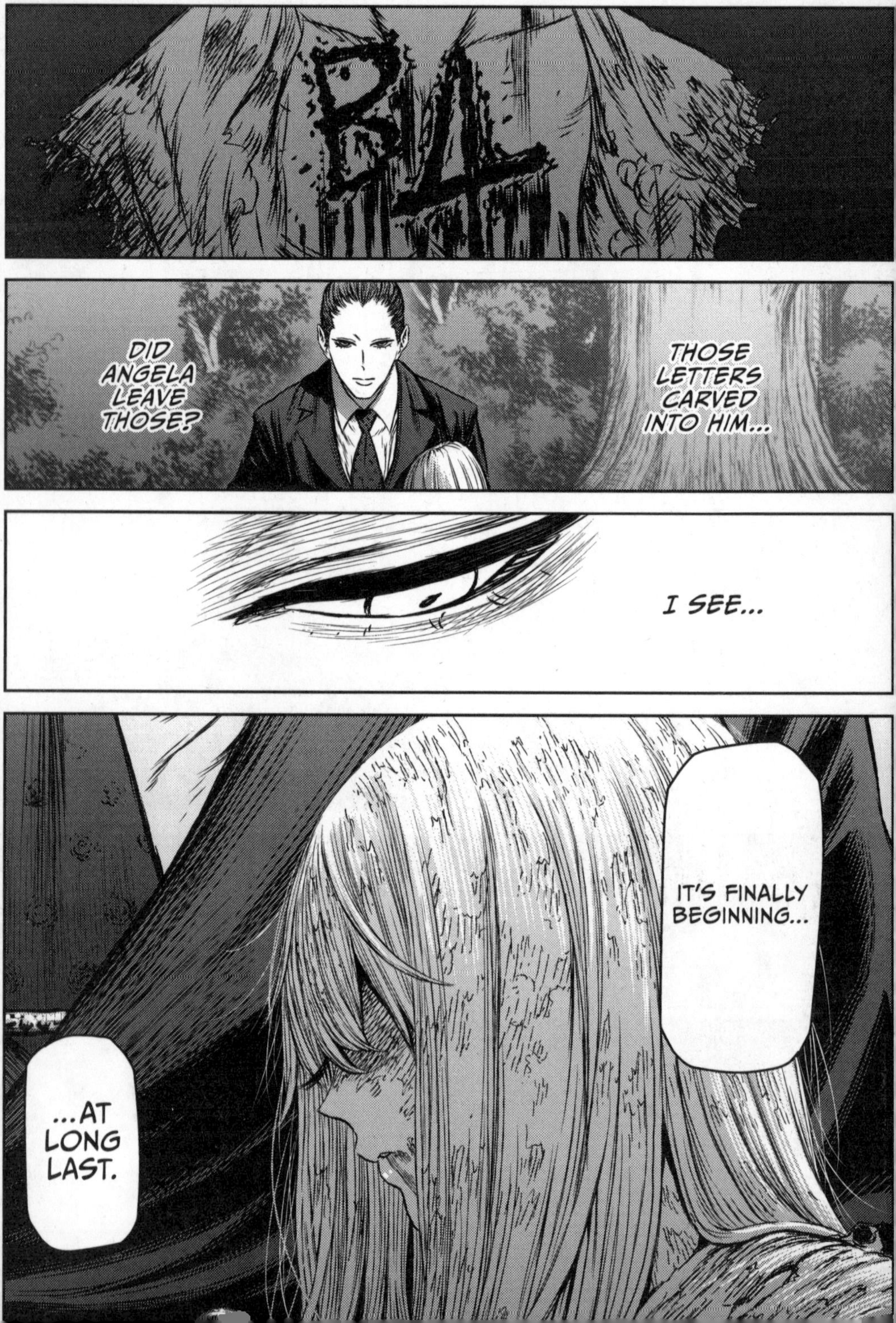
BILL
THOSE LETTERS CARVED INTO HIM...
DID ANGELA LEAVE THOSE?
I SEE...
IT'S FINALLY BEGINNING...
...AT LONG LAST.

THE WITCH AND THE BEAST

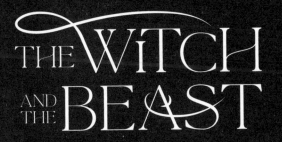

THE WITCH AND THE BEAST

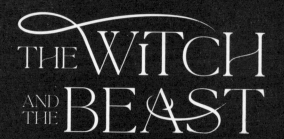

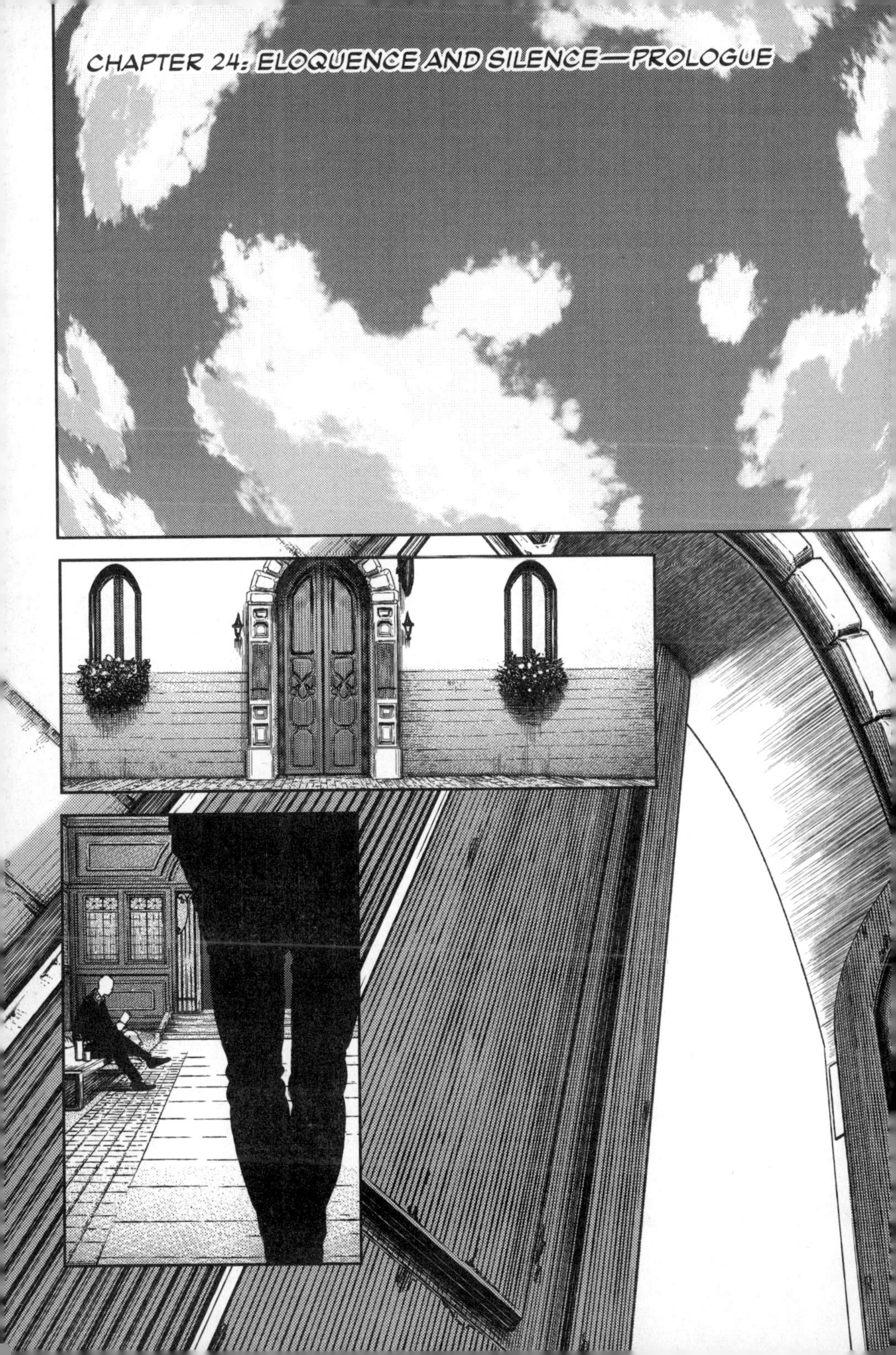
CHAPTER 24: ELOQUENCE AND SILENCE—PROLOGUE

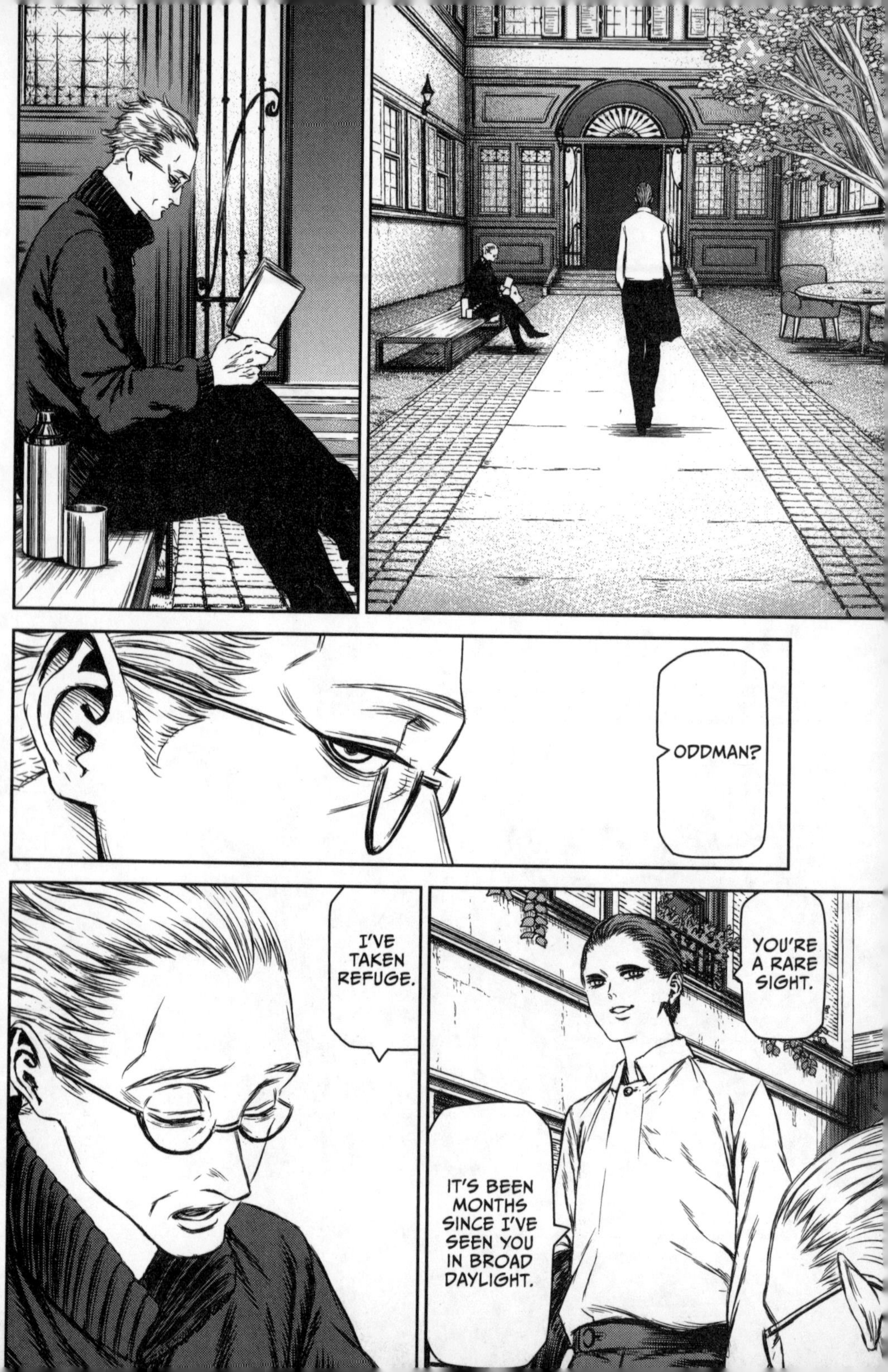
ODDMAN?
YOU'RE A RARE SIGHT.
IT'S BEEN MONTHS SINCE I'VE SEEN YOU IN BROAD DAYLIGHT.
I'VE TAKEN REFUGE.

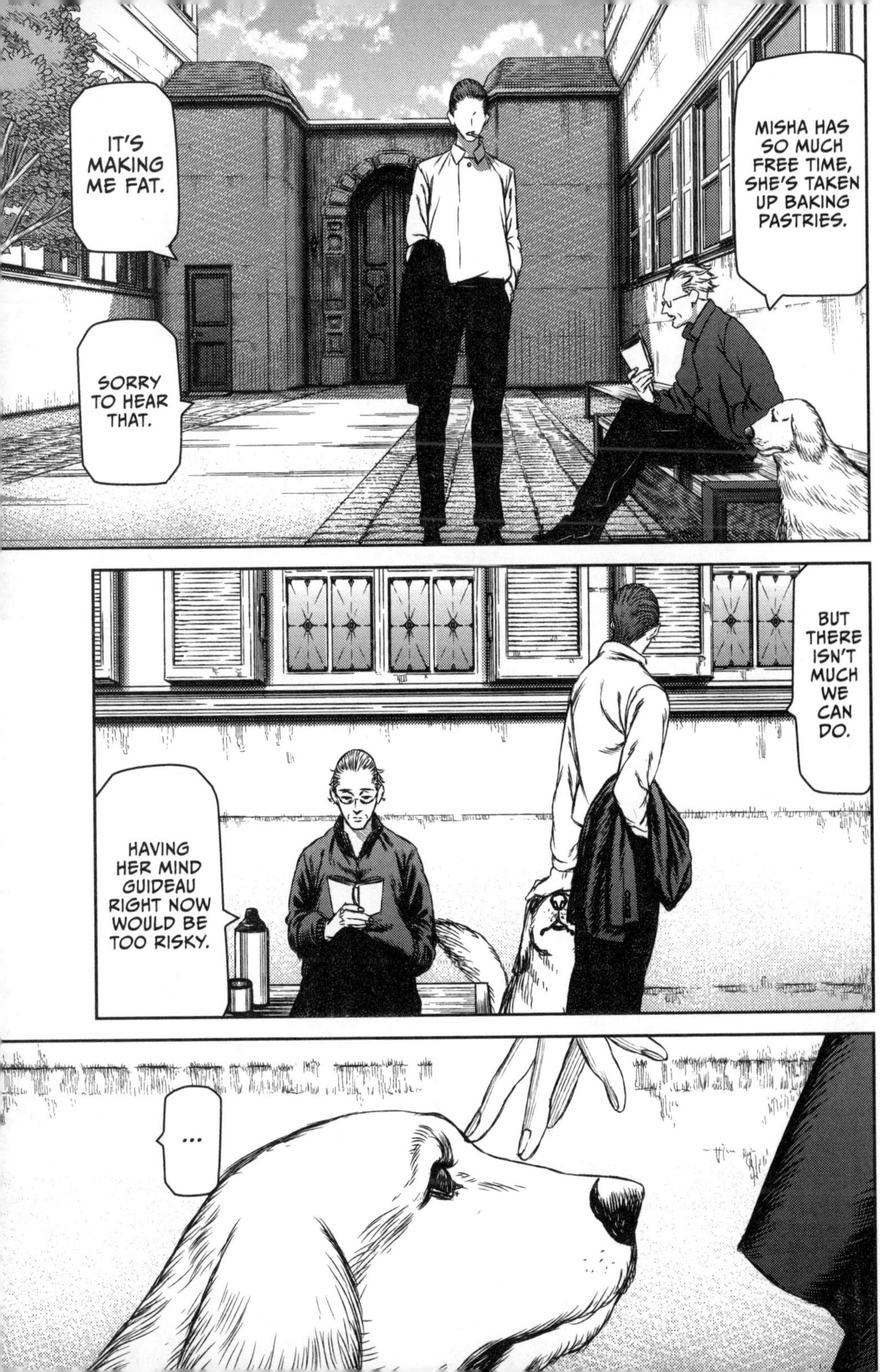
MISHA HAS SO MUCH FREE TIME, SHE'S TAKEN UP BAKING PASTRIES.
IT'S MAKING ME FAT.
SORRY TO HEAR THAT.
BUT THERE ISN'T MUCH WE CAN DO.
HAVING HER MIND GUIDEAU RIGHT NOW WOULD BE TOO RISKY.
...

CRASSSH

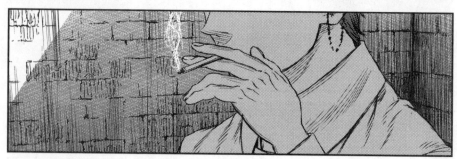

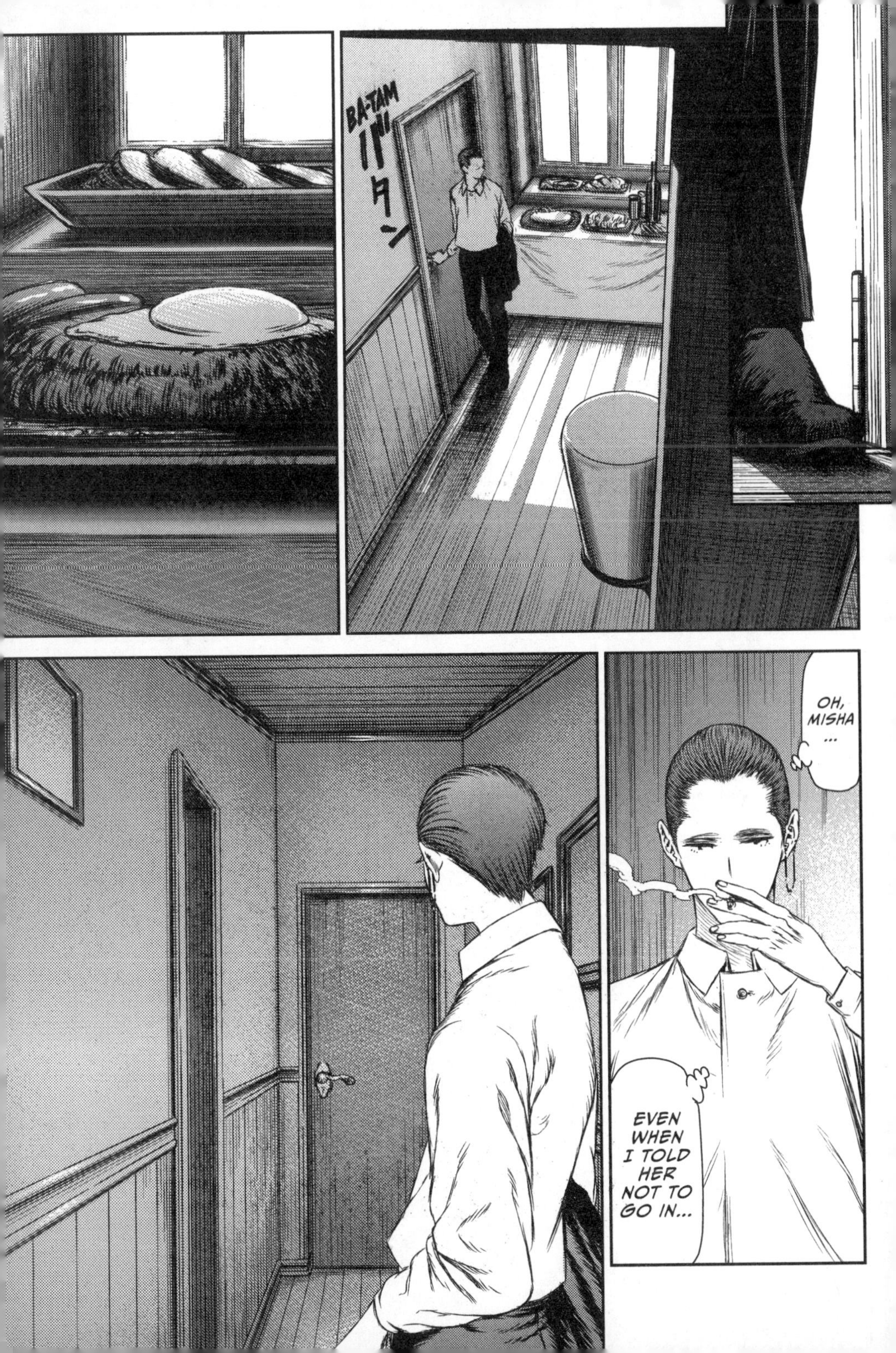
BA-TAM
バタン
OH, MISHA...
EVEN WHEN I TOLD HER NOT TO GO IN...

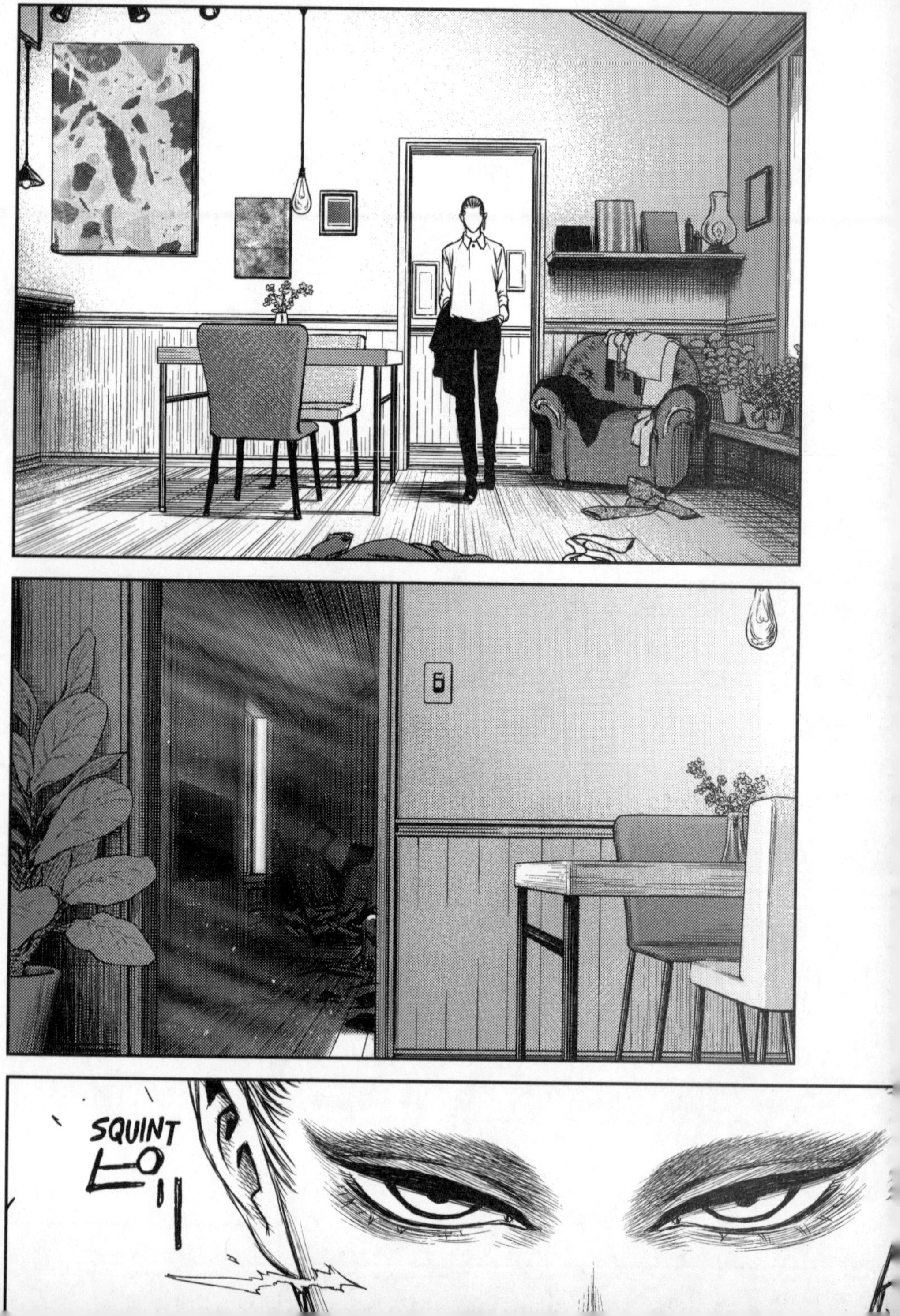
SQUINT

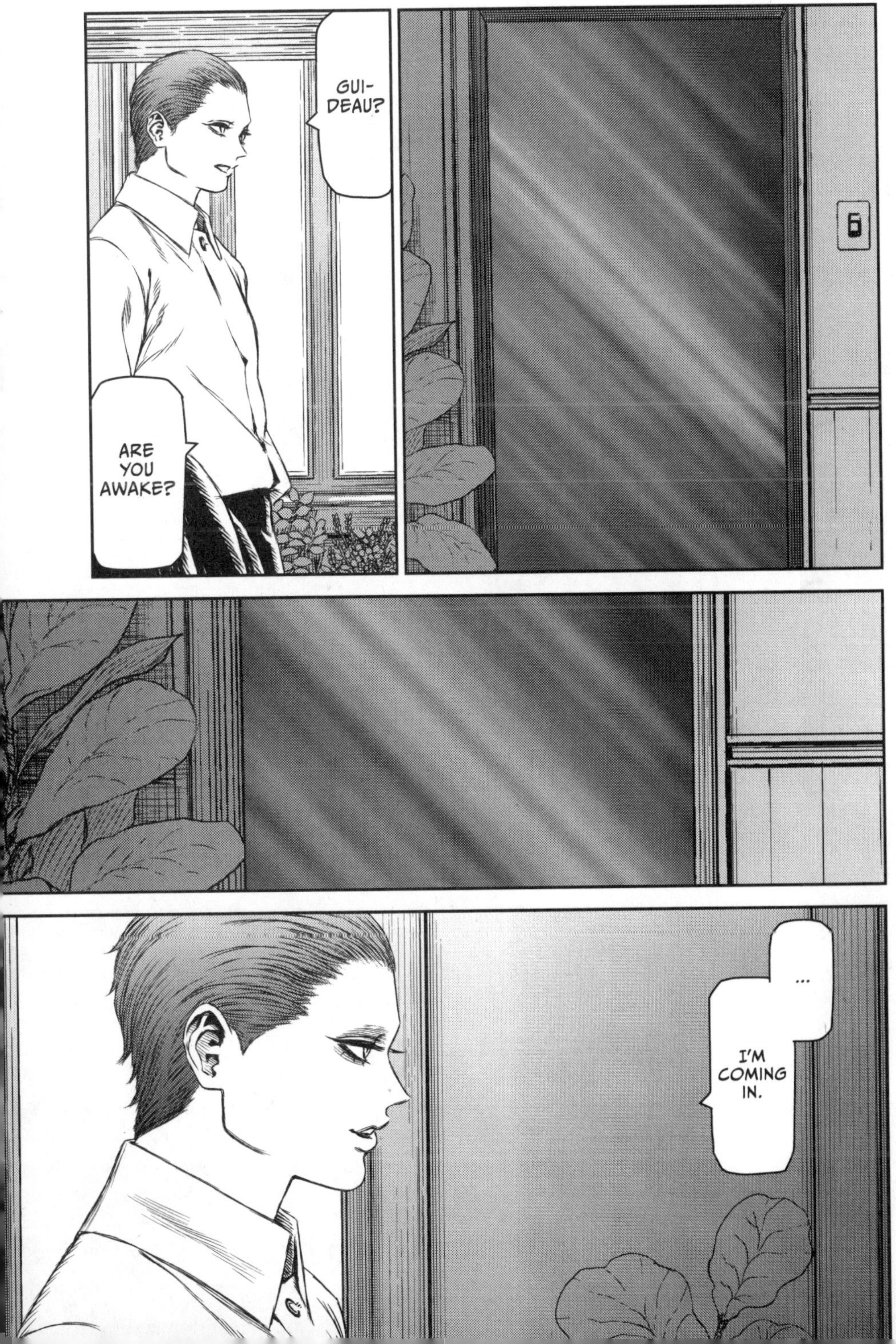
6
GUI-DEAU?
ARE YOU AWAKE?
...
I'M COMING IN.

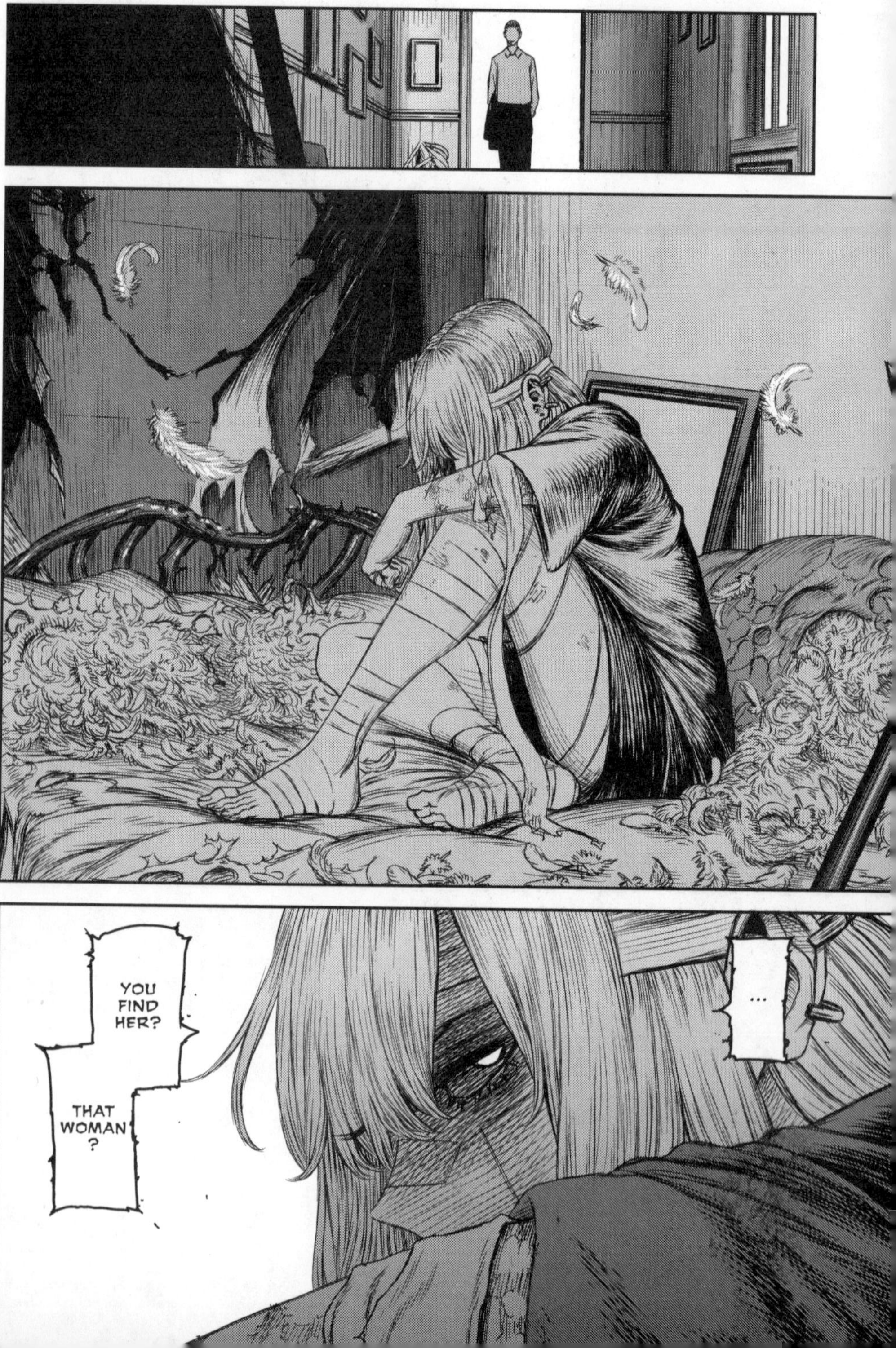
...
YOU FIND HER?
THAT WOMAN?

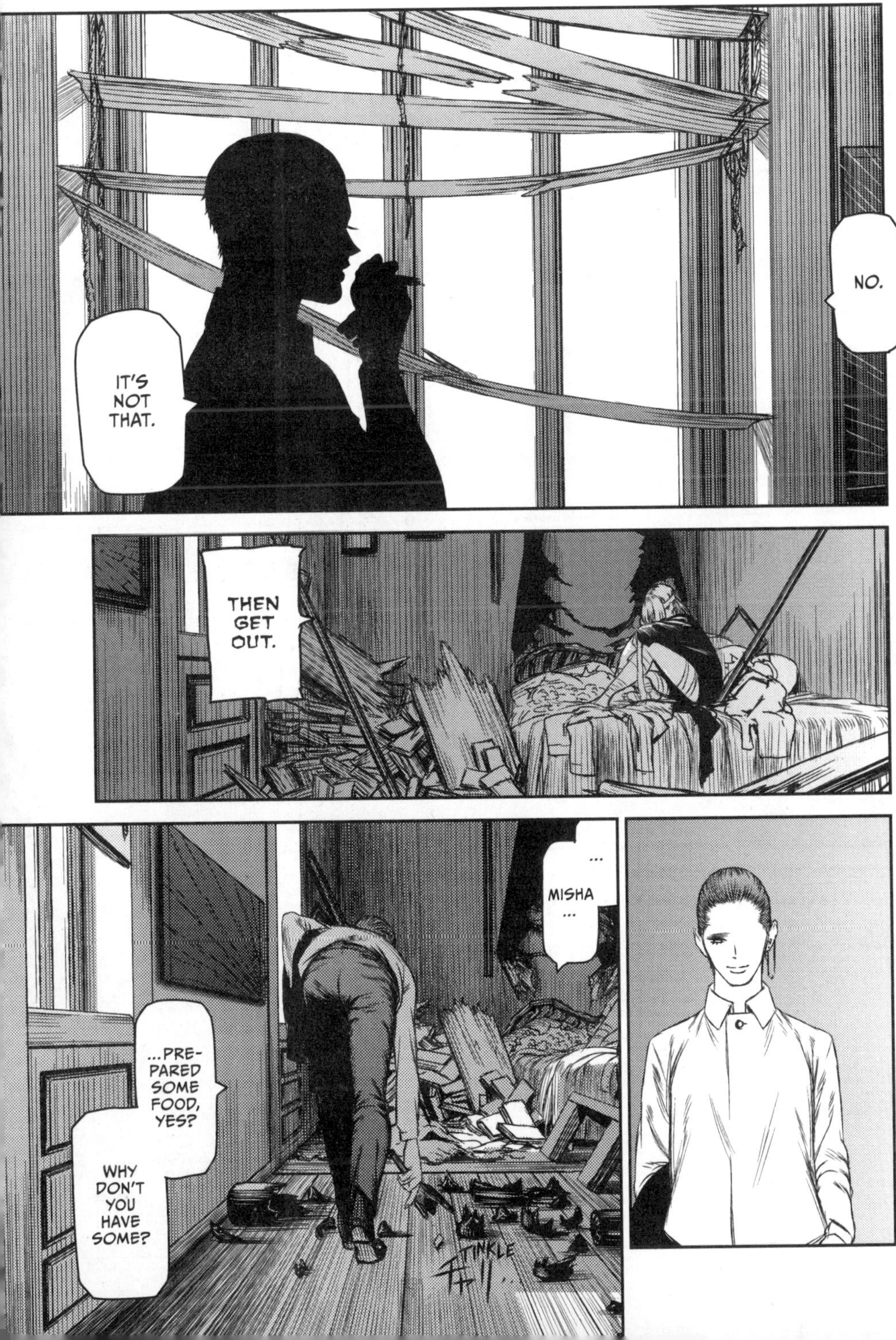
NO.
IT'S NOT THAT.
THEN GET OUT.
... MISHA ...
...PRE-PARED SOME FOOD, YES?
WHY DON'T YOU HAVE SOME?
TINKLE

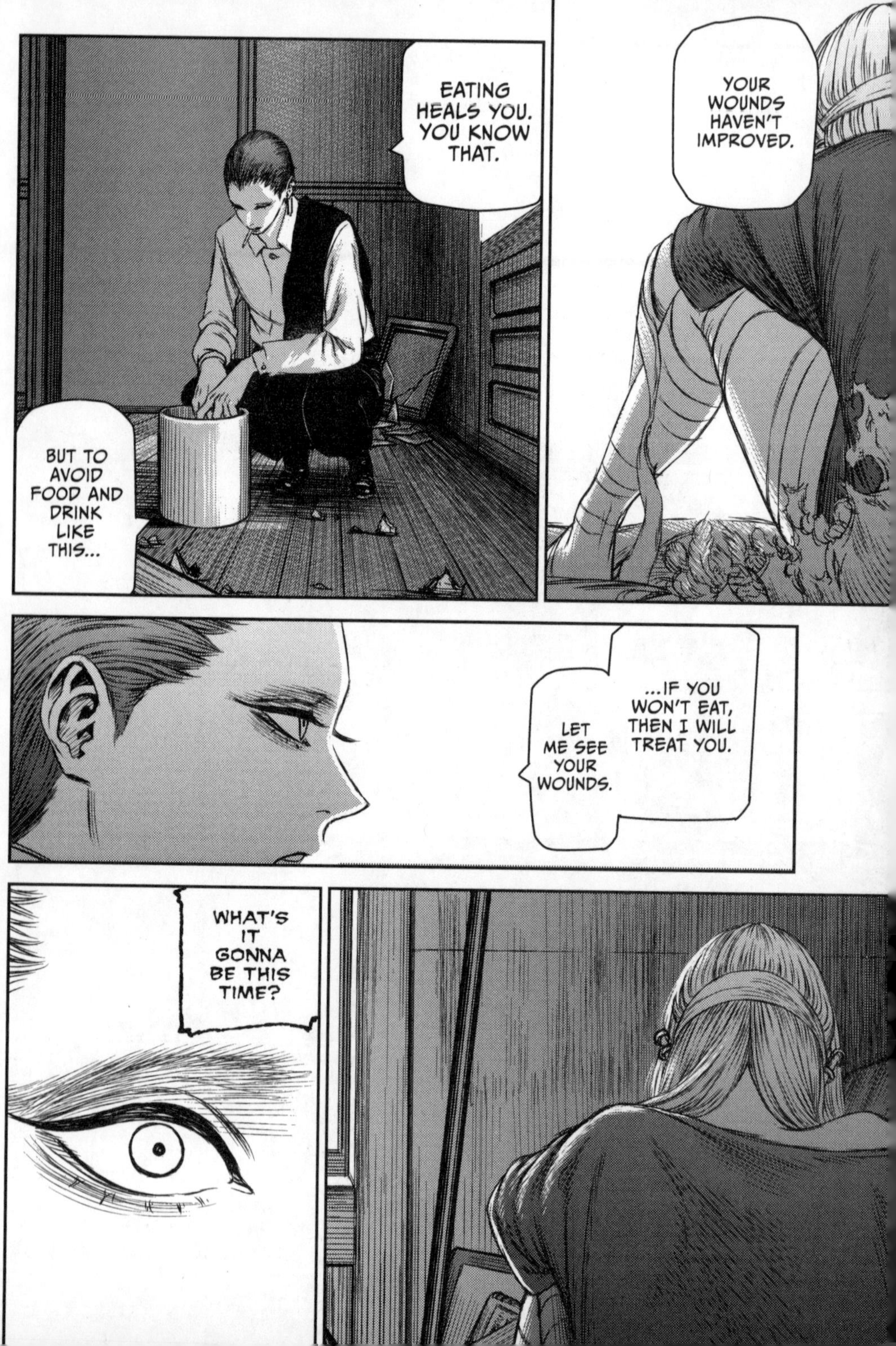
YOUR WOUNDS HAVEN'T IMPROVED.
EATING HEALS YOU. YOU KNOW THAT.
BUT TO AVOID FOOD AND DRINK LIKE THIS...
...IF YOU WON'T EAT, THEN I WILL TREAT YOU.
LET ME SEE YOUR WOUNDS.
WHAT'S IT GONNA BE THIS TIME?

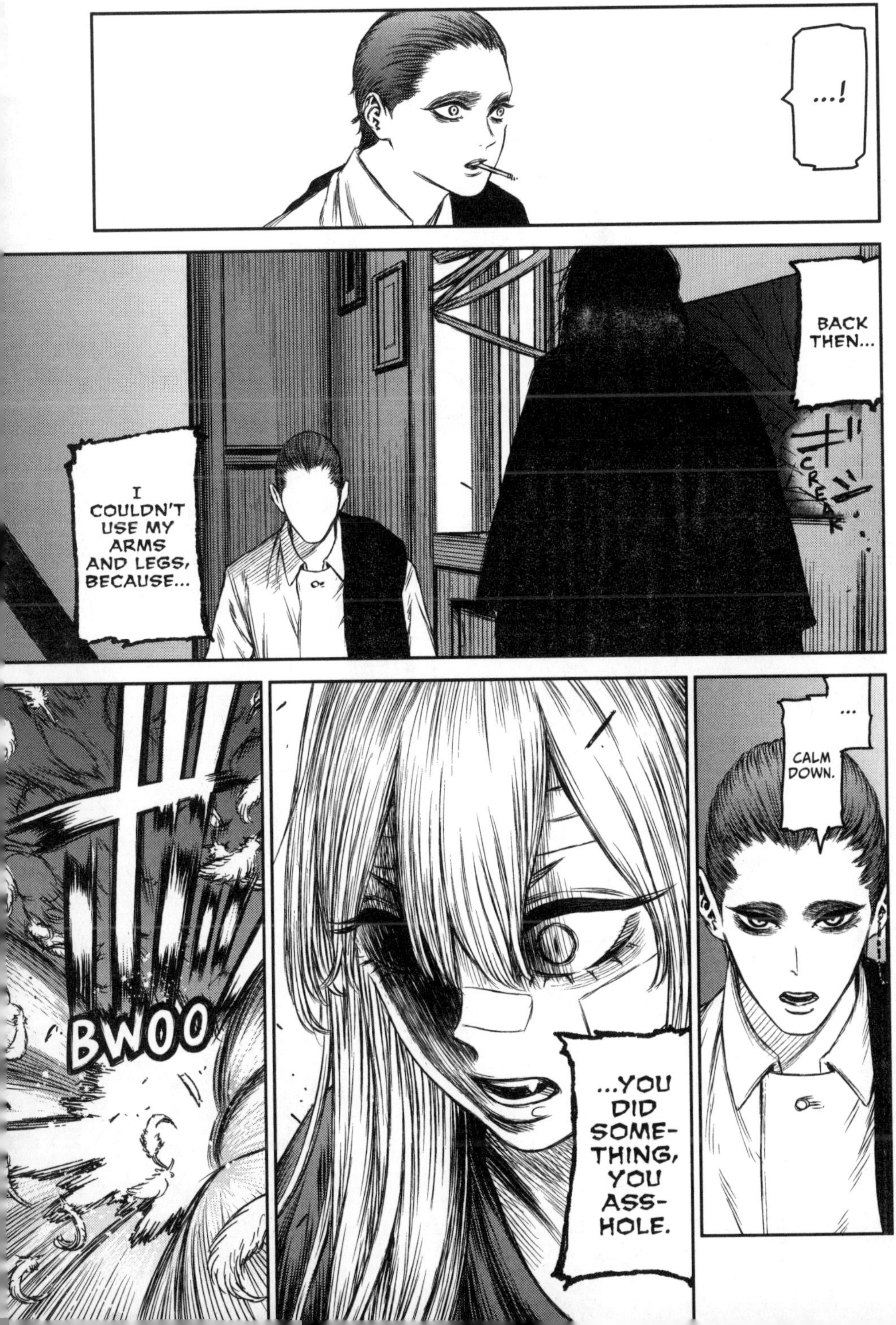
...!
BACK THEN...
CREAK
I COULDN'T USE MY ARMS AND LEGS, BECAUSE...
... CALM DOWN.
...YOU DID SOMETHING, YOU ASSHOLE.
BWOO

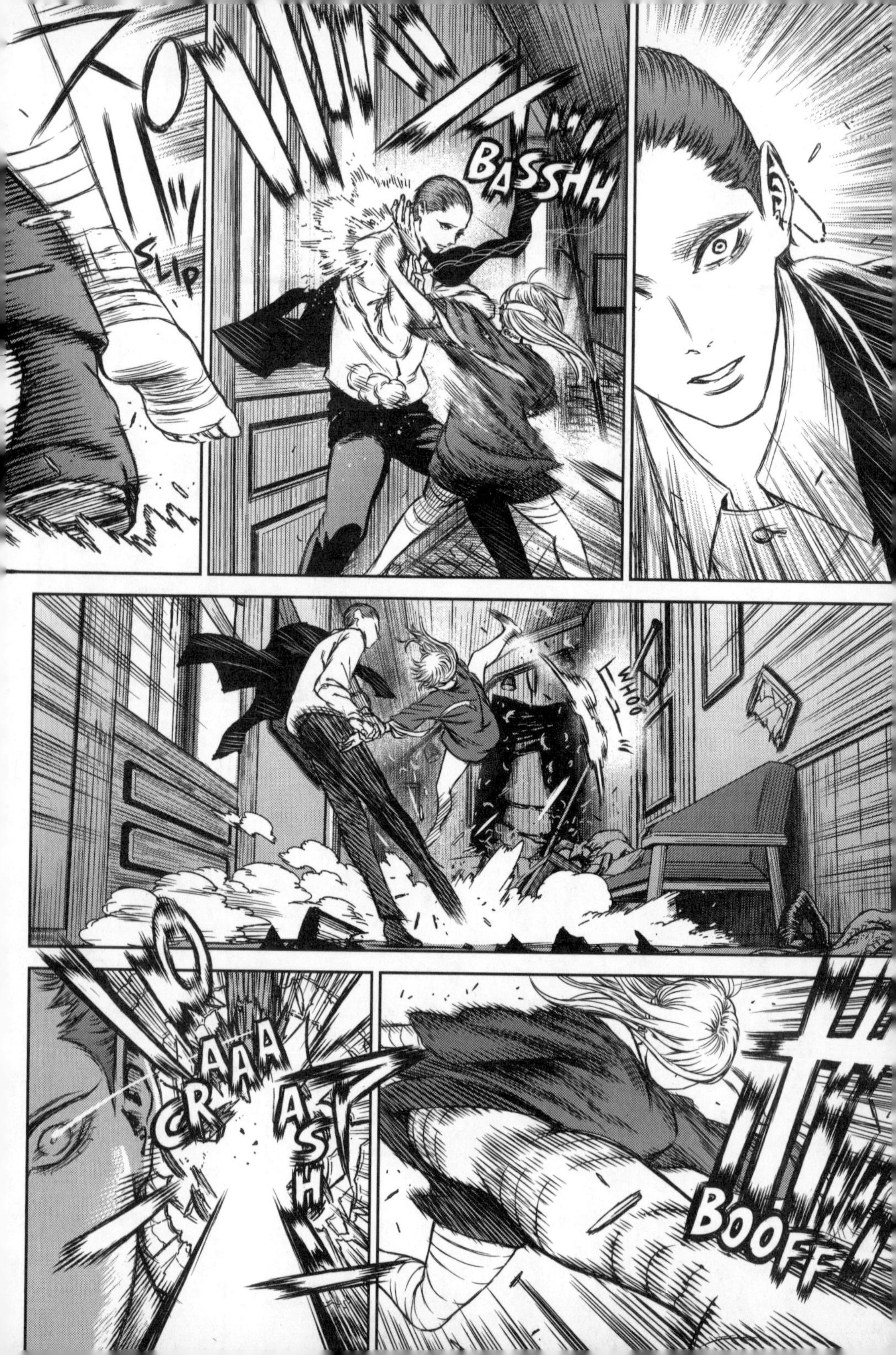
BASSHH
SLIP
WHOO
CRAAASH
BOOFF

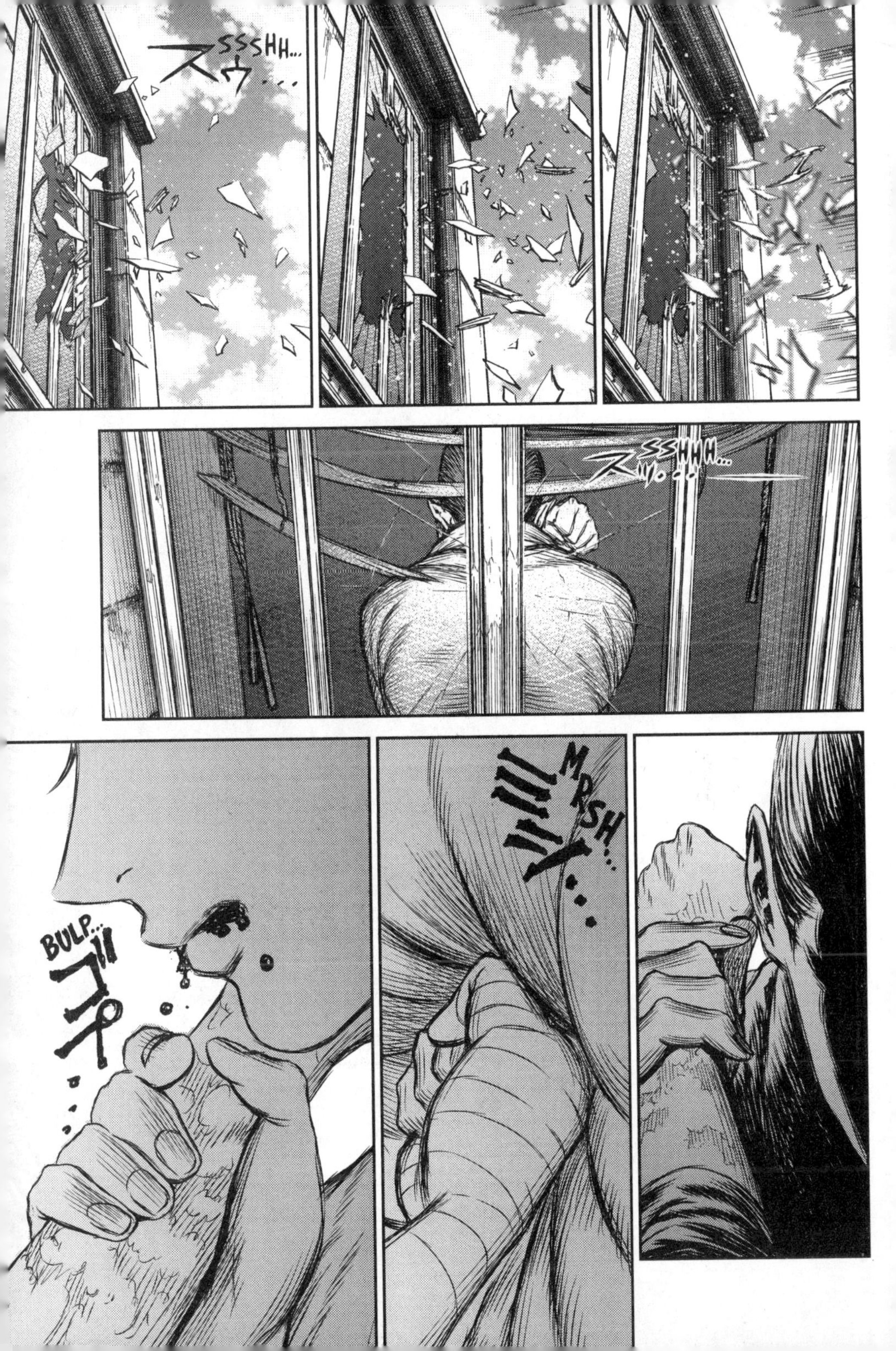

SSSHH...
スゥ...
SSHHH...
スゥ...
MRSH...
ミシ...
BULP...
ゴプ...

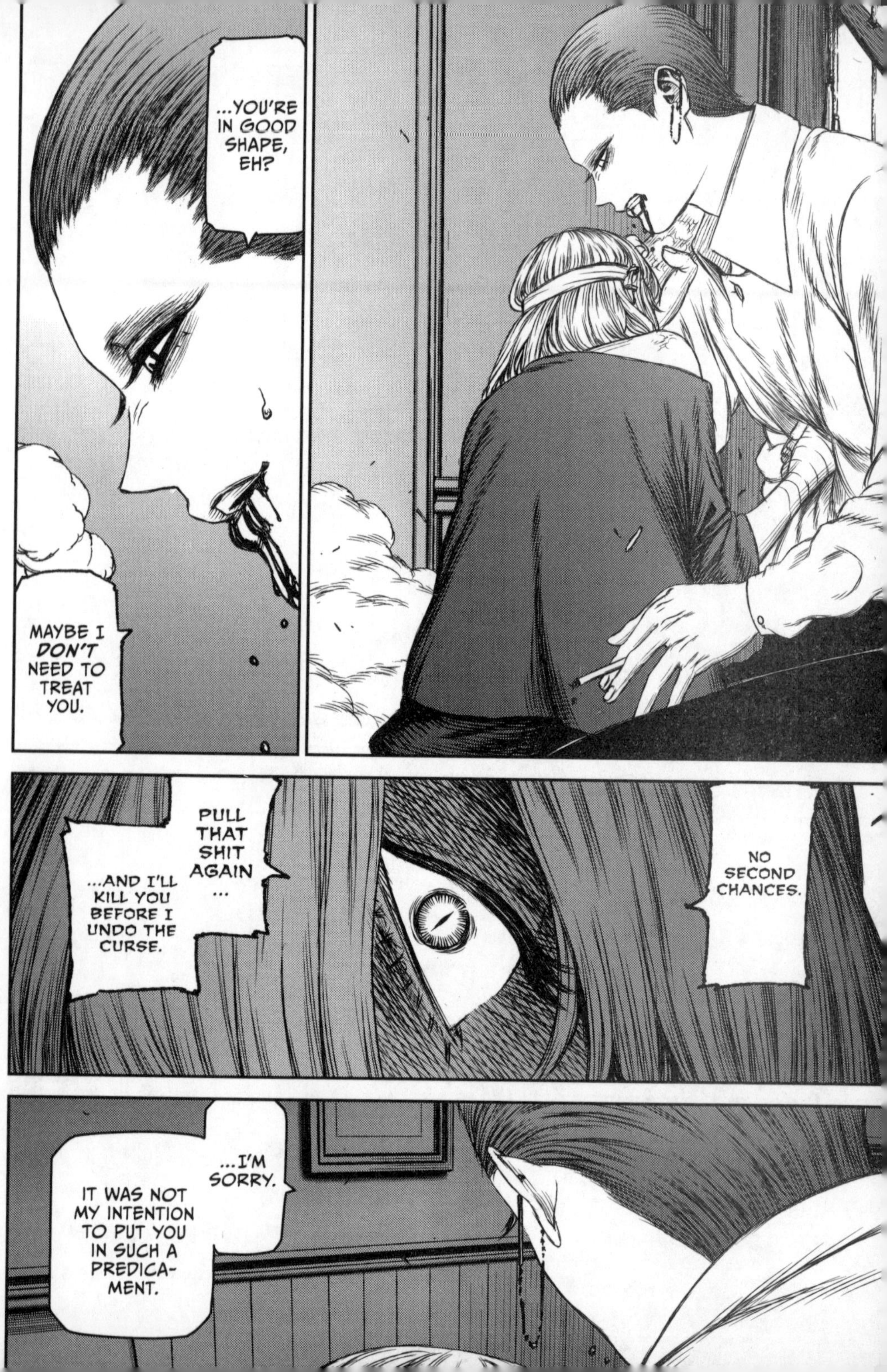
...YOU'RE IN GOOD SHAPE, EH?
MAYBE I *DON'T* NEED TO TREAT YOU.
NO SECOND CHANCES.
PULL THAT SHIT AGAIN ...
...AND I'LL KILL YOU BEFORE I UNDO THE CURSE.
...I'M SORRY.
IT WAS NOT MY INTENTION TO PUT YOU IN SUCH A PREDICA-MENT.

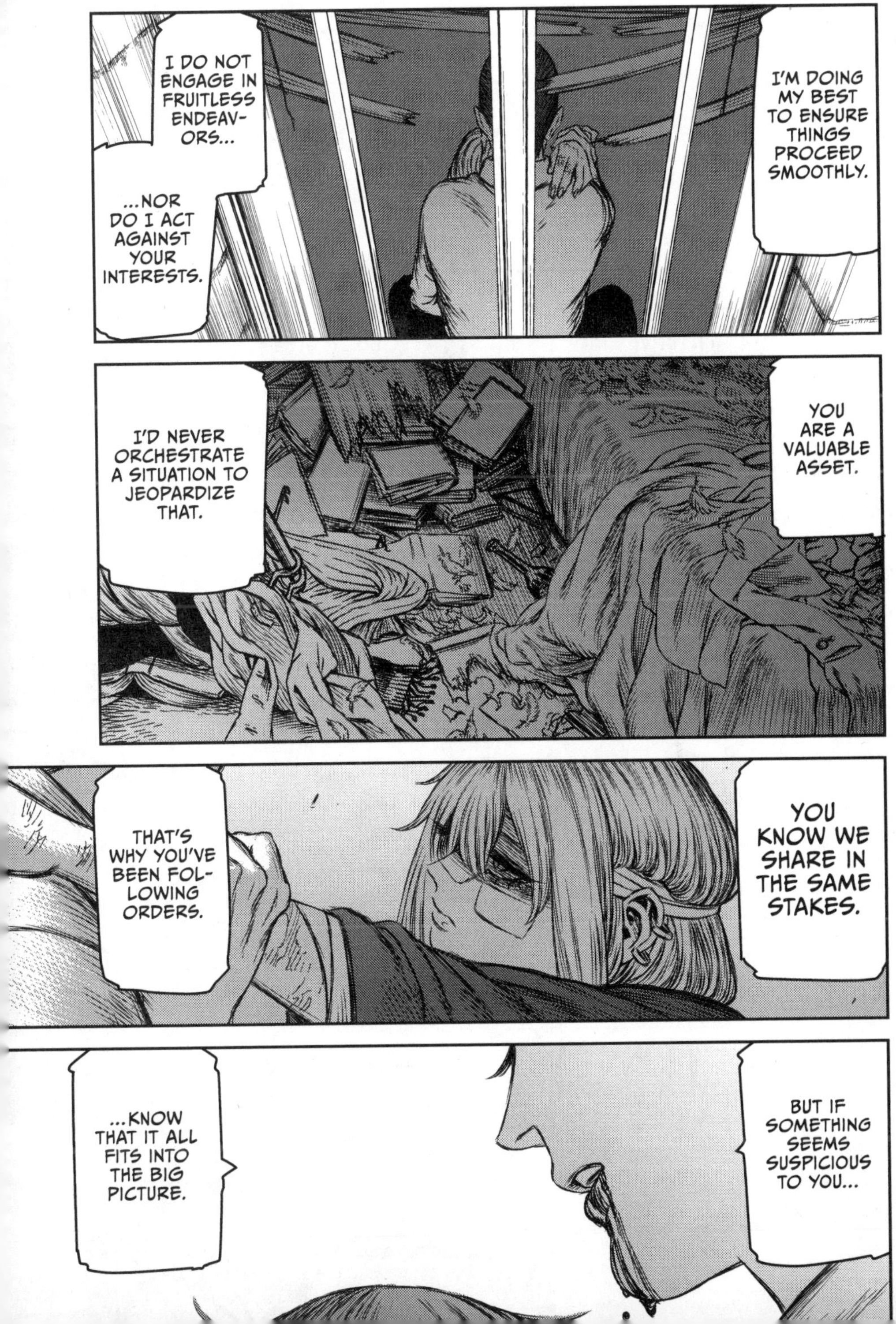
I'M DOING MY BEST TO ENSURE THINGS PROCEED SMOOTHLY.
I DO NOT ENGAGE IN FRUITLESS ENDEAV-ORS...
...NOR DO I ACT AGAINST YOUR INTERESTS.
YOU ARE A VALUABLE ASSET.
I'D NEVER ORCHESTRATE A SITUATION TO JEOPARDIZE THAT.
YOU KNOW WE SHARE IN THE SAME STAKES.
THAT'S WHY YOU'VE BEEN FOL-LOWING ORDERS.
BUT IF SOMETHING SEEMS SUSPICIOUS TO YOU...
...KNOW THAT IT ALL FITS INTO THE BIG PICTURE.

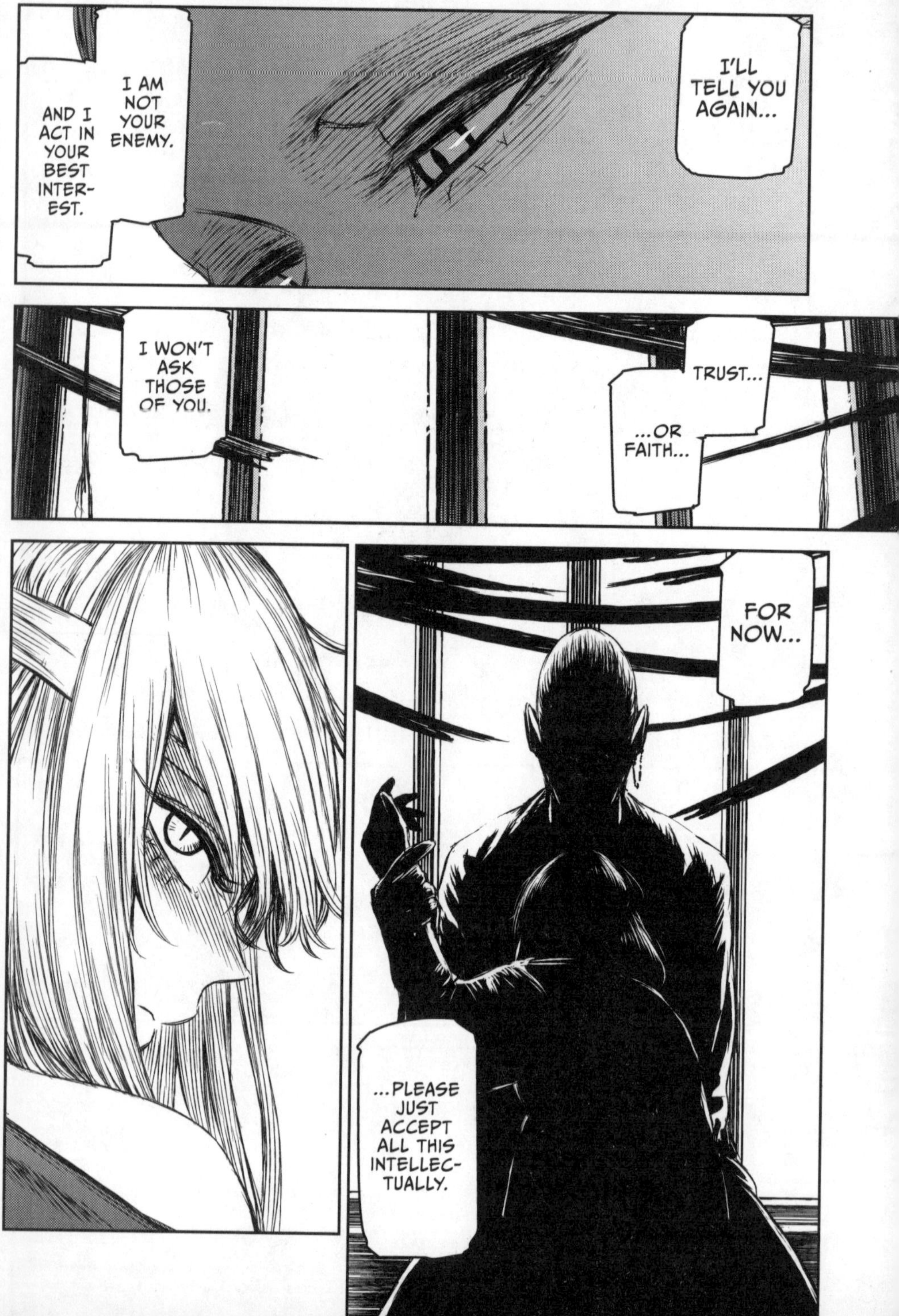
I'LL TELL YOU AGAIN...
I AM NOT YOUR ENEMY.
AND I ACT IN YOUR BEST INTER-EST.
TRUST...
...OR FAITH...
I WON'T ASK THOSE OF YOU.
FOR NOW...
...PLEASE JUST ACCEPT ALL THIS INTELLEC-TUALLY.

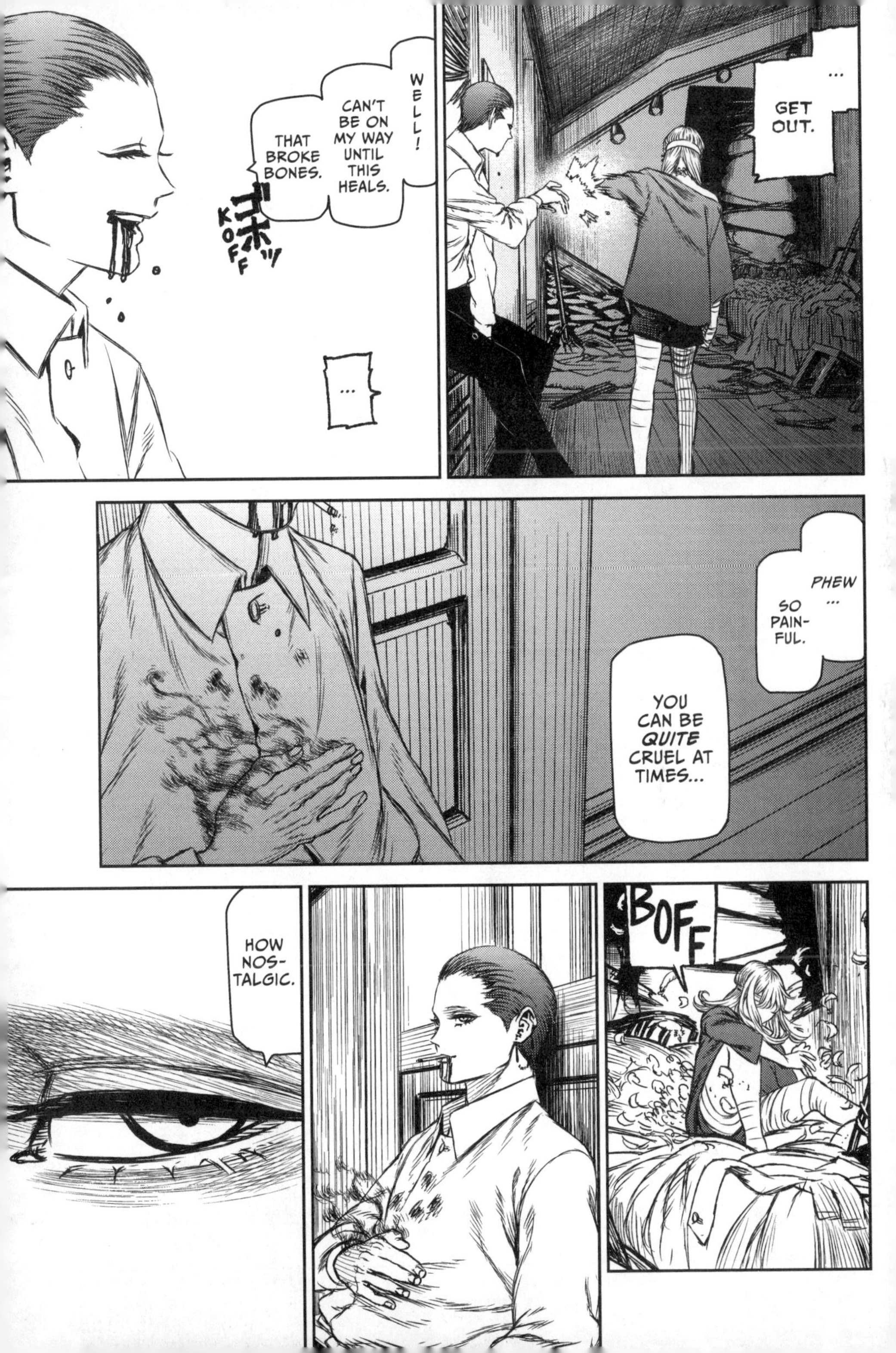
... GET OUT.
WELL!
CAN'T BE ON MY WAY UNTIL THIS HEALS.
THAT BROKE BONES.
ゴホッ KOFF
...
PHEW ...
SO PAINFUL.
YOU CAN BE *QUITE* CRUEL AT TIMES...
BOFF
HOW NOSTALGIC.

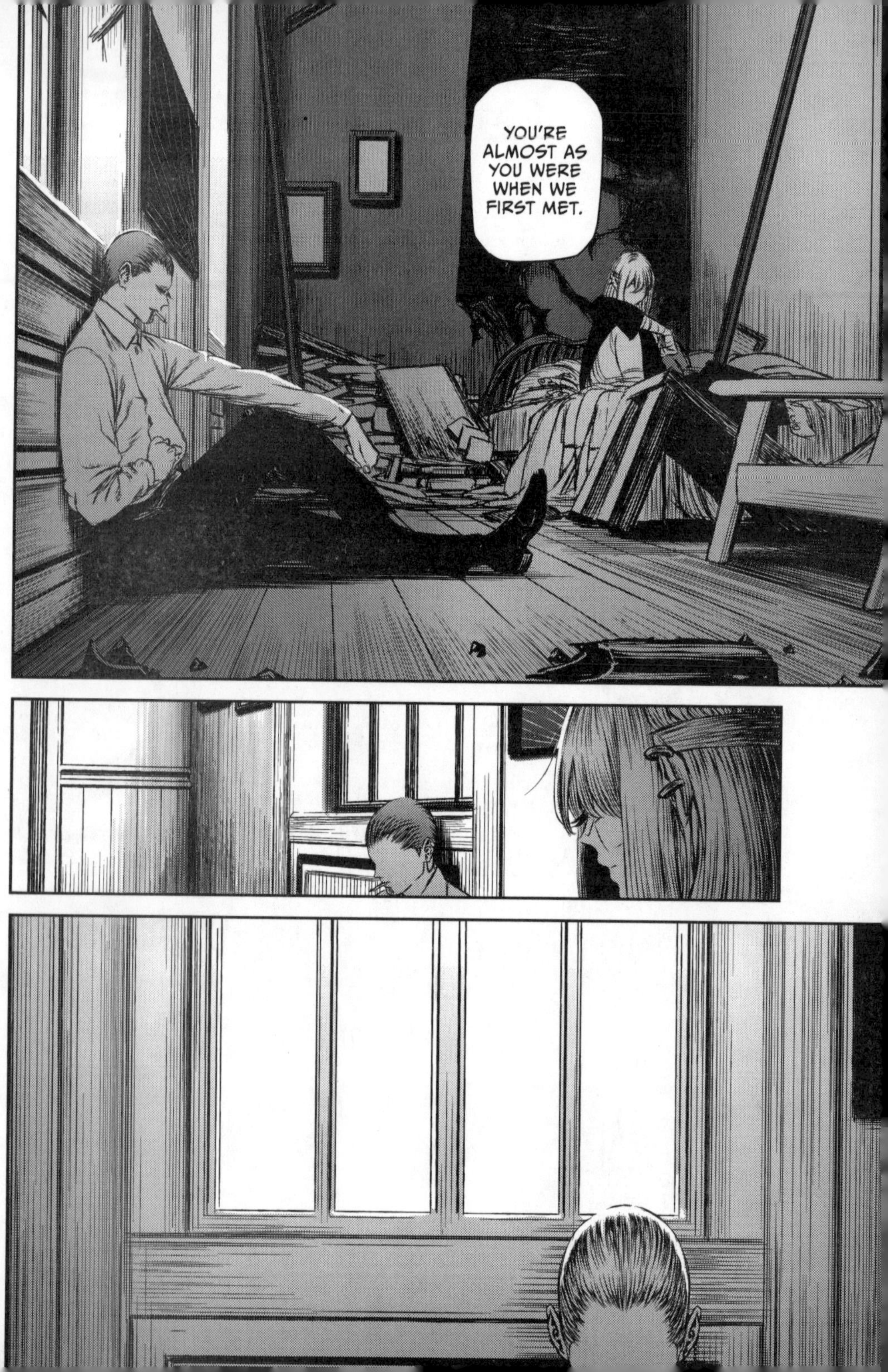
YOU'RE ALMOST AS YOU WERE WHEN WE FIRST MET.

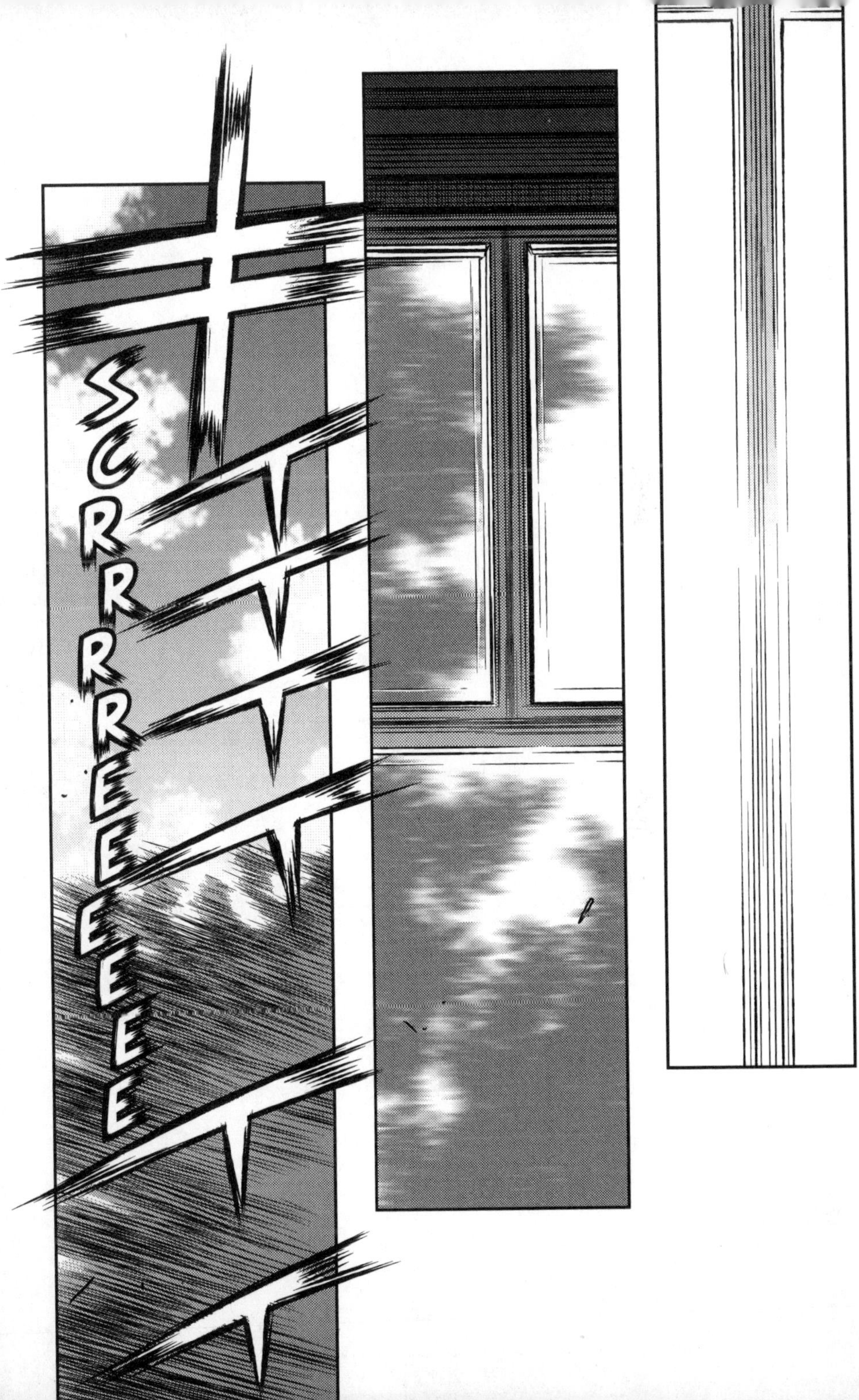
SCRREEEEE

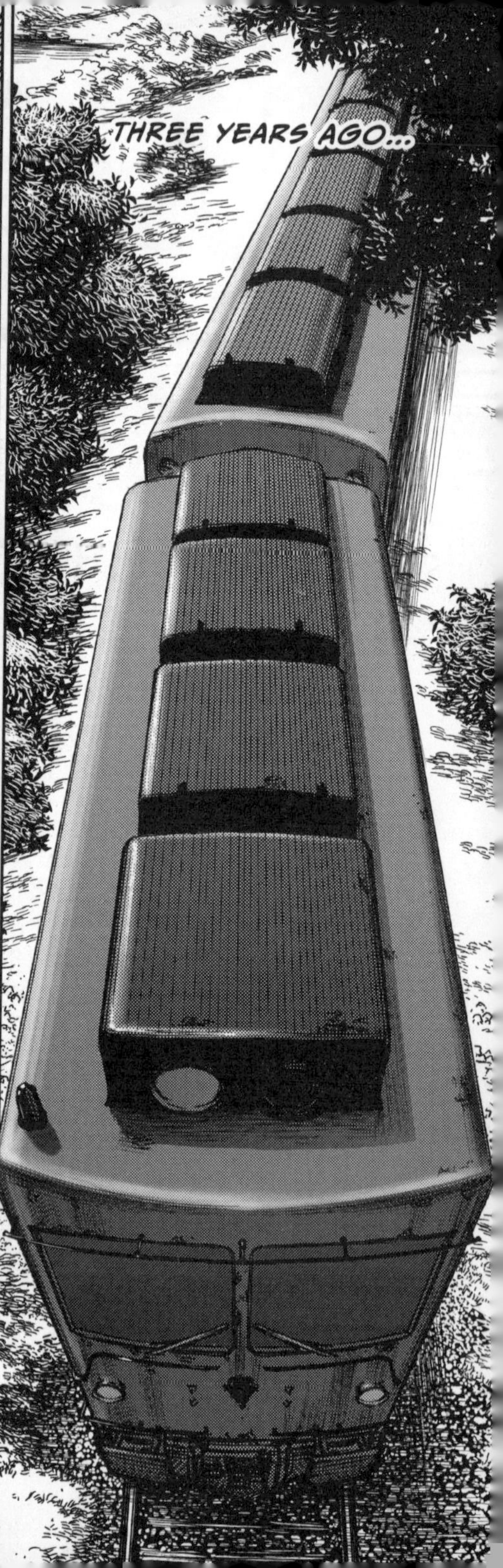
THREE YEARS AGO...
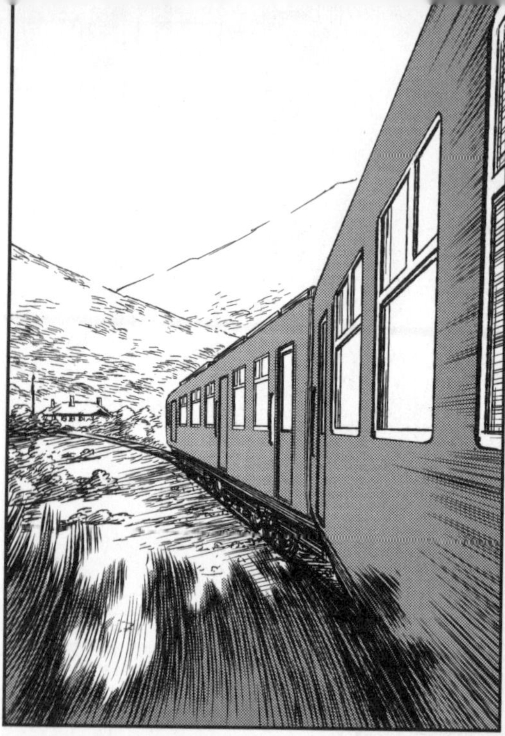
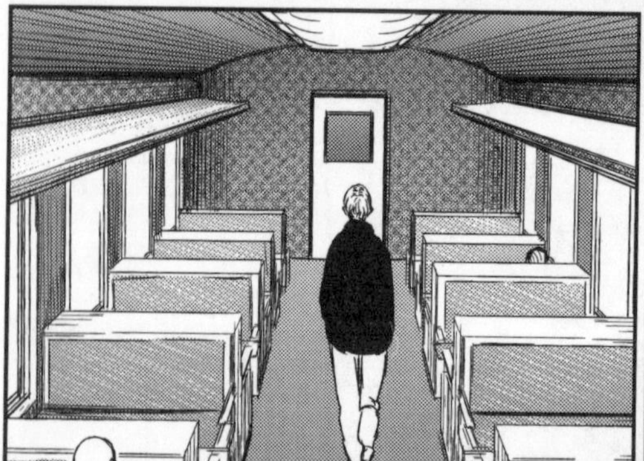
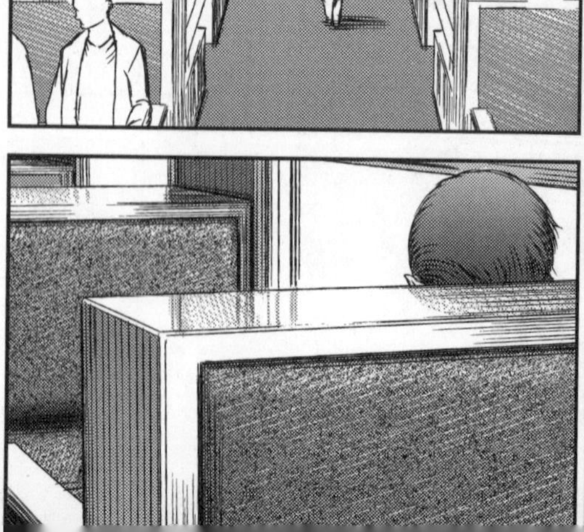

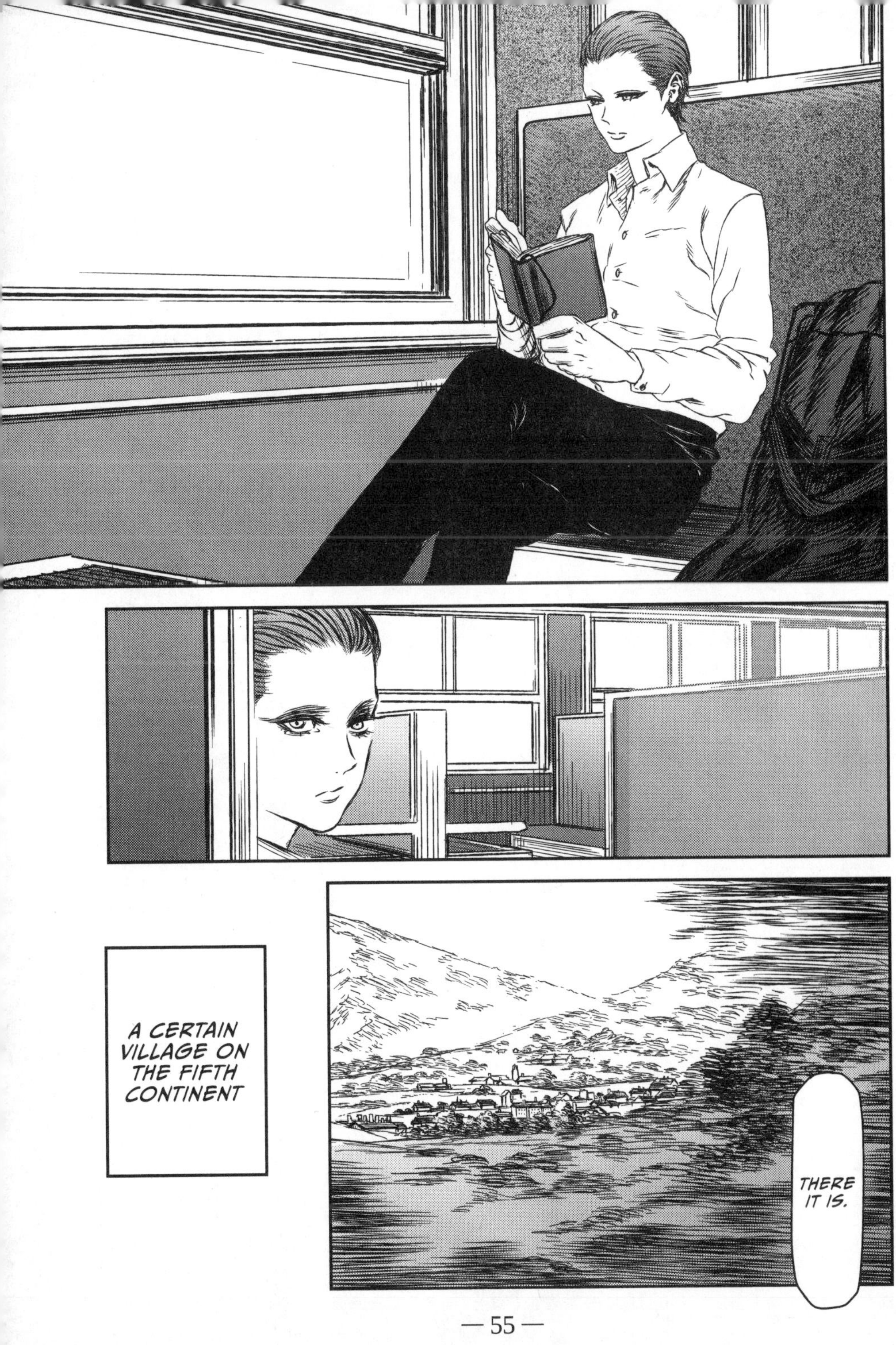
THERE IT IS.
A CERTAIN VILLAGE ON THE FIFTH CONTINENT

HERE, FAR FROM THE GLOBAL HOLY CHURCH'S HEADQUARTERS ON THE FIRST CONTINENT...

...A CULTURE OF MAGIC HAS YET TO DEVELOP.

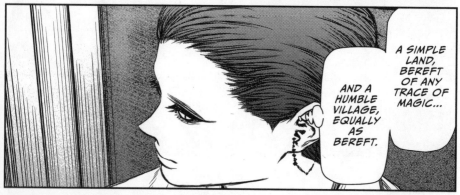

A SIMPLE LAND, BEREFT OF ANY TRACE OF MAGIC...

AND A HUMBLE VILLAGE, EQUALLY AS BEREFT.

...?

HEY...

THAT WAS A COFFIN JUST NOW, RIGHT?

A COFFIN!

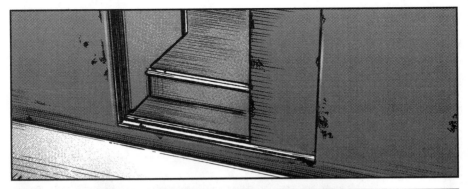

PHEW
...

IT'S BRAC-INGLY EMPTY.

BUT THIS VILLAGE IS HOME TO A WITCH.

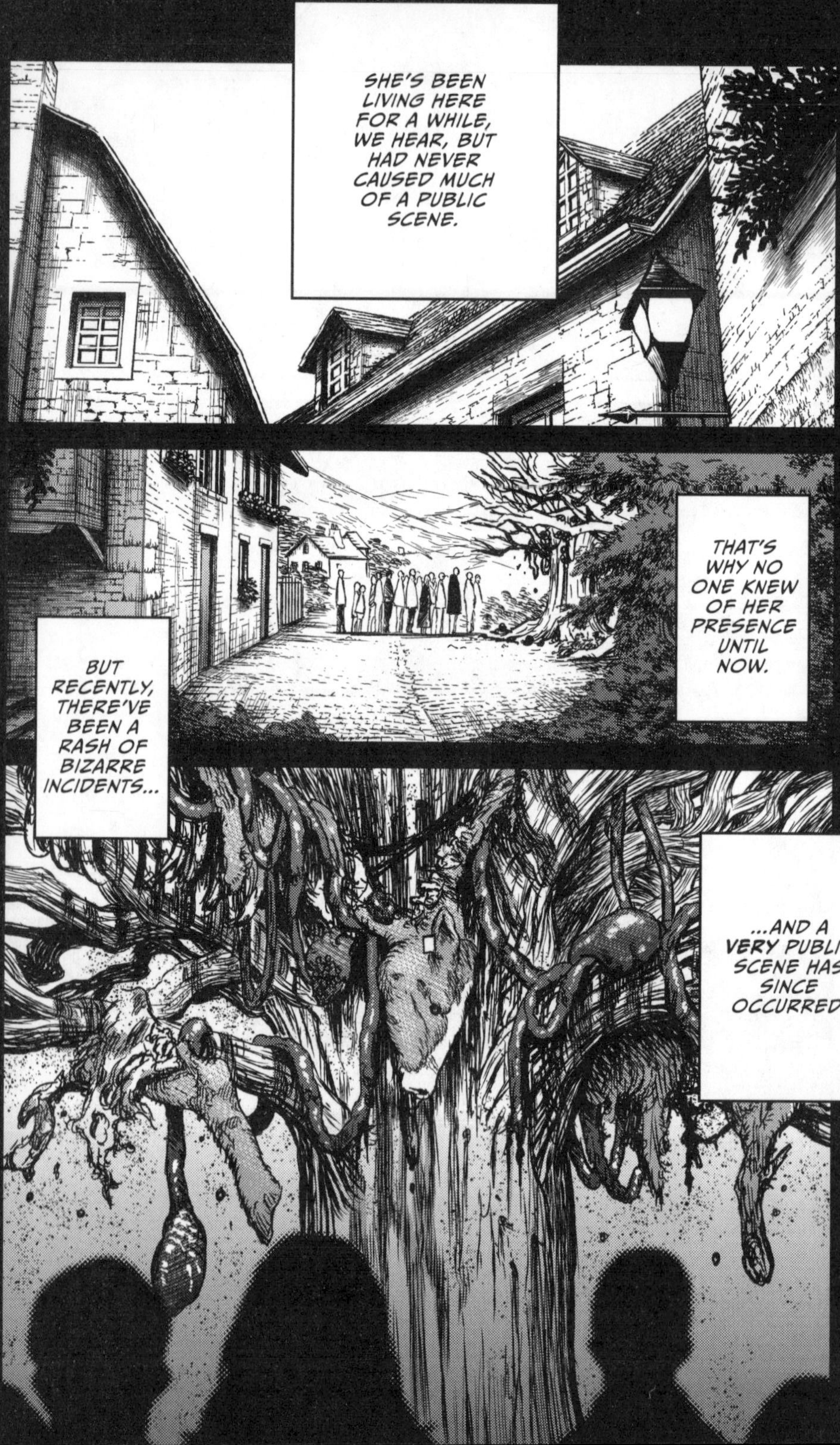
SHE'S BEEN LIVING HERE FOR A WHILE, WE HEAR, BUT HAD NEVER CAUSED MUCH OF A PUBLIC SCENE.
THAT'S WHY NO ONE KNEW OF HER PRESENCE UNTIL NOW.
BUT RECENTLY, THERE'VE BEEN A RASH OF BIZARRE INCIDENTS...
...AND A **VERY** PUBLIC SCENE HAS SINCE OCCURRED.

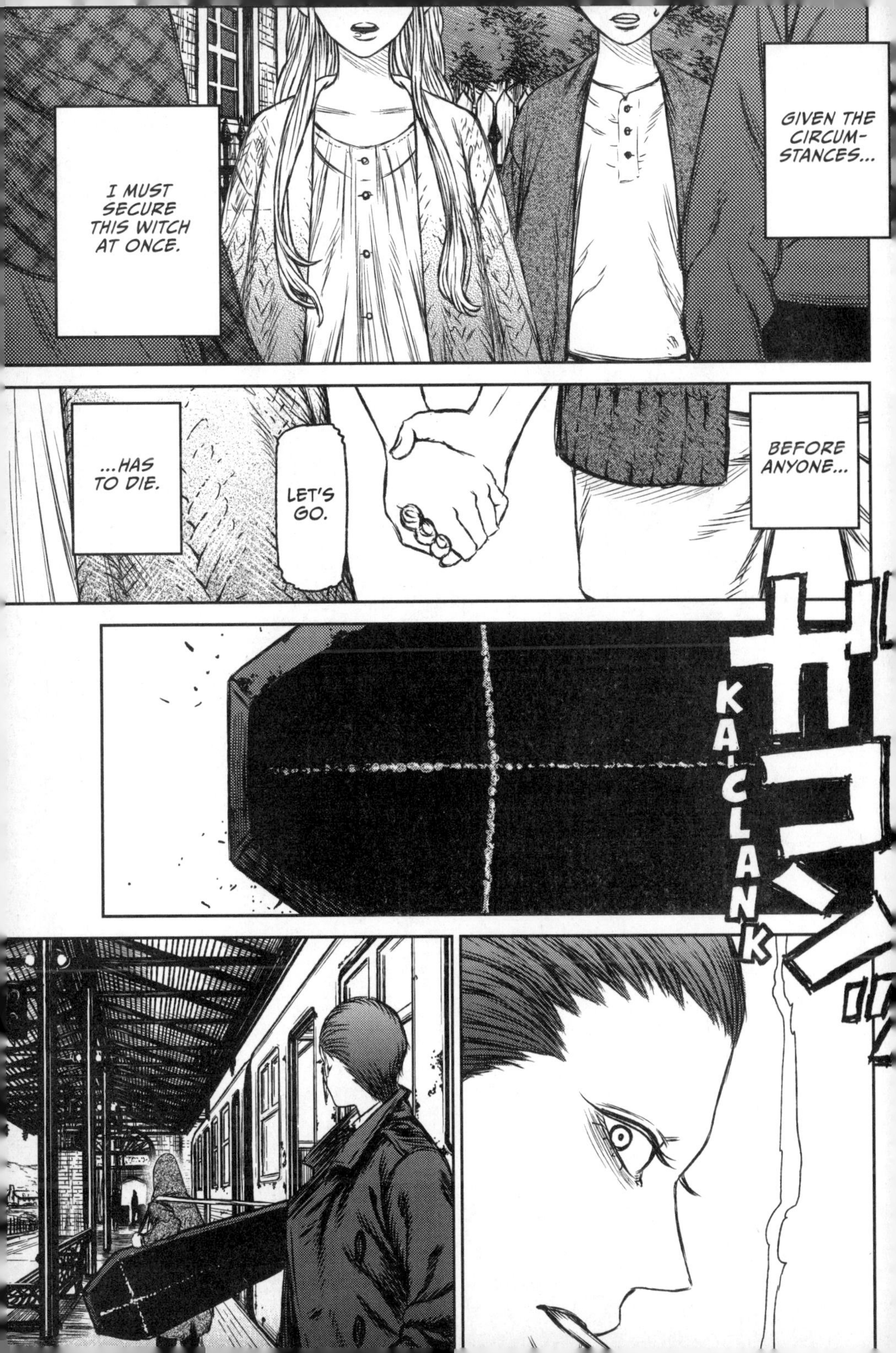
GIVEN THE CIRCUM-STANCES...
I MUST SECURE THIS WITCH AT ONCE.
BEFORE ANYONE...
LET'S GO.
...HAS TO DIE.
KA-CLANK

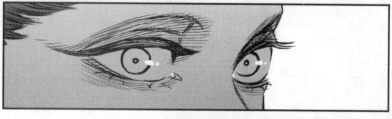

THE WITCH AND THE BEAST

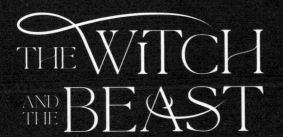

THE WITCH AND THE BEAST

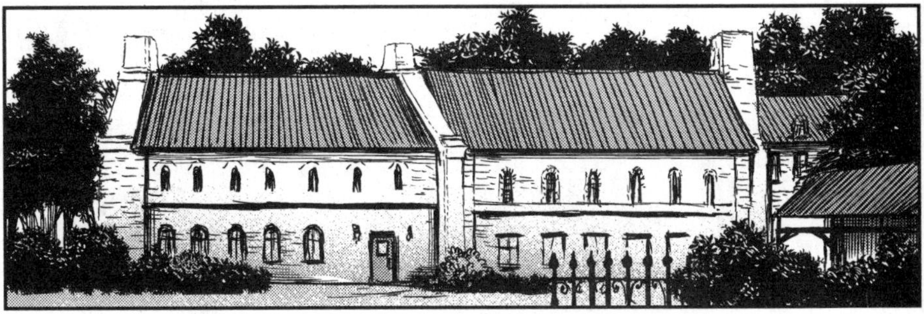

CHAPTER 25

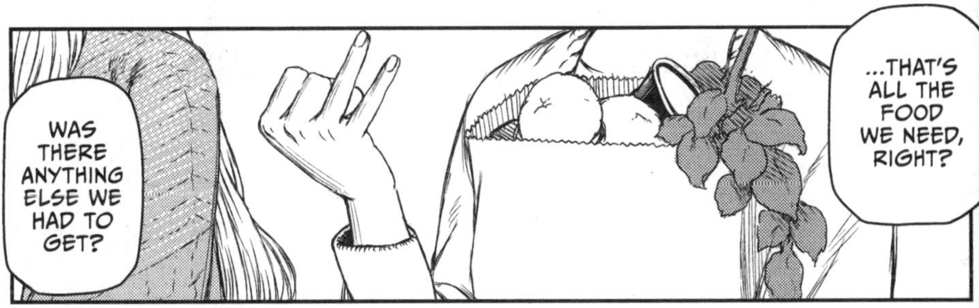
...THAT'S ALL THE FOOD WE NEED, RIGHT?
WAS THERE ANYTHING ELSE WE HAD TO GET?

ELOQUENCE AND SILENCE

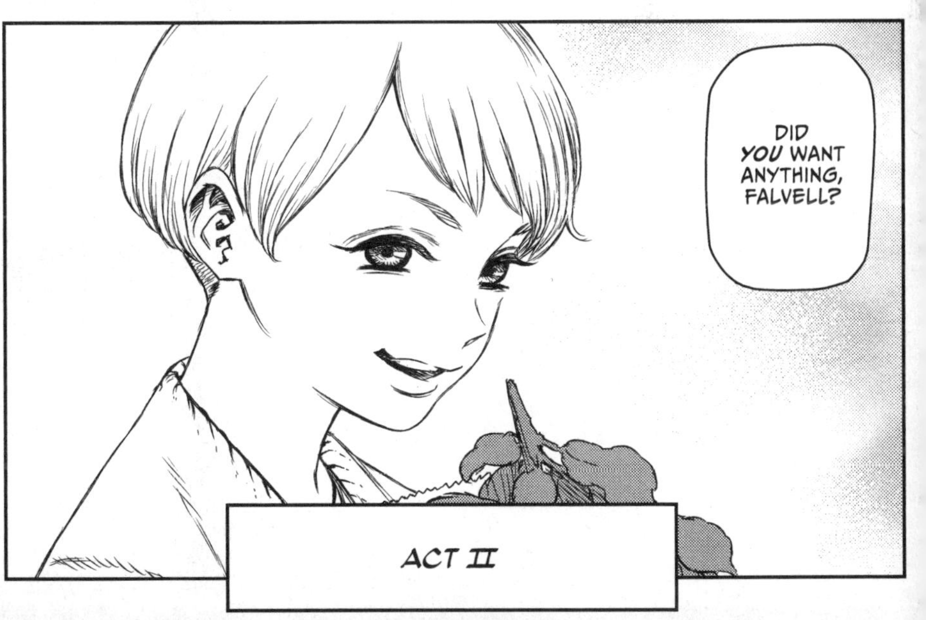
DID *YOU* WANT ANYTHING, FALVELL?

ACT II

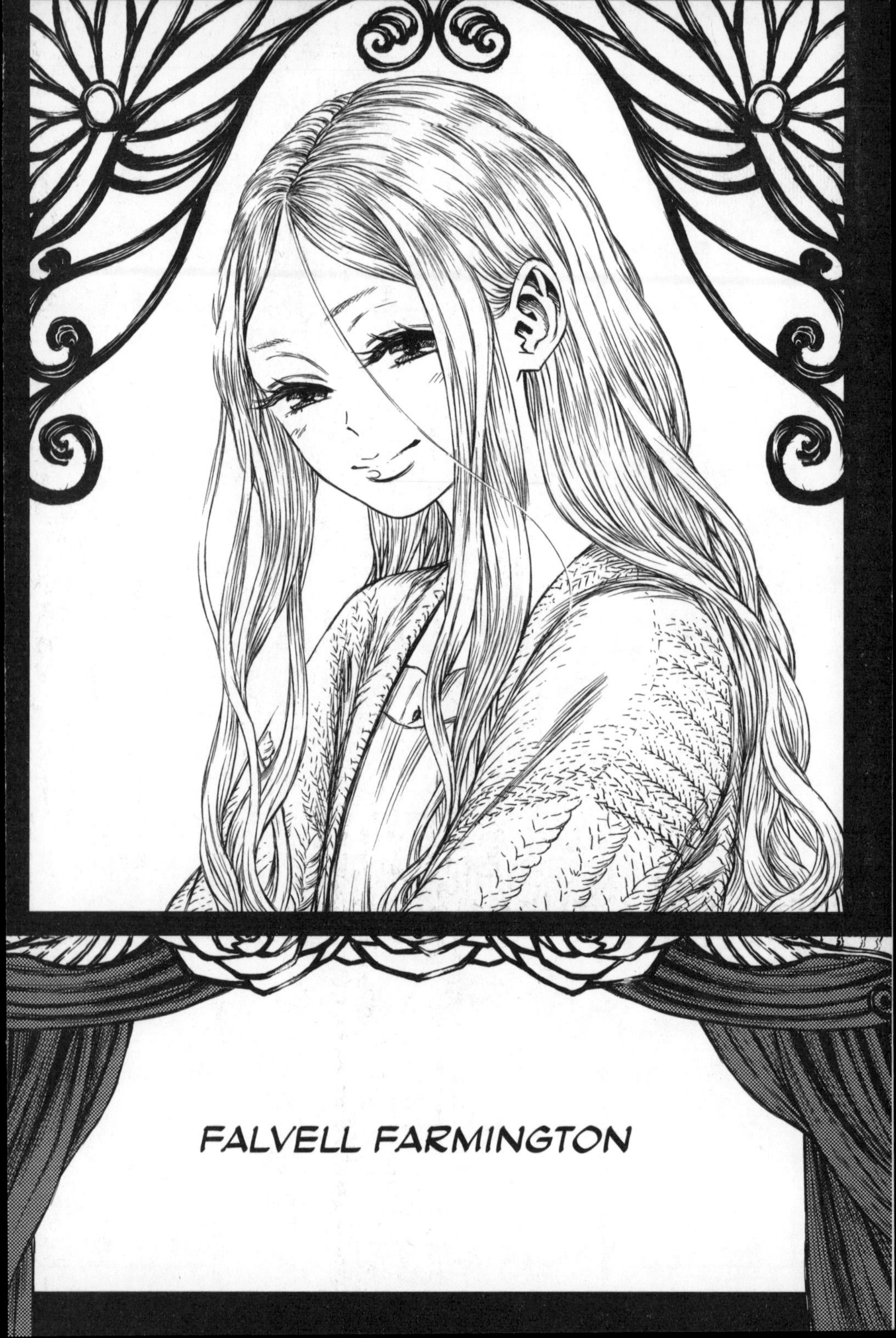
FALVELL FARMINGTON

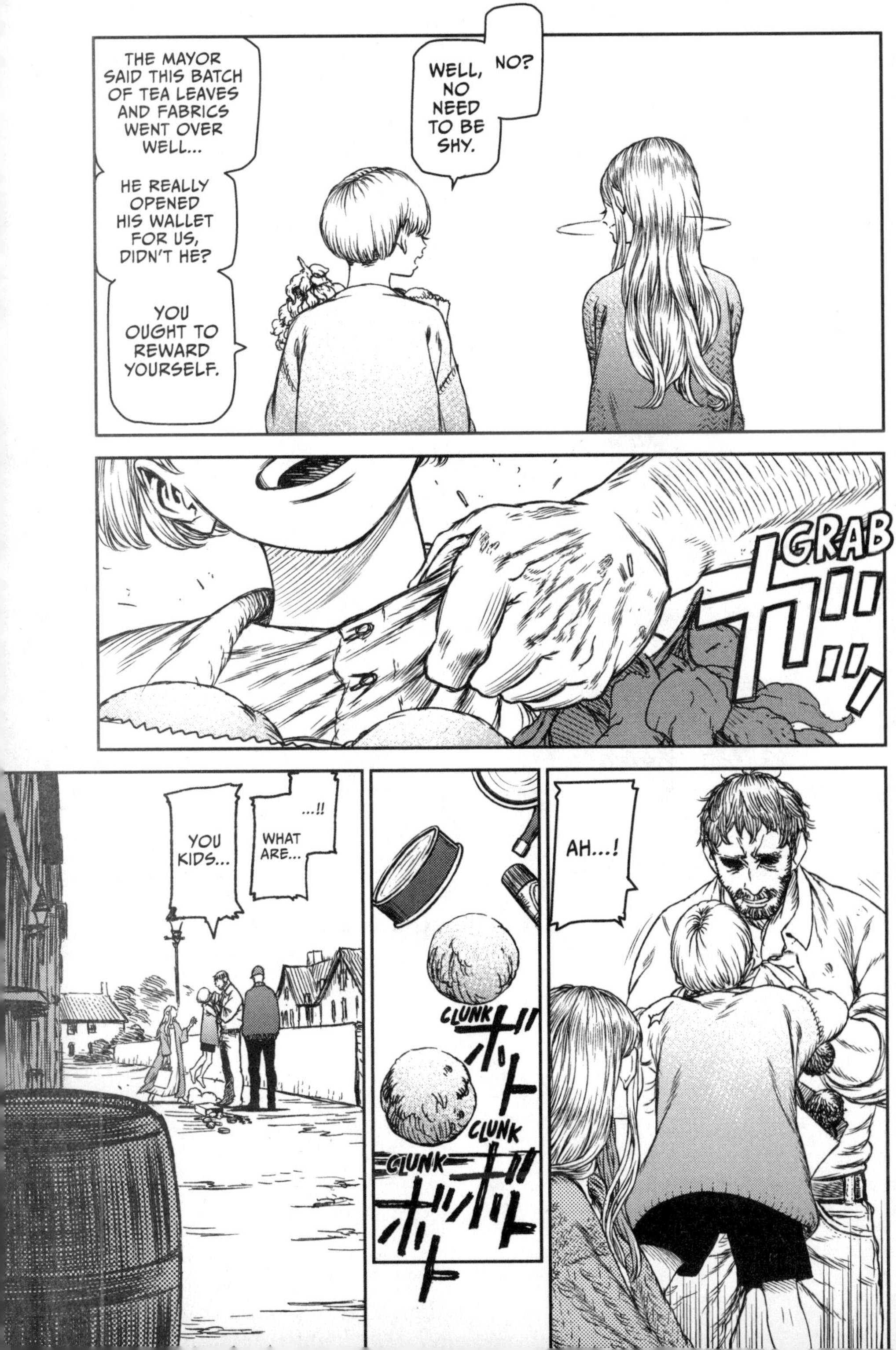

NO?
WELL, NO NEED TO BE SHY.
THE MAYOR SAID THIS BATCH OF TEA LEAVES AND FABRICS WENT OVER WELL...
HE REALLY OPENED HIS WALLET FOR US, DIDN'T HE?
YOU OUGHT TO REWARD YOURSELF.
GRAB
AH...!
CLUNK
CLUNK
CLUNK
...!!
WHAT ARE...
YOU KIDS...

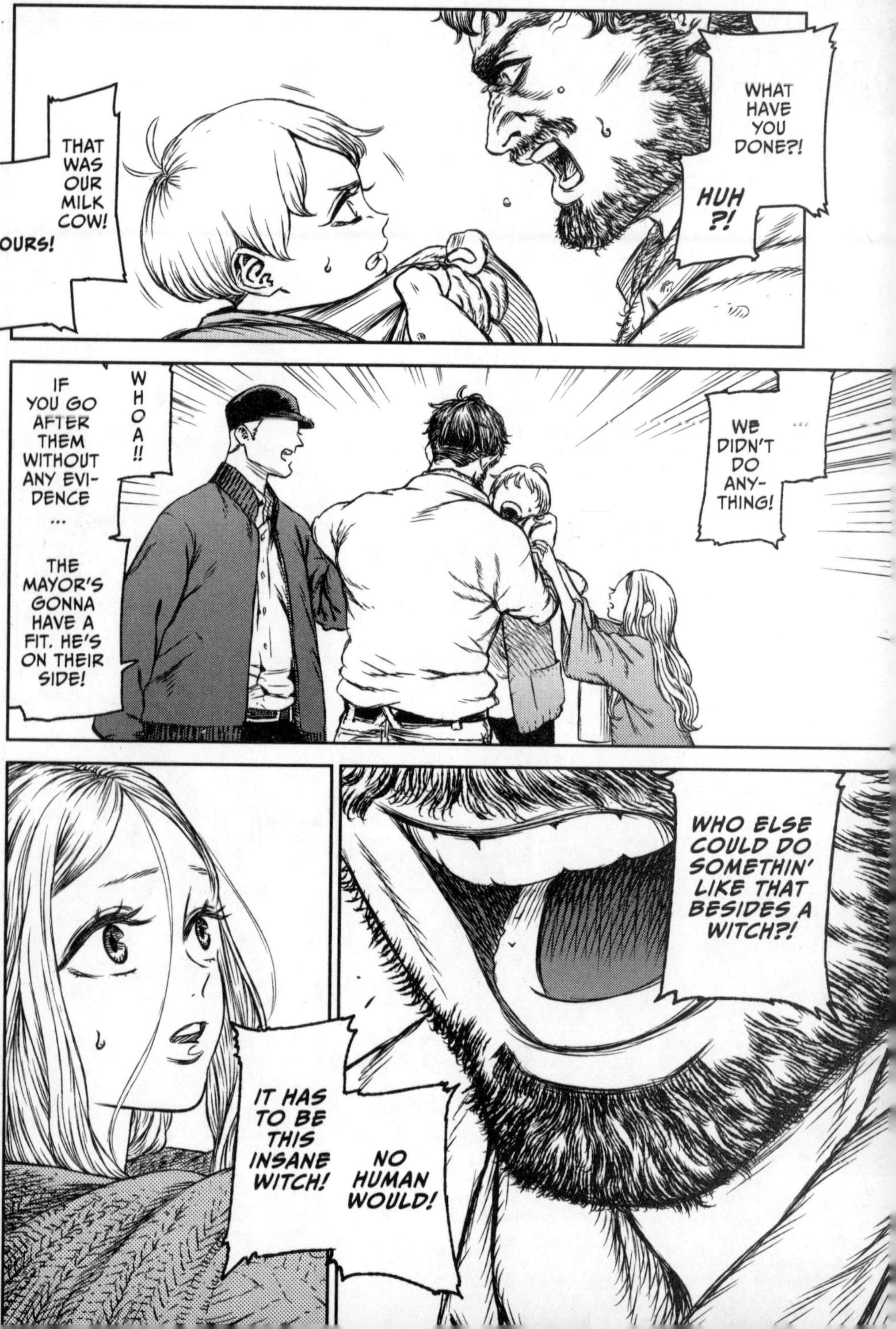
WHAT HAVE YOU DONE?!
HUH ?!
THAT WAS OUR MILK COW!
OURS!
WE DIDN'T DO ANYTHING!
WHOA!!
IF YOU GO AFTER THEM WITHOUT ANY EVIDENCE ...
THE MAYOR'S GONNA HAVE A FIT. HE'S ON THEIR SIDE!
WHO ELSE COULD DO SOMETHIN' LIKE THAT BESIDES A WITCH?!
NO HUMAN WOULD!
IT HAS TO BE THIS INSANE WITCH!

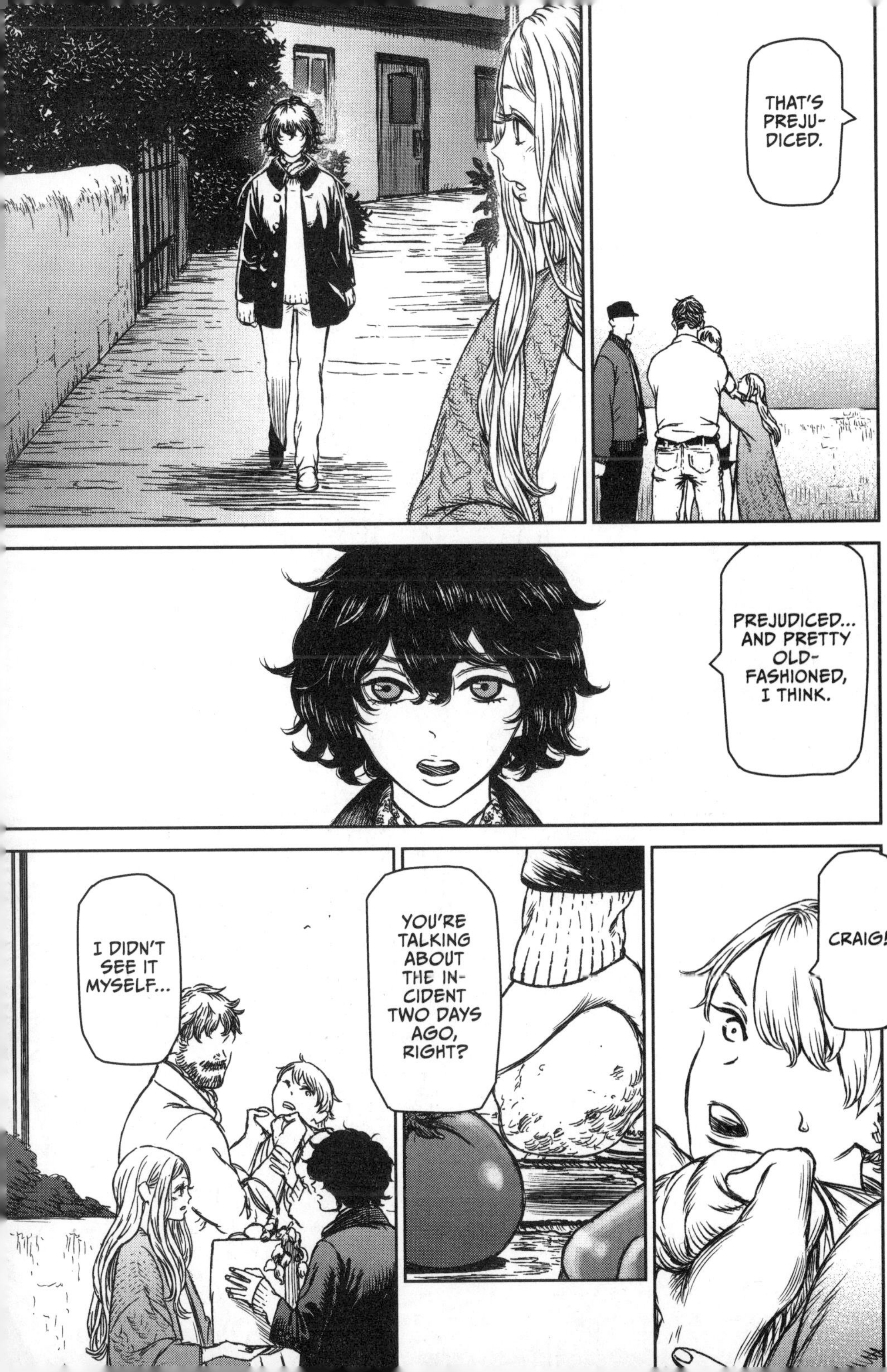
THAT'S PREJUDICED.
PREJUDICED... AND PRETTY OLD-FASHIONED, I THINK.
CRAIG!
YOU'RE TALKING ABOUT THE INCIDENT TWO DAYS AGO, RIGHT?
I DIDN'T SEE IT MYSELF...

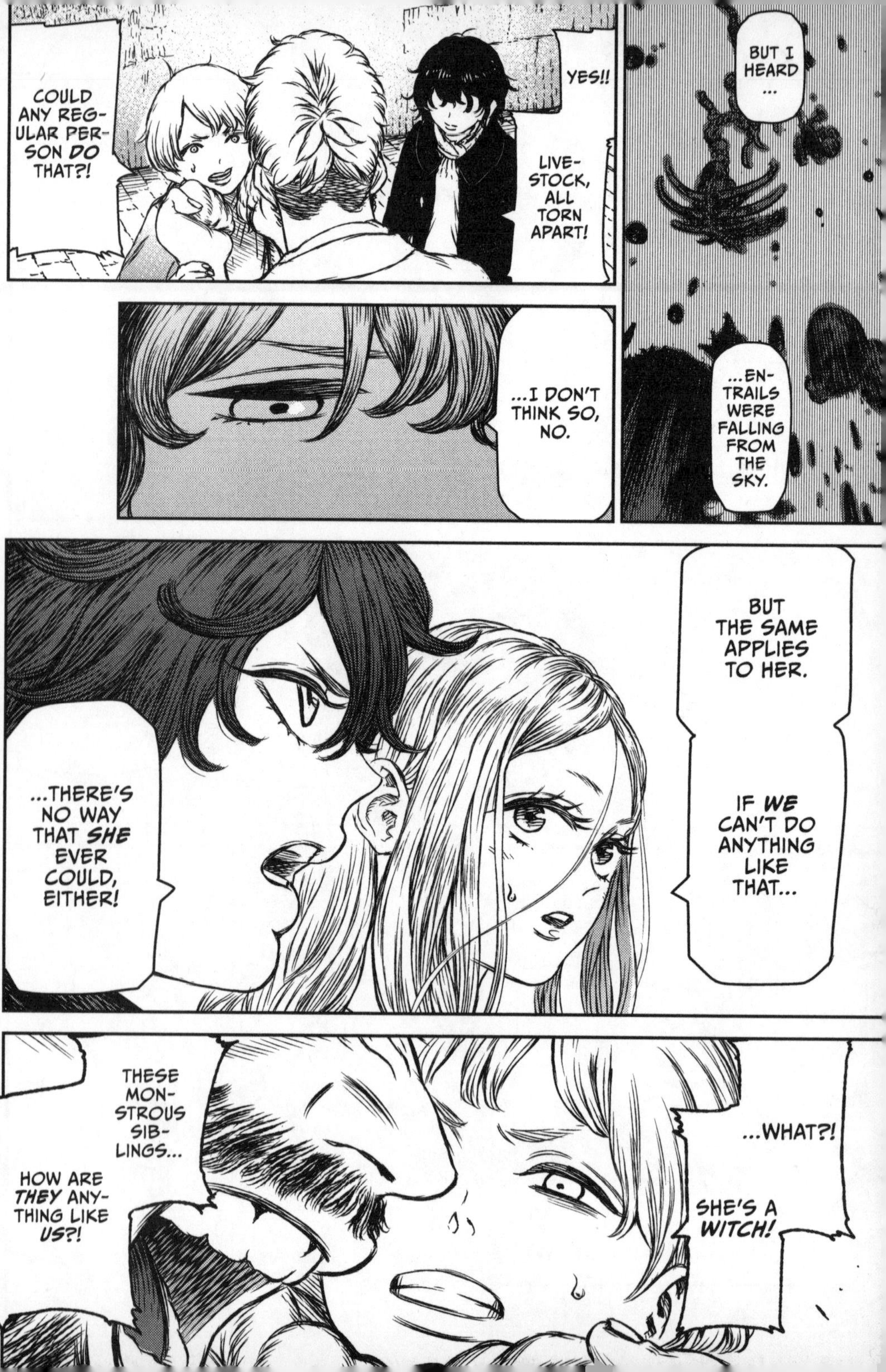
BUT I HEARD ...
...EN-TRAILS WERE FALLING FROM THE SKY.
YES!!
LIVE-STOCK, ALL TORN APART!
COULD ANY REG-ULAR PER-SON DO THAT?!
...I DON'T THINK SO, NO.
BUT THE SAME APPLIES TO HER.
IF WE CAN'T DO ANYTHING LIKE THAT...
...THERE'S NO WAY THAT SHE EVER COULD, EITHER!
...WHAT?!
SHE'S A WITCH!
THESE MON-STROUS SIB-LINGS...
HOW ARE THEY ANY-THING LIKE US?!

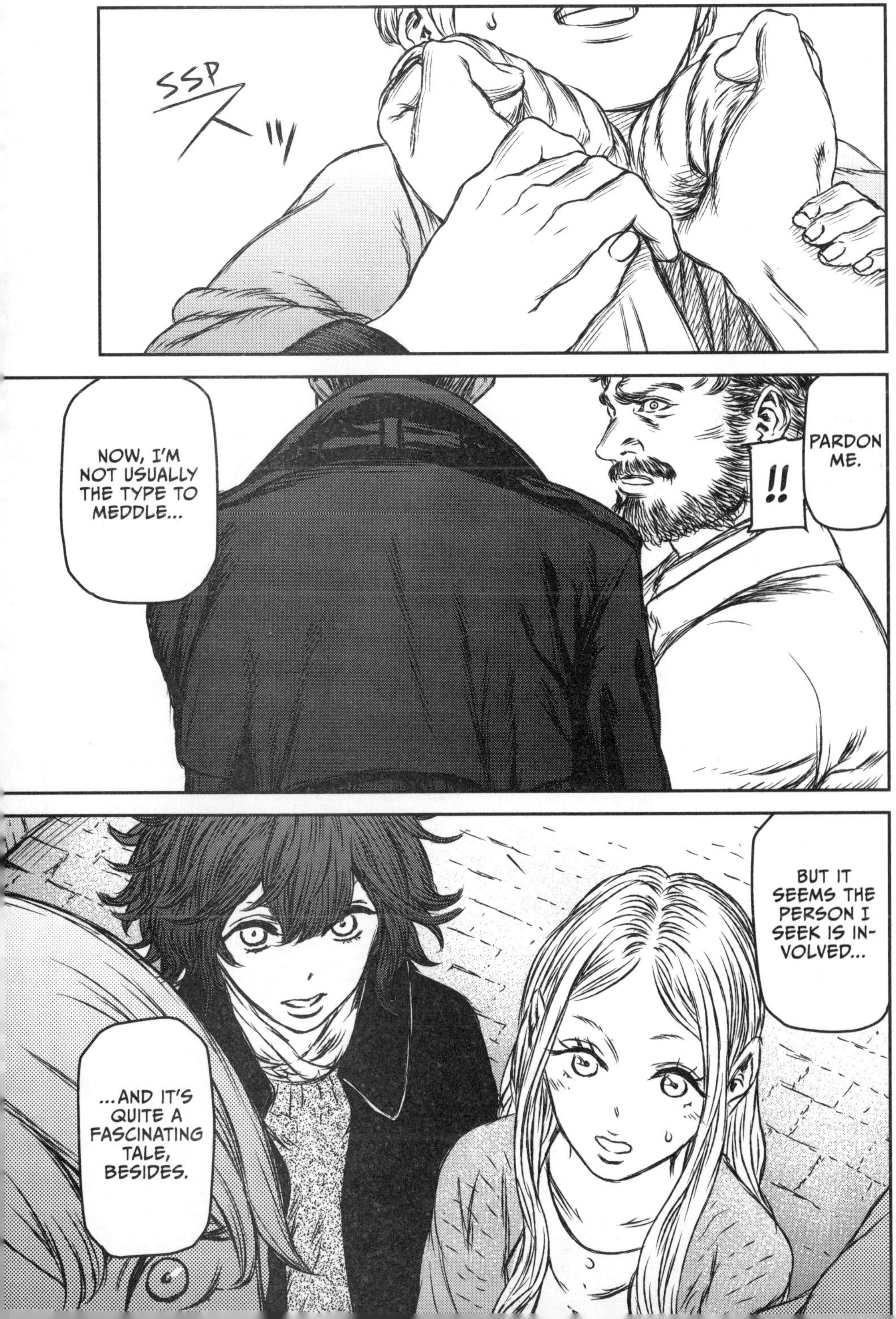
SSP
スッ
PARDON ME.
!!
NOW, I'M NOT USUALLY THE TYPE TO MEDDLE...
BUT IT SEEMS THE PERSON I SEEK IS INVOLVED...
...AND IT'S QUITE A FASCINATING TALE, BESIDES.

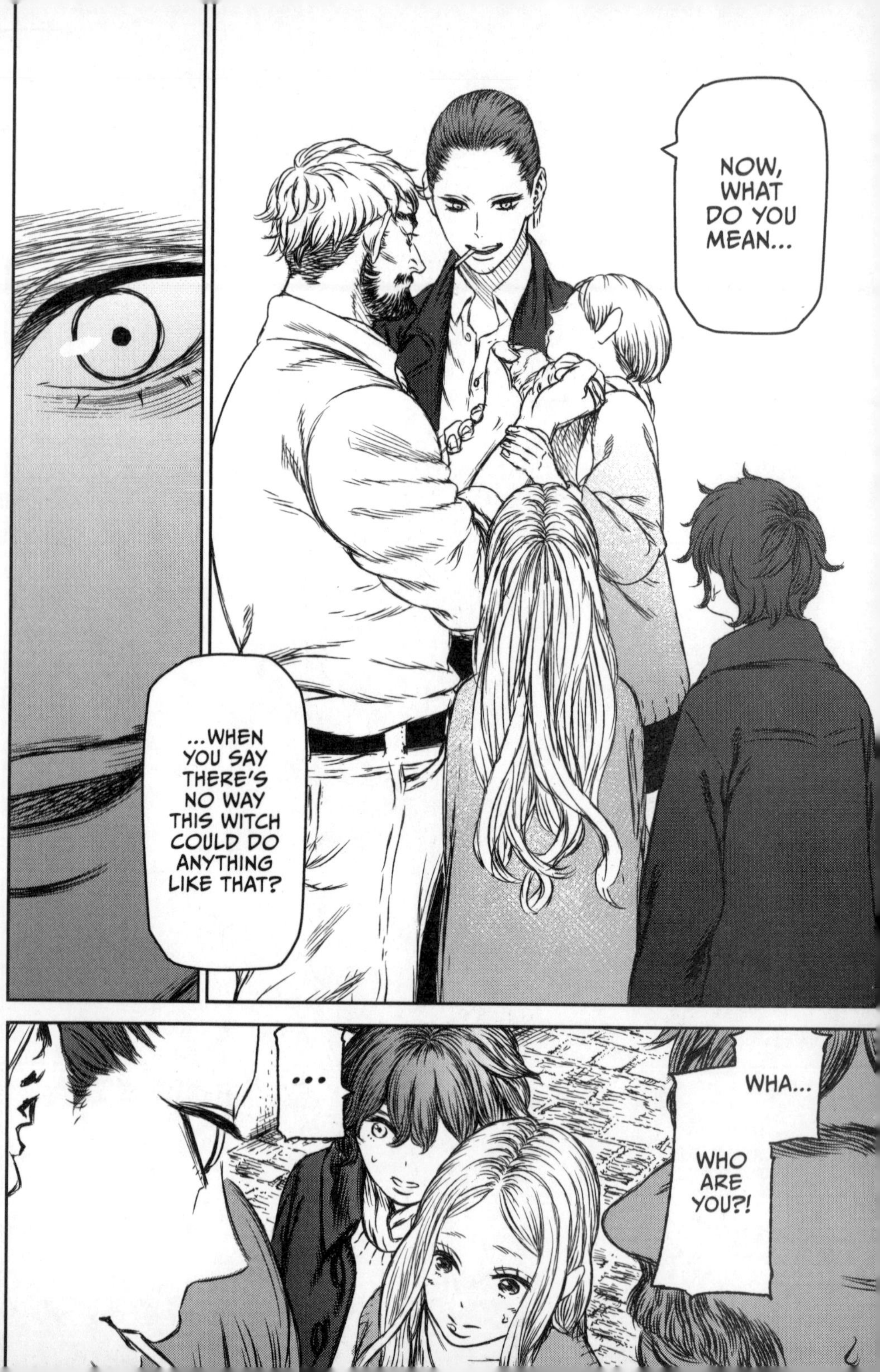
NOW, WHAT DO YOU MEAN...
...WHEN YOU SAY THERE'S NO WAY THIS WITCH COULD DO ANYTHING LIKE THAT?
WHA... WHO ARE YOU?!
...

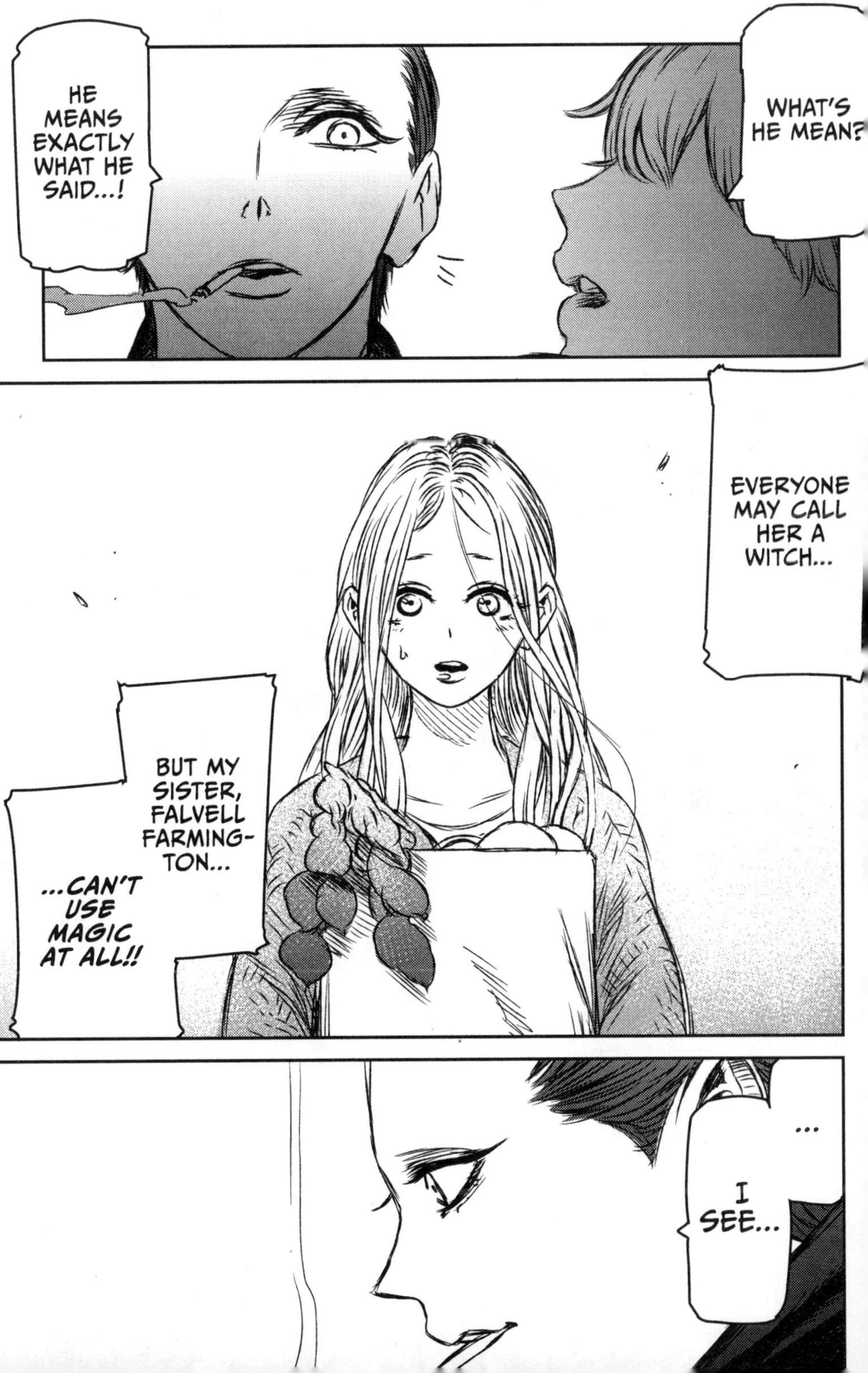
WHAT'S HE MEAN?
HE MEANS EXACTLY WHAT HE SAID...!
EVERYONE MAY CALL HER A WITCH...
BUT MY SISTER, FALVELL FARMINGTON...
...CAN'T USE MAGIC AT ALL!!
...
I SEE...

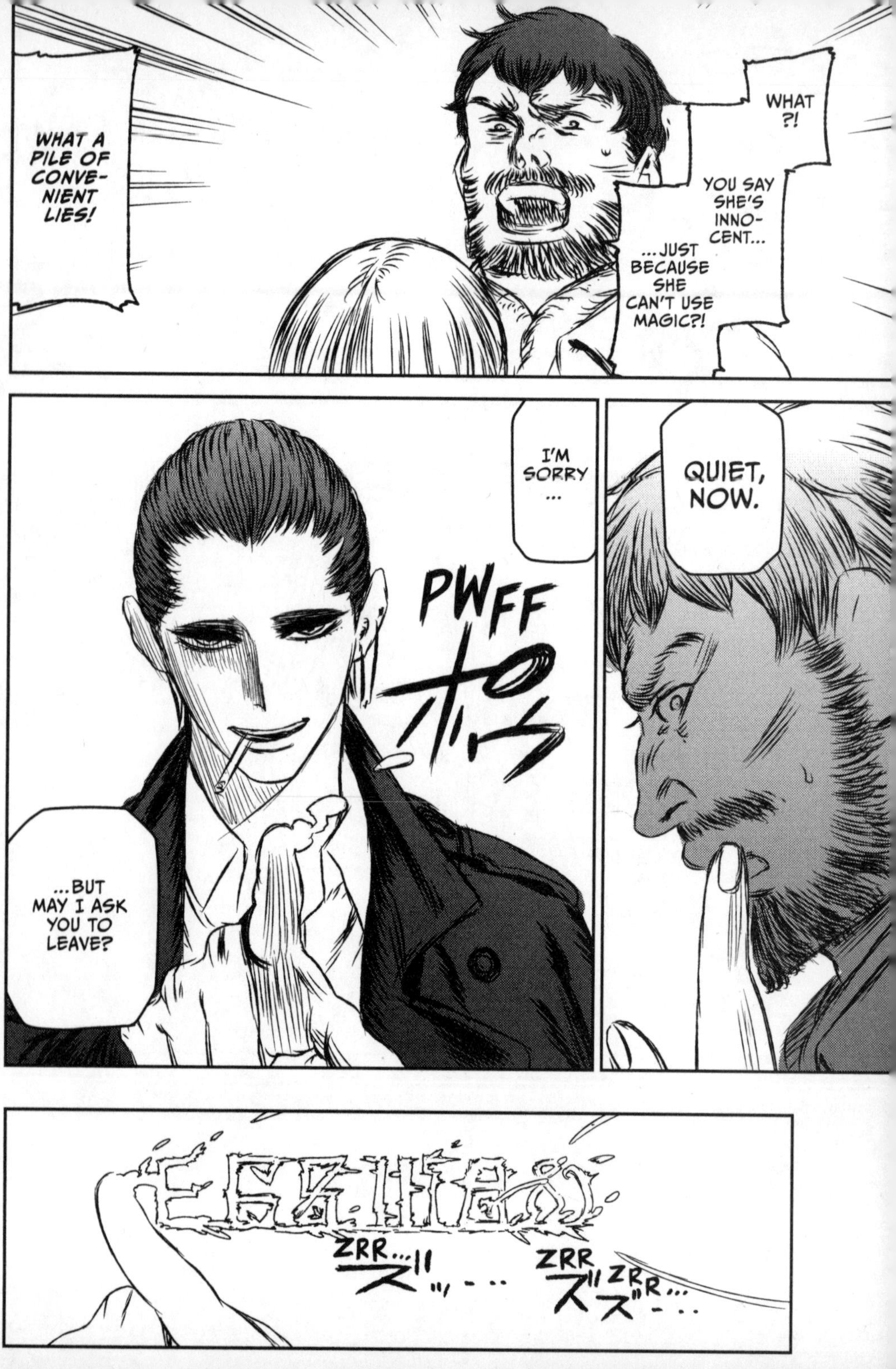
WHAT ?!
YOU SAY SHE'S INNO-CENT...
...JUST BECAUSE SHE CAN'T USE MAGIC?!
WHAT A PILE OF CONVE-NIENT LIES!
QUIET, NOW.
I'M SORRY ...
PWFF
...BUT MAY I ASK YOU TO LEAVE?
ZRR
ZRR...
ZRR...

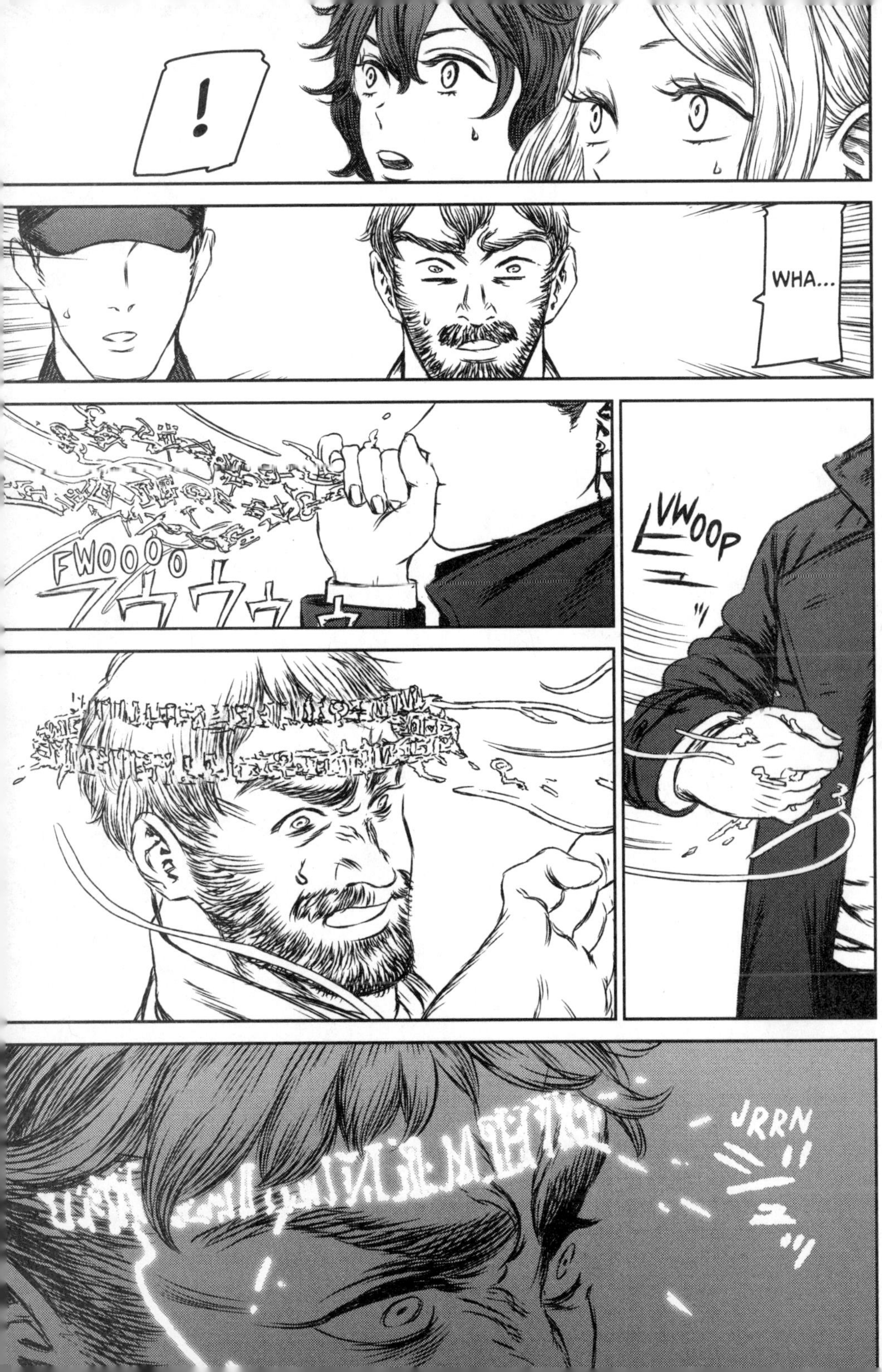
!
WHA...
VWOOP
FWOOOO
JRRN

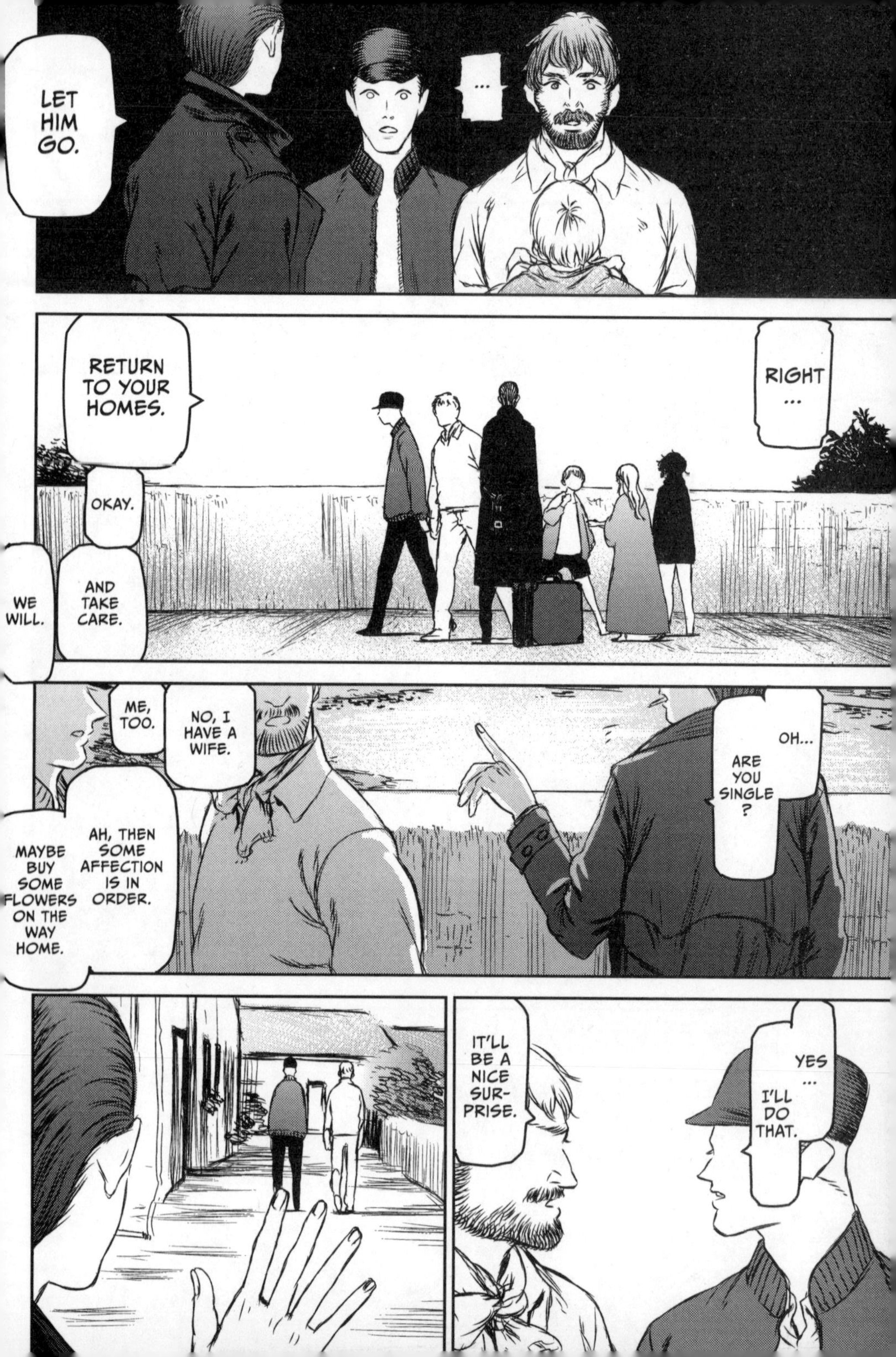
...
LET HIM GO.
RIGHT ...
RETURN TO YOUR HOMES.
OKAY.
AND TAKE CARE.
WE WILL.
OH... ARE YOU SINGLE?
NO, I HAVE A WIFE.
ME, TOO.
AH, THEN SOME AFFECTION IS IN ORDER.
MAYBE BUY SOME FLOWERS ON THE WAY HOME.
YES ... I'LL DO THAT.
IT'LL BE A NICE SUR-PRISE.

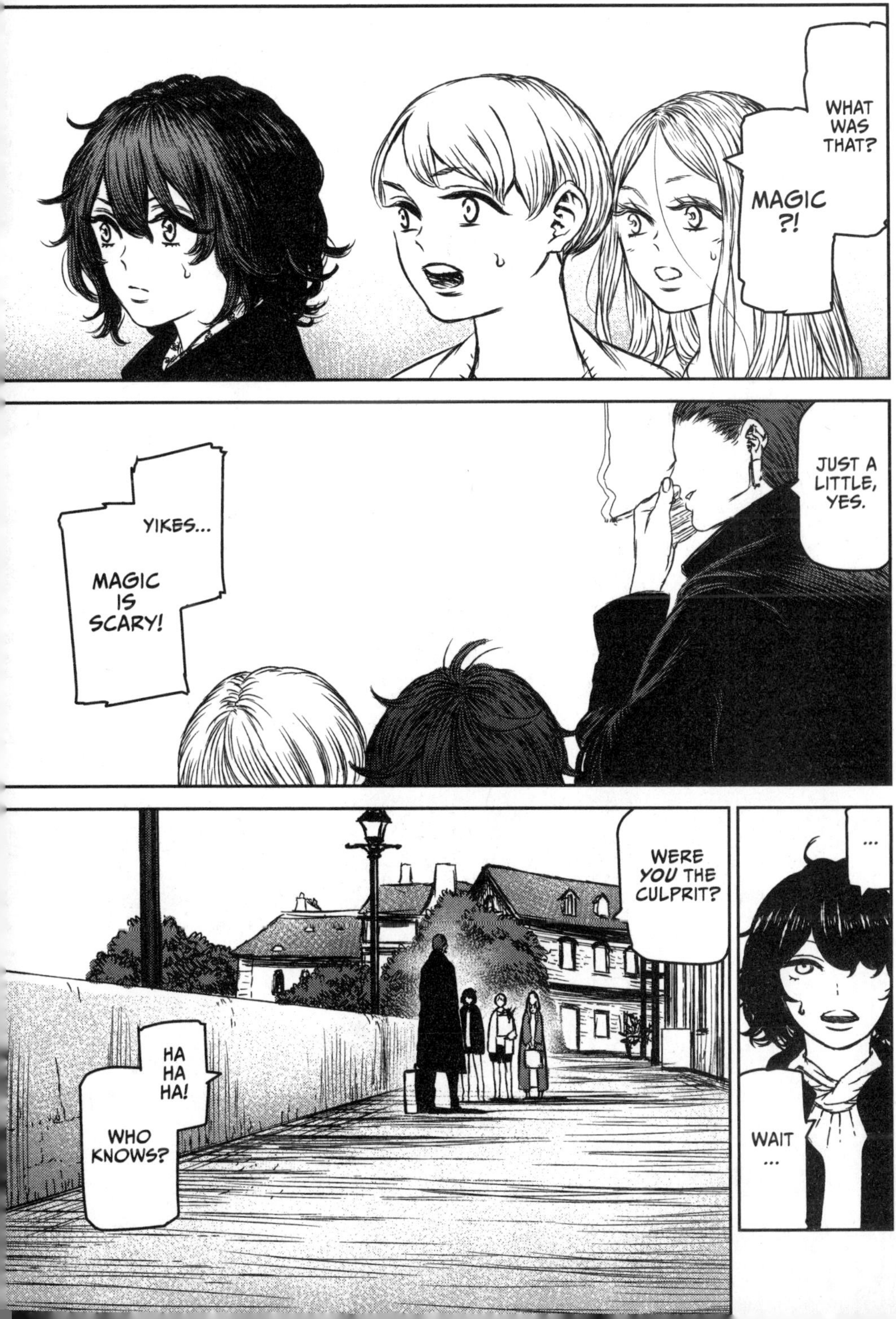
WHAT WAS THAT?
MAGIC ?!
JUST A LITTLE, YES.
YIKES...
MAGIC IS SCARY!
...
WAIT ...
WERE *YOU* THE CULPRIT?
HA HA HA!
WHO KNOWS?

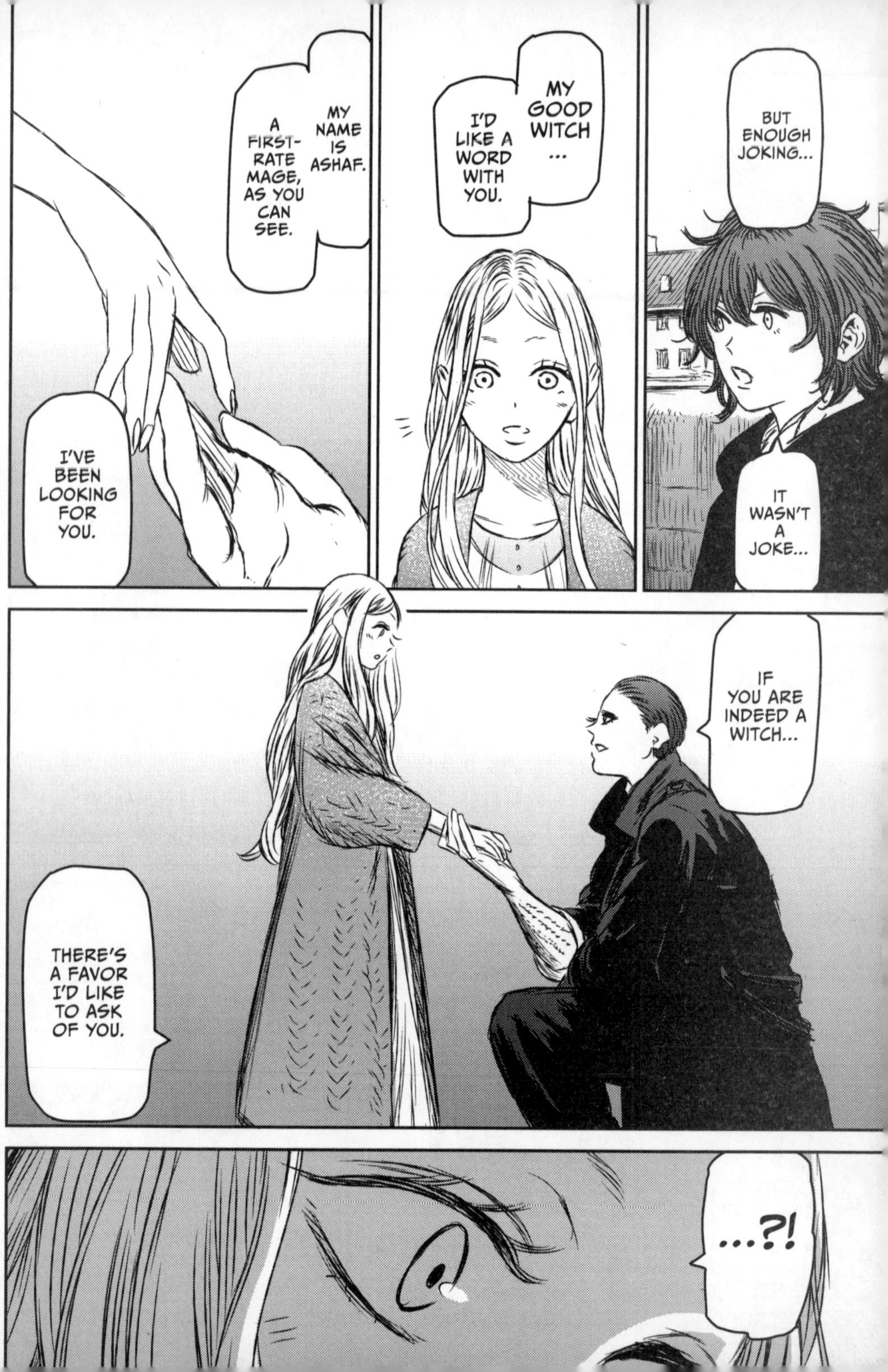
BUT ENOUGH JOKING...
IT WASN'T A JOKE...
MY GOOD WITCH...
I'D LIKE A WORD WITH YOU.
MY NAME IS ASHAF.
A FIRST-RATE MAGE, AS YOU CAN SEE.
I'VE BEEN LOOKING FOR YOU.
IF YOU ARE INDEED A WITCH...
THERE'S A FAVOR I'D LIKE TO ASK OF YOU.
...?!

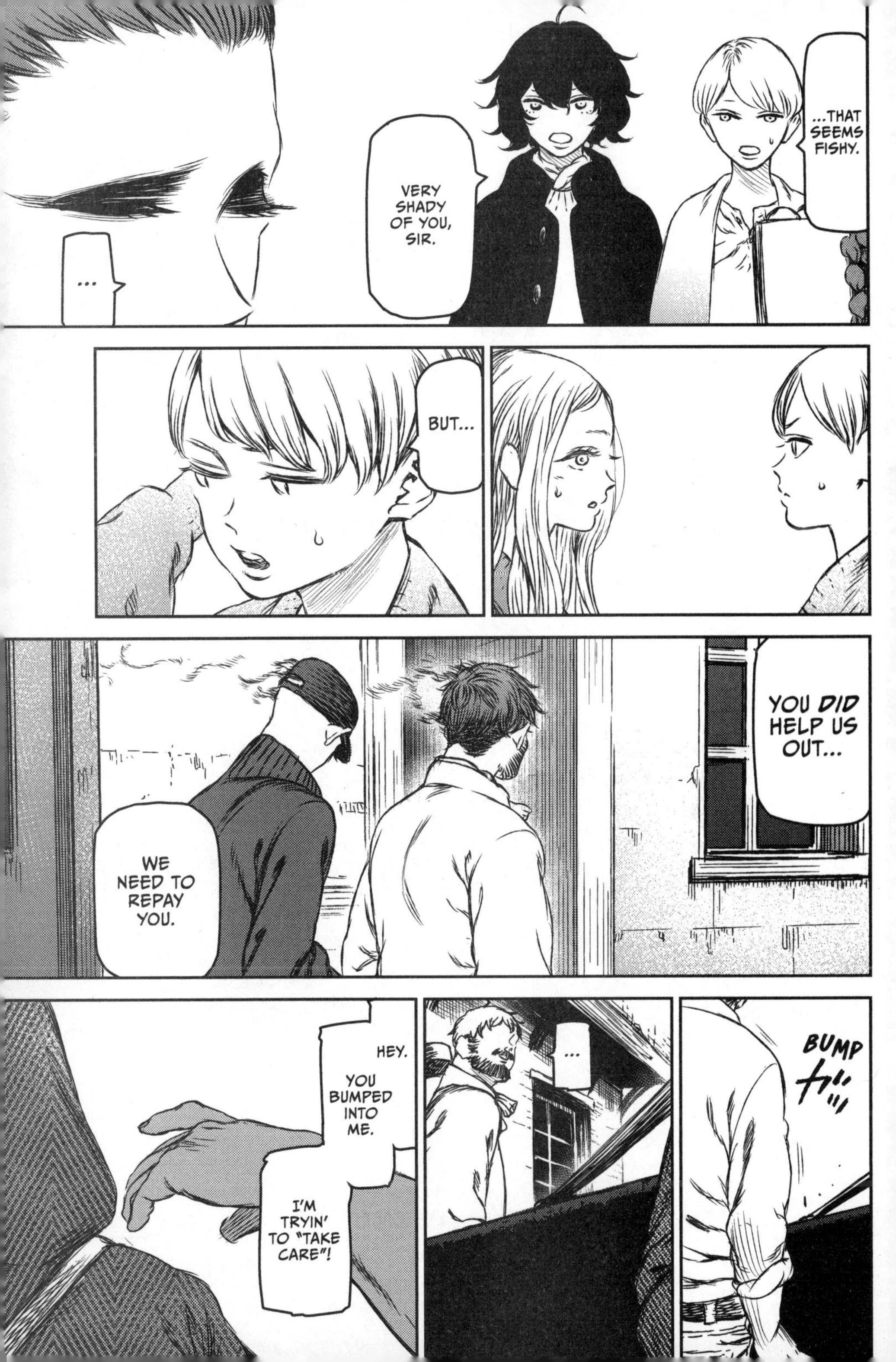
...THAT SEEMS FISHY.
VERY SHADY OF YOU, SIR.
...
BUT...
YOU *DID* HELP US OUT...
WE NEED TO REPAY YOU.
BUMP
ガッ
...
HEY. YOU BUMPED INTO ME.
I'M TRYIN' TO "TAKE CARE"!

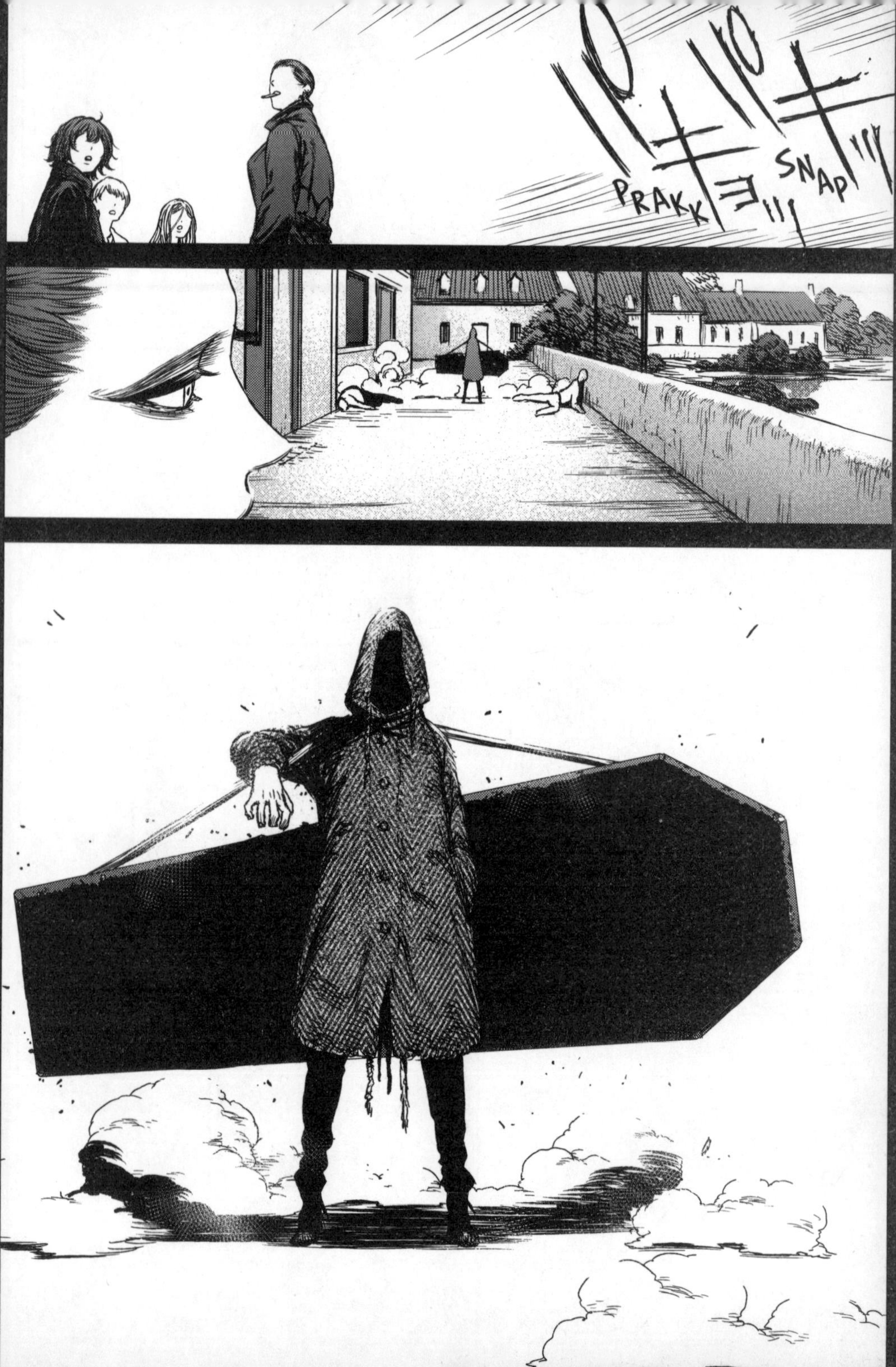
SNAP
PRAKK

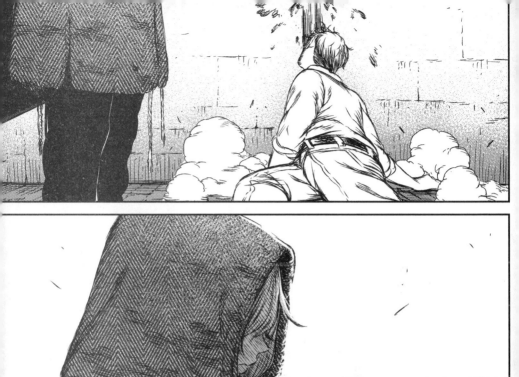

....?

GRIT

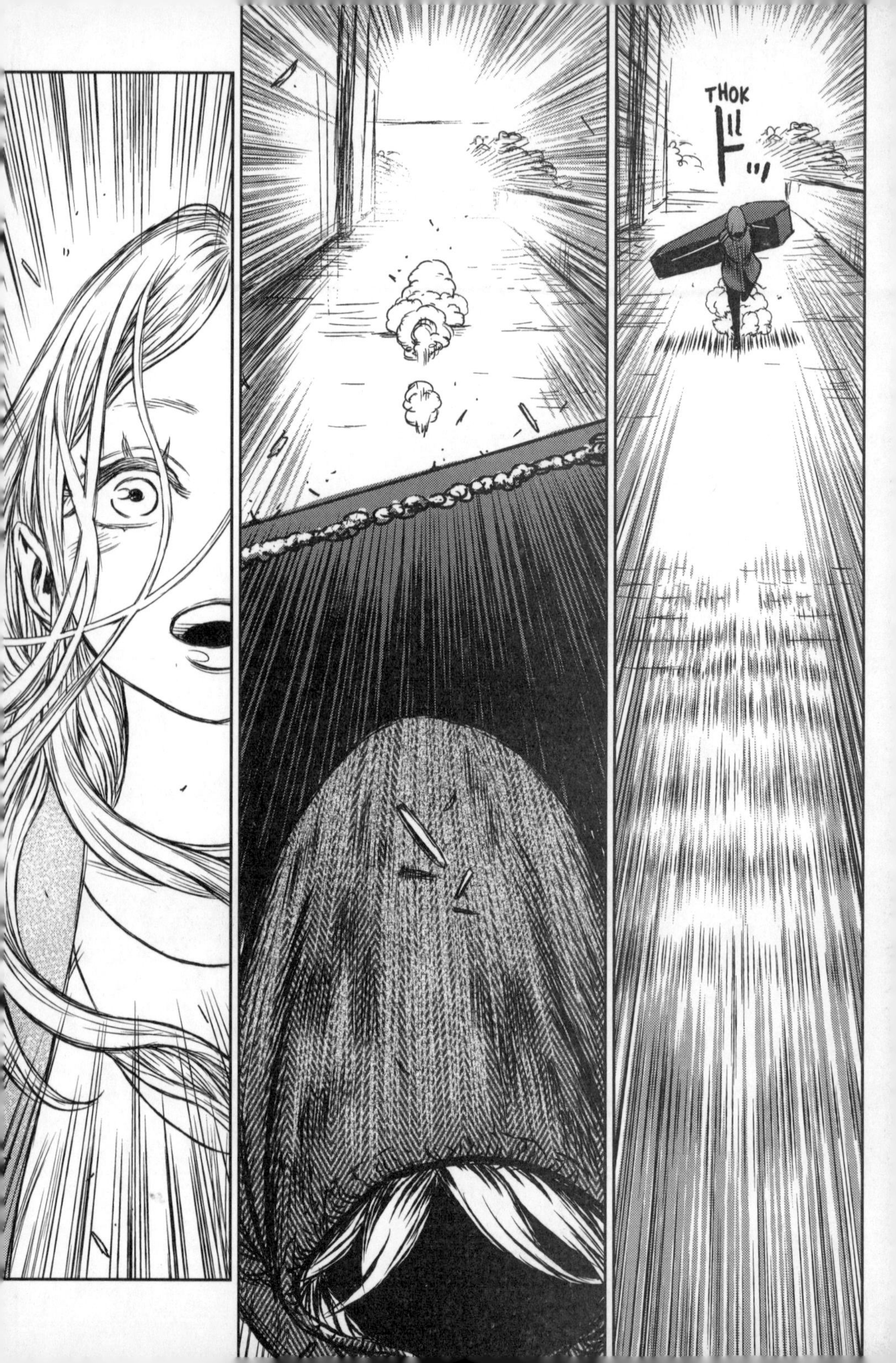
THOK
ドッ

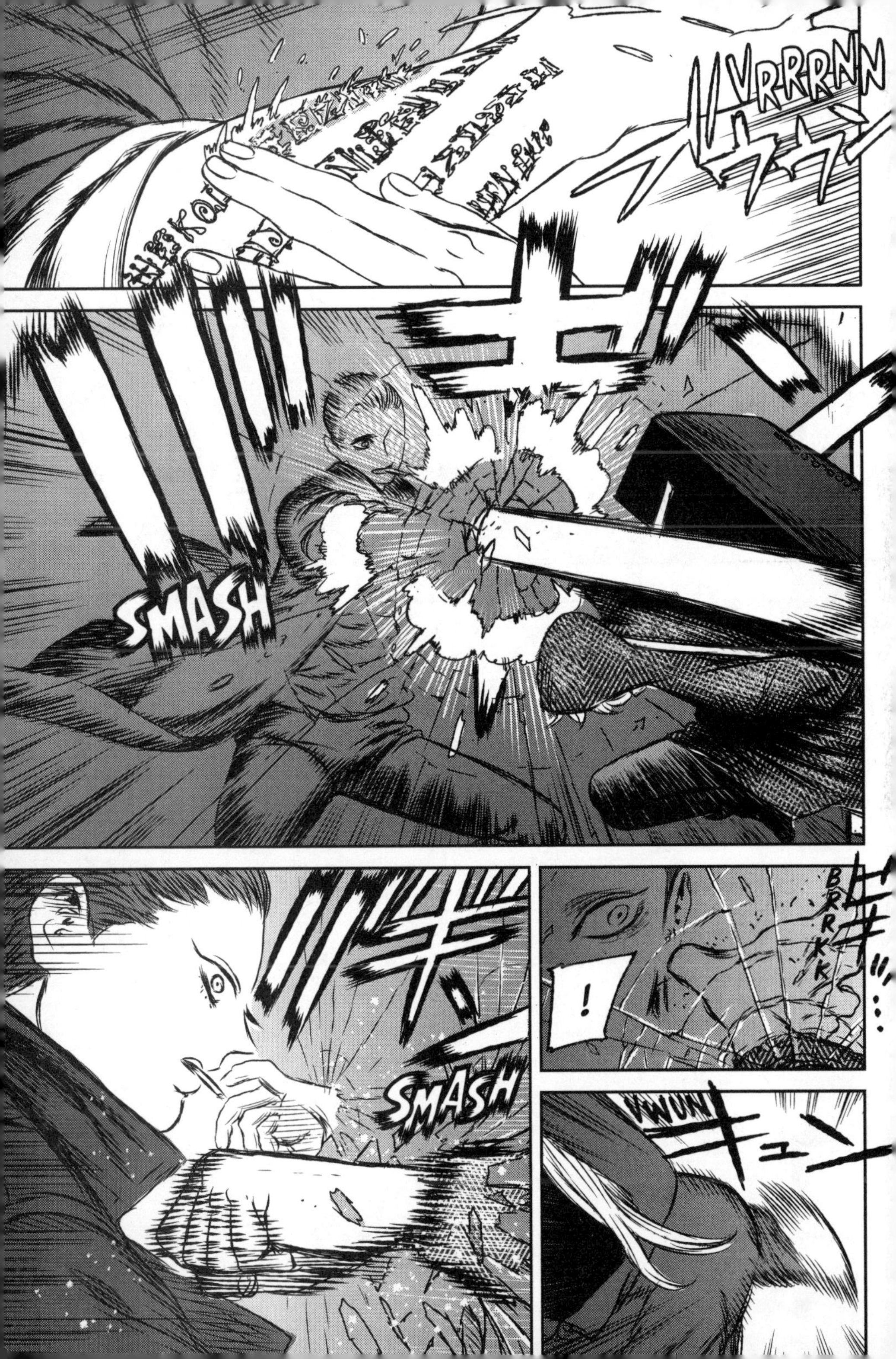
VRRRNN
SMASH
BRRKK
!
VWUN
SMASH

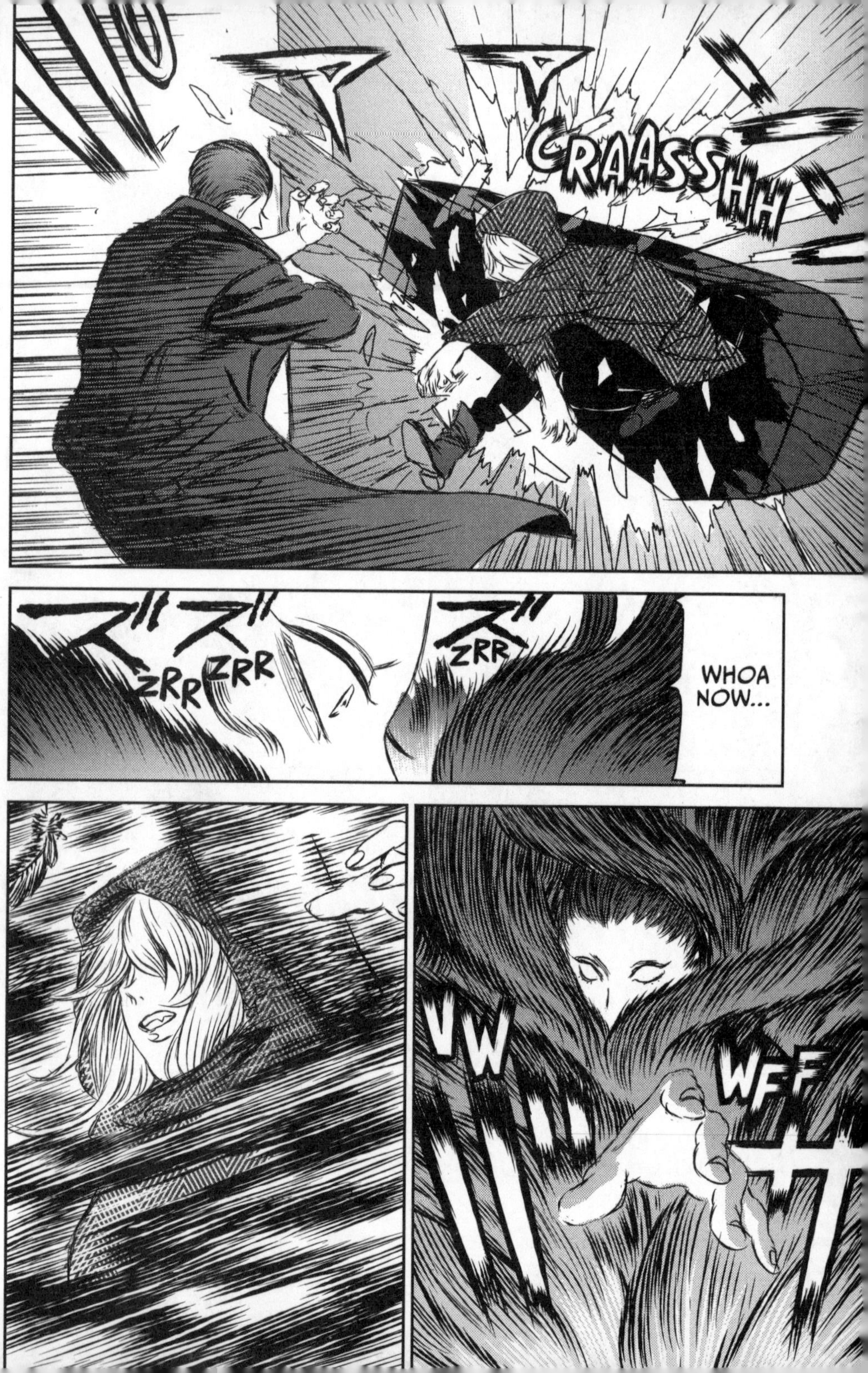
CRAASSHH
WHOA NOW...
ZRR
ZRR
ZRR
WFF
VW

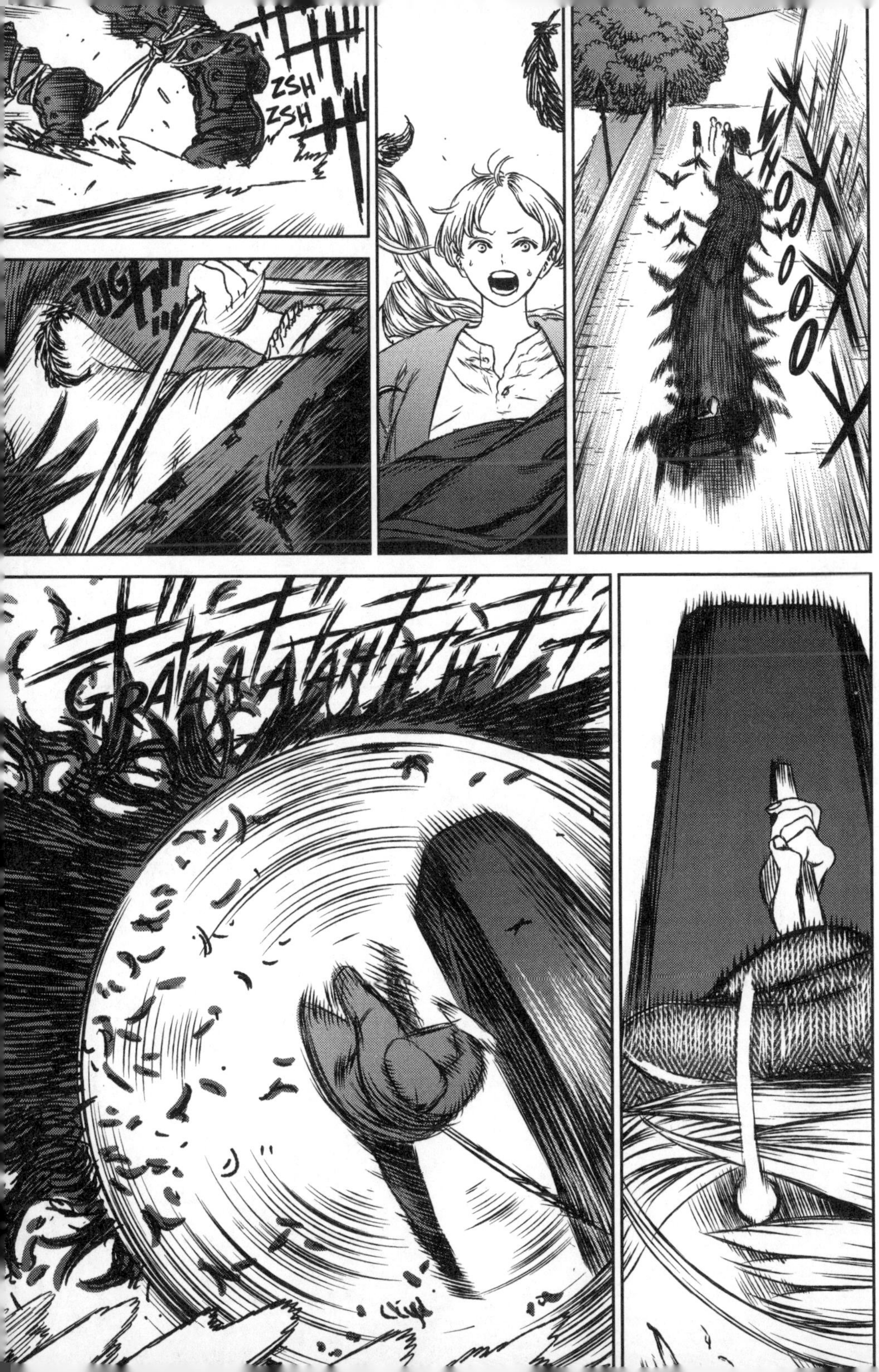
WHOOOOOOO
ZSH
ZSH
ZSH
TUG!!
GRAAAAAHHH

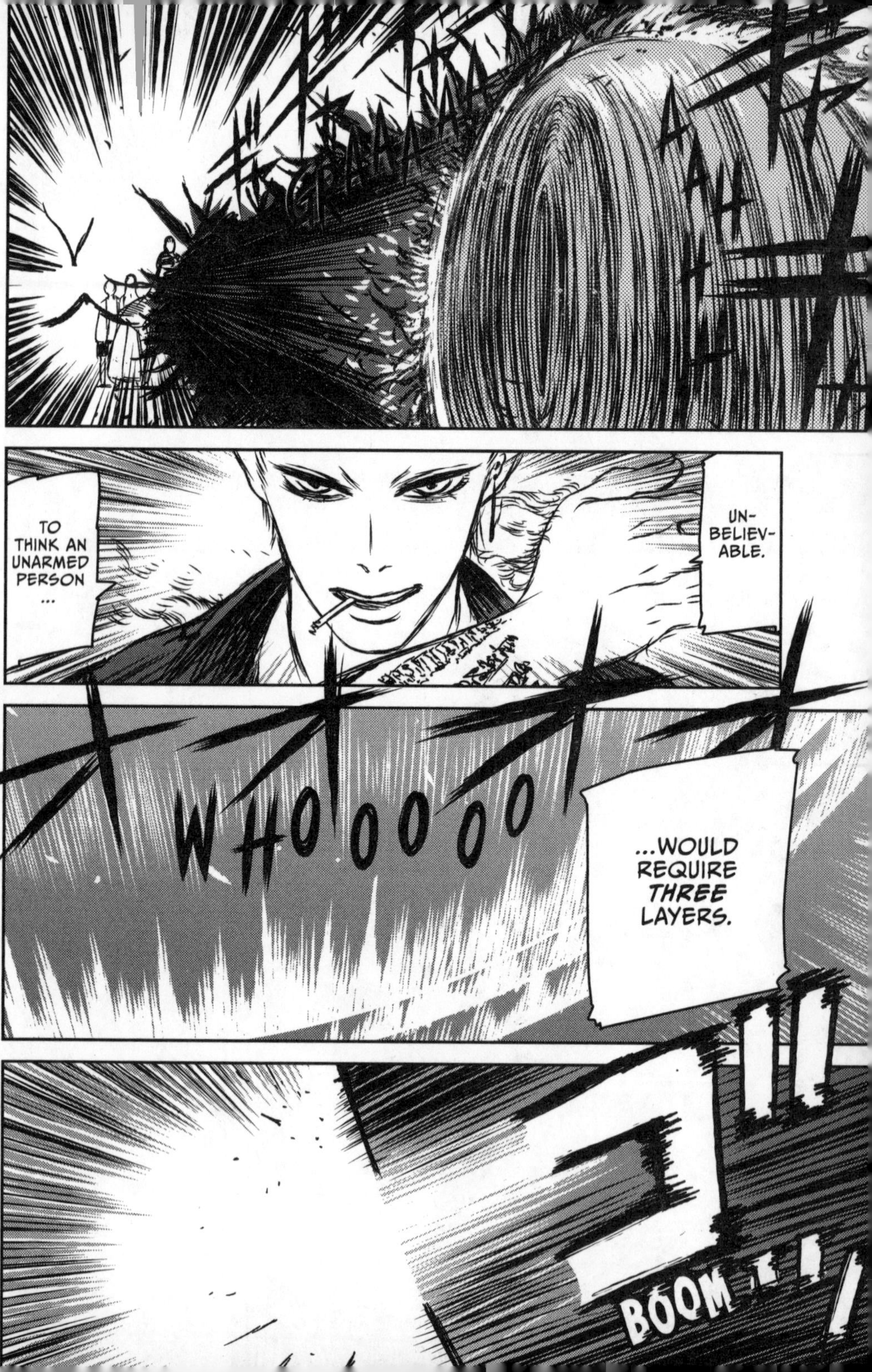
UN-BELIEV-ABLE.
TO THINK AN UNARMED PERSON ...
WHOOOOO
...WOULD REQUIRE *THREE* LAYERS.
BOOM

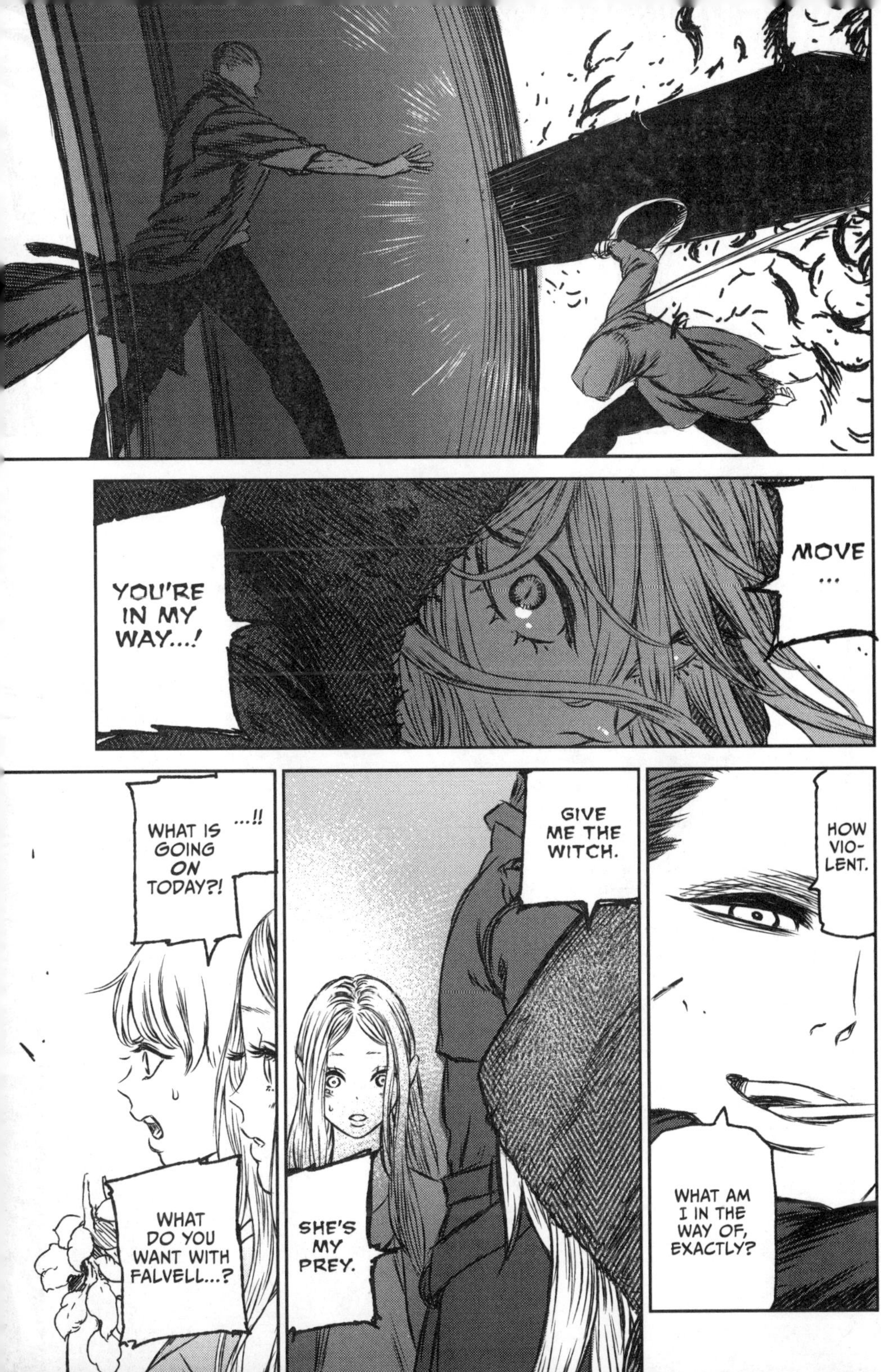
MOVE...
YOU'RE IN MY WAY...!
HOW VIO-LENT.
WHAT AM I IN THE WAY OF, EXACTLY?
GIVE ME THE WITCH.
SHE'S MY PREY.
...!!
WHAT IS GOING ON TODAY?!
WHAT DO YOU WANT WITH FALVELL...?

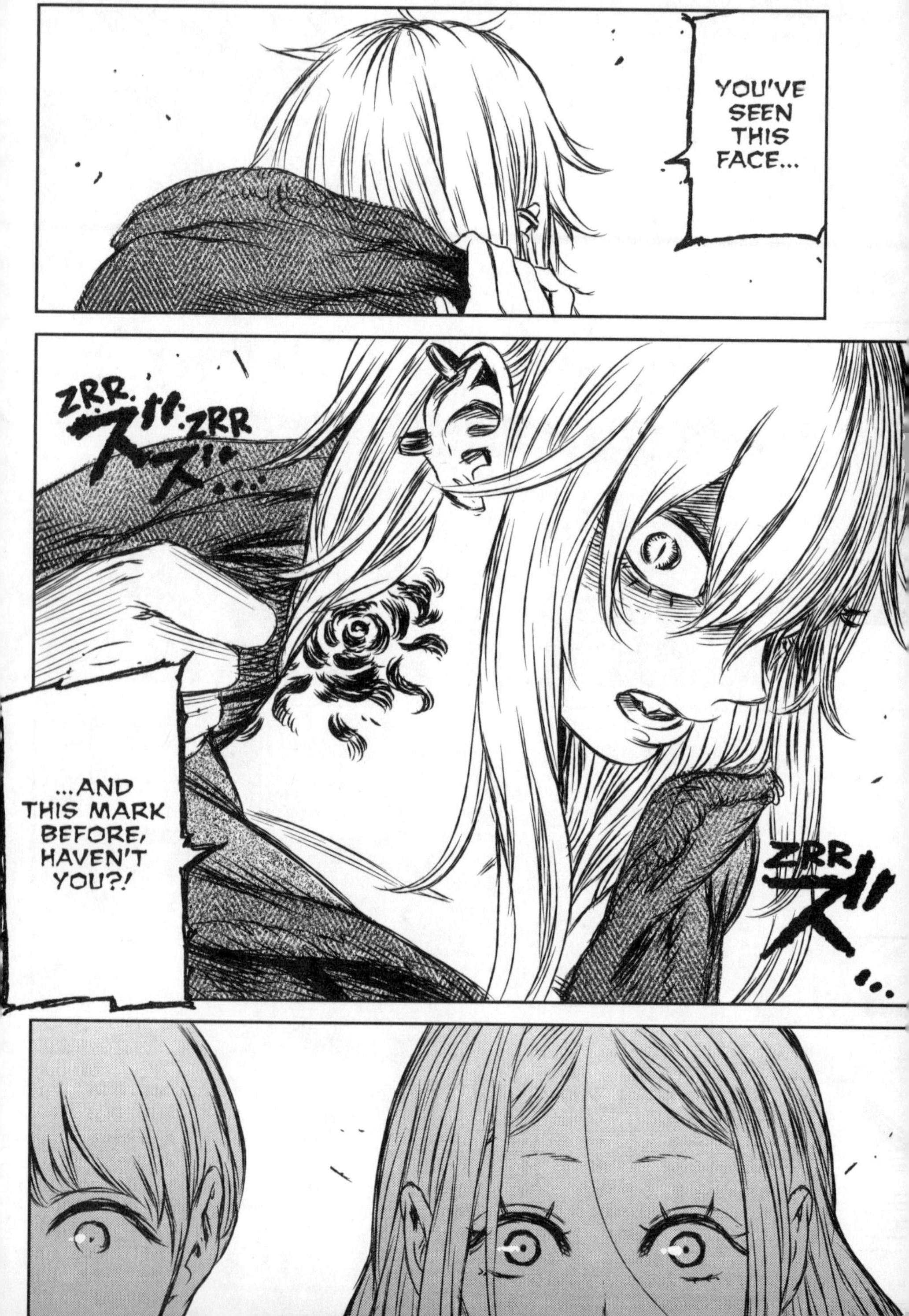

YOU'VE SEEN THIS FACE...
ZRR. ZRR
...AND THIS MARK BEFORE, HAVEN'T YOU?!
ZRR

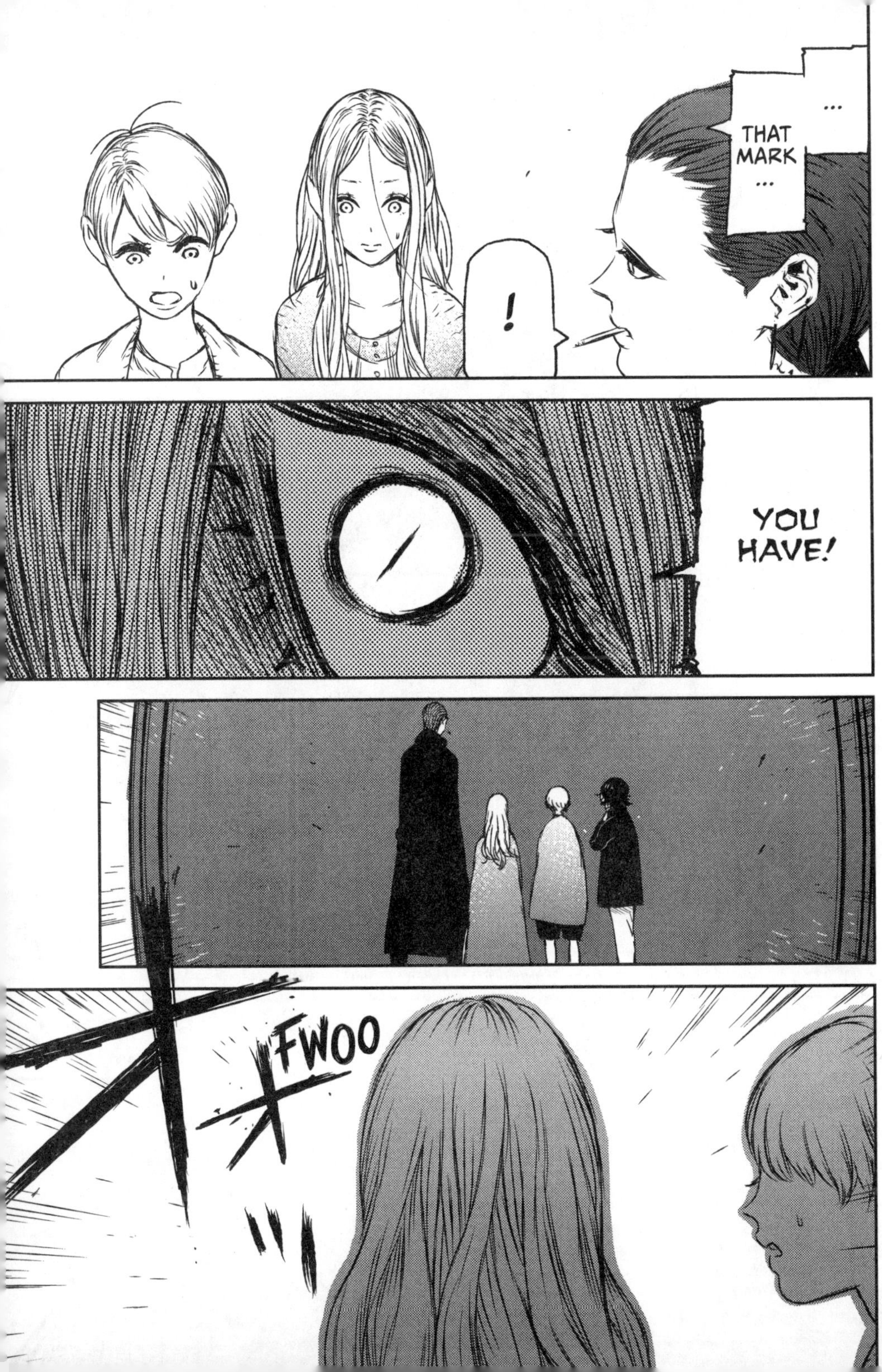
...
THAT MARK ...
!
YOU HAVE!
FWOO

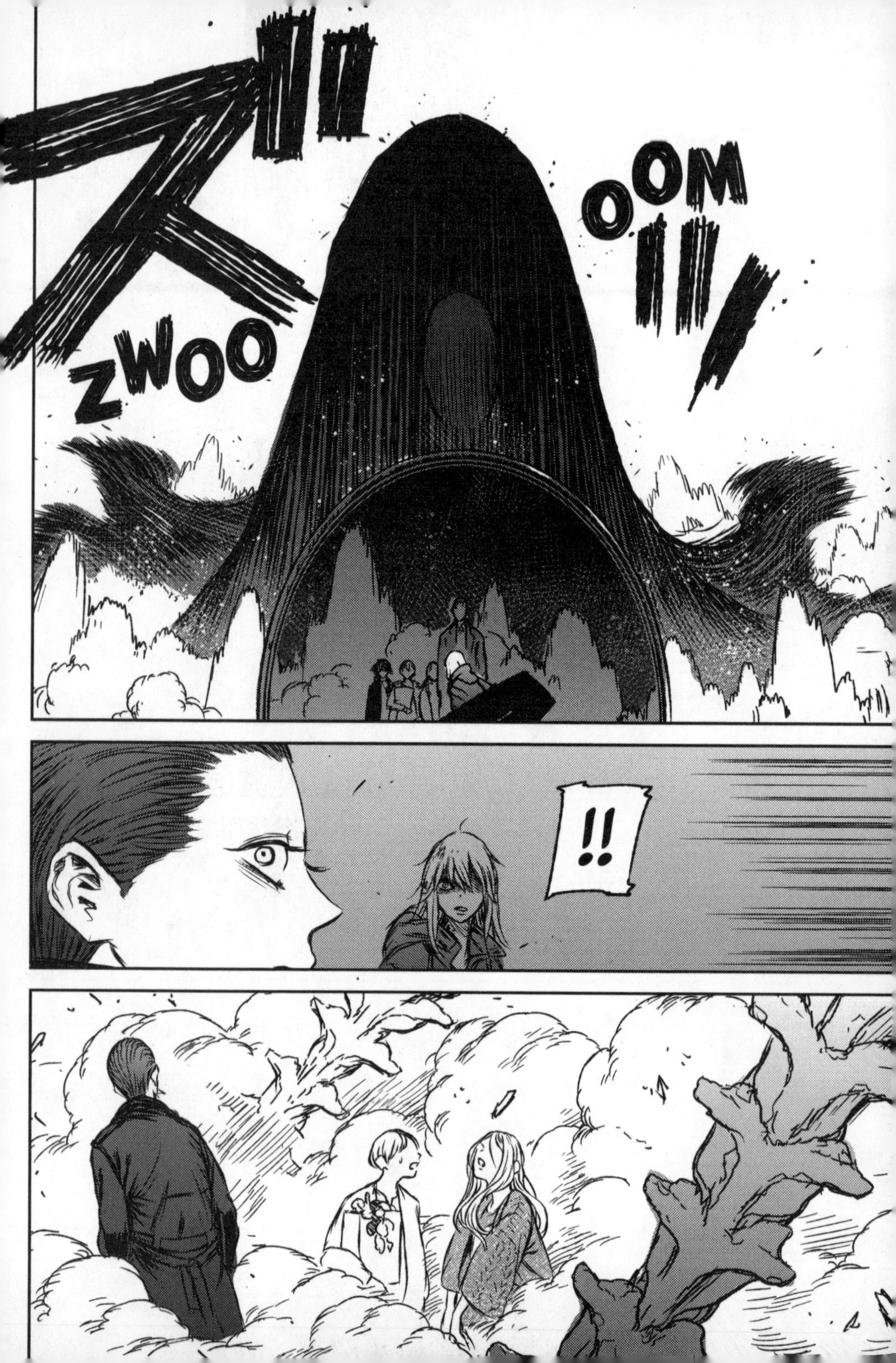
ZWOO
OOM
!!

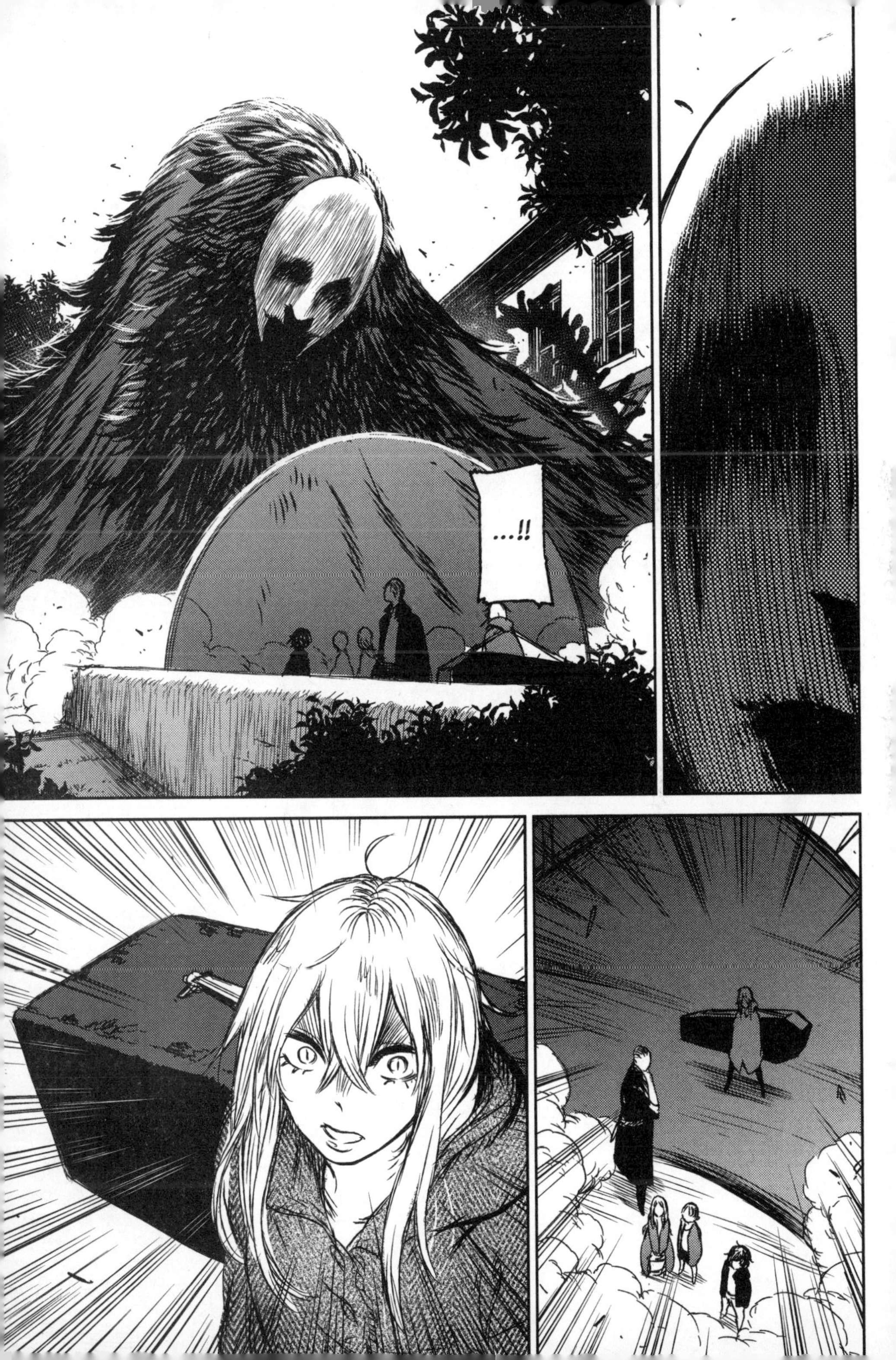
...!!

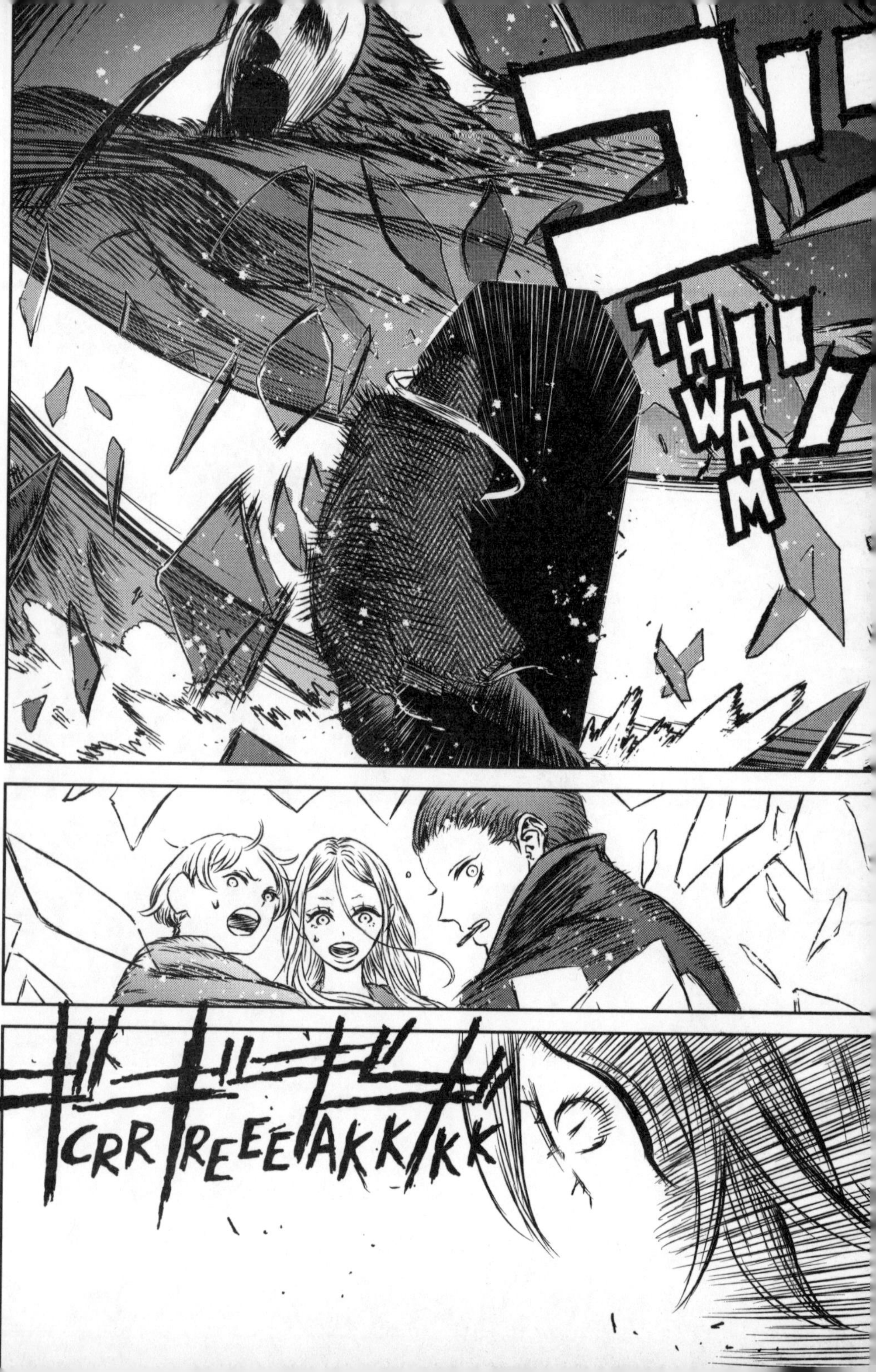
THWAM
CRRREEEAKKKK

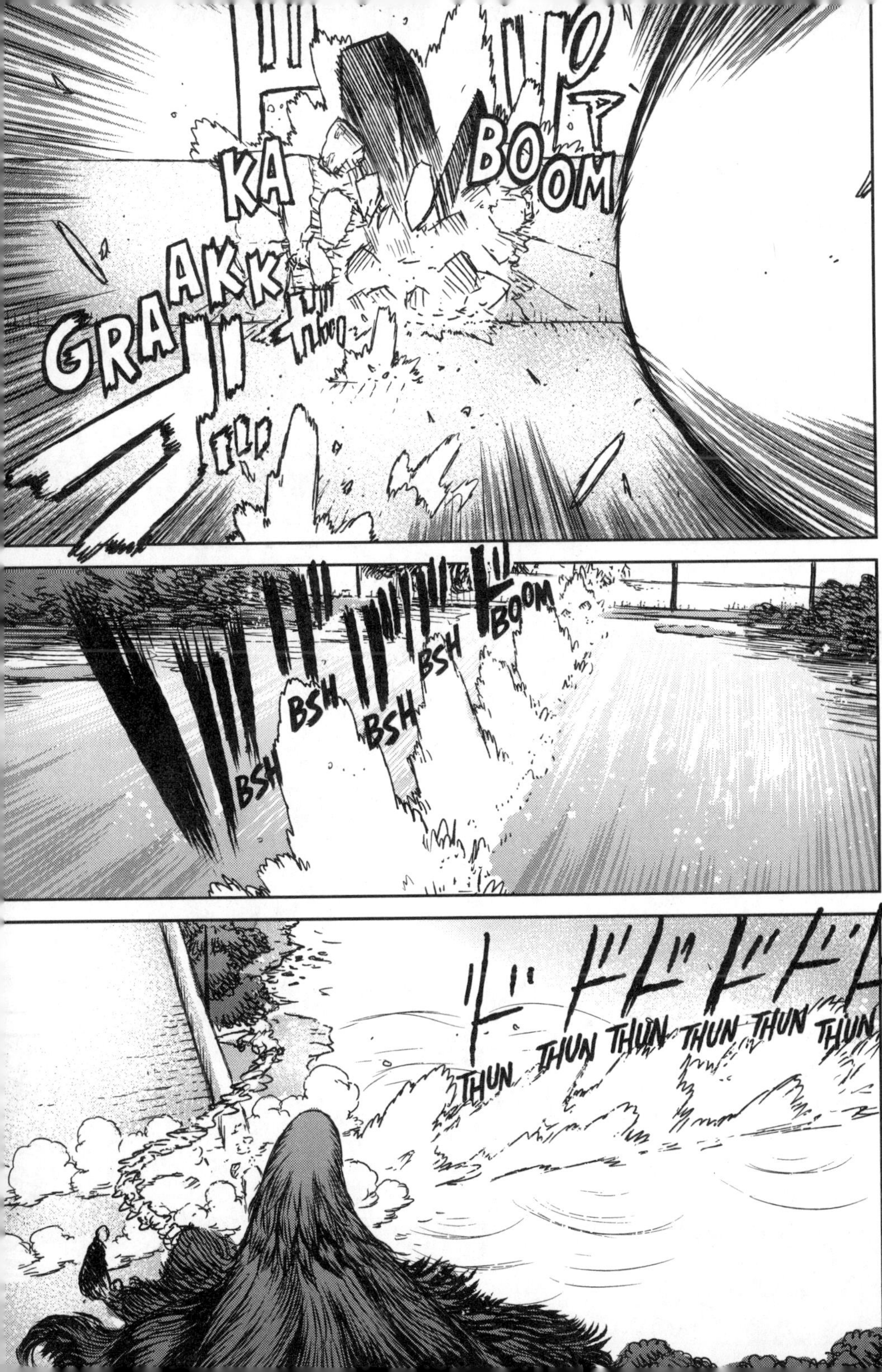
BOOM
KA
GRAAKK
BOOM
BSH
BSH
BSH
BSH
BSH
THUN
THUN
THUN
THUN
THUN
THUN

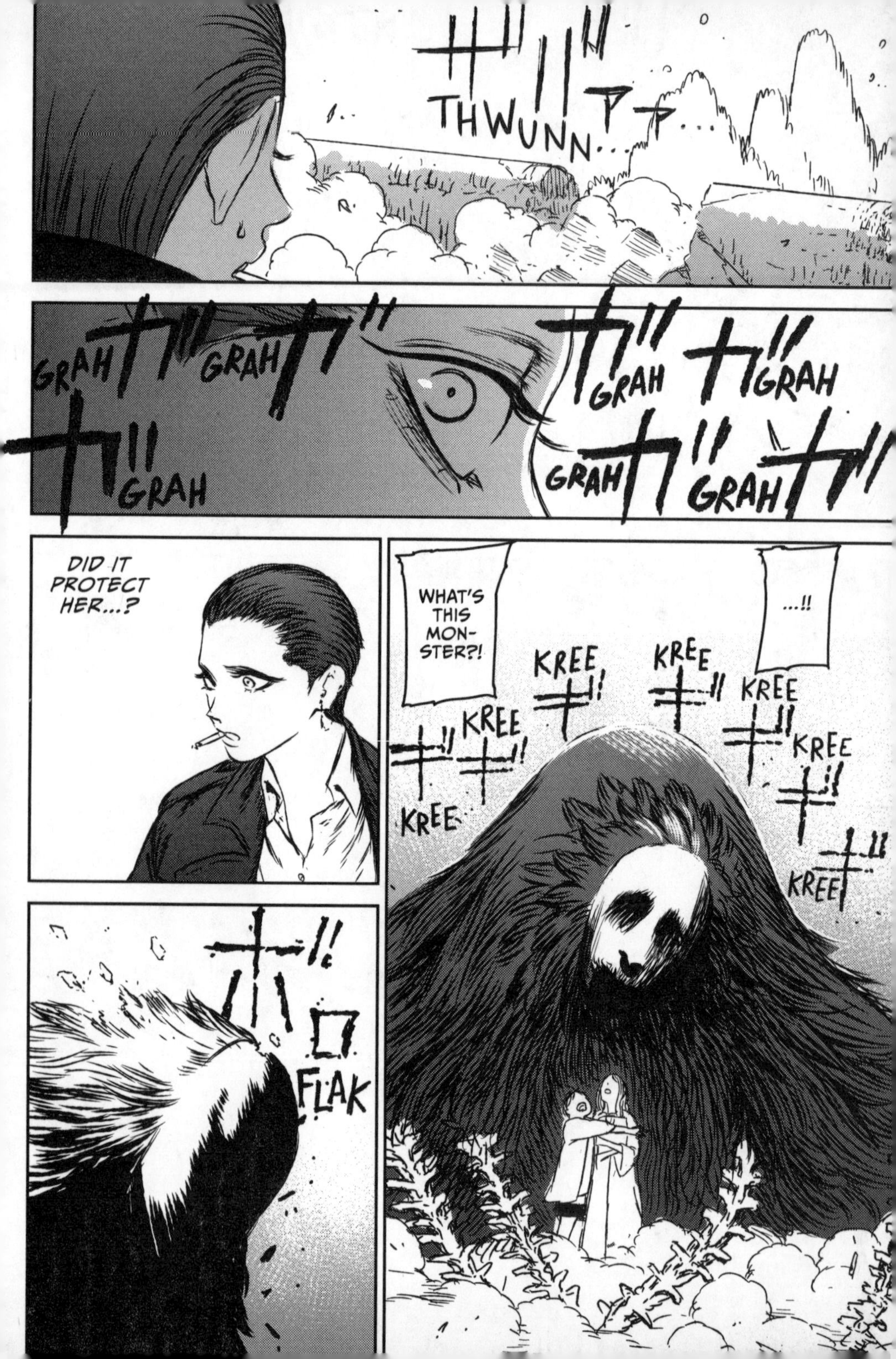
THWUNN...
GRAH GRAH GRAH GRAH GRAH GRAH GRAH
...!!
WHAT'S THIS MON-STER?!
KREE KREE KREE KREE KREE KREE KREE
DID IT PROTECT HER...?
FLAK

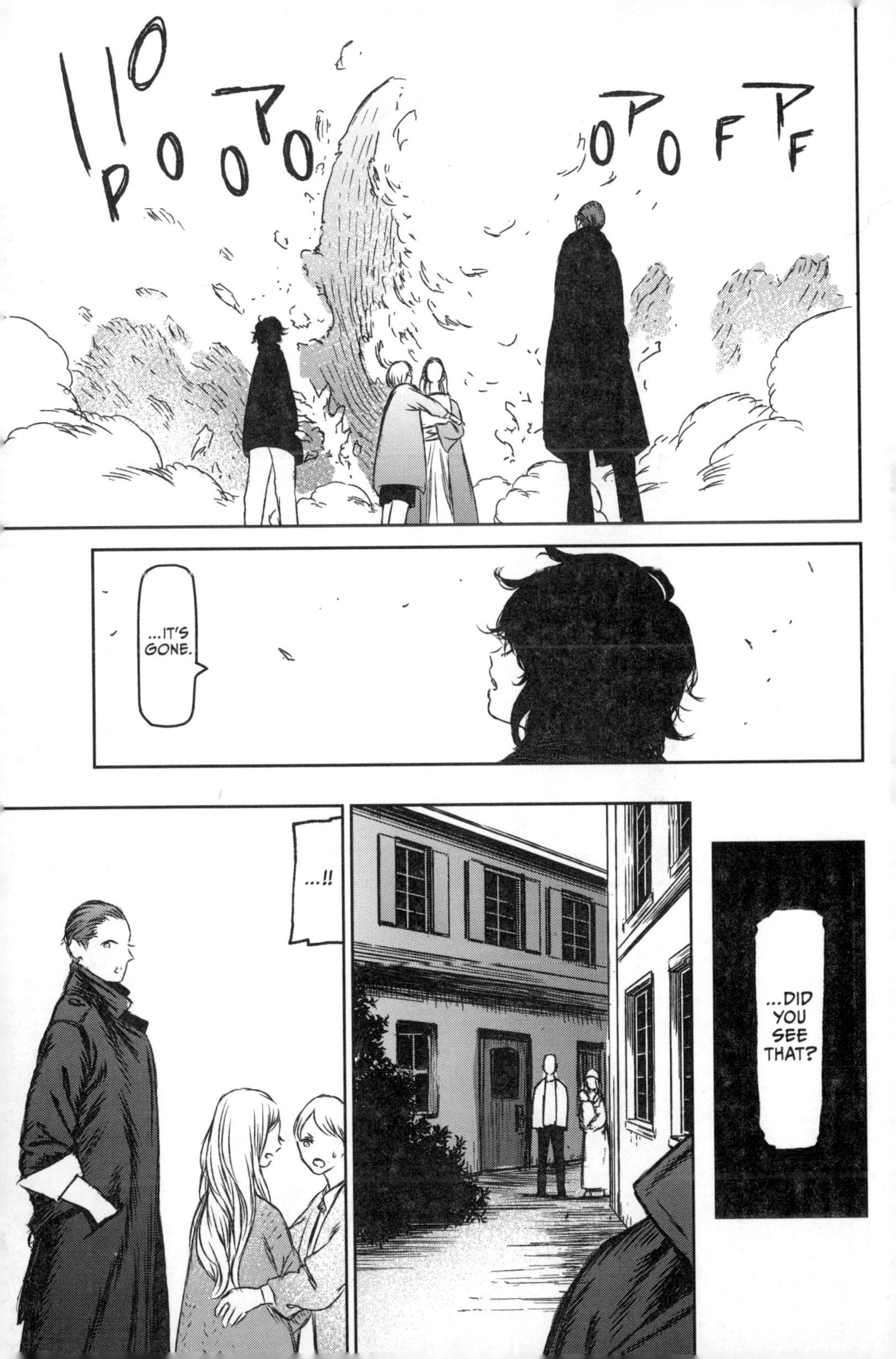
POOOO
OOFF
...IT'S GONE.
...DID YOU SEE THAT?
...!!

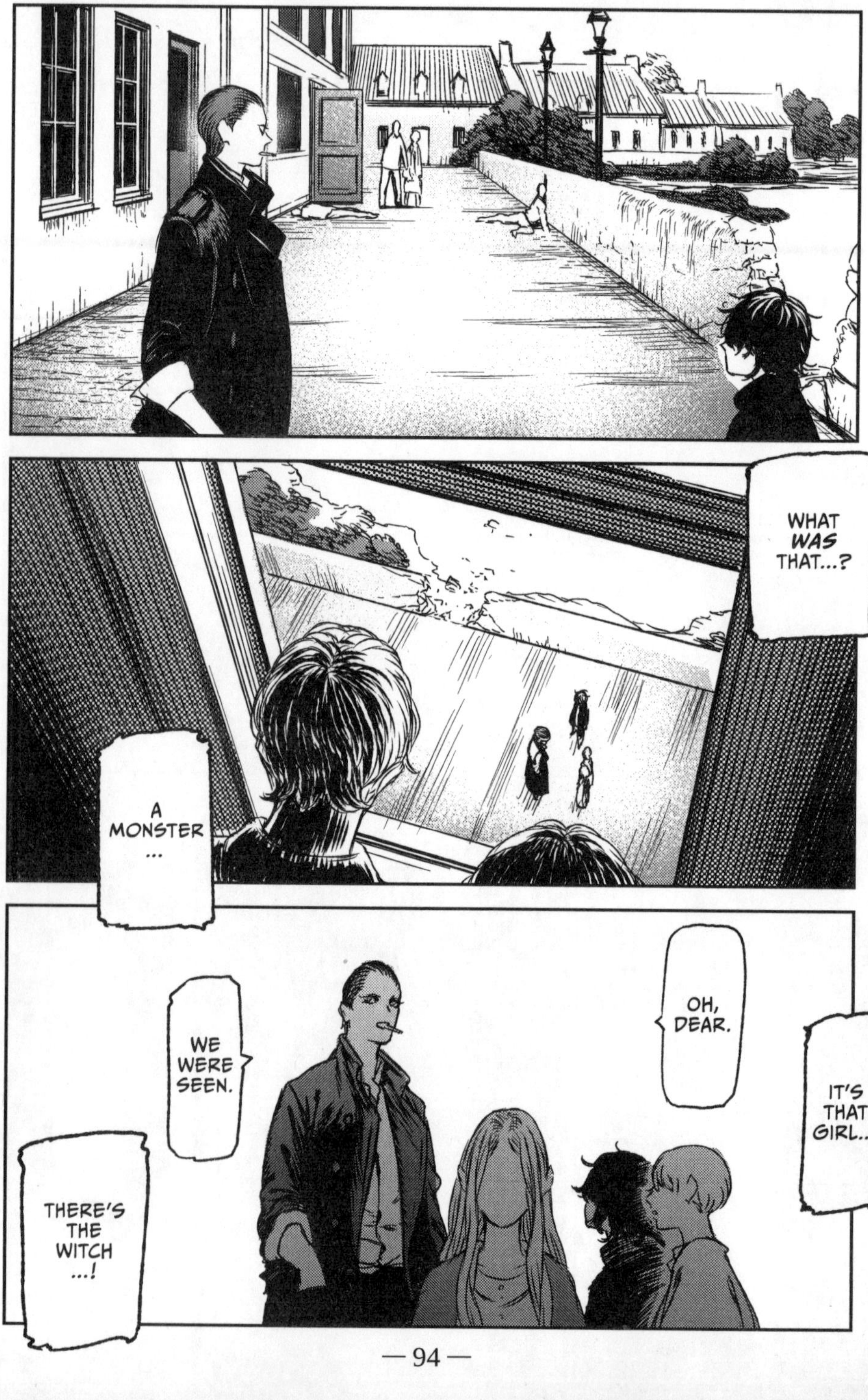
WHAT *WAS* THAT...?
A MONSTER ...
OH, DEAR.
IT'S THAT GIRL...
WE WERE SEEN.
THERE'S THE WITCH ...!

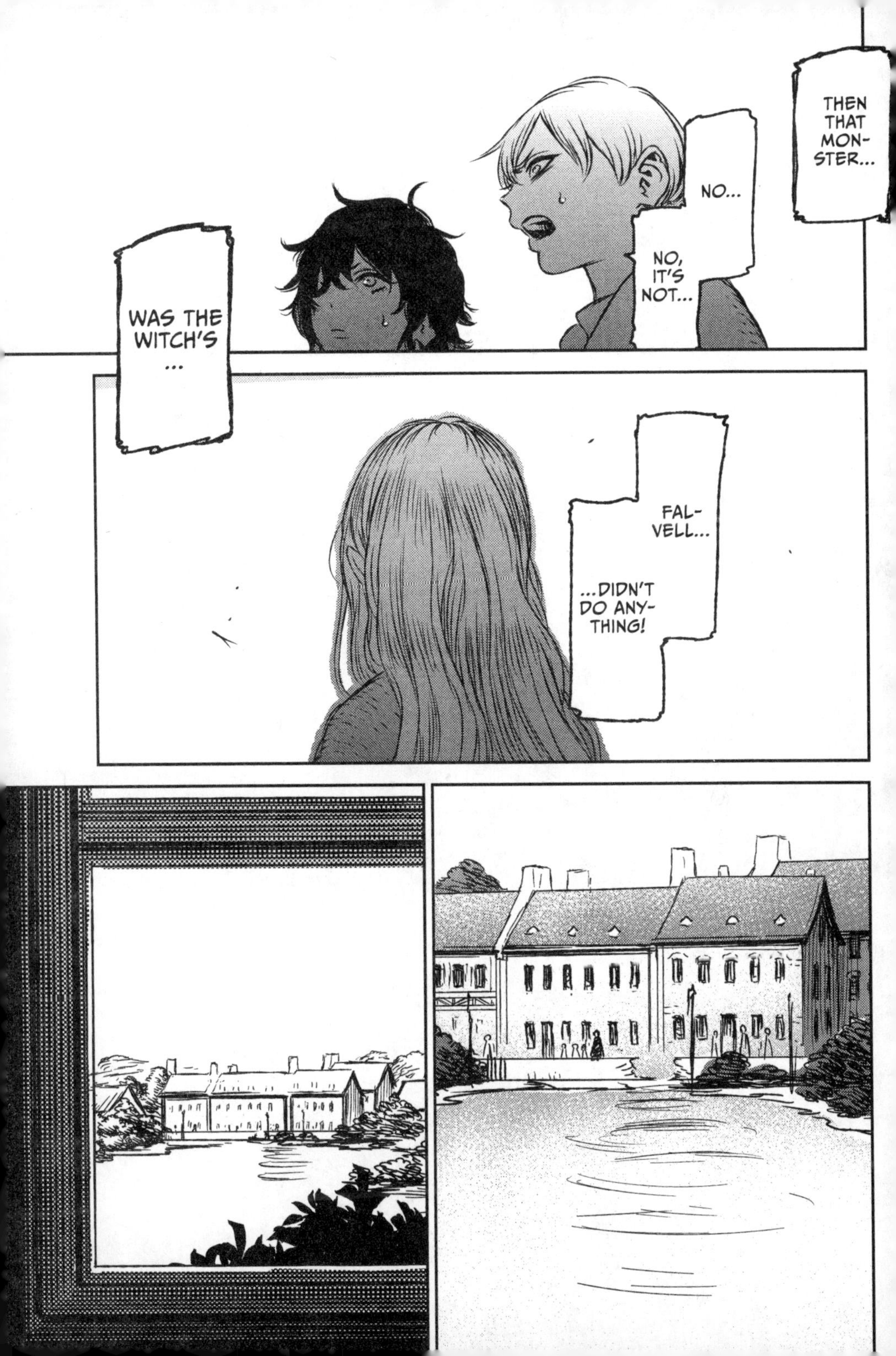
THEN THAT MON-STER...
NO...
NO, IT'S NOT...
WAS THE WITCH'S ...
FAL-VELL...
...DIDN'T DO ANY-THING!

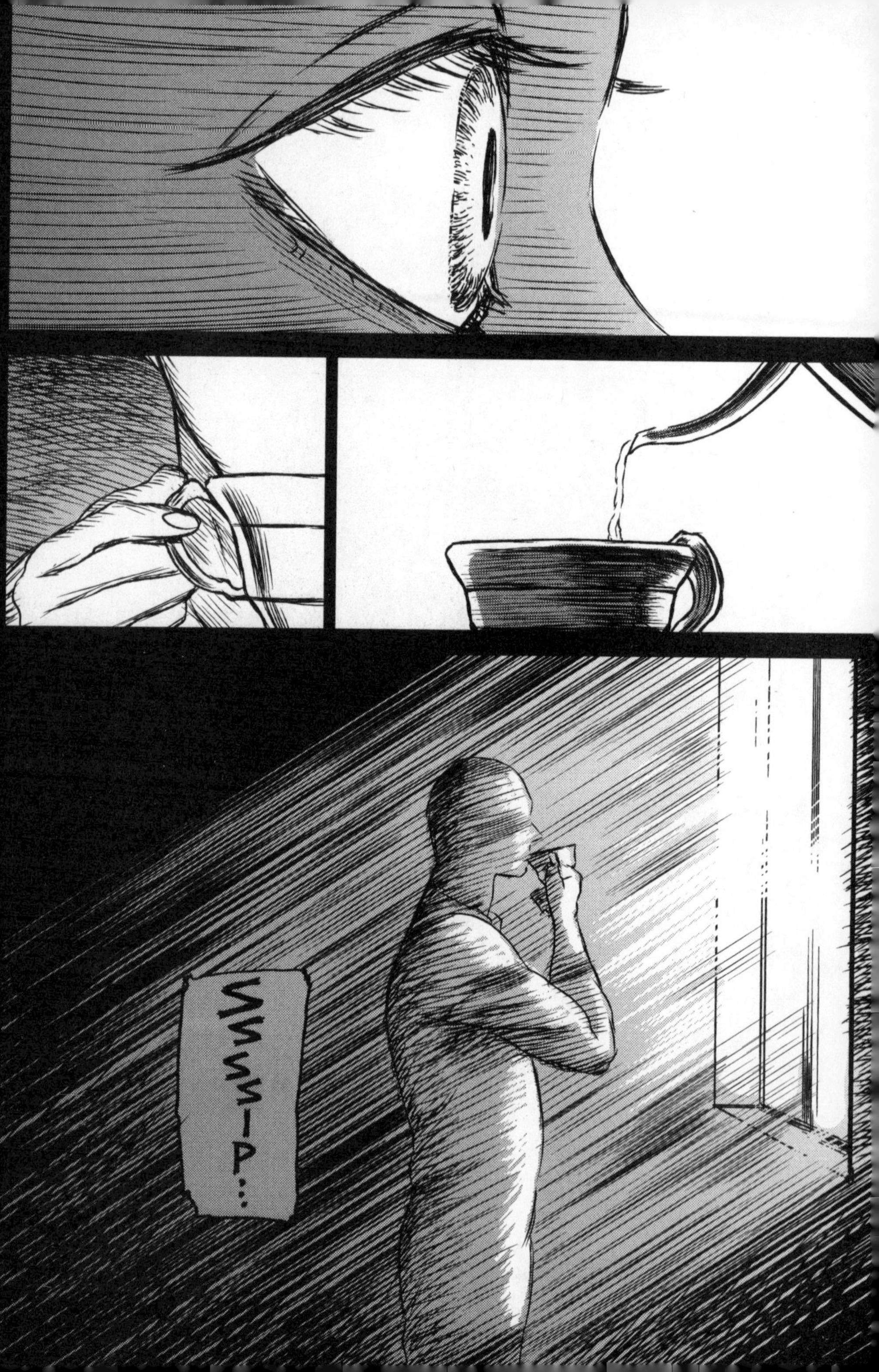
SSSSIP...

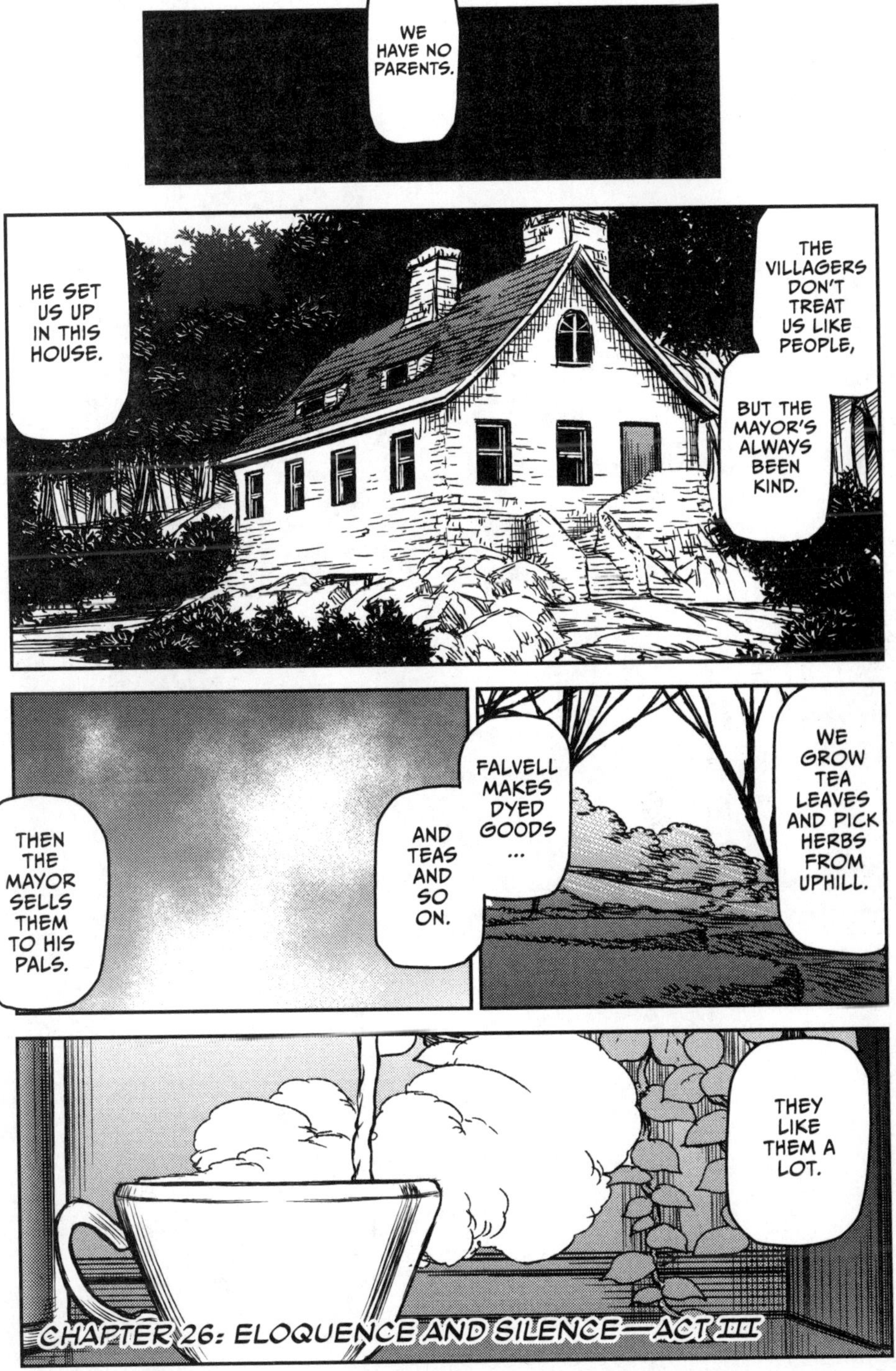
WE HAVE NO PARENTS.
THE VILLAGERS DON'T TREAT US LIKE PEOPLE,
BUT THE MAYOR'S ALWAYS BEEN KIND.
HE SET US UP IN THIS HOUSE.
WE GROW TEA LEAVES AND PICK HERBS FROM UPHILL.
FALVELL MAKES DYED GOODS ...
AND TEAS AND SO ON.
THEN THE MAYOR SELLS THEM TO HIS PALS.
THEY LIKE THEM A LOT.
CHAPTER 26: ELOQUENCE AND SILENCE—ACT III

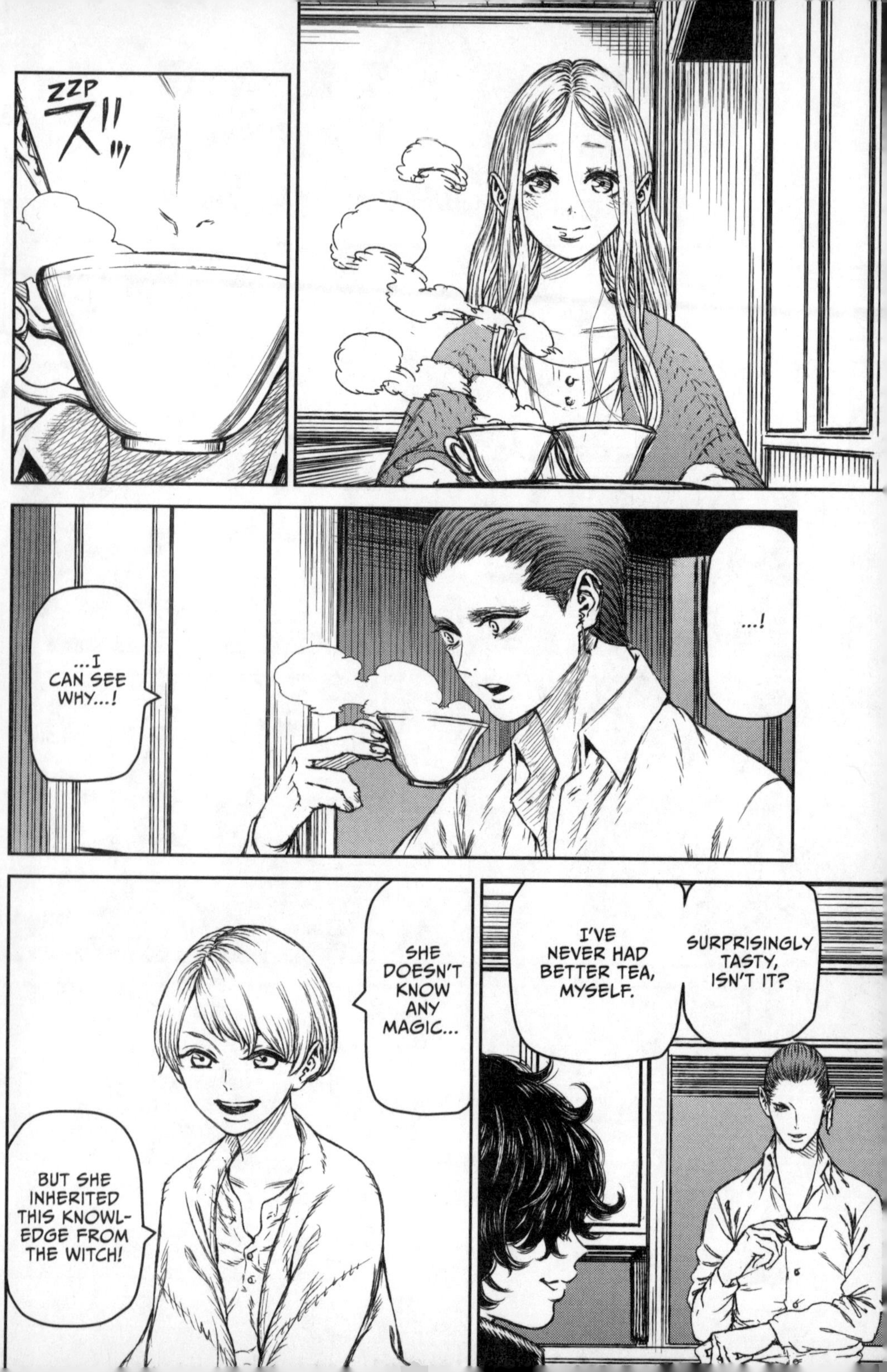
ZZP
ズッ
...!
...I CAN SEE WHY...!
SURPRISINGLY TASTY, ISN'T IT?
I'VE NEVER HAD BETTER TEA, MYSELF.
SHE DOESN'T KNOW ANY MAGIC...
BUT SHE INHERITED THIS KNOWLEDGE FROM THE WITCH!

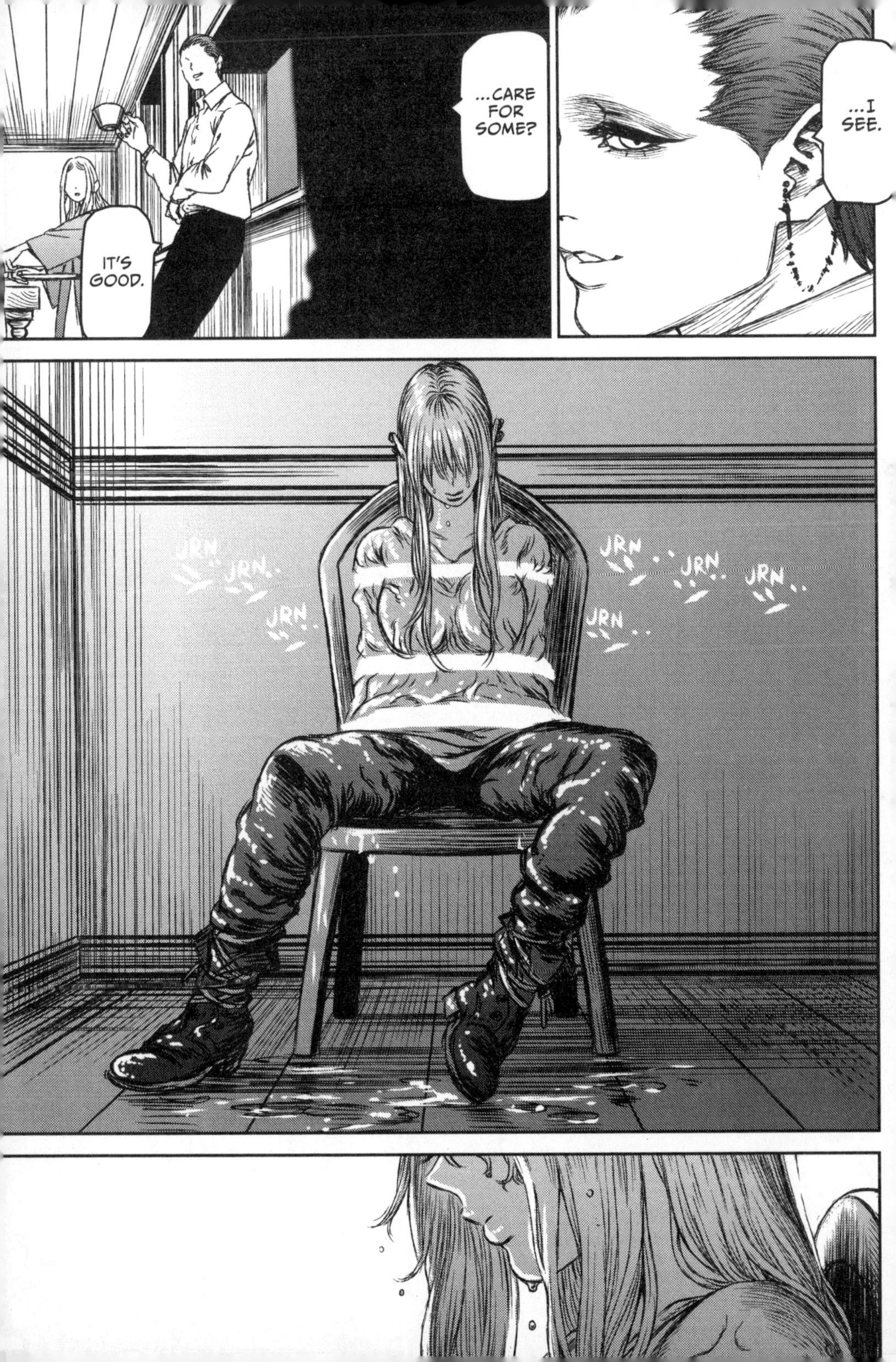
...I SEE.
...CARE FOR SOME?
IT'S GOOD.
JRN..
JRN..
JRN..
JRN..
JRN..
JRN..
JRN..

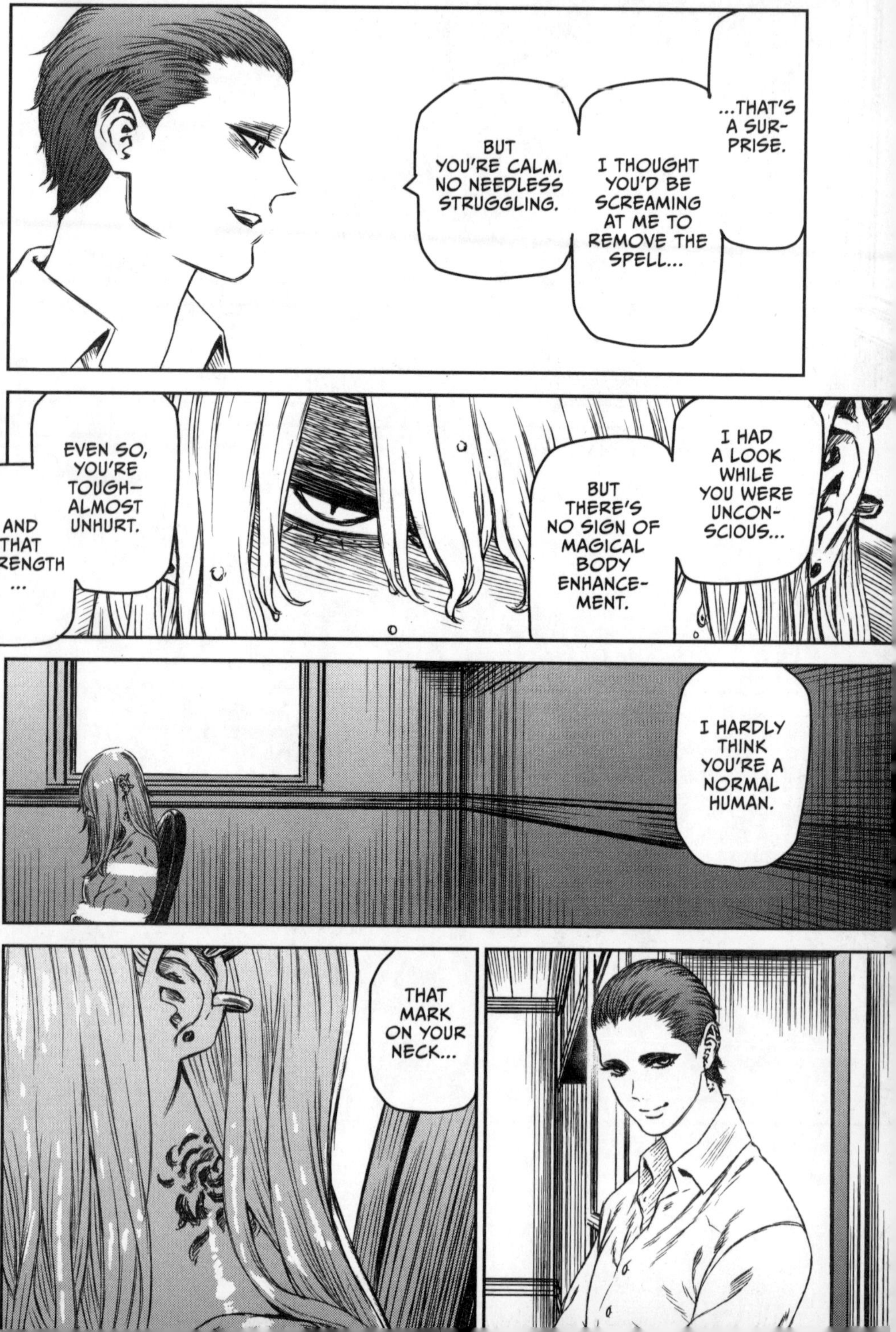
...THAT'S A SUR-PRISE.
I THOUGHT YOU'D BE SCREAMING AT ME TO REMOVE THE SPELL...
BUT YOU'RE CALM. NO NEEDLESS STRUGGLING.
I HAD A LOOK WHILE YOU WERE UNCON-SCIOUS...
BUT THERE'S NO SIGN OF MAGICAL BODY ENHANCE-MENT.
EVEN SO, YOU'RE TOUGH—ALMOST UNHURT.
AND THAT TRENGTH ...
I HARDLY THINK YOU'RE A NORMAL HUMAN.
THAT MARK ON YOUR NECK...

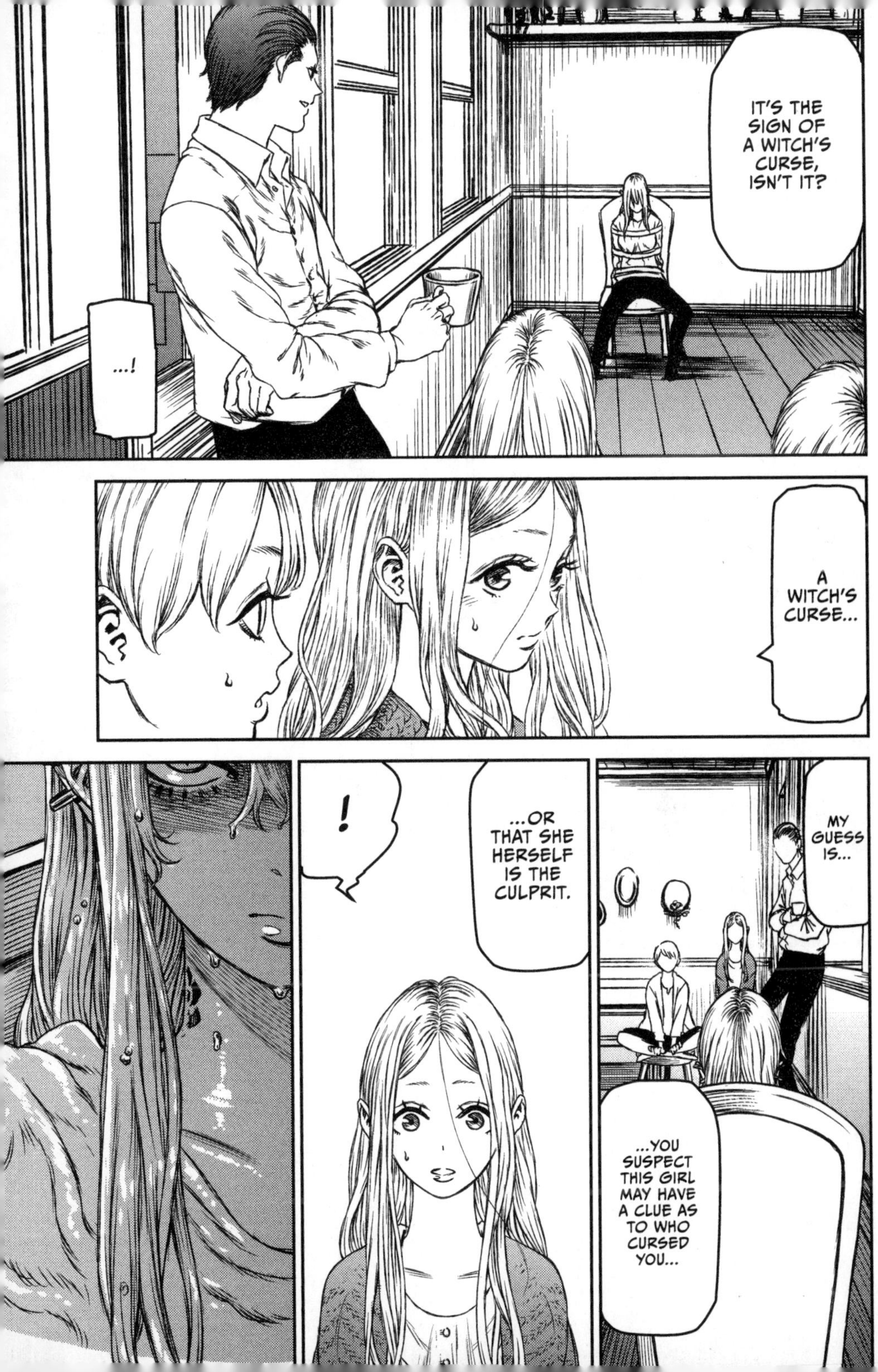
IT'S THE SIGN OF A WITCH'S CURSE, ISN'T IT?
...!
A WITCH'S CURSE...
MY GUESS IS...
...YOU SUSPECT THIS GIRL MAY HAVE A CLUE AS TO WHO CURSED YOU...
...OR THAT SHE HERSELF IS THE CULPRIT.
!

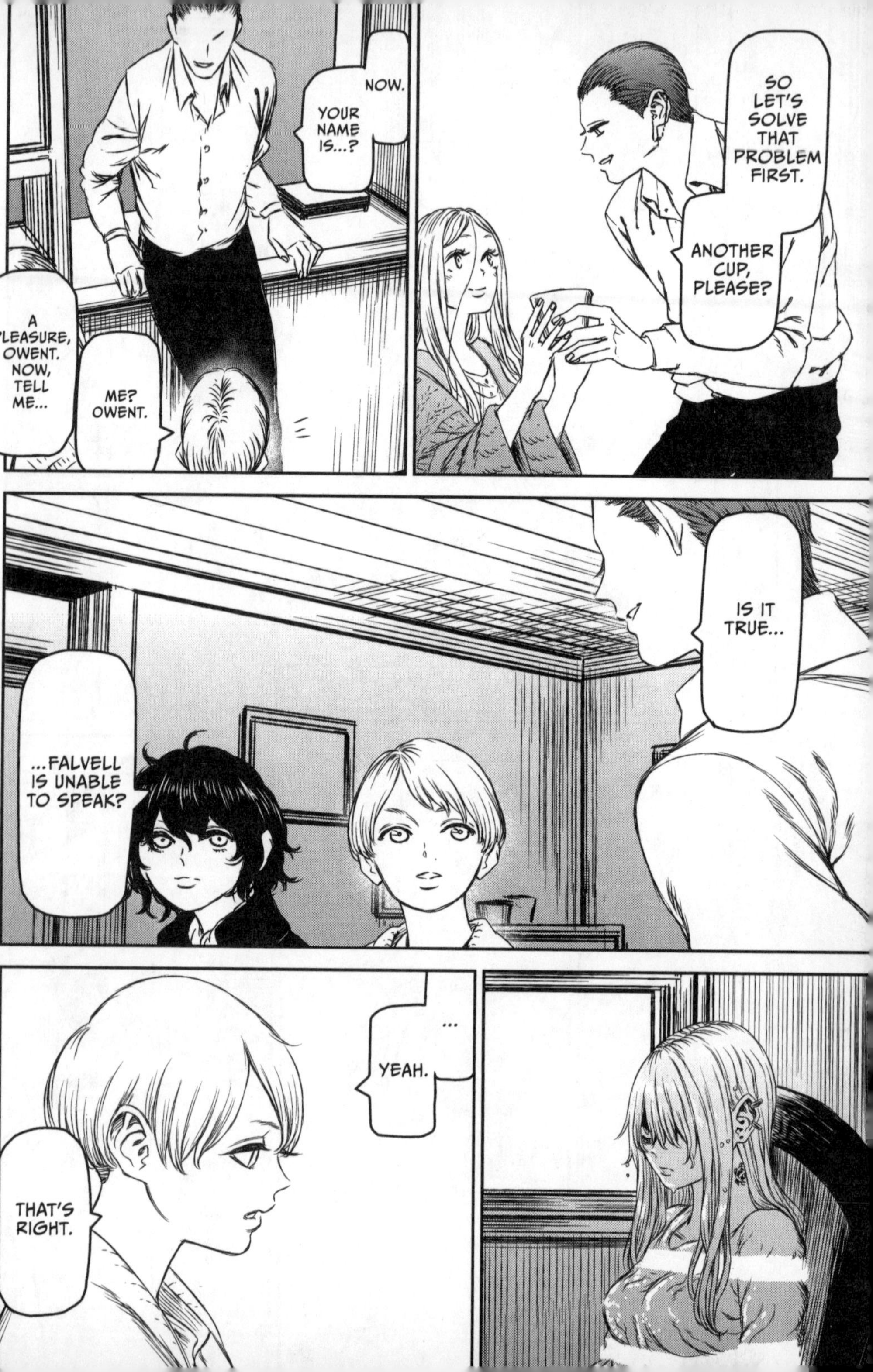
SO LET'S SOLVE THAT PROBLEM FIRST.
ANOTHER CUP, PLEASE?
NOW.
YOUR NAME IS...?
ME? OWENT.
A PLEASURE, OWENT. NOW, TELL ME...
IS IT TRUE...
...FALVELL IS UNABLE TO SPEAK?
...
YEAH.
THAT'S RIGHT.

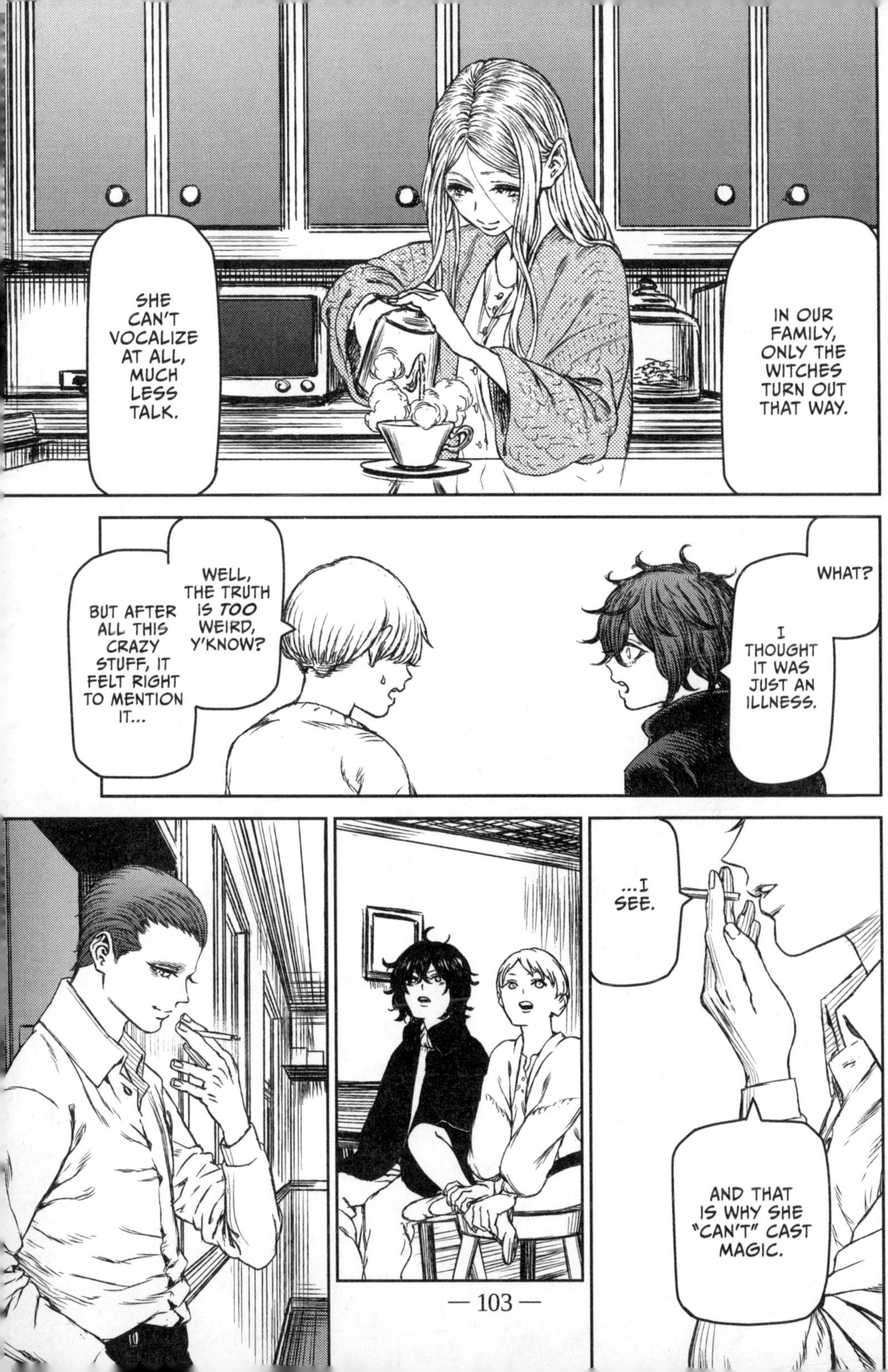
IN OUR FAMILY, ONLY THE WITCHES TURN OUT THAT WAY.
SHE CAN'T VOCALIZE AT ALL, MUCH LESS TALK.
WHAT?
I THOUGHT IT WAS JUST AN ILLNESS.
WELL, THE TRUTH IS *TOO* WEIRD, Y'KNOW?
BUT AFTER ALL THIS CRAZY STUFF, IT FELT RIGHT TO MENTION IT...
...I SEE.
AND THAT IS WHY SHE "CAN'T" CAST MAGIC.

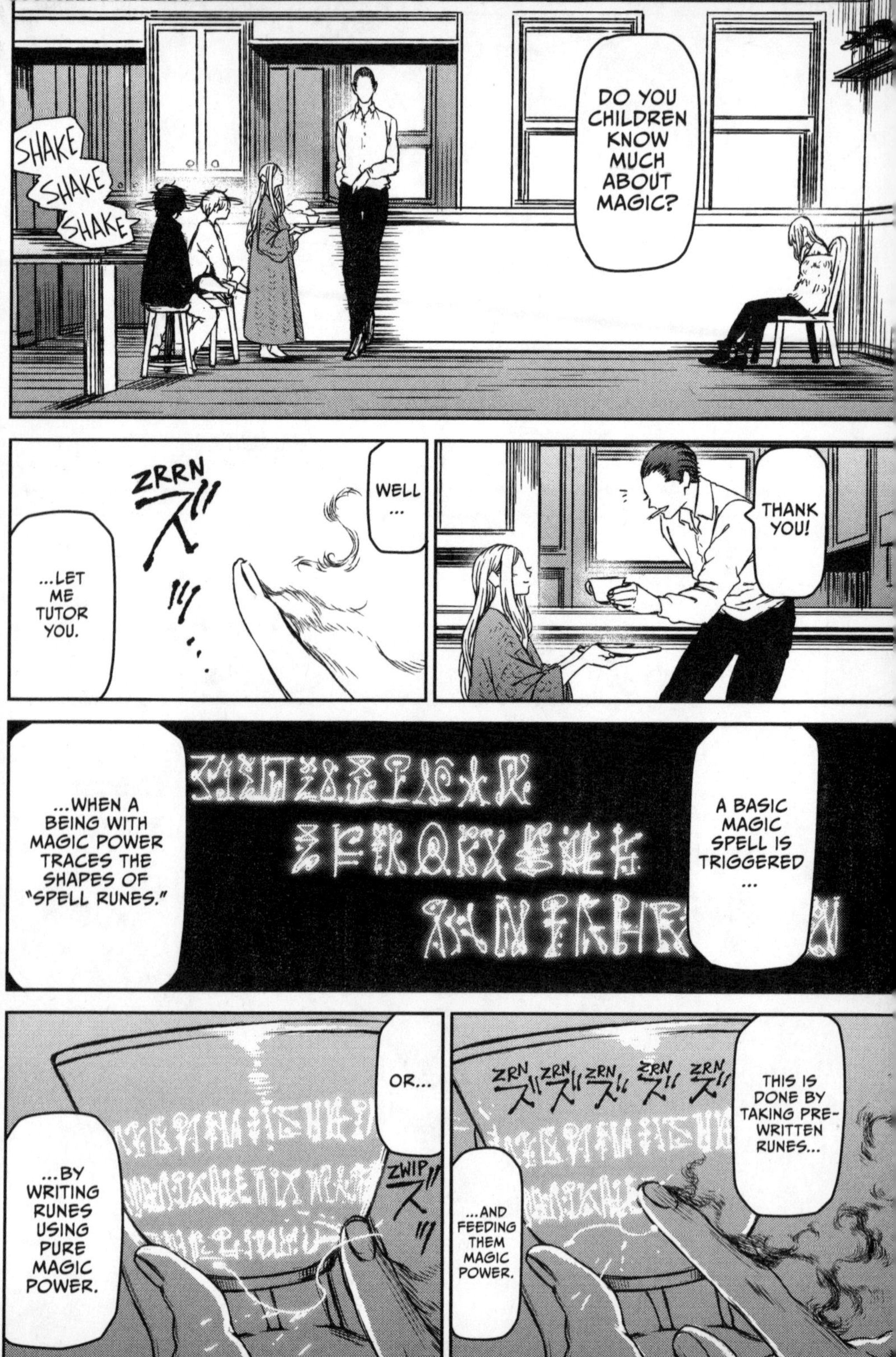
DO YOU CHILDREN KNOW MUCH ABOUT MAGIC?
SHAKE SHAKE SHAKE
THANK YOU!
WELL ...
ZRRN
...LET ME TUTOR YOU.
A BASIC MAGIC SPELL IS TRIGGERED ...
...WHEN A BEING WITH MAGIC POWER TRACES THE SHAPES OF "SPELL RUNES."
THIS IS DONE BY TAKING PRE-WRITTEN RUNES...
ZRN ZRN ZRN ZRN ZRN
...AND FEEDING THEM MAGIC POWER.
OR...
ZWIP
...BY WRITING RUNES USING PURE MAGIC POWER.

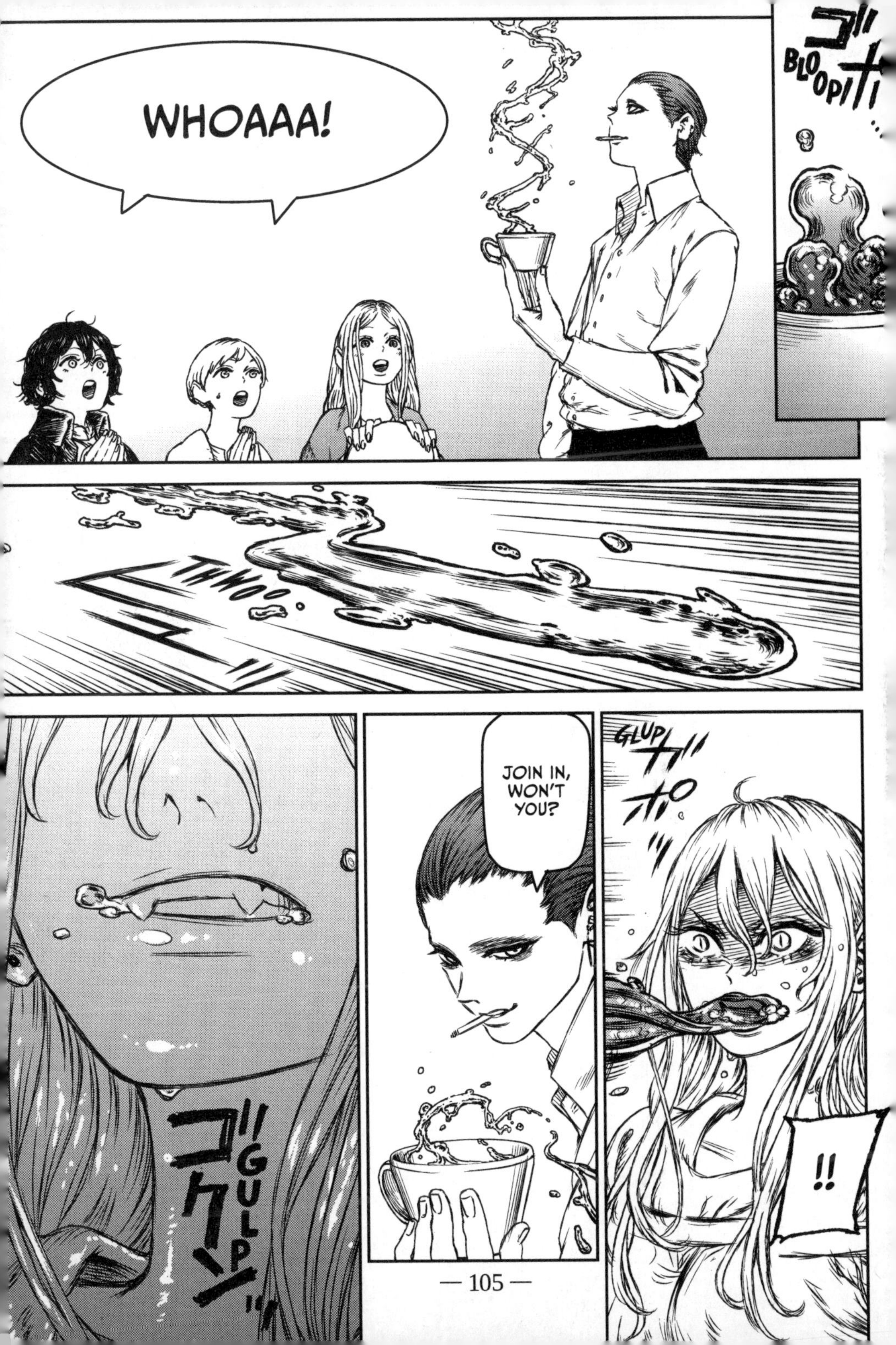
BLOOP!
WHOAAA!
THWOOO
GLUP
!!
JOIN IN, WON'T YOU?
GULP

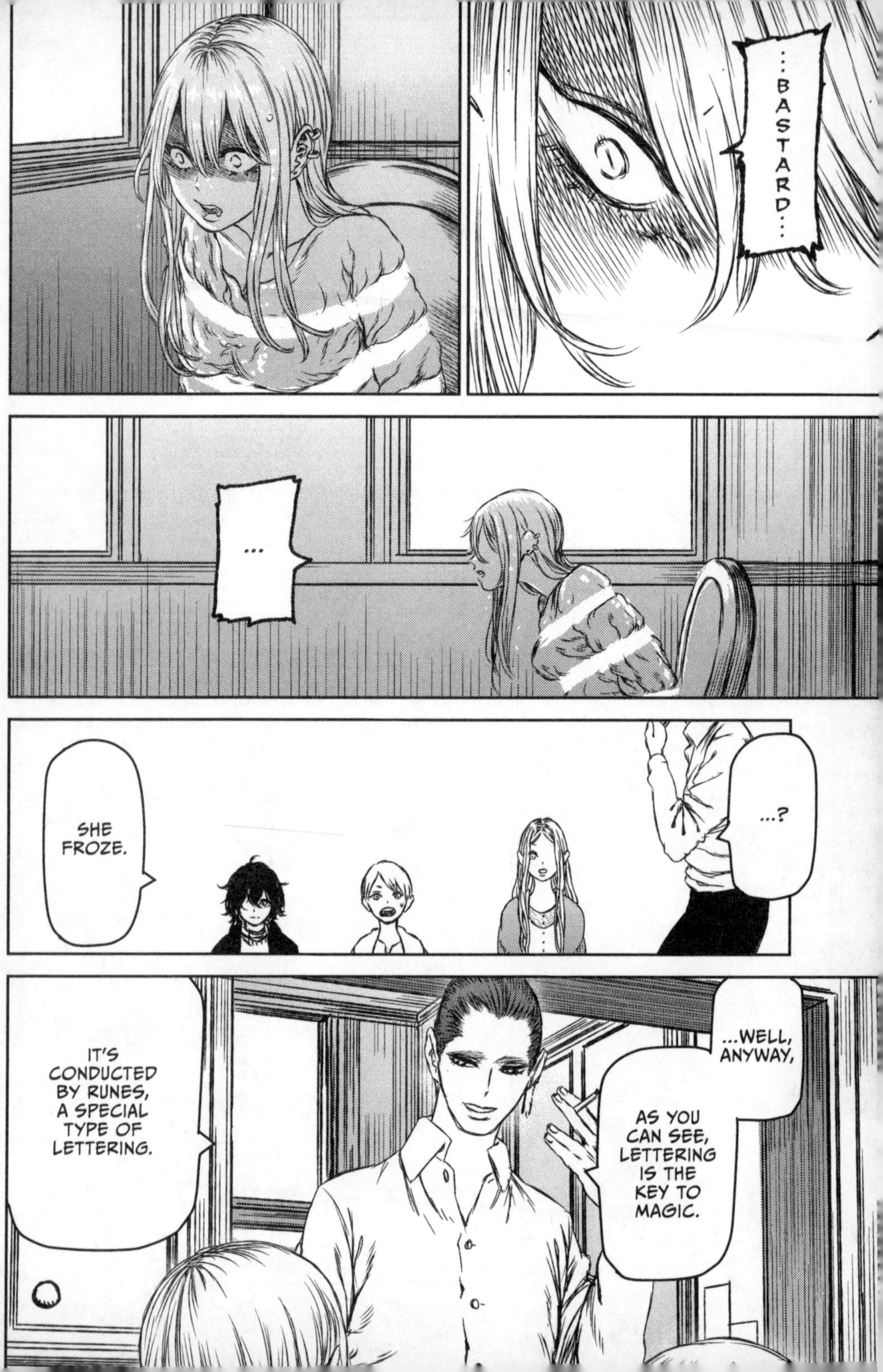
...BASTARD...
...
...?
SHE FROZE.
...WELL, ANYWAY,
AS YOU CAN SEE, LETTERING IS THE KEY TO MAGIC.
IT'S CONDUCTED BY RUNES, A SPECIAL TYPE OF LETTERING.

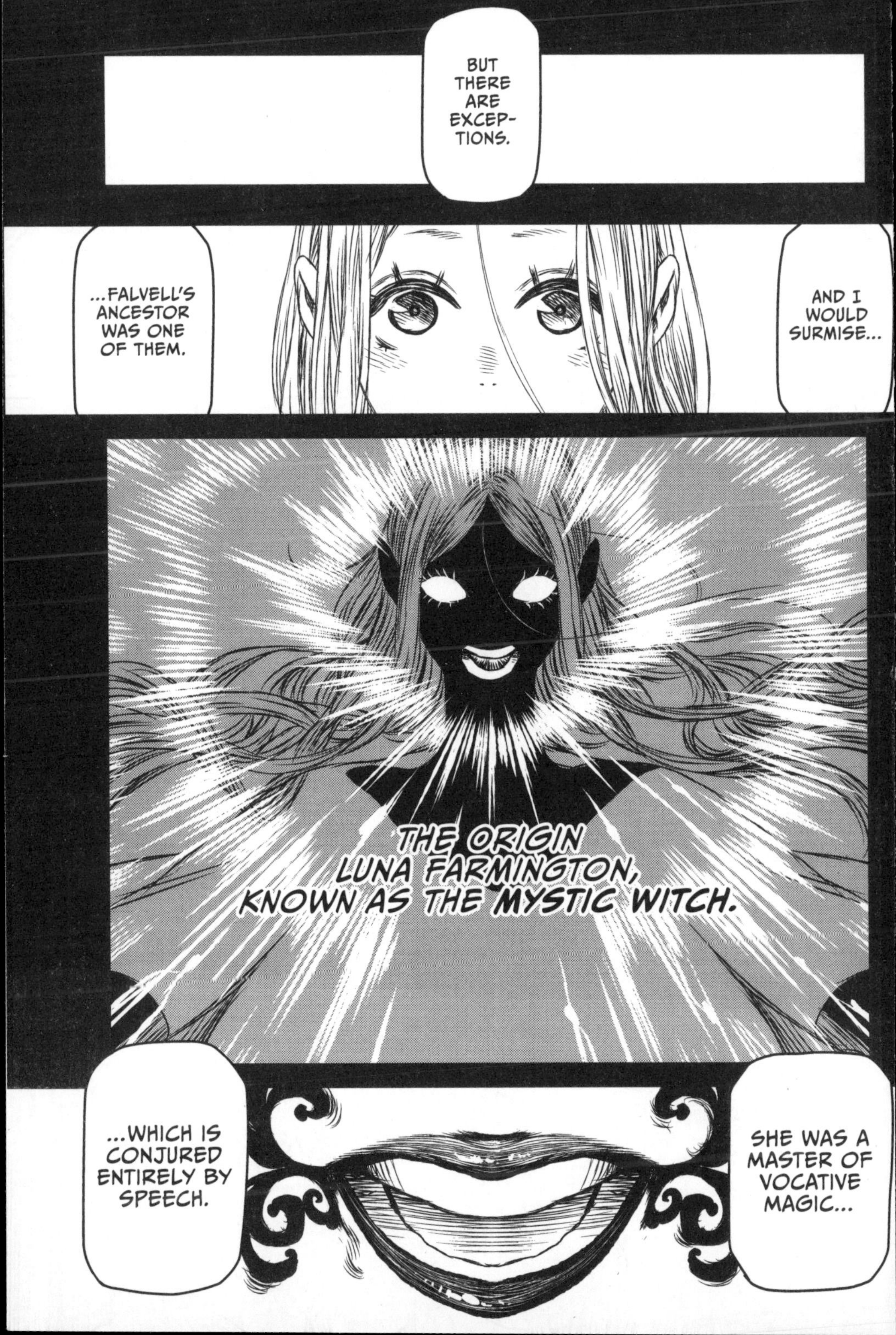
BUT THERE ARE EXCEPTIONS.
AND I WOULD SURMISE...
...FALVELL'S ANCESTOR WAS ONE OF THEM.
THE ORIGIN LUNA FARMINGTON, KNOWN AS THE MYSTIC WITCH.
SHE WAS A MASTER OF VOCATIVE MAGIC...
...WHICH IS CONJURED ENTIRELY BY SPEECH.

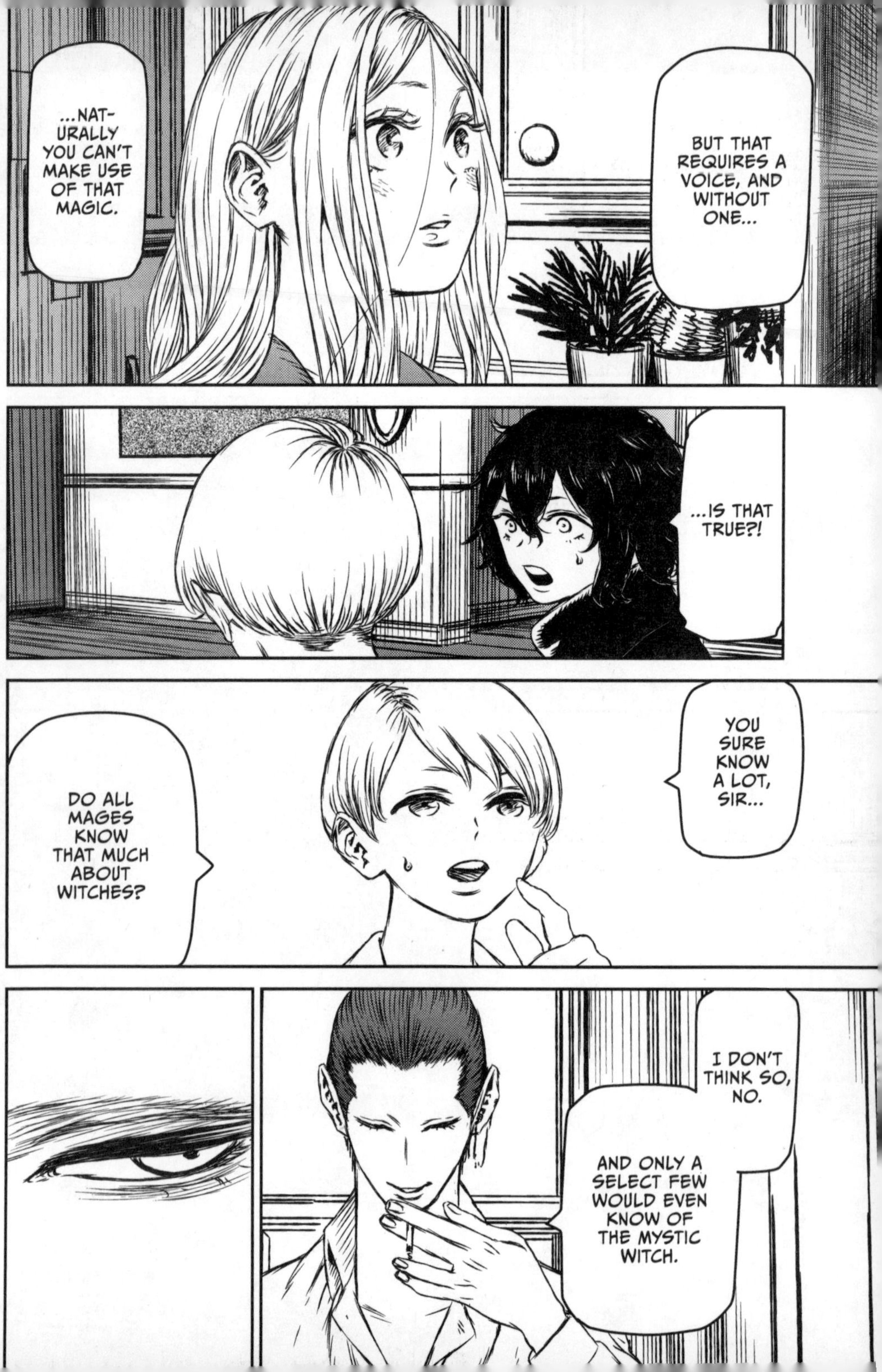
BUT THAT REQUIRES A VOICE, AND WITHOUT ONE...
...NAT-URALLY YOU CAN'T MAKE USE OF THAT MAGIC.
...IS THAT TRUE?!
YOU SURE KNOW A LOT, SIR...
DO ALL MAGES KNOW THAT MUCH ABOUT WITCHES?
I DON'T THINK SO, NO.
AND ONLY A SELECT FEW WOULD EVEN KNOW OF THE MYSTIC WITCH.

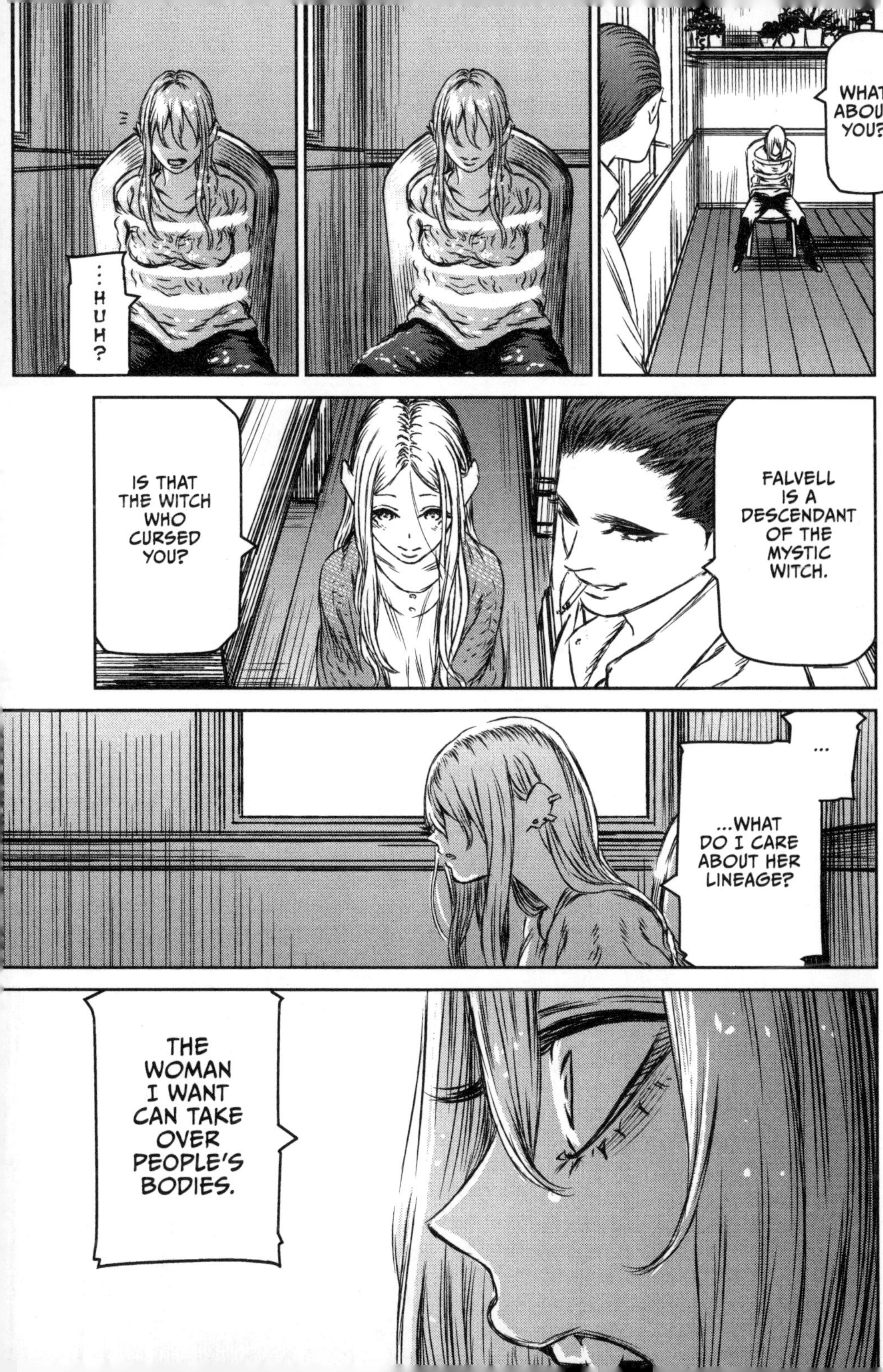
WHAT ABOUT YOU?
...HUH?
FALVELL IS A DESCENDANT OF THE MYSTIC WITCH.
IS THAT THE WITCH WHO CURSED YOU?
...
...WHAT DO I CARE ABOUT HER LINEAGE?
THE WOMAN I WANT CAN TAKE OVER PEOPLE'S BODIES.

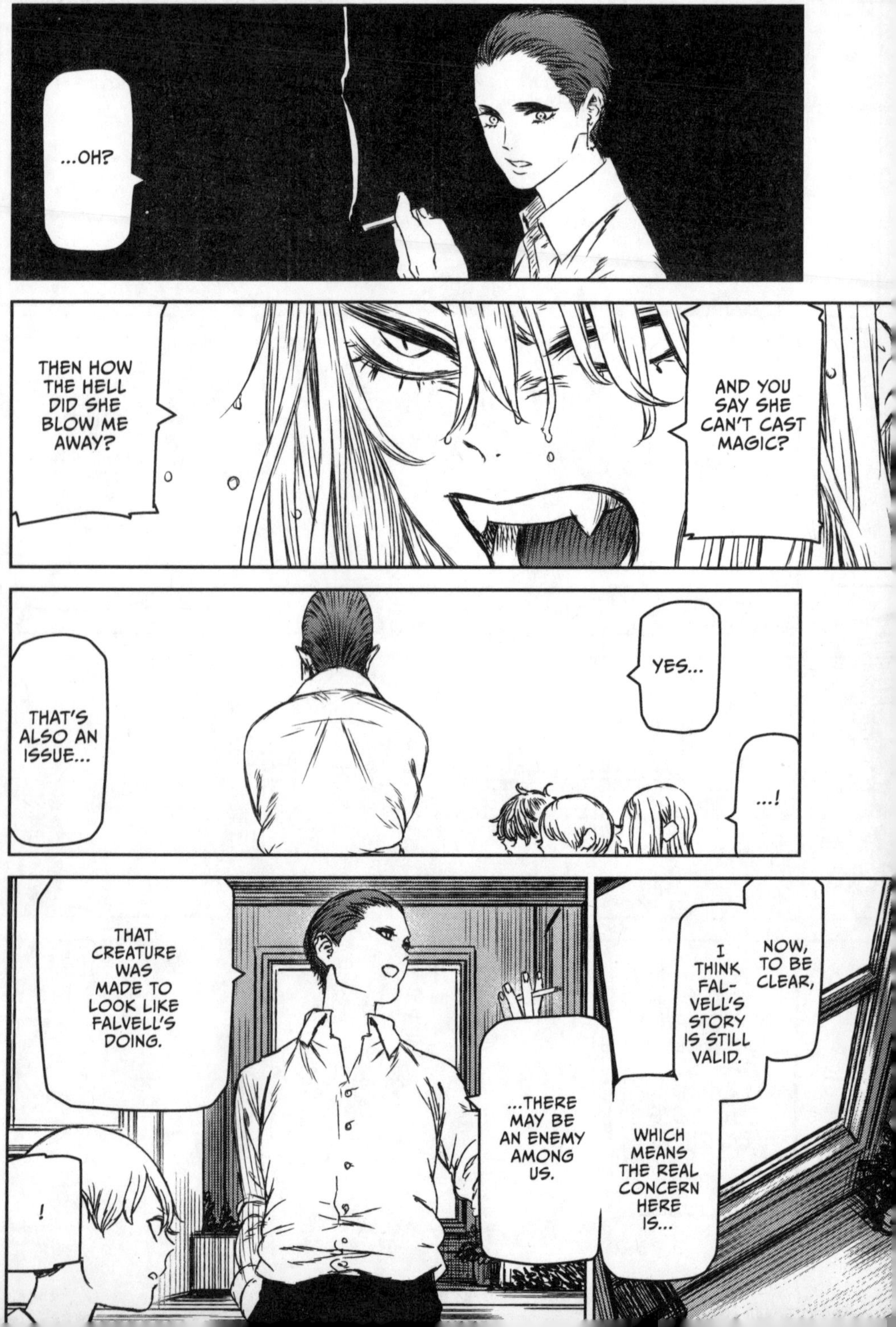
...OH?
AND YOU SAY SHE CAN'T CAST MAGIC?
THEN HOW THE HELL DID SHE BLOW ME AWAY?
YES...
...!
THAT'S ALSO AN ISSUE...
NOW, TO BE CLEAR,
I THINK FAL-VELL'S STORY IS STILL VALID.
THAT CREATURE WAS MADE TO LOOK LIKE FALVELL'S DOING.
WHICH MEANS THE REAL CONCERN HERE IS...
...THERE MAY BE AN ENEMY AMONG US.
!

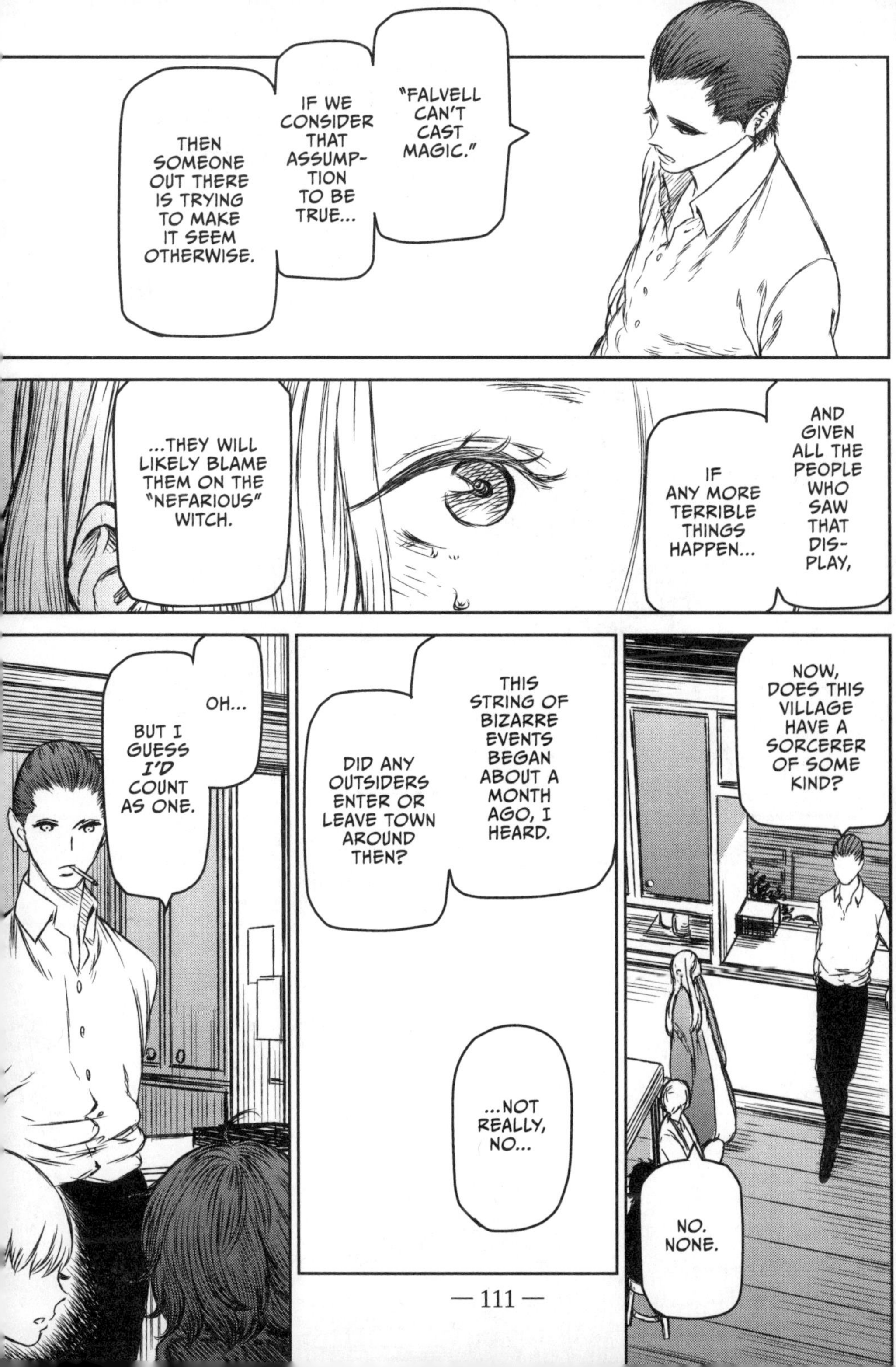
"FALVELL CAN'T CAST MAGIC."
IF WE CONSIDER THAT ASSUMPTION TO BE TRUE...
THEN SOMEONE OUT THERE IS TRYING TO MAKE IT SEEM OTHERWISE.
AND GIVEN ALL THE PEOPLE WHO SAW THAT DISPLAY,
IF ANY MORE TERRIBLE THINGS HAPPEN...
...THEY WILL LIKELY BLAME THEM ON THE "NEFARIOUS" WITCH.
NOW, DOES THIS VILLAGE HAVE A SORCERER OF SOME KIND?
NO. NONE.
THIS STRING OF BIZARRE EVENTS BEGAN ABOUT A MONTH AGO, I HEARD.
DID ANY OUTSIDERS ENTER OR LEAVE TOWN AROUND THEN?
...NOT REALLY, NO...
OH...
BUT I GUESS *I'D* COUNT AS ONE.

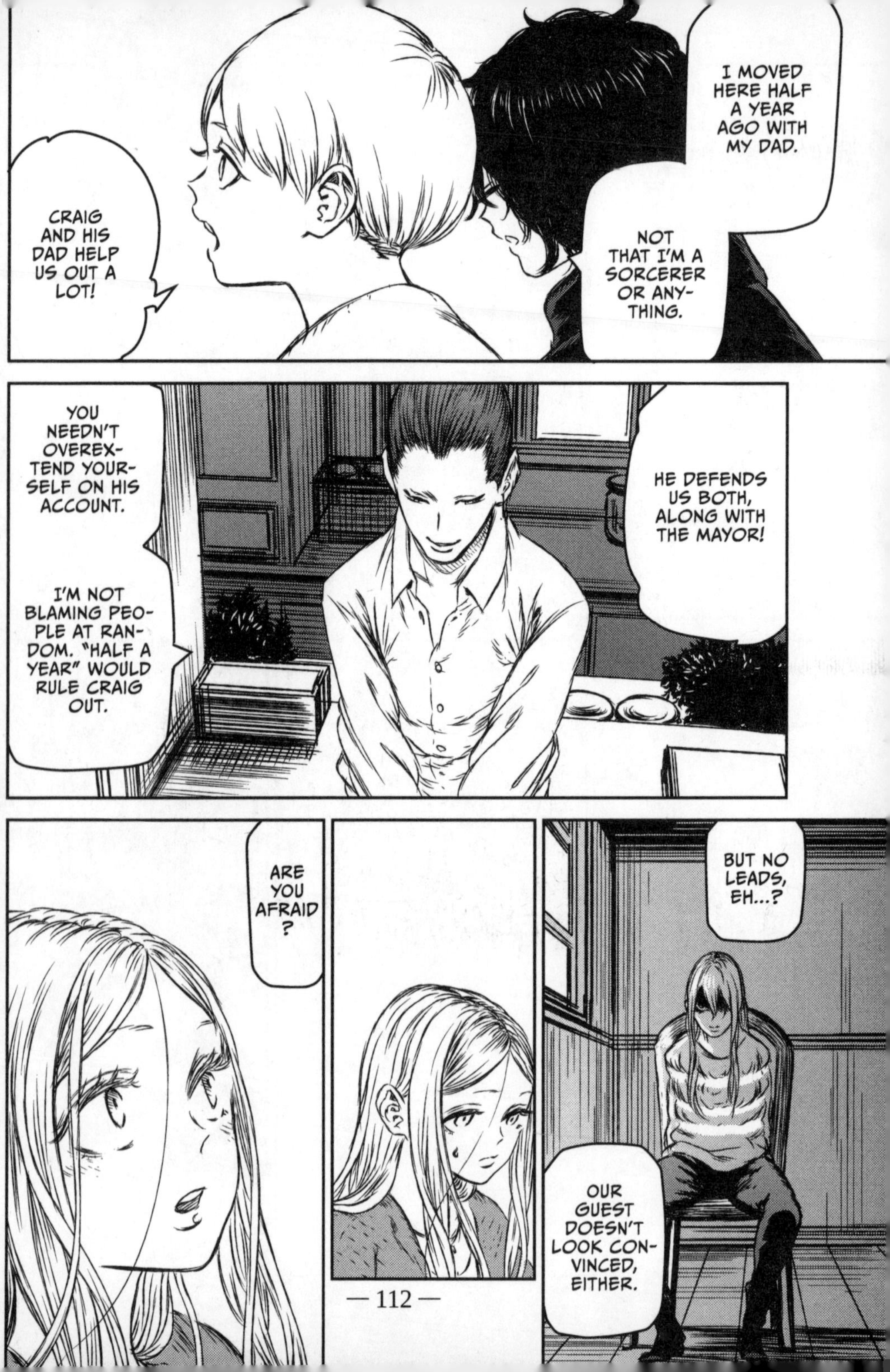
I MOVED HERE HALF A YEAR AGO WITH MY DAD.
NOT THAT I'M A SORCERER OR ANYTHING.
CRAIG AND HIS DAD HELP US OUT A LOT!
HE DEFENDS US BOTH, ALONG WITH THE MAYOR!
YOU NEEDN'T OVEREXTEND YOURSELF ON HIS ACCOUNT.
I'M NOT BLAMING PEOPLE AT RANDOM. "HALF A YEAR" WOULD RULE CRAIG OUT.
BUT NO LEADS, EH...?
OUR GUEST DOESN'T LOOK CONVINCED, EITHER.
ARE YOU AFRAID?

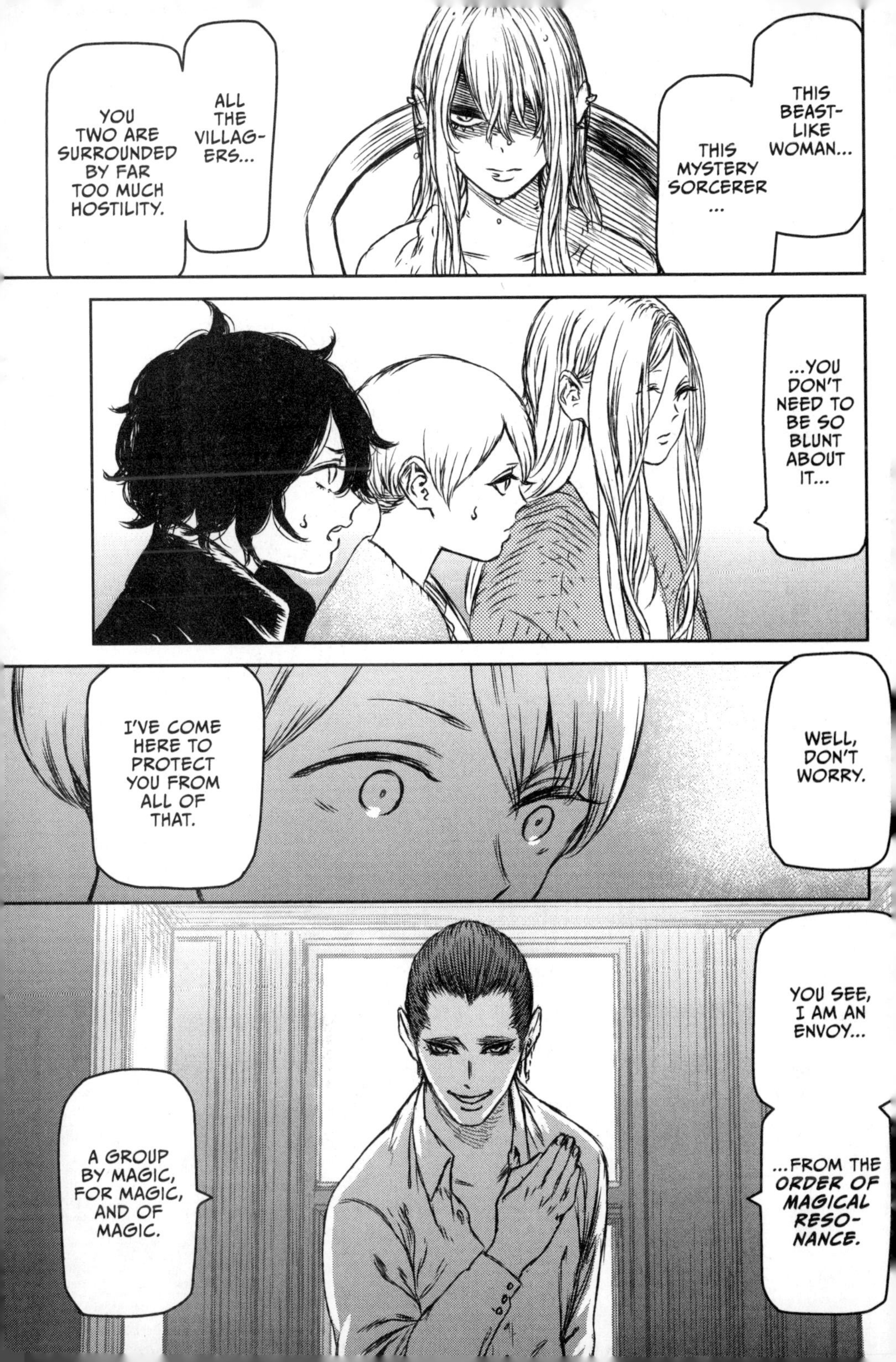
THIS BEAST-LIKE WOMAN...
THIS MYSTERY SORCERER ...
ALL THE VILLAGERS...
YOU TWO ARE SURROUNDED BY FAR TOO MUCH HOSTILITY.
...YOU DON'T NEED TO BE SO BLUNT ABOUT IT...
WELL, DON'T WORRY.
I'VE COME HERE TO PROTECT YOU FROM ALL OF THAT.
YOU SEE, I AM AN ENVOY...
...FROM THE *ORDER OF MAGICAL RESONANCE.*
A GROUP BY MAGIC, FOR MAGIC, AND OF MAGIC.

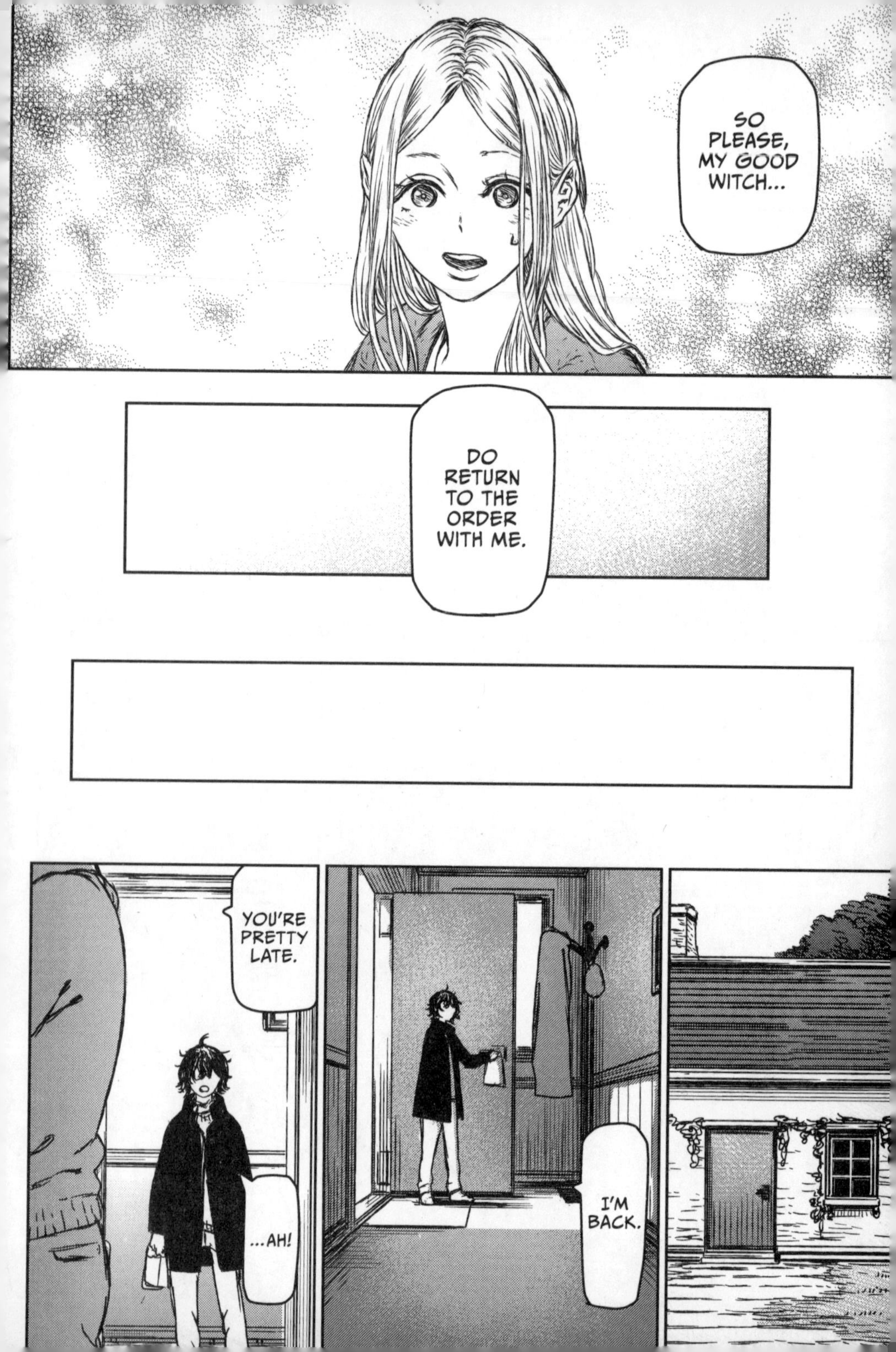
SO PLEASE, MY GOOD WITCH...
DO RETURN TO THE ORDER WITH ME.
I'M BACK.
YOU'RE PRETTY LATE.
...AH!

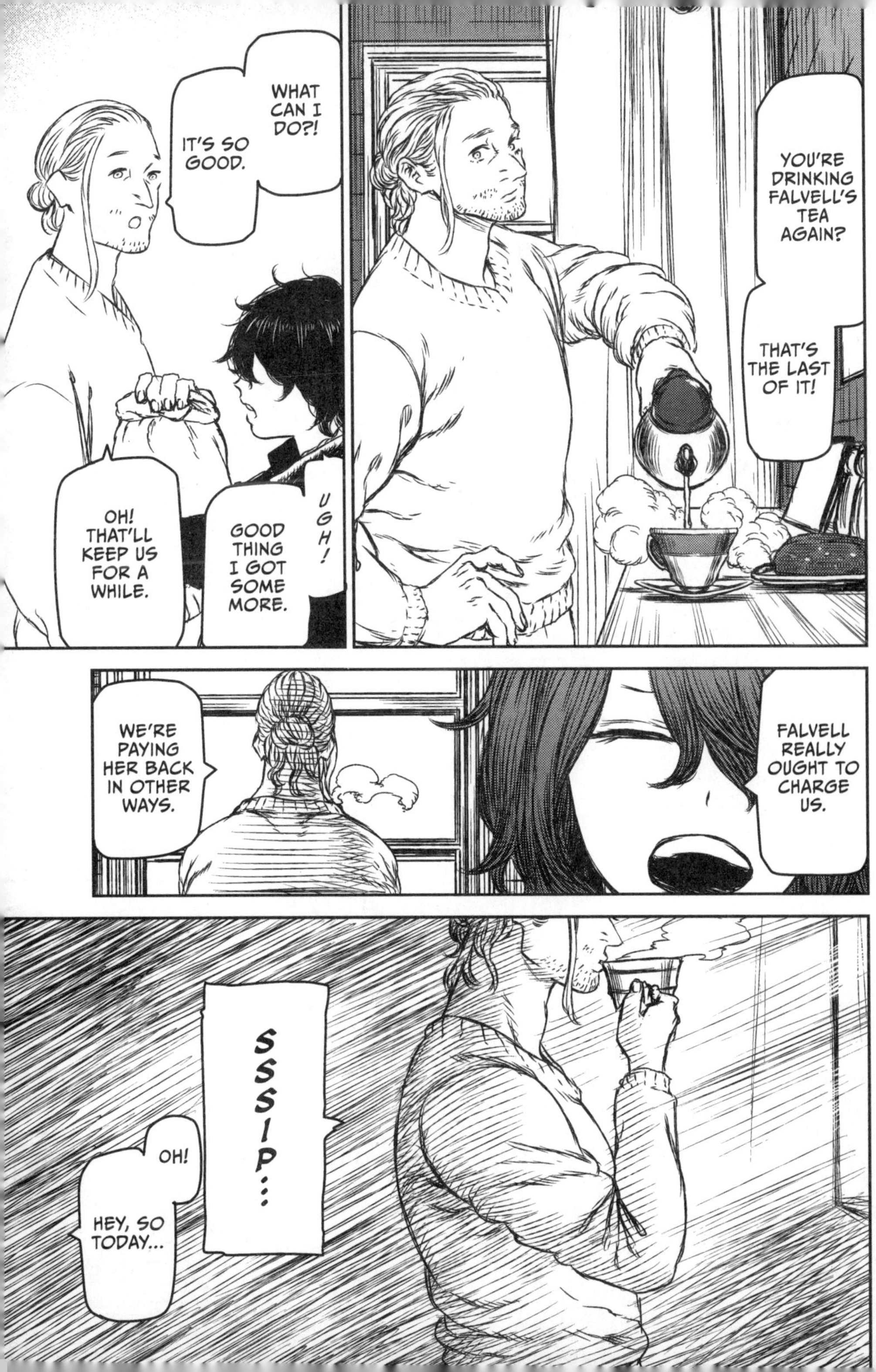
YOU'RE DRINKING FALVELL'S TEA AGAIN?
THAT'S THE LAST OF IT!
WHAT CAN I DO?!
IT'S SO GOOD.
UGH!
GOOD THING I GOT SOME MORE.
OH! THAT'LL KEEP US FOR A WHILE.
FALVELL REALLY OUGHT TO CHARGE US.
WE'RE PAYING HER BACK IN OTHER WAYS.
SSSIP...
OH!
HEY, SO TODAY...

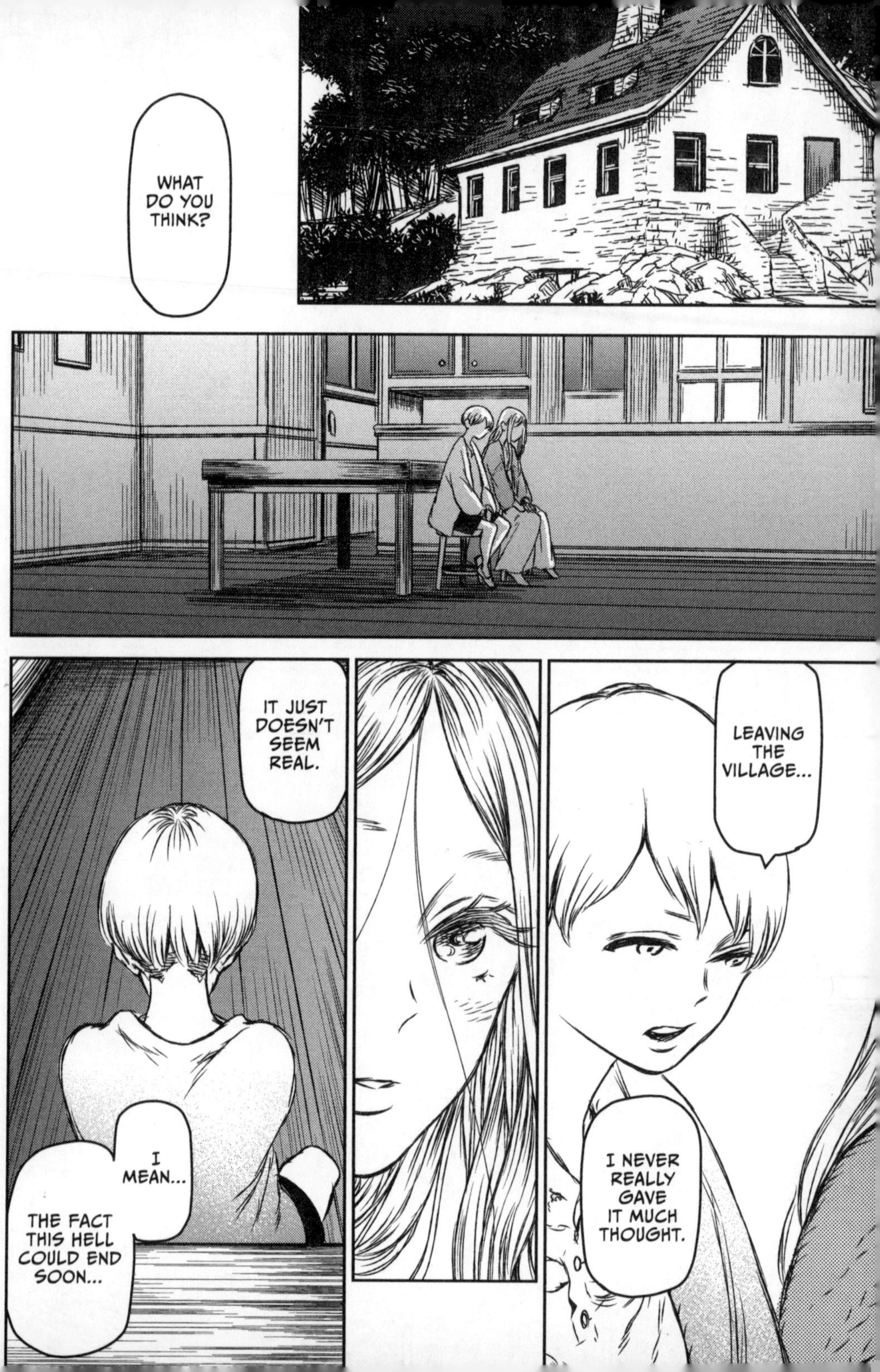
WHAT DO YOU THINK?
LEAVING THE VILLAGE...
I NEVER REALLY GAVE IT MUCH THOUGHT.
IT JUST DOESN'T SEEM REAL.
I MEAN...
THE FACT THIS HELL COULD END SOON...

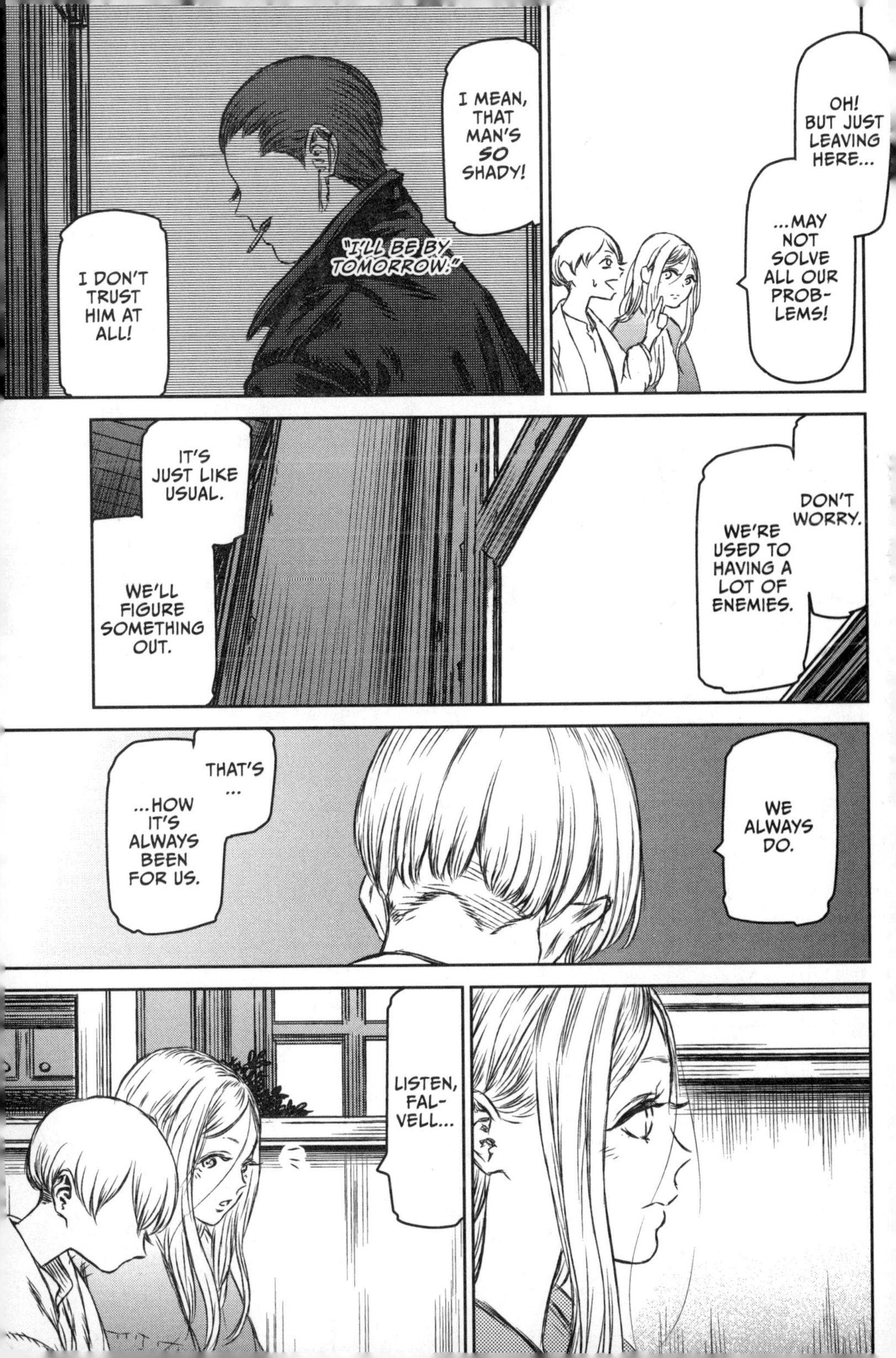
OH! BUT JUST LEAVING HERE...
...MAY NOT SOLVE ALL OUR PROB-LEMS!
I MEAN, THAT MAN'S *SO* SHADY!
"I'LL BE BY TOMORROW."
I DON'T TRUST HIM AT ALL!
DON'T WORRY.
WE'RE USED TO HAVING A LOT OF ENEMIES.
IT'S JUST LIKE USUAL.
WE'LL FIGURE SOMETHING OUT.
WE ALWAYS DO.
THAT'S...
...HOW IT'S ALWAYS BEEN FOR US.
LISTEN, FAL-VELL...

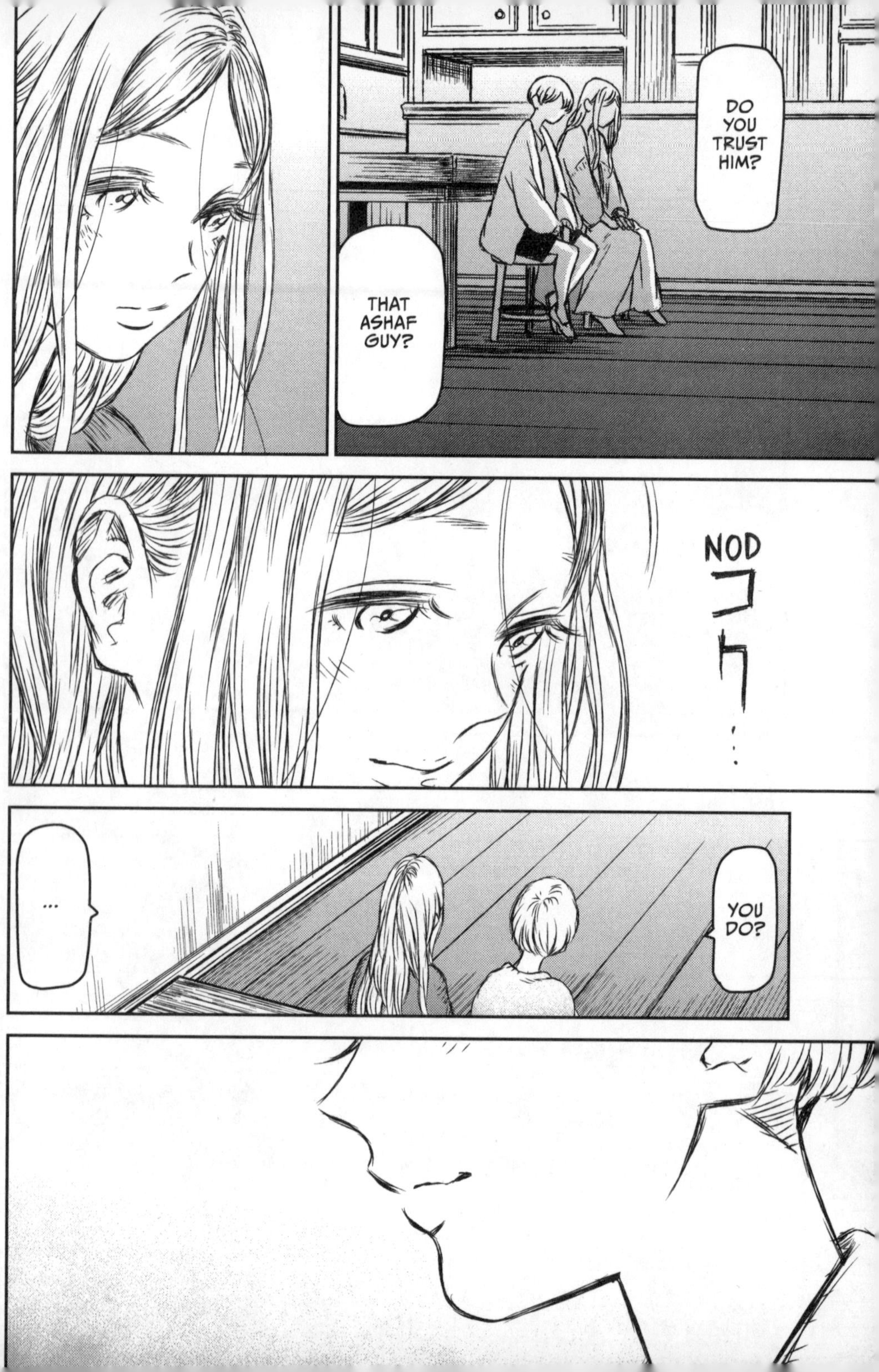
DO YOU TRUST HIM?
THAT ASHAF GUY?
NOD
コク
YOU DO?
...

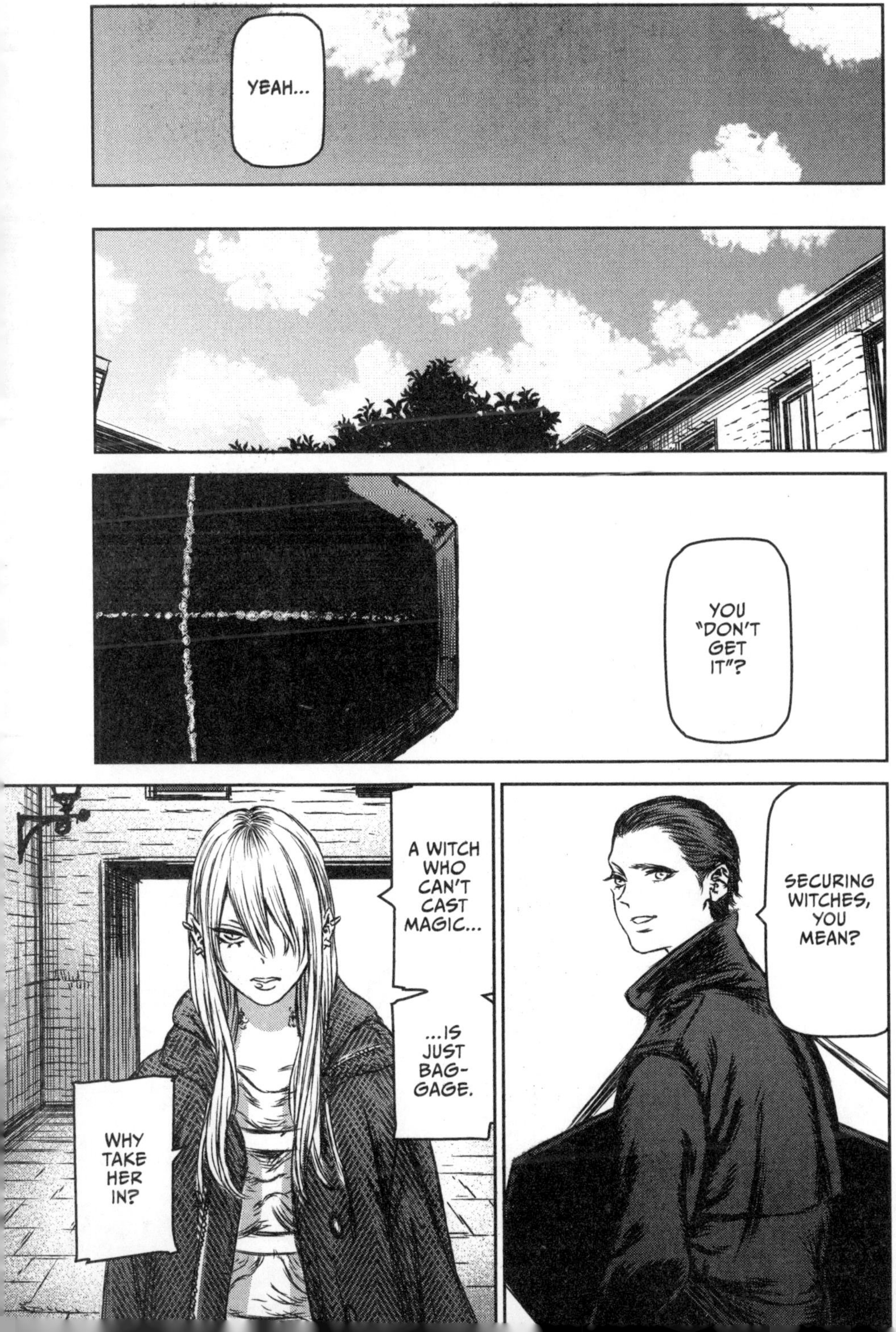
YEAH...
YOU "DON'T GET IT"?
SECURING WITCHES, YOU MEAN?
A WITCH WHO CAN'T CAST MAGIC...
...IS JUST BAGGAGE.
WHY TAKE HER IN?

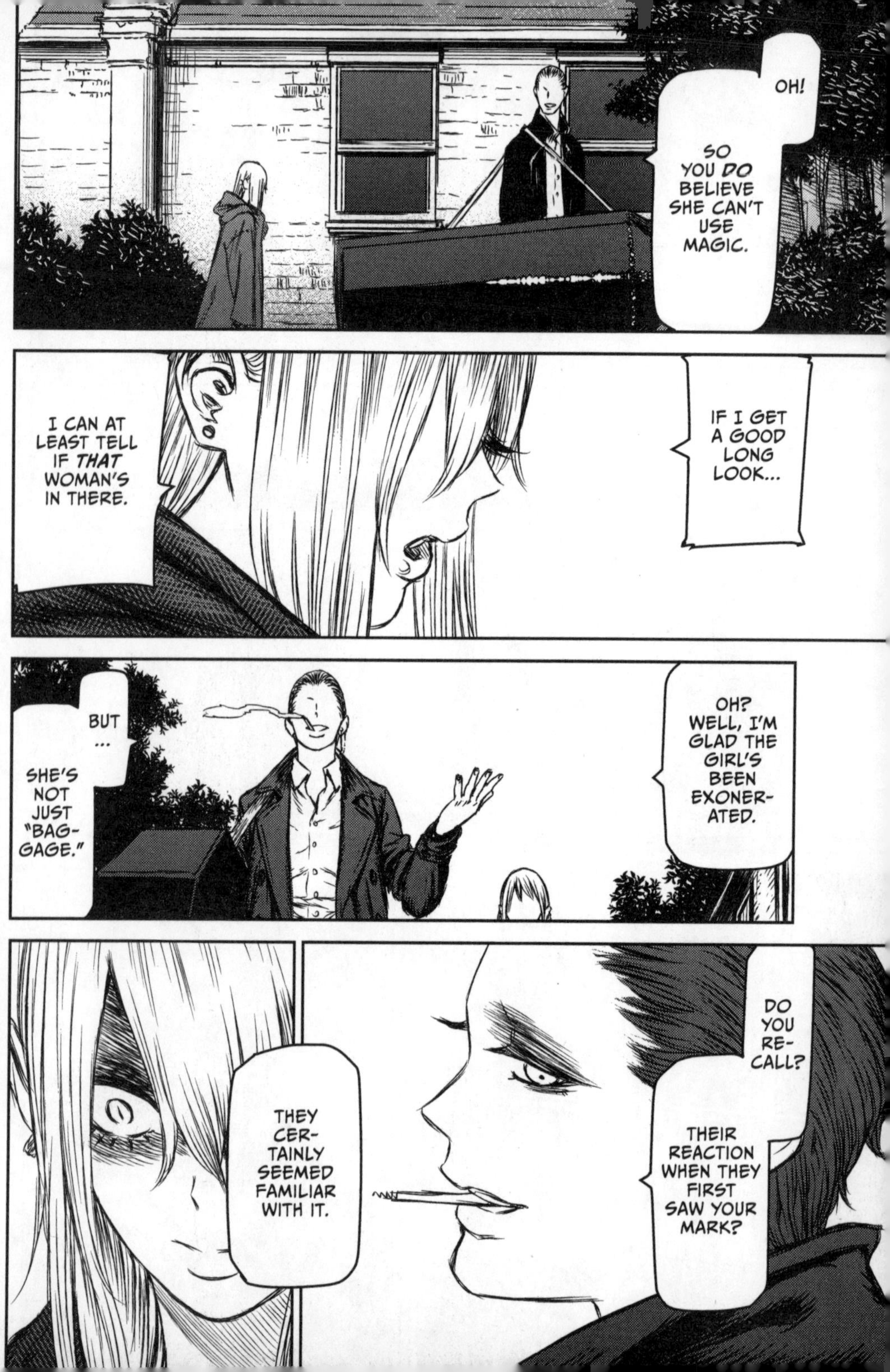
OH!
SO YOU *DO* BELIEVE SHE CAN'T USE MAGIC.
IF I GET A GOOD LONG LOOK...
I CAN AT LEAST TELL IF *THAT* WOMAN'S IN THERE.
OH? WELL, I'M GLAD THE GIRL'S BEEN EXONER-ATED.
BUT ...
SHE'S NOT JUST "BAG-GAGE."
DO YOU RE-CALL?
THEIR REACTION WHEN THEY FIRST SAW YOUR MARK?
THEY CER-TAINLY SEEMED FAMILIAR WITH IT.

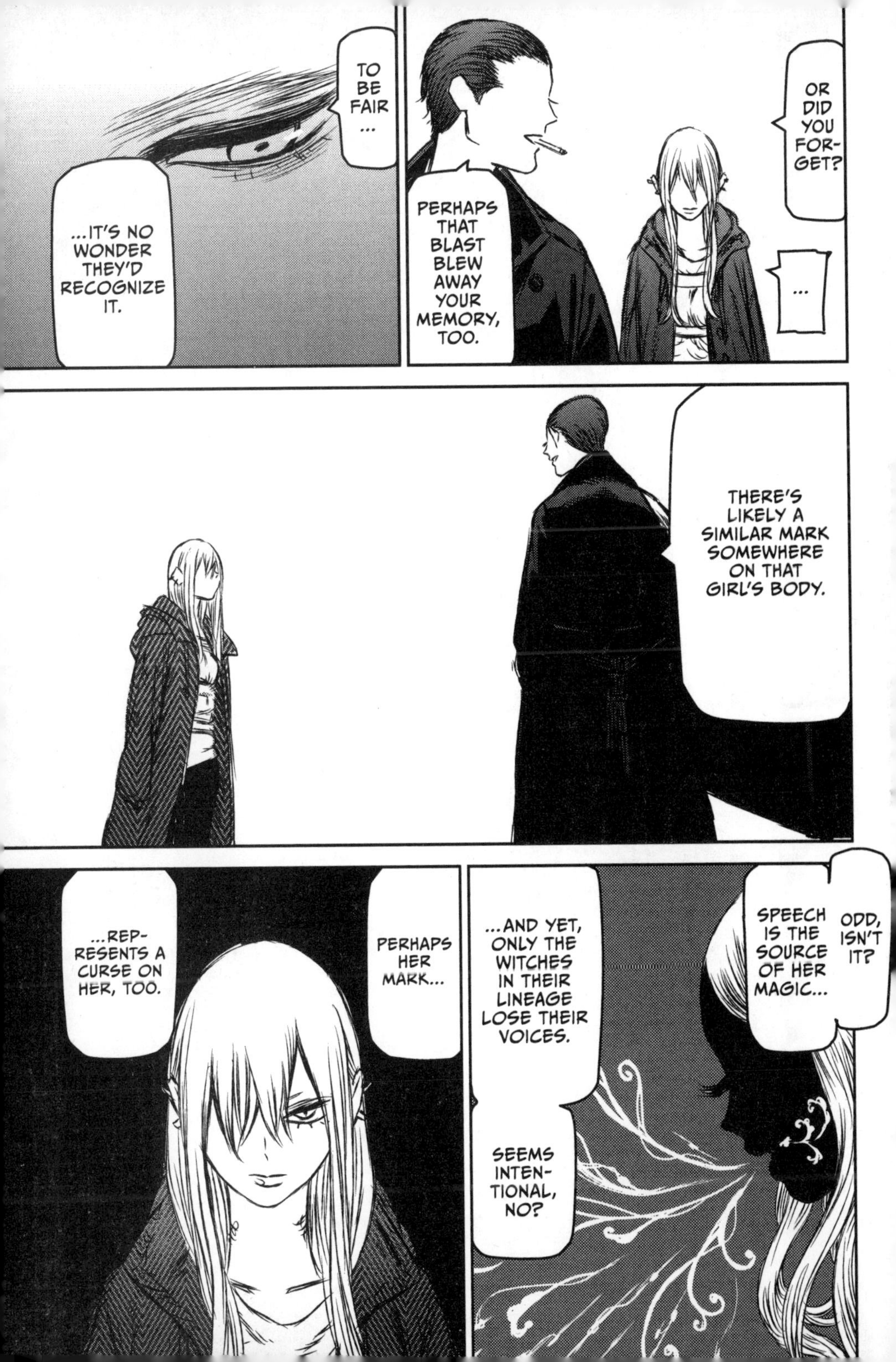
OR DID YOU FORGET?
...
PERHAPS THAT BLAST BLEW AWAY YOUR MEMORY, TOO.
TO BE FAIR...
...IT'S NO WONDER THEY'D RECOGNIZE IT.
THERE'S LIKELY A SIMILAR MARK SOMEWHERE ON THAT GIRL'S BODY.
ODD, ISN'T IT?
SPEECH IS THE SOURCE OF HER MAGIC...
...AND YET, ONLY THE WITCHES IN THEIR LINEAGE LOSE THEIR VOICES.
SEEMS INTENTIONAL, NO?
PERHAPS HER MARK...
...REPRESENTS A CURSE ON HER, TOO.

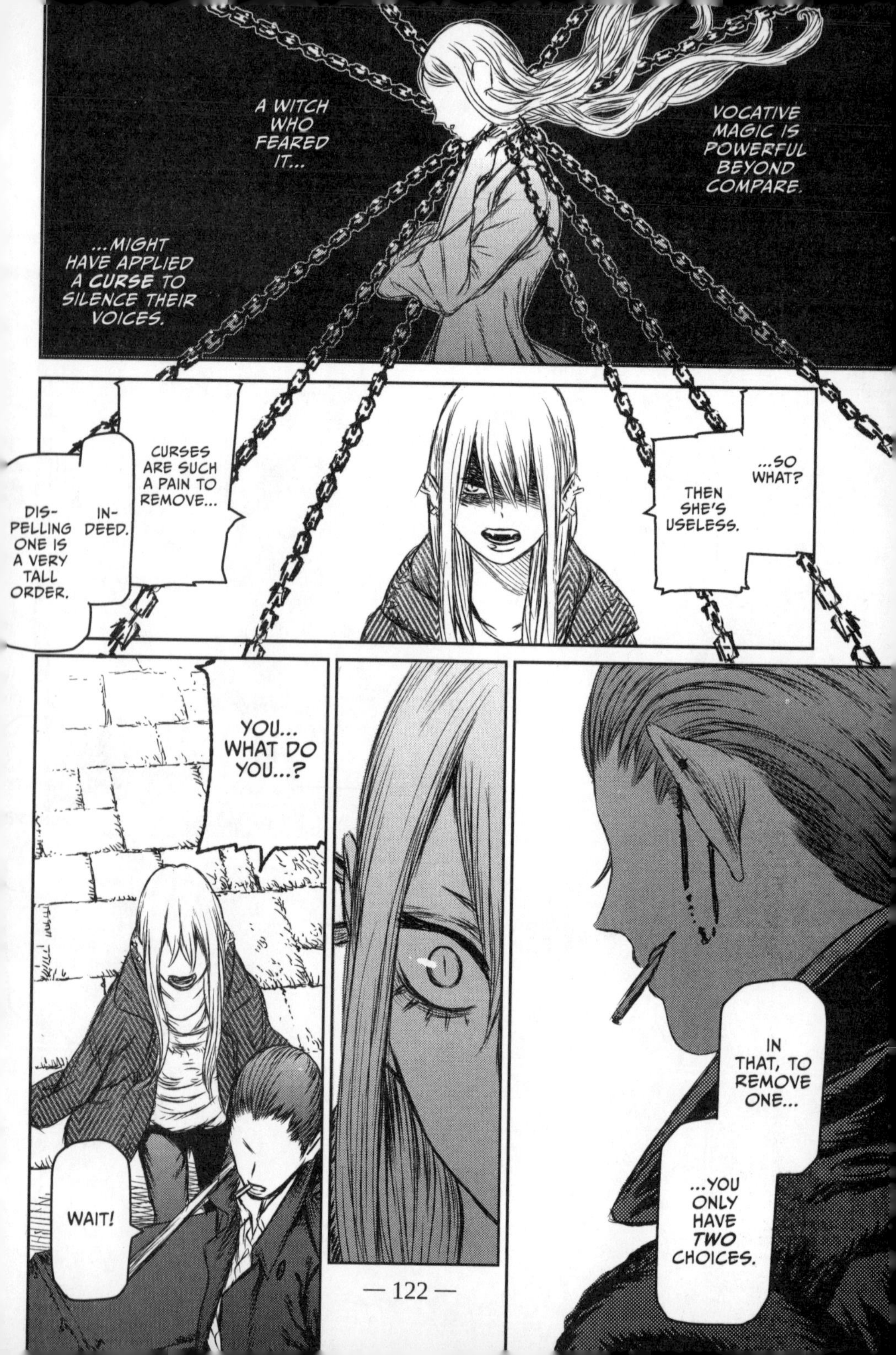
VOCATIVE MAGIC IS POWERFUL BEYOND COMPARE.
A WITCH WHO FEARED IT...
...MIGHT HAVE APPLIED A **CURSE** TO SILENCE THEIR VOICES.
...SO WHAT?
THEN SHE'S USELESS.
CURSES ARE SUCH A PAIN TO REMOVE...
IN- DEED.
DIS- PELLING ONE IS A VERY TALL ORDER.
IN THAT, TO REMOVE ONE...
...YOU ONLY HAVE ***TWO*** CHOICES.
YOU... WHAT DO YOU...?
WAIT!

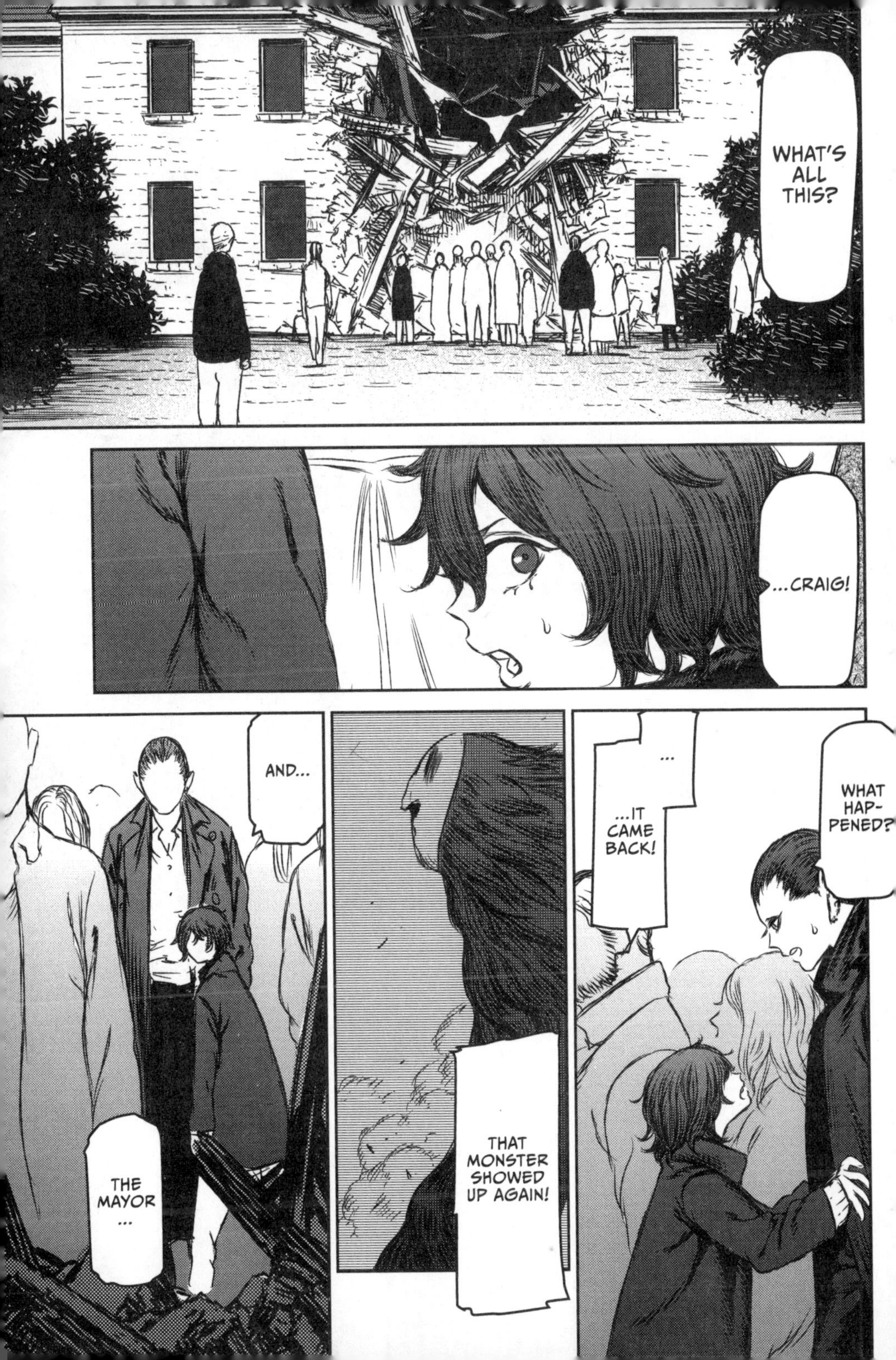
WHAT'S ALL THIS?
...CRAIG!
WHAT HAP-PENED?
... ...IT CAME BACK!
THAT MONSTER SHOWED UP AGAIN!
AND...
THE MAYOR ...

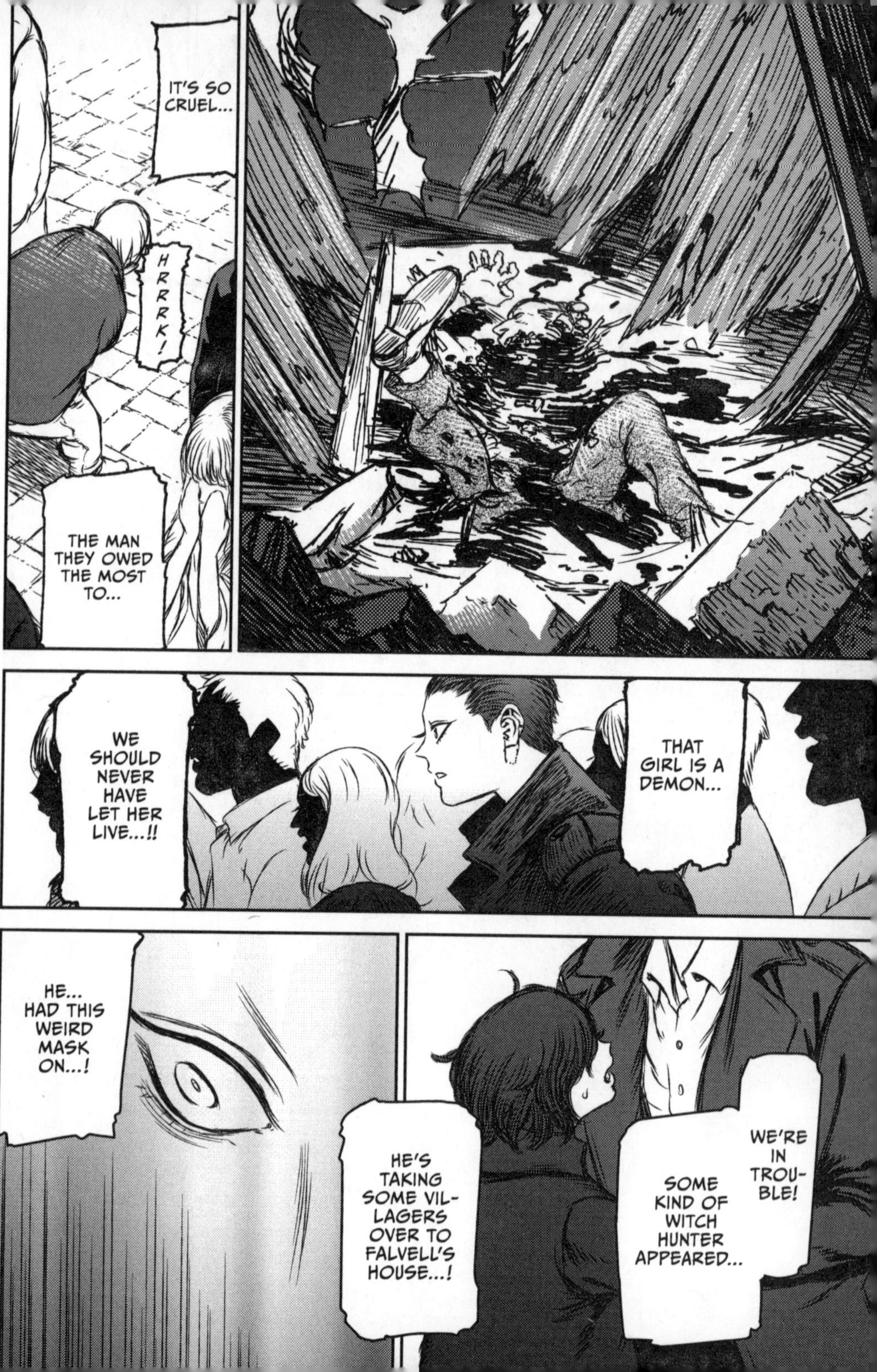
IT'S SO CRUEL...
HRRRK!
THE MAN THEY OWED THE MOST TO...
THAT GIRL IS A DEMON...
WE SHOULD NEVER HAVE LET HER LIVE...!!
WE'RE IN TROU-BLE!
SOME KIND OF WITCH HUNTER APPEARED...
HE'S TAKING SOME VIL-LAGERS OVER TO FALVELL'S HOUSE...!
HE... HAD THIS WEIRD MASK ON...!

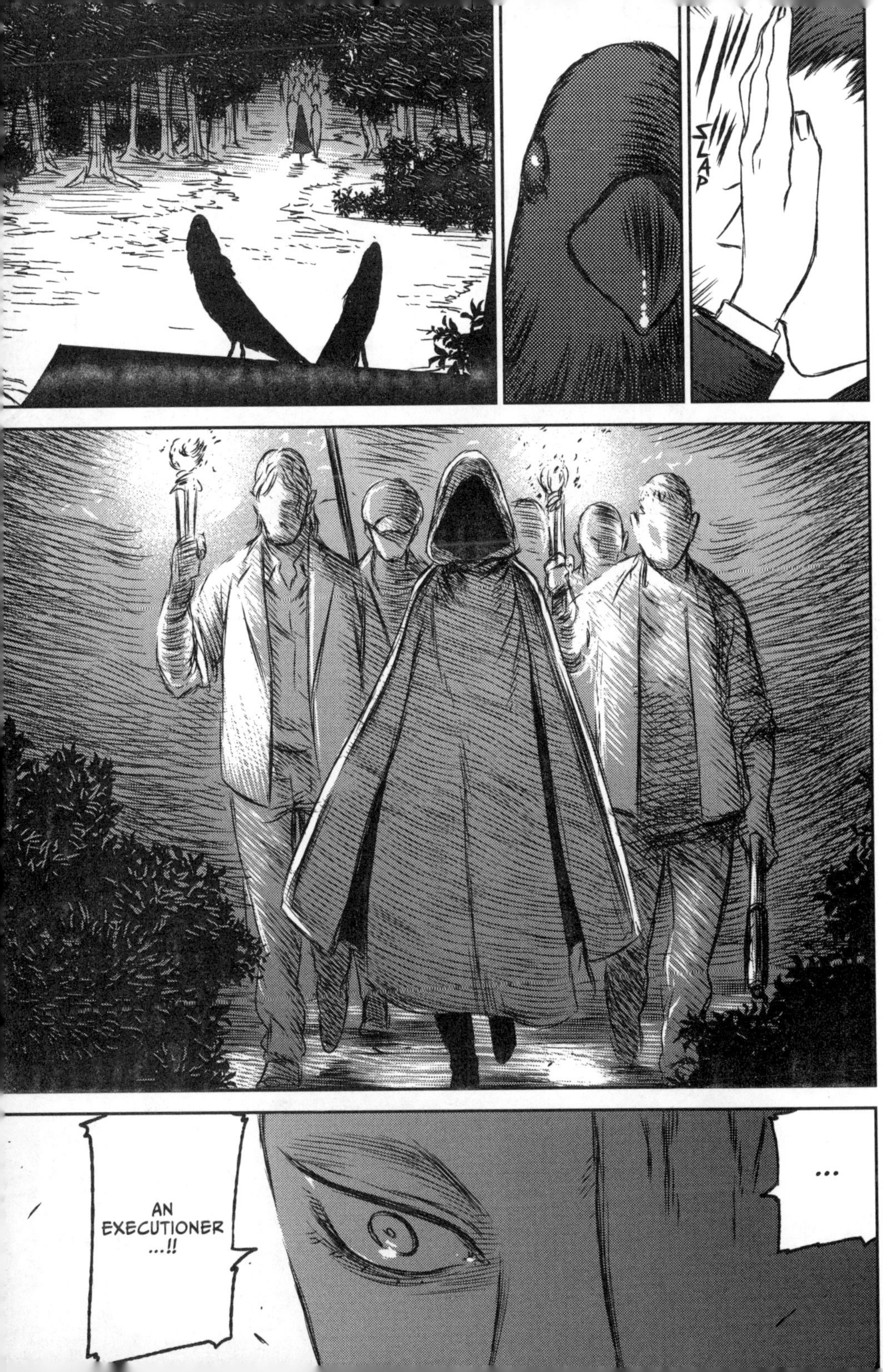
SLAP
...
AN EXECUTIONER ...!!

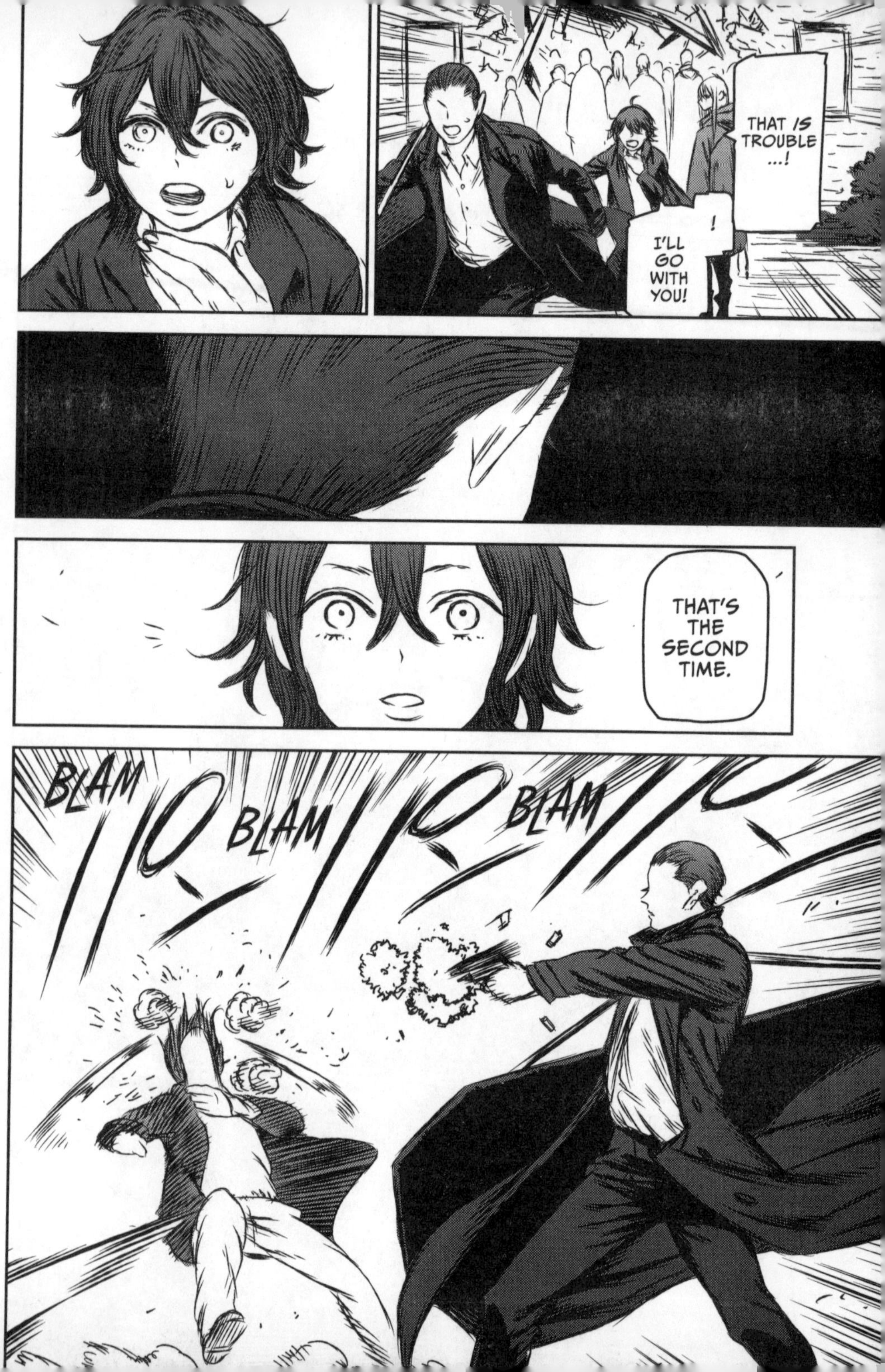
THAT *IS* TROUBLE ...!
!
I'LL GO WITH YOU!
THAT'S THE SECOND TIME.
BLAM
BLAM
BLAM

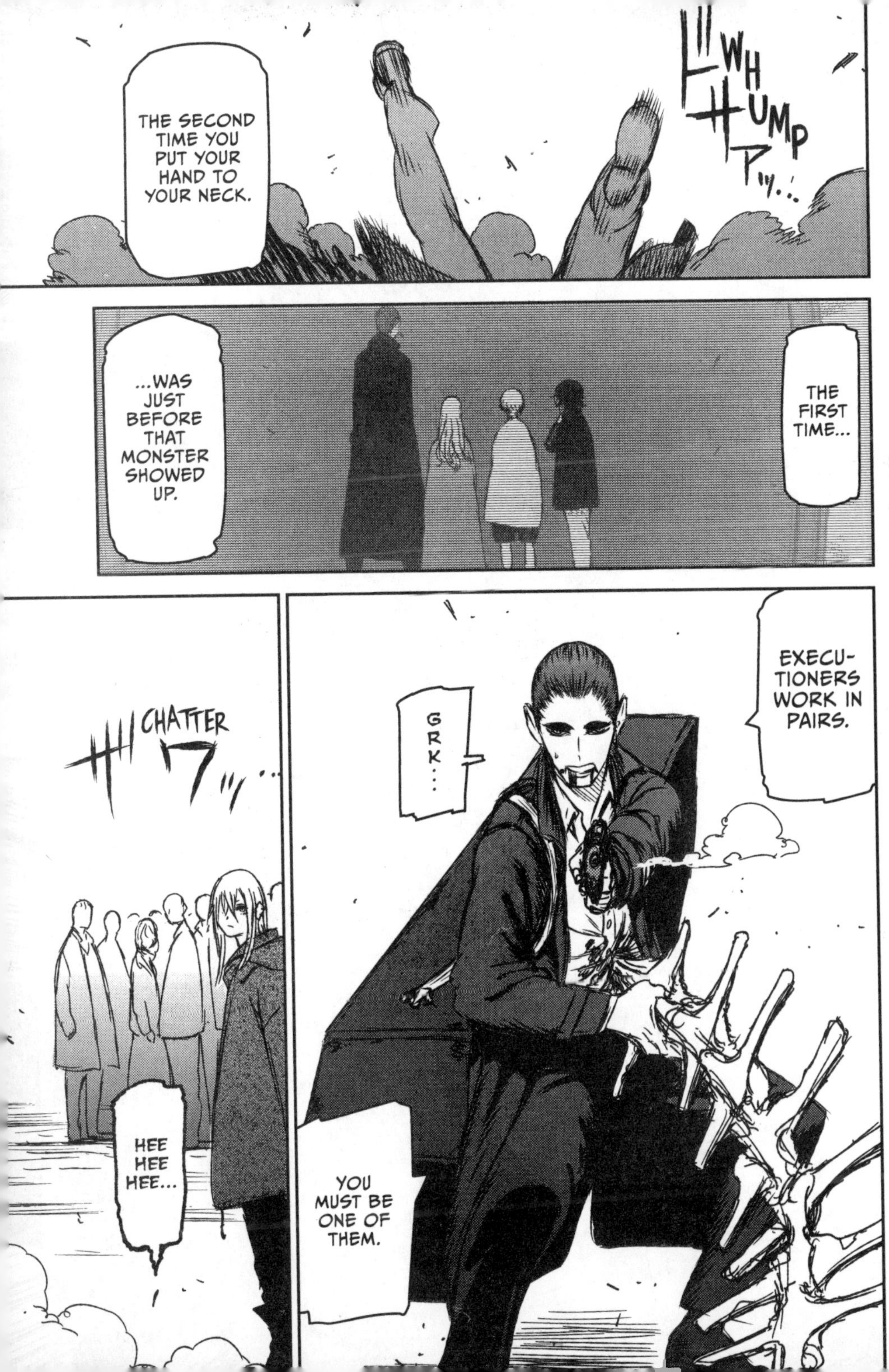
WHUMP
THE SECOND TIME YOU PUT YOUR HAND TO YOUR NECK.
THE FIRST TIME...
...WAS JUST BEFORE THAT MONSTER SHOWED UP.
EXECU-TIONERS WORK IN PAIRS.
GRK...
YOU MUST BE ONE OF THEM.
CHATTER
HEE HEE HEE...

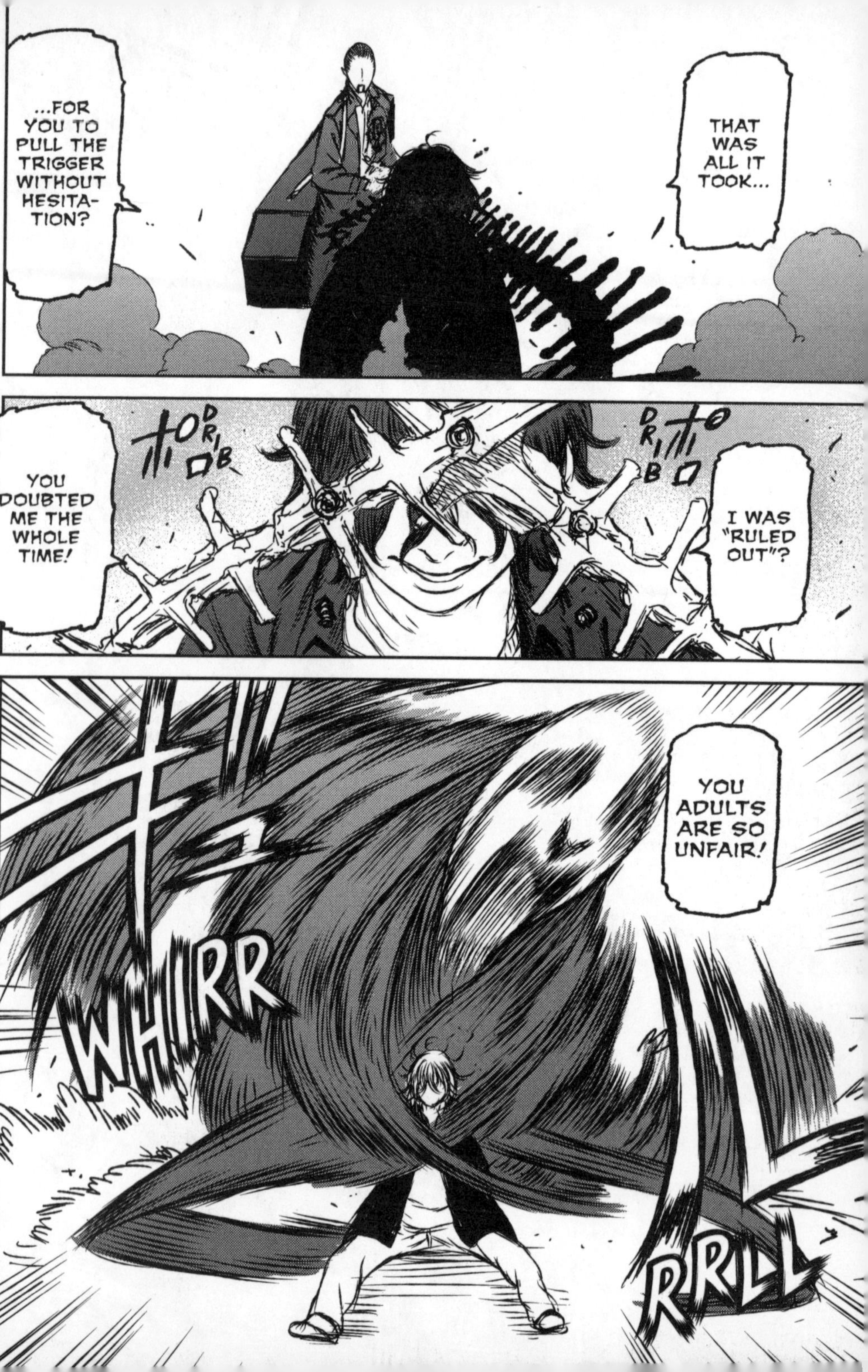

THAT WAS ALL IT TOOK...
...FOR YOU TO PULL THE TRIGGER WITHOUT HESITATION?
DRIB
I WAS "RULED OUT"?
DRIB
YOU DOUBTED ME THE WHOLE TIME!
YOU ADULTS ARE SO UNFAIR!
WHIRR
RRLL

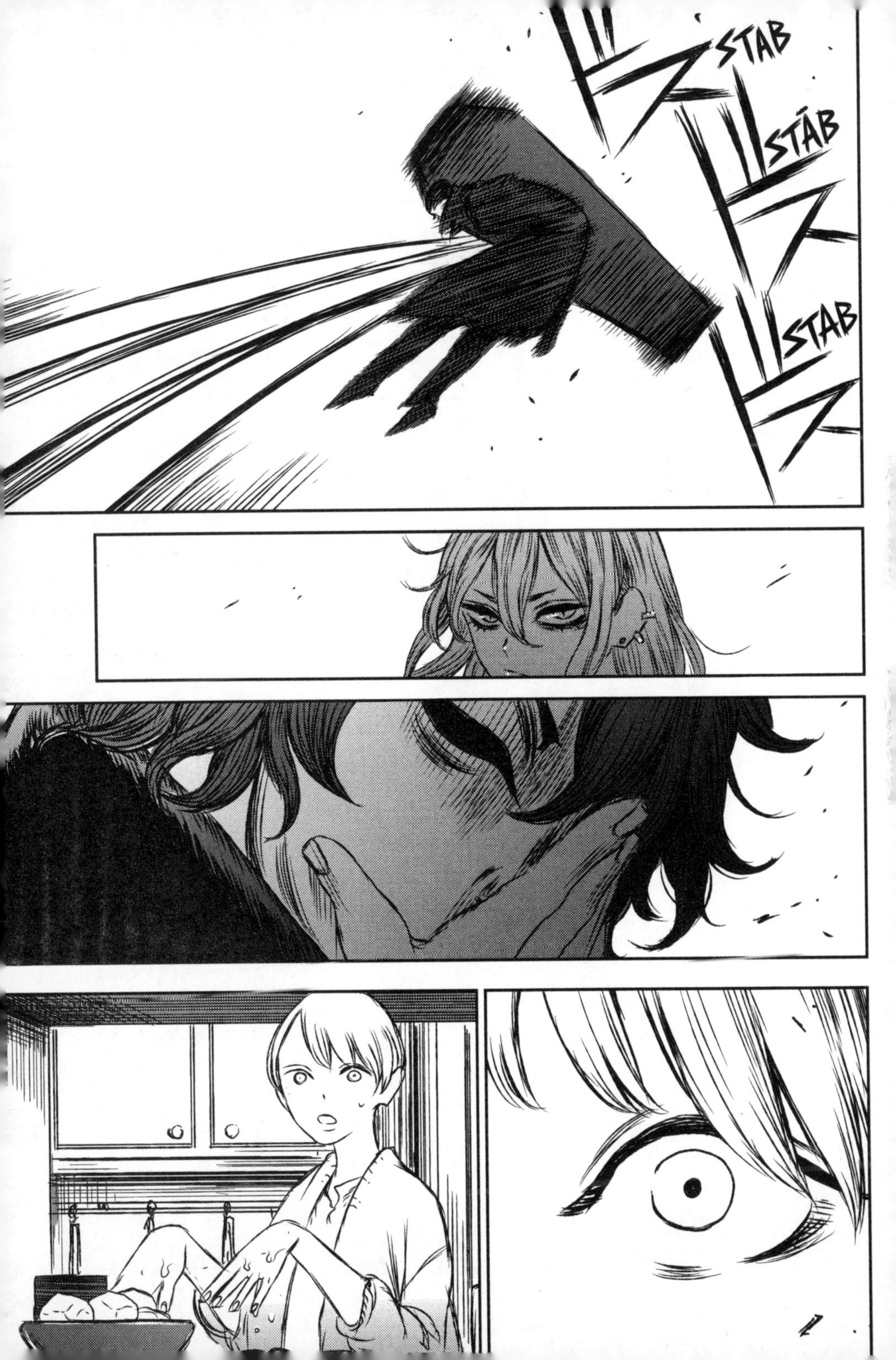
STAB
STAB
STAB

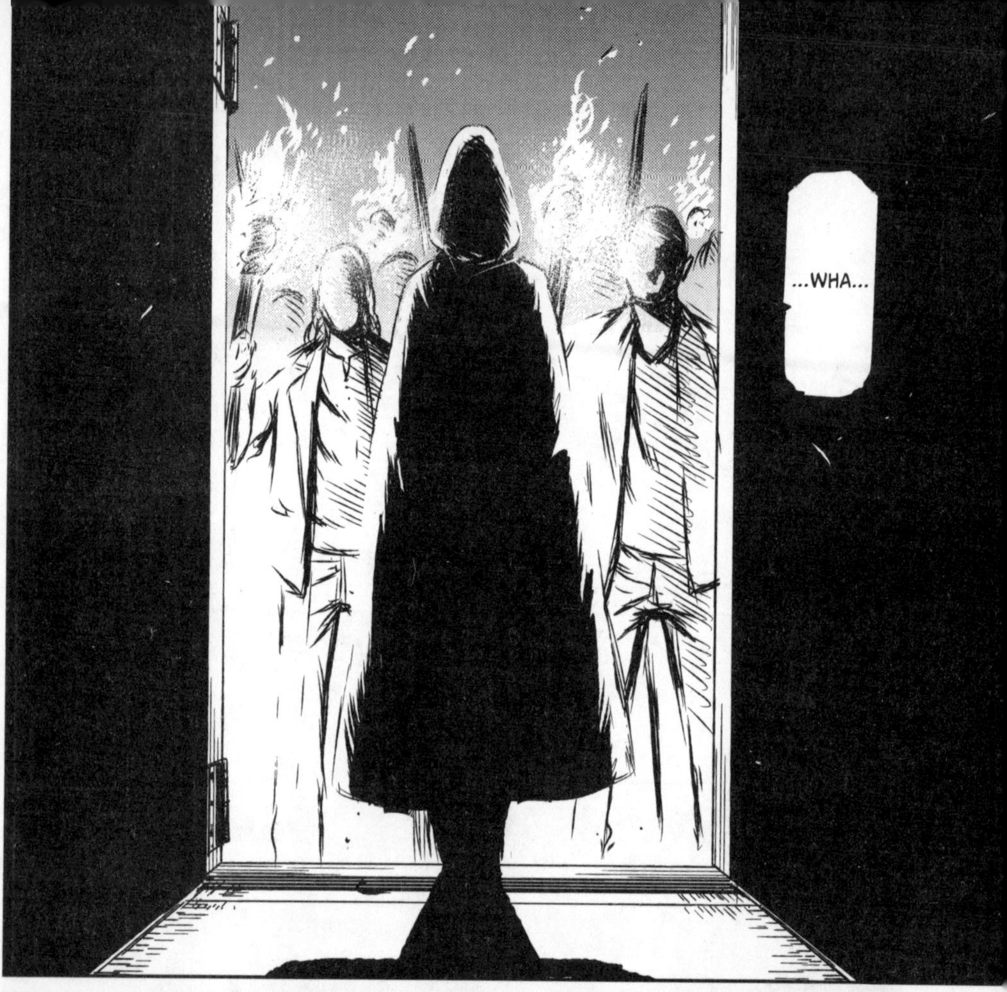
...WHA...
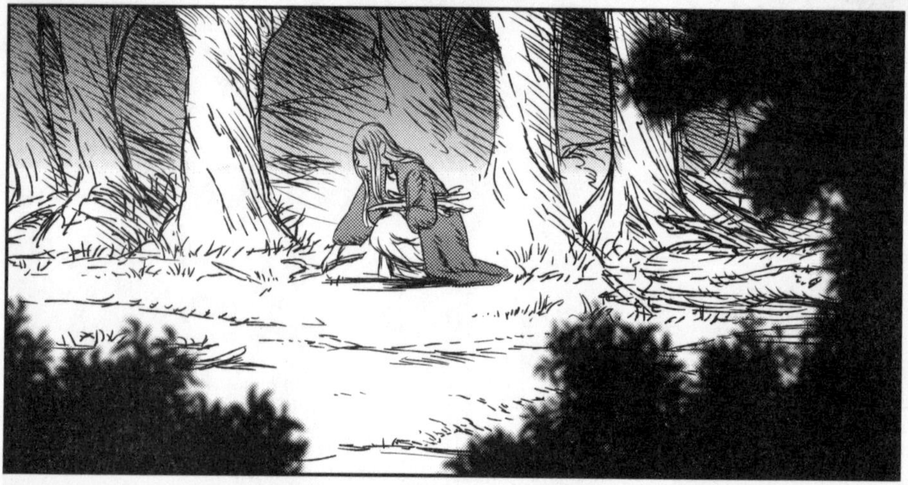

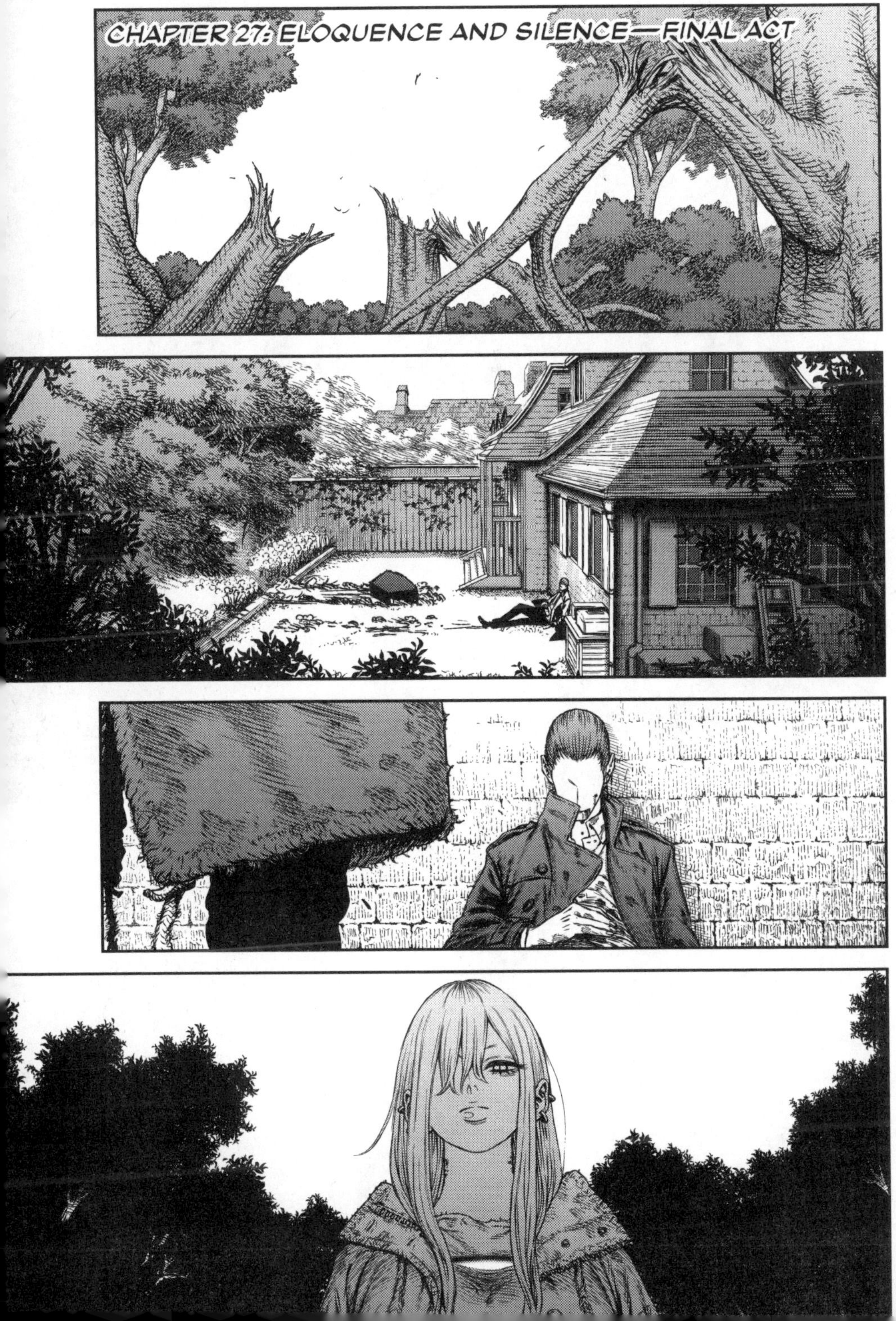
CHAPTER 27: ELOQUENCE AND SILENCE—FINAL ACT

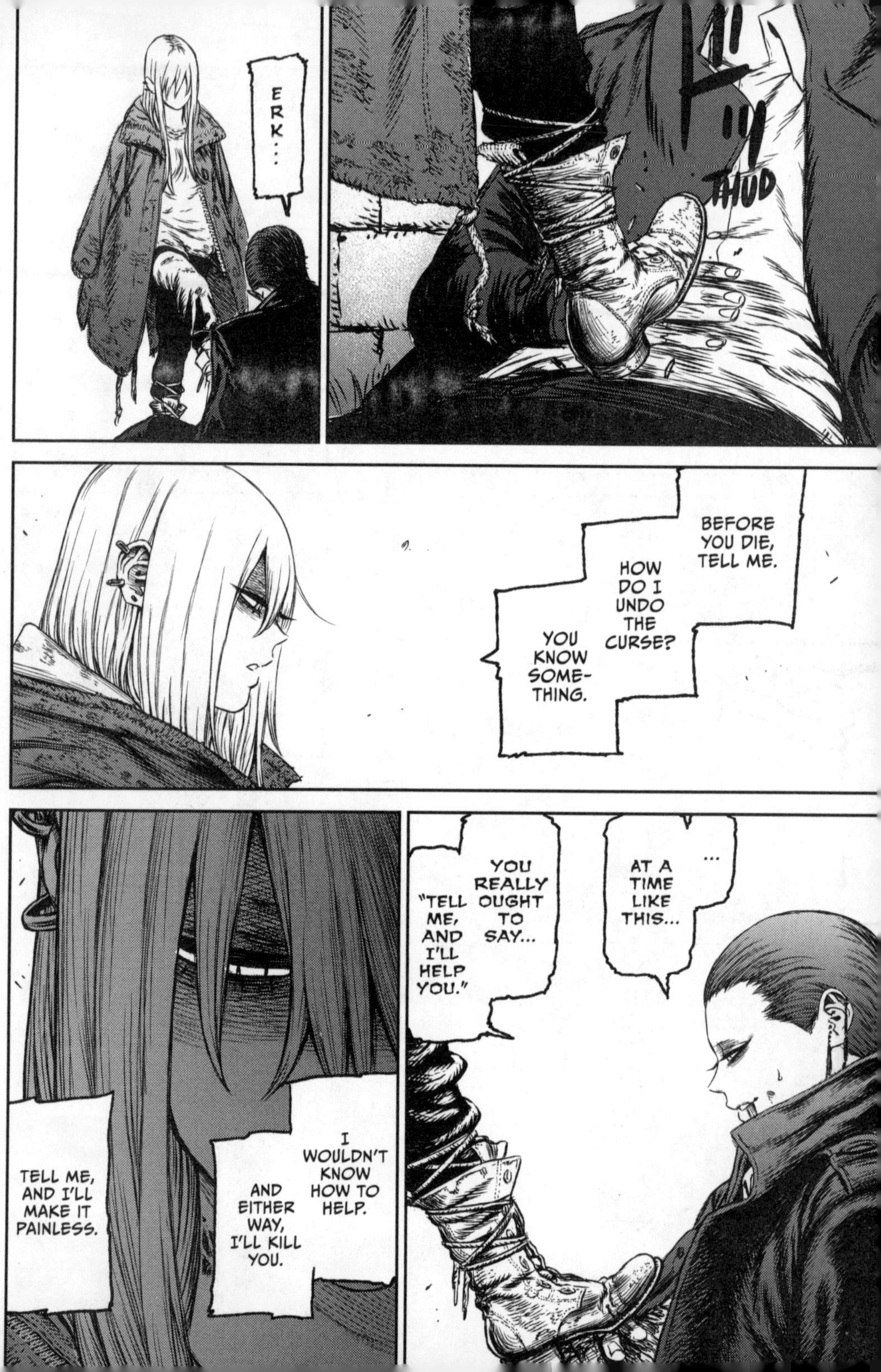
THUD
ERK...
BEFORE YOU DIE, TELL ME.
HOW DO I UNDO THE CURSE?
YOU KNOW SOMETHING.
...
AT A TIME LIKE THIS...
YOU REALLY OUGHT TO SAY...
"TELL ME, AND I'LL HELP YOU."
I WOULDN'T KNOW HOW TO HELP.
AND EITHER WAY, I'LL KILL YOU.
TELL ME, AND I'LL MAKE IT PAINLESS.

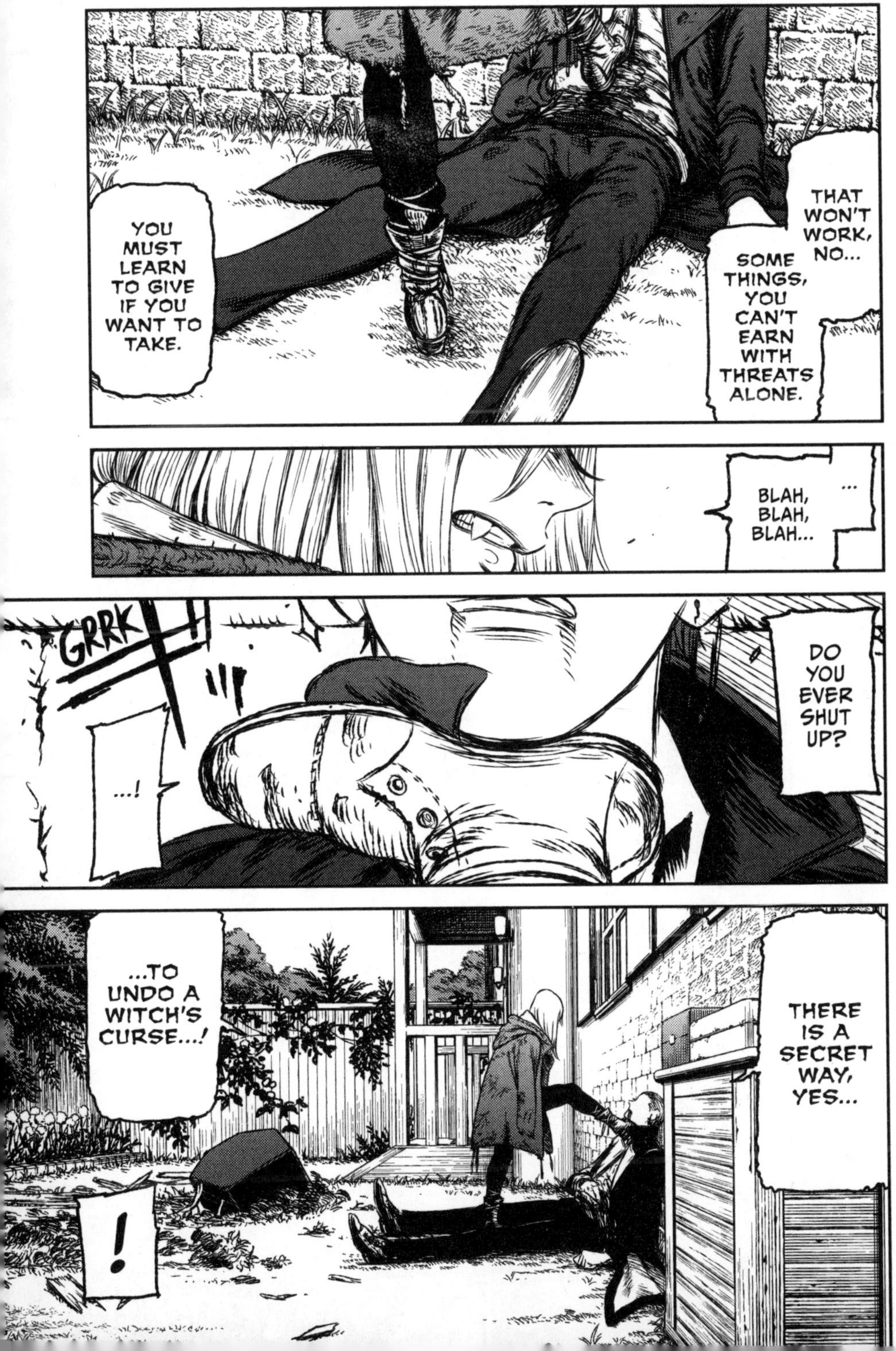
THAT WON'T WORK, NO...
SOME THINGS, YOU CAN'T EARN WITH THREATS ALONE.
YOU MUST LEARN TO GIVE IF YOU WANT TO TAKE.
...
BLAH, BLAH, BLAH...
DO YOU EVER SHUT UP?
GRRK
...!
THERE IS A SECRET WAY, YES...
...TO UNDO A WITCH'S CURSE...!
!

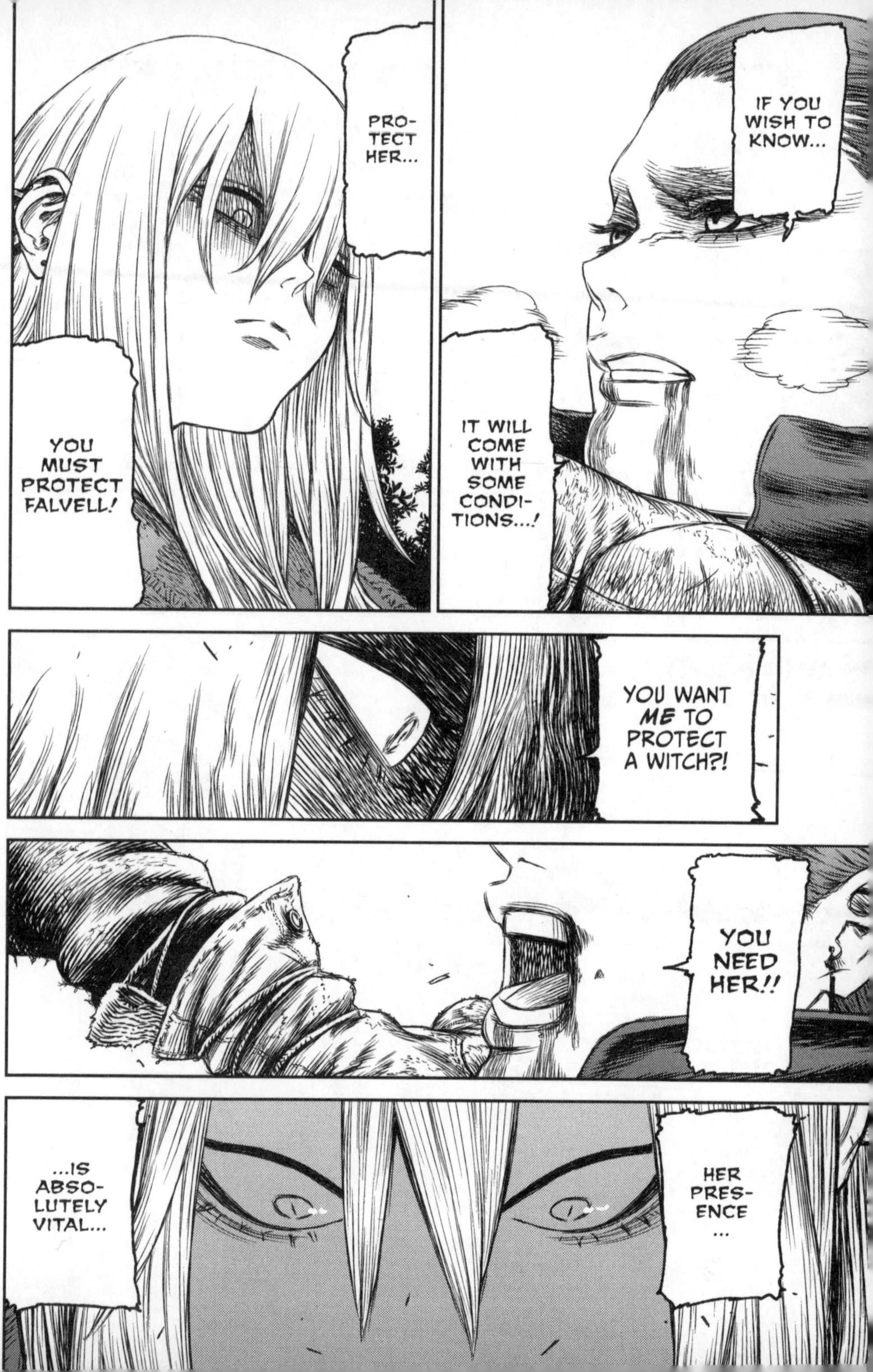
IF YOU WISH TO KNOW...
IT WILL COME WITH SOME CONDITIONS...!
PROTECT HER...
YOU MUST PROTECT FALVELL!
YOU WANT *ME* TO PROTECT A WITCH?!
YOU NEED HER!!
HER PRESENCE...
...IS ABSOLUTELY VITAL...

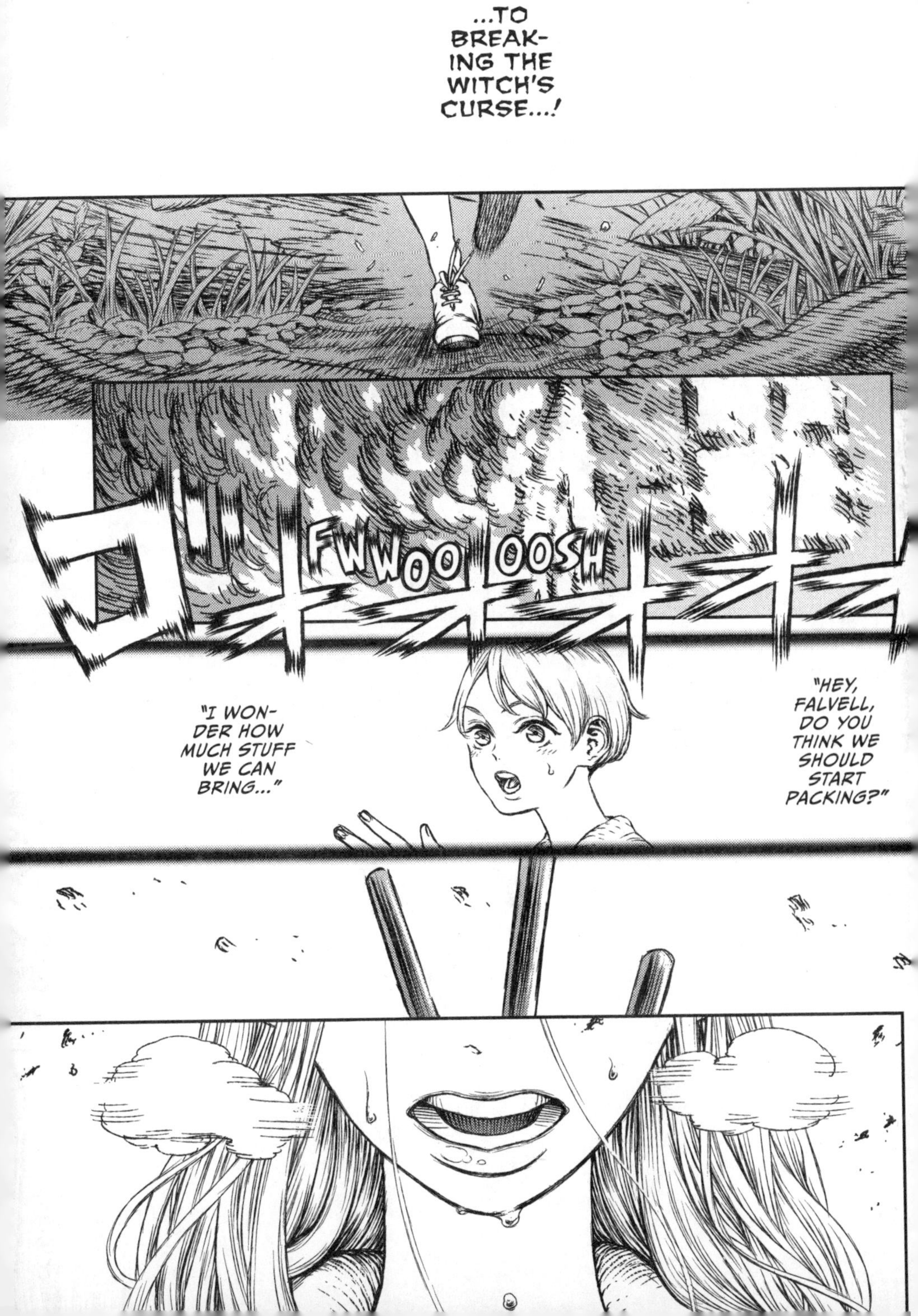
...TO BREAKING THE WITCH'S CURSE...!
FWWOO OOSH
"HEY, FALVELL, DO YOU THINK WE SHOULD START PACKING?"
"I WONDER HOW MUCH STUFF WE CAN BRING..."

YOU'RE LATE.

HELLO.

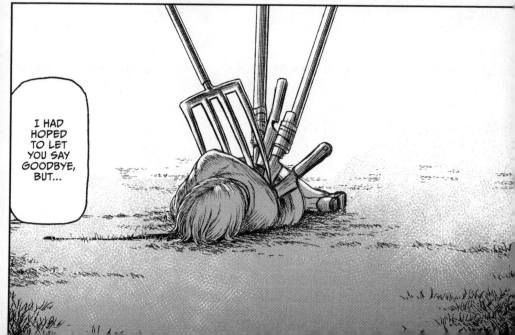

I HAD HOPED TO LET YOU SAY GOODBYE, BUT...

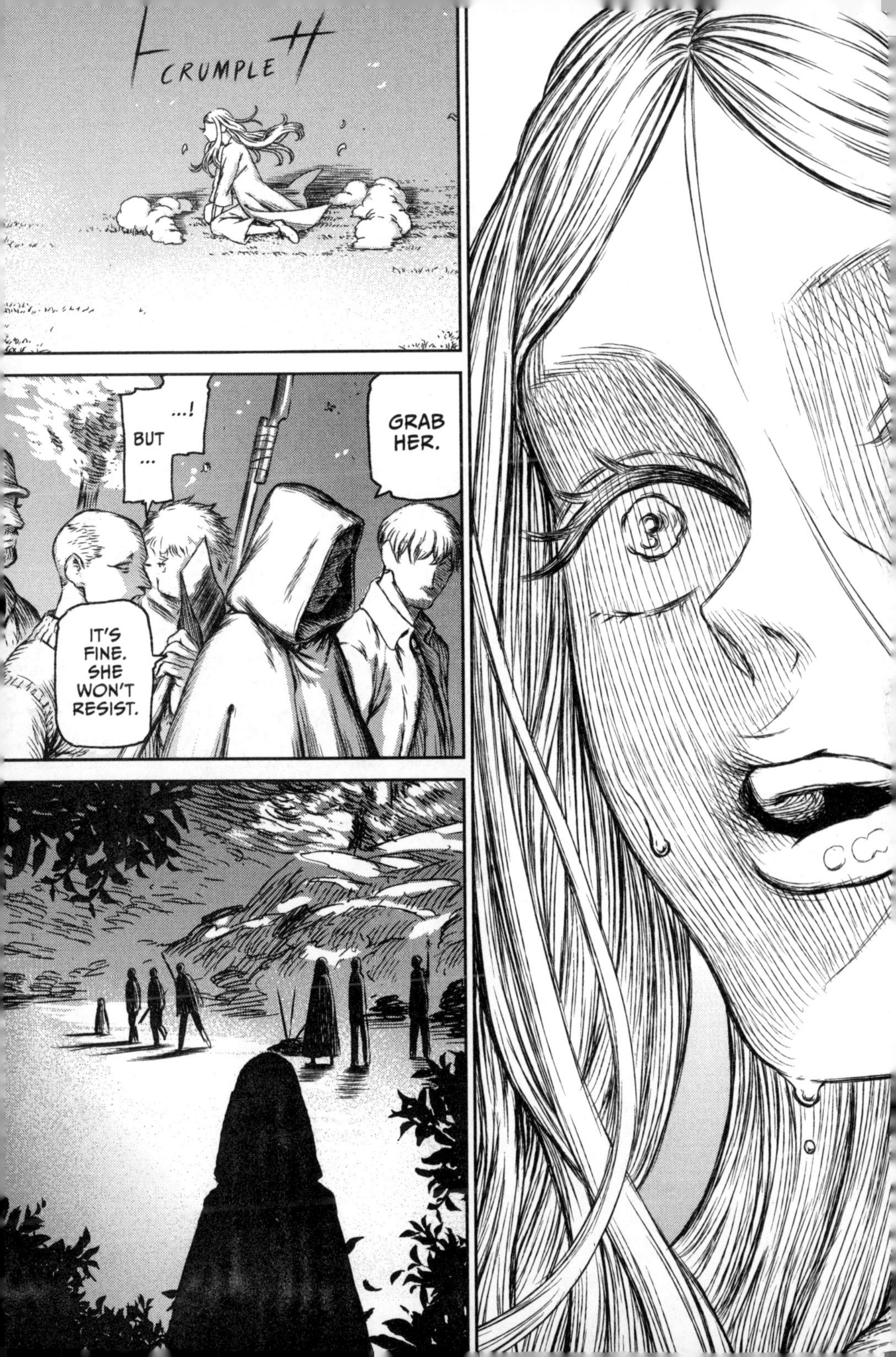
CRUMPLE
GRAB HER.
...! BUT ...
IT'S FINE. SHE WON'T RESIST.

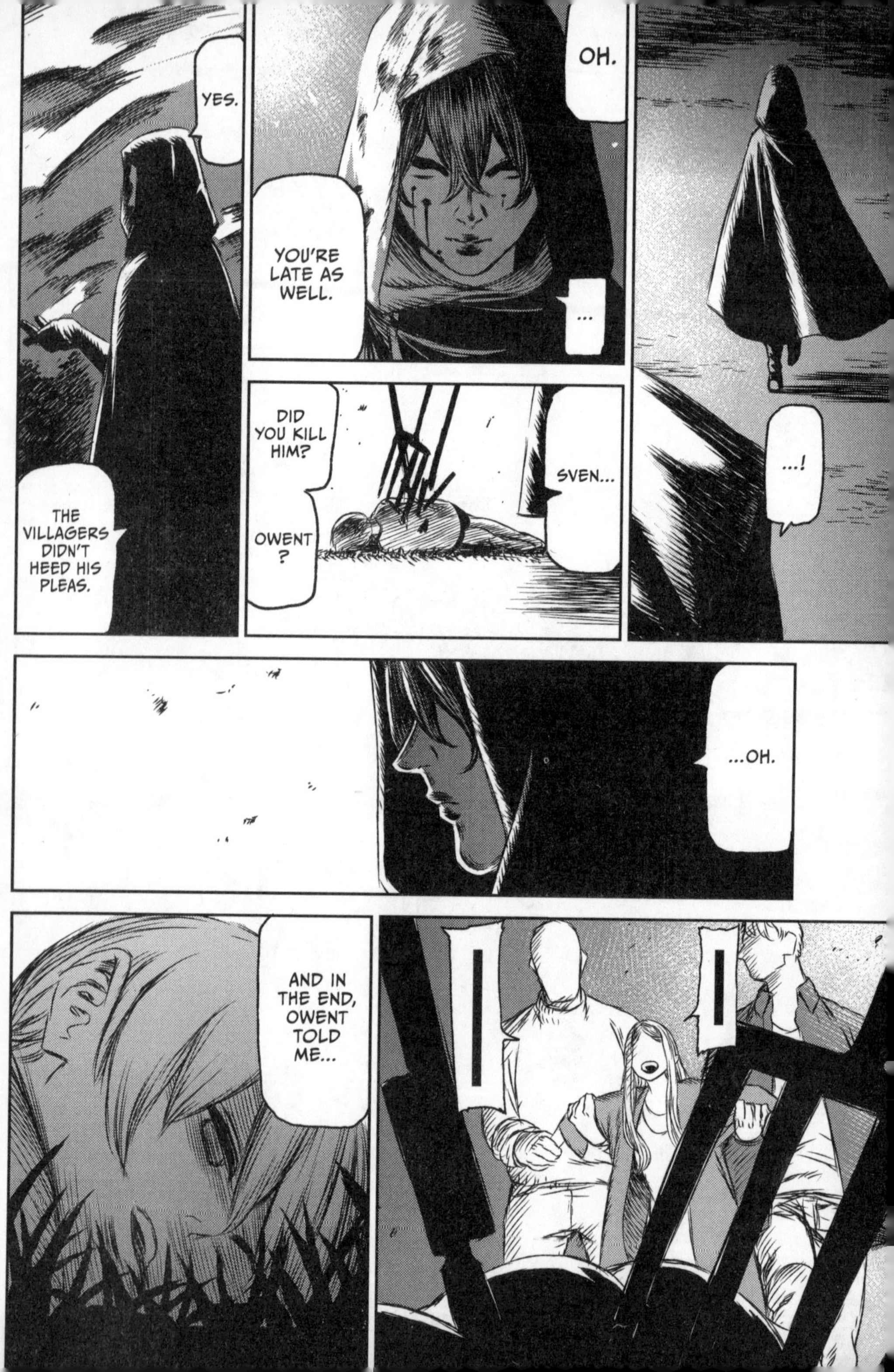
OH.
...!
...
YOU'RE LATE AS WELL.
SVEN...
DID YOU KILL HIM?
OWENT?
YES.
THE VILLAGERS DIDN'T HEED HIS PLEAS.
...OH.
AND IN THE END, OWENT TOLD ME...

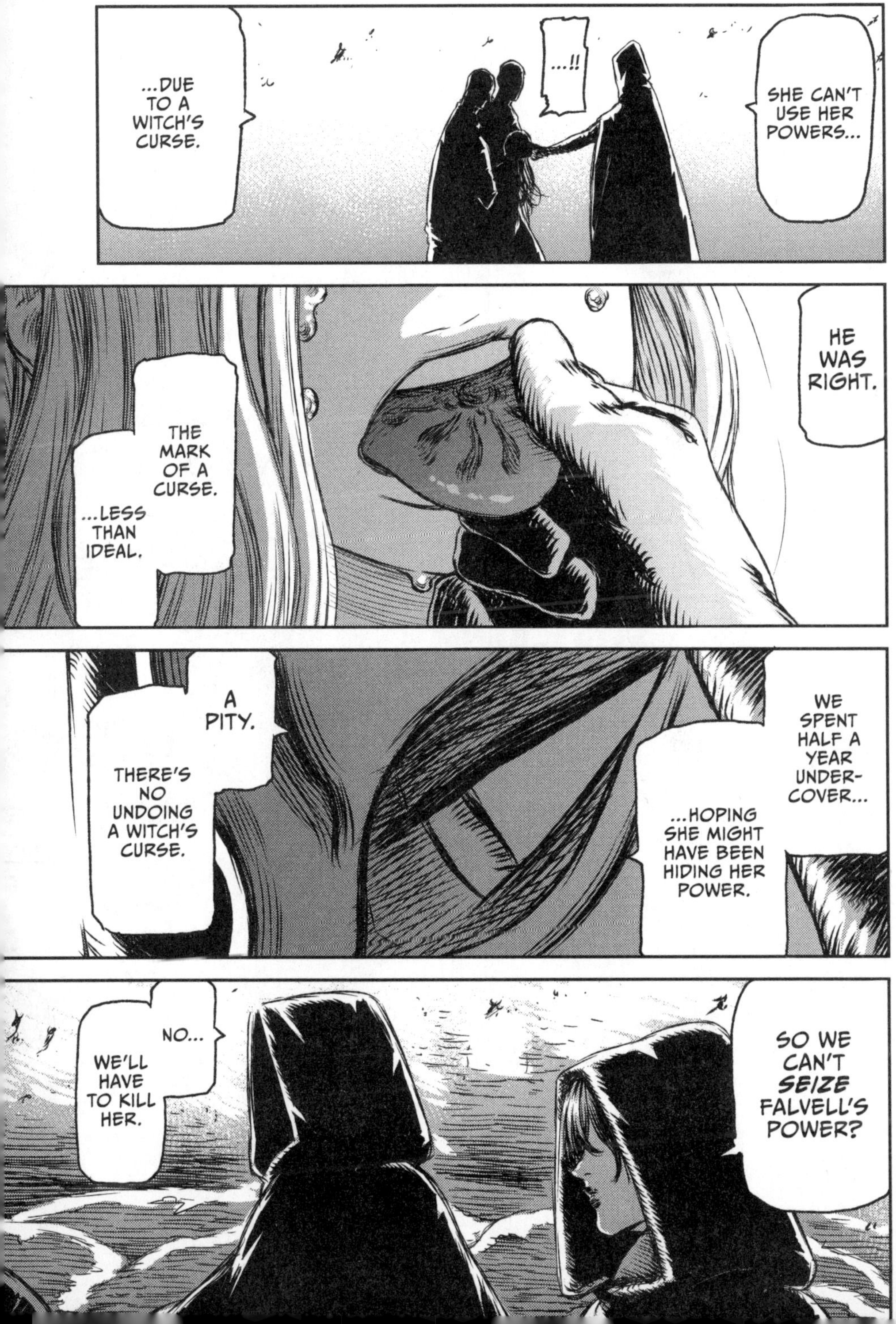
SHE CAN'T USE HER POWERS...
...!!
...DUE TO A WITCH'S CURSE.
HE WAS RIGHT.
THE MARK OF A CURSE.
...LESS THAN IDEAL.
WE SPENT HALF A YEAR UNDER-COVER...
...HOPING SHE MIGHT HAVE BEEN HIDING HER POWER.
A PITY.
THERE'S NO UNDOING A WITCH'S CURSE.
SO WE CAN'T *SEIZE* FALVELL'S POWER?
NO...
WE'LL HAVE TO KILL HER.

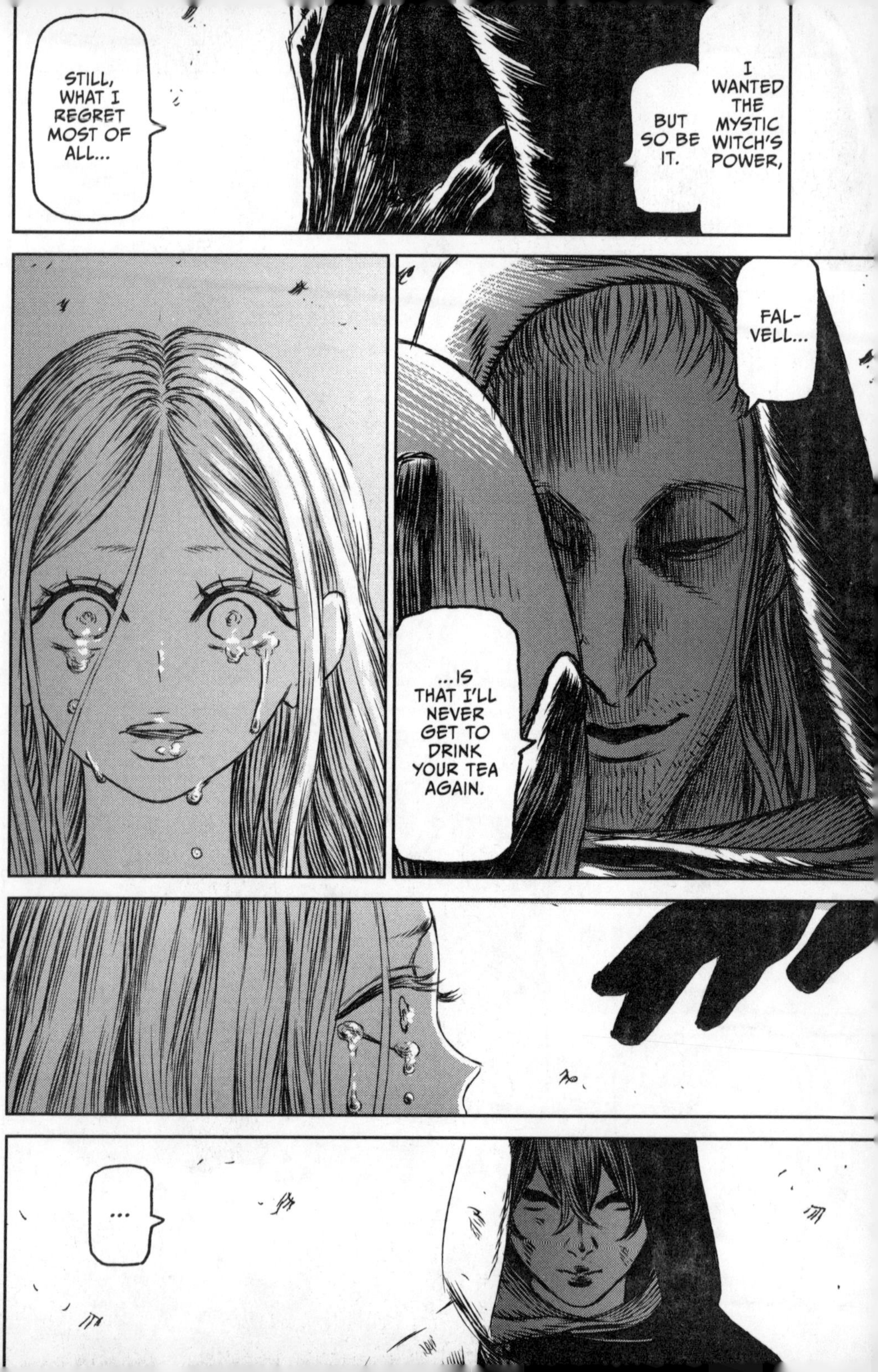
I WANTED THE MYSTIC WITCH'S POWER,
BUT SO BE IT.
STILL, WHAT I REGRET MOST OF ALL...
FAL-VELL...
...IS THAT I'LL NEVER GET TO DRINK YOUR TEA AGAIN.
...

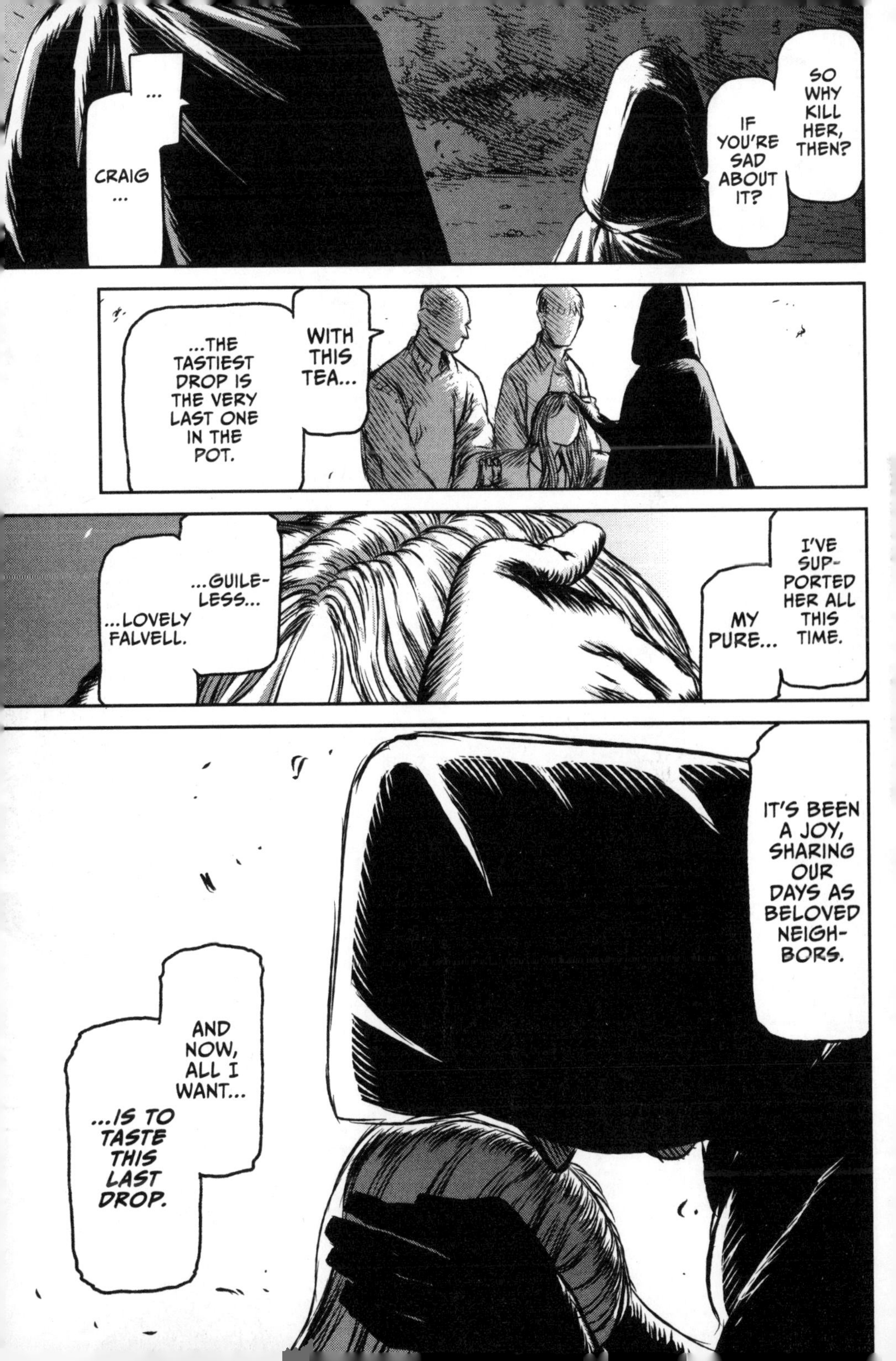
SO WHY KILL HER, THEN?
IF YOU'RE SAD ABOUT IT?
... CRAIG ...
WITH THIS TEA...
...THE TASTIEST DROP IS THE VERY LAST ONE IN THE POT.
I'VE SUP-PORTED HER ALL THIS TIME.
MY PURE...
...GUILE-LESS...
...LOVELY FALVELL.
IT'S BEEN A JOY, SHARING OUR DAYS AS BELOVED NEIGH-BORS.
AND NOW, ALL I WANT...
...IS TO TASTE THIS LAST DROP.

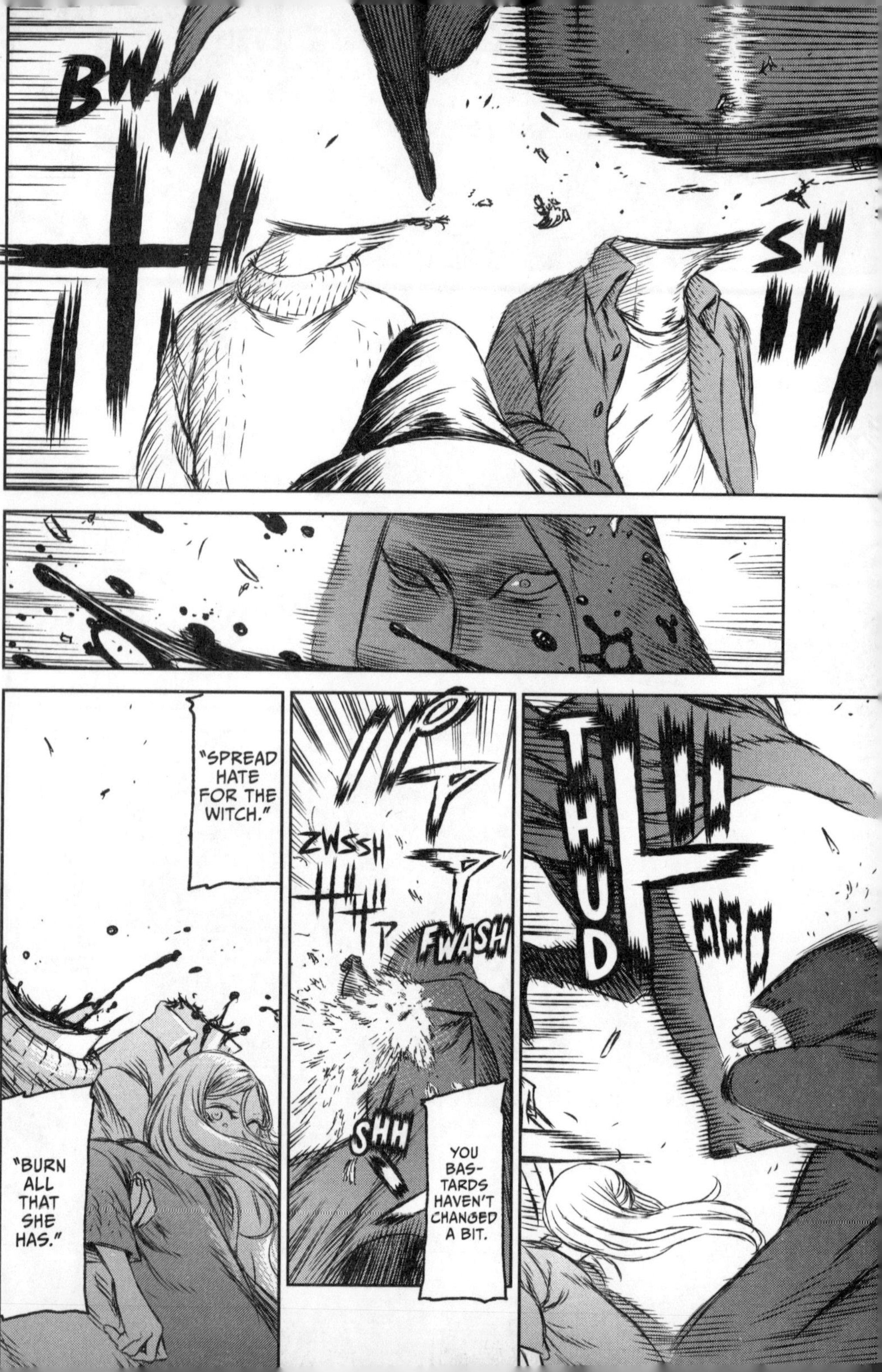
SH
BWW
THUD
ZWSSH
FWASH
SHH
YOU BAS-TARDS HAVEN'T CHANGED A BIT.
"SPREAD HATE FOR THE WITCH."
"BURN ALL THAT SHE HAS."

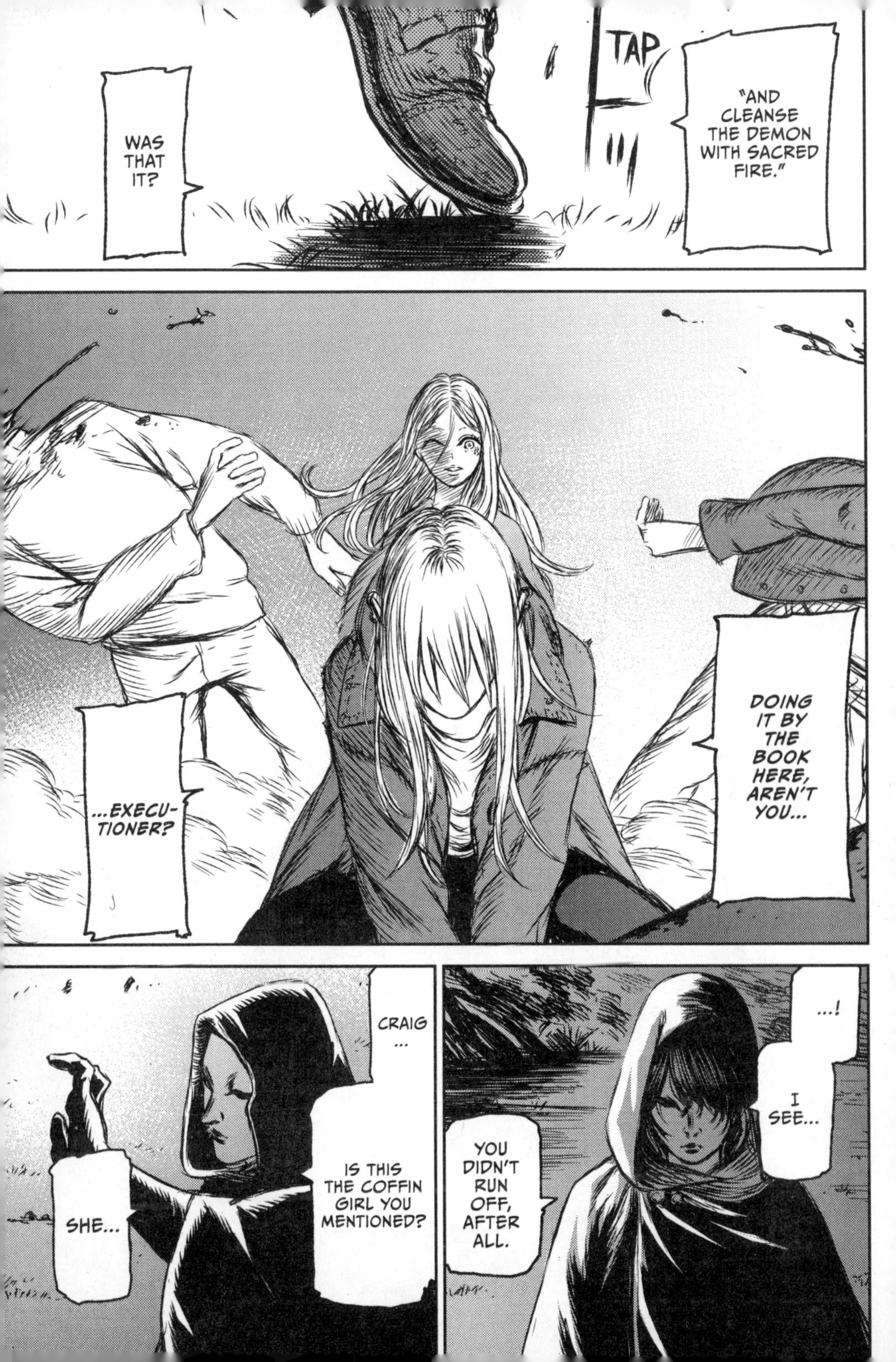
"AND CLEANSE THE DEMON WITH SACRED FIRE."
TAP
WAS THAT IT?
DOING IT BY THE BOOK HERE, AREN'T YOU...
...EXECUTIONER?
...!
I SEE...
YOU DIDN'T RUN OFF, AFTER ALL.
CRAIG...
IS THIS THE COFFIN GIRL YOU MENTIONED?
SHE...

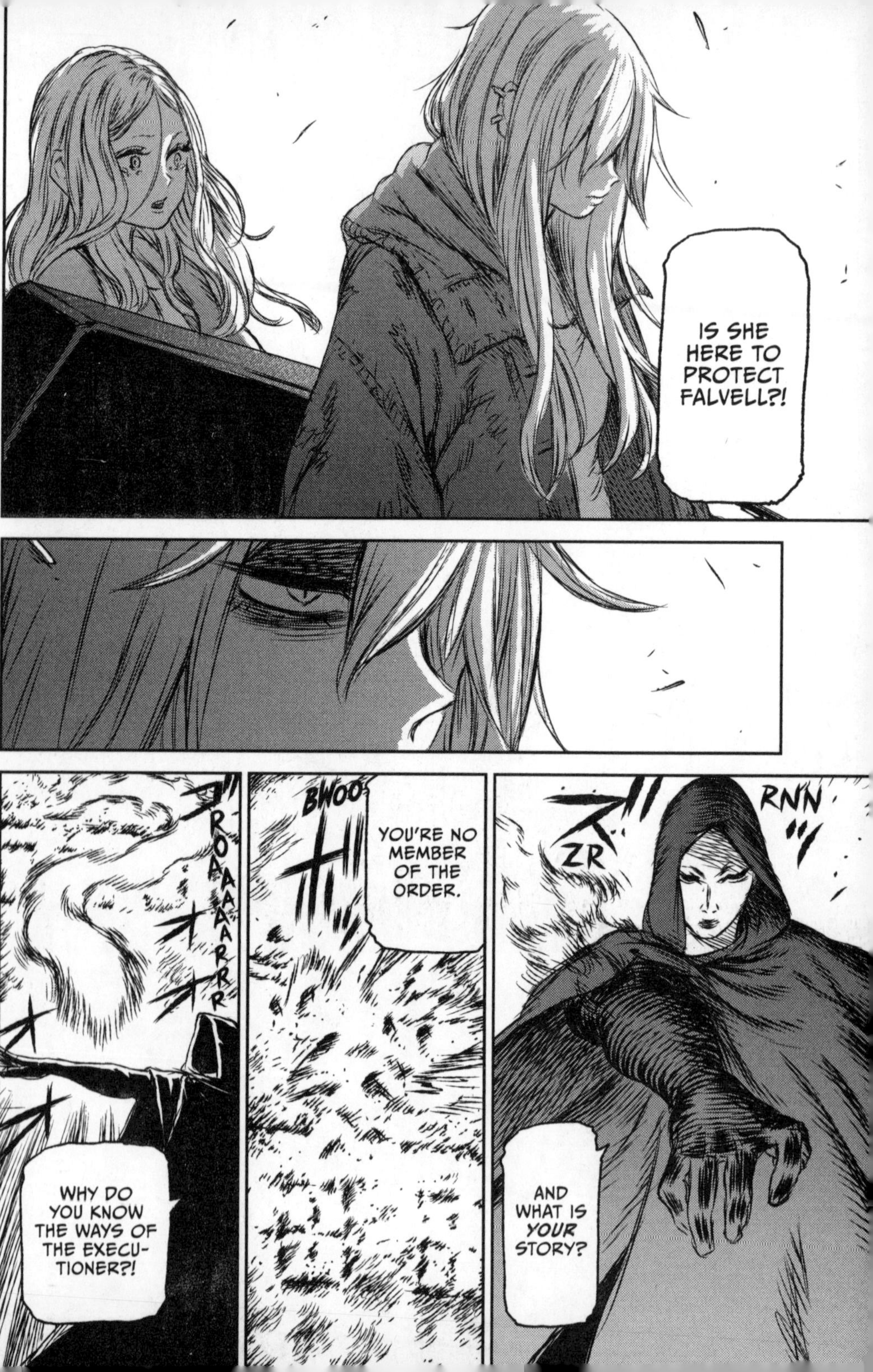
IS SHE HERE TO PROTECT FALVELL?!
RNN
ZR
AND WHAT IS *YOUR* STORY?
BWOO
YOU'RE NO MEMBER OF THE ORDER.
ROAAAARRR
WHY DO YOU KNOW THE WAYS OF THE EXECU-TIONER?!

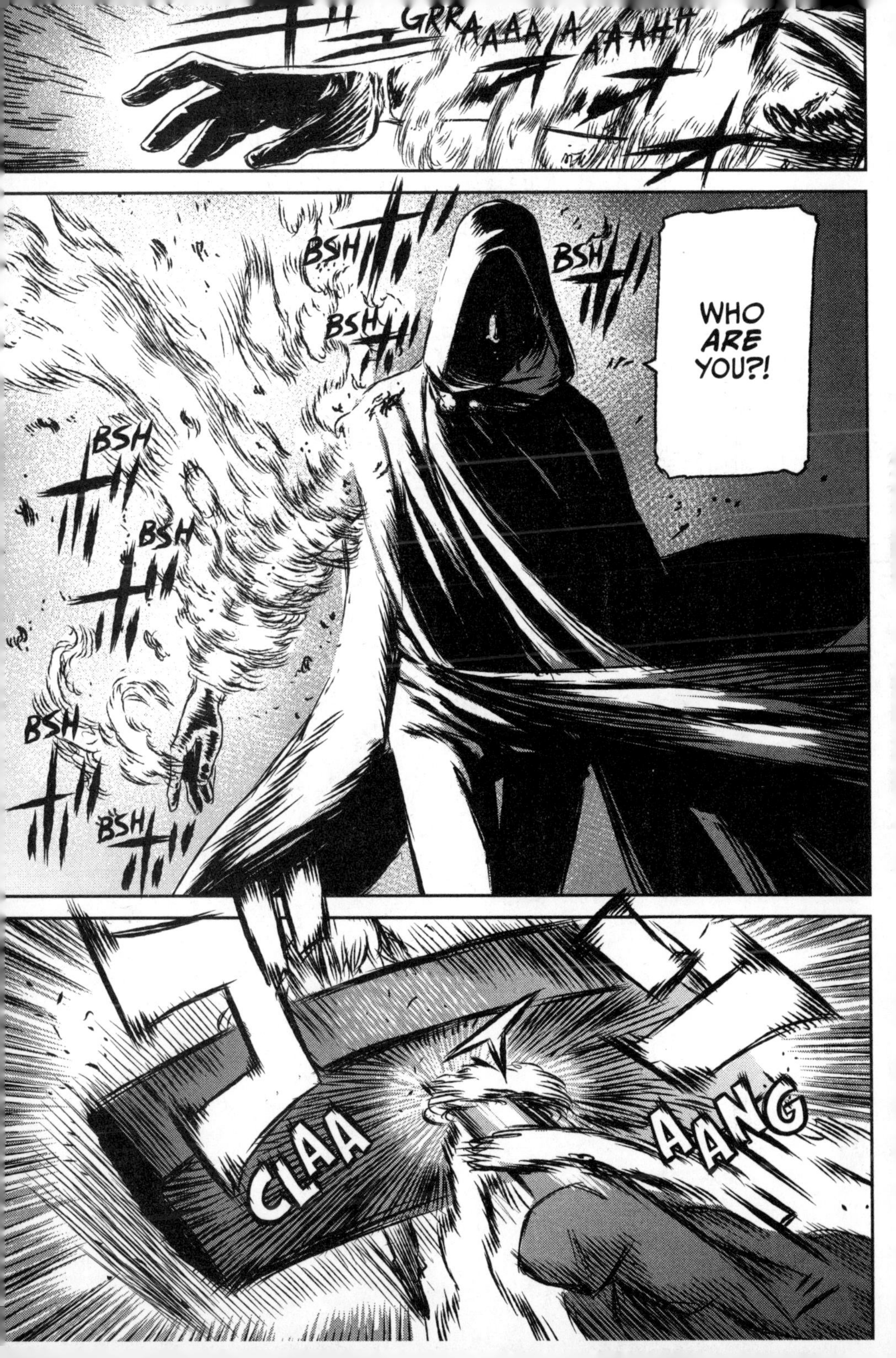
GRRAAAAAAAH
BSH
BSH
BSH
WHO ARE YOU?!
BSH
BSH
BSH
BSH
CLAA
AANG

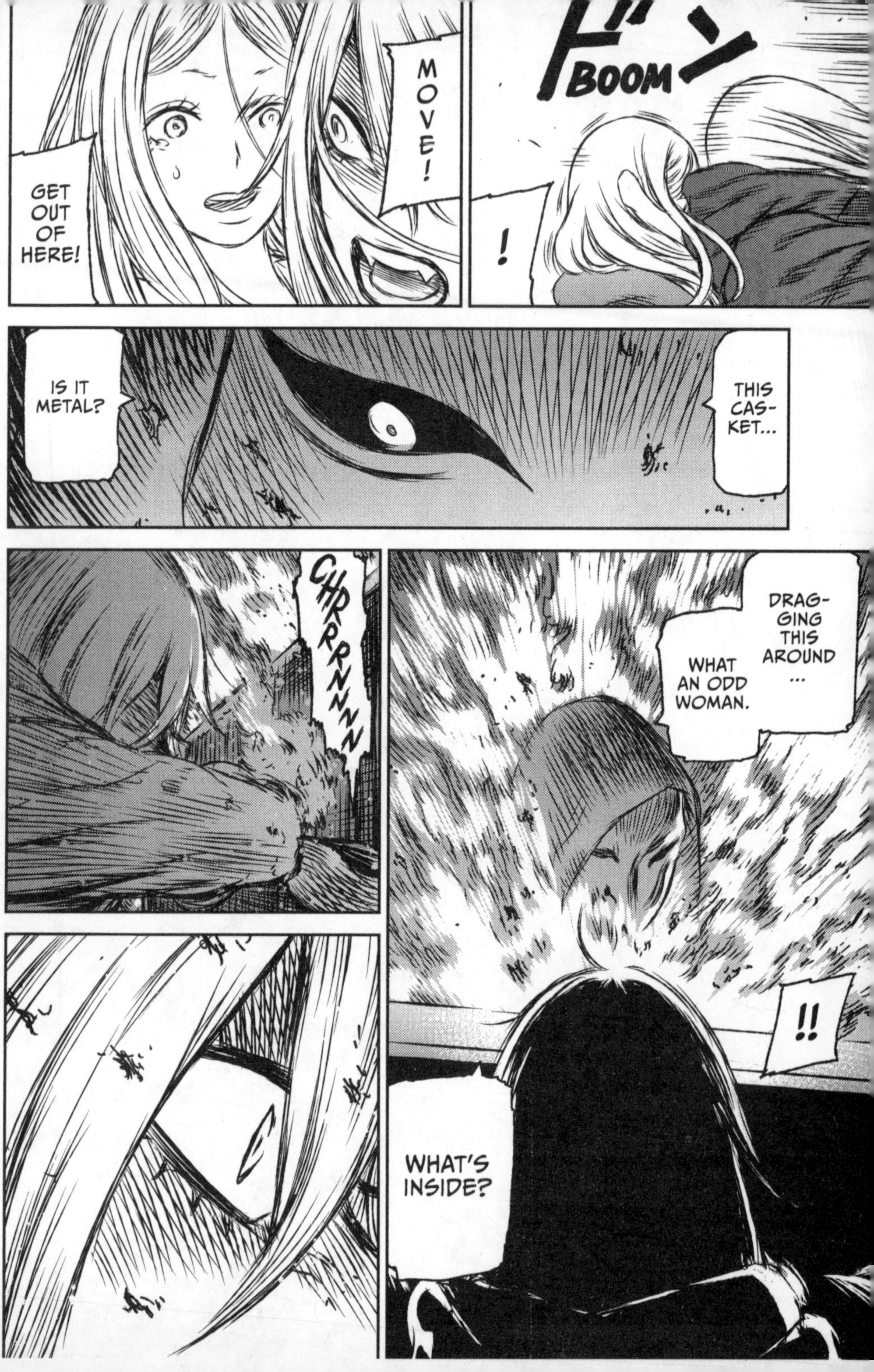
ドン
BOOM
!
MOVE!
GET OUT OF HERE!
THIS CASKET...
IS IT METAL?
DRAGGING THIS AROUND...
WHAT AN ODD WOMAN.
!!
WHAT'S INSIDE?
CHRRRNNNN

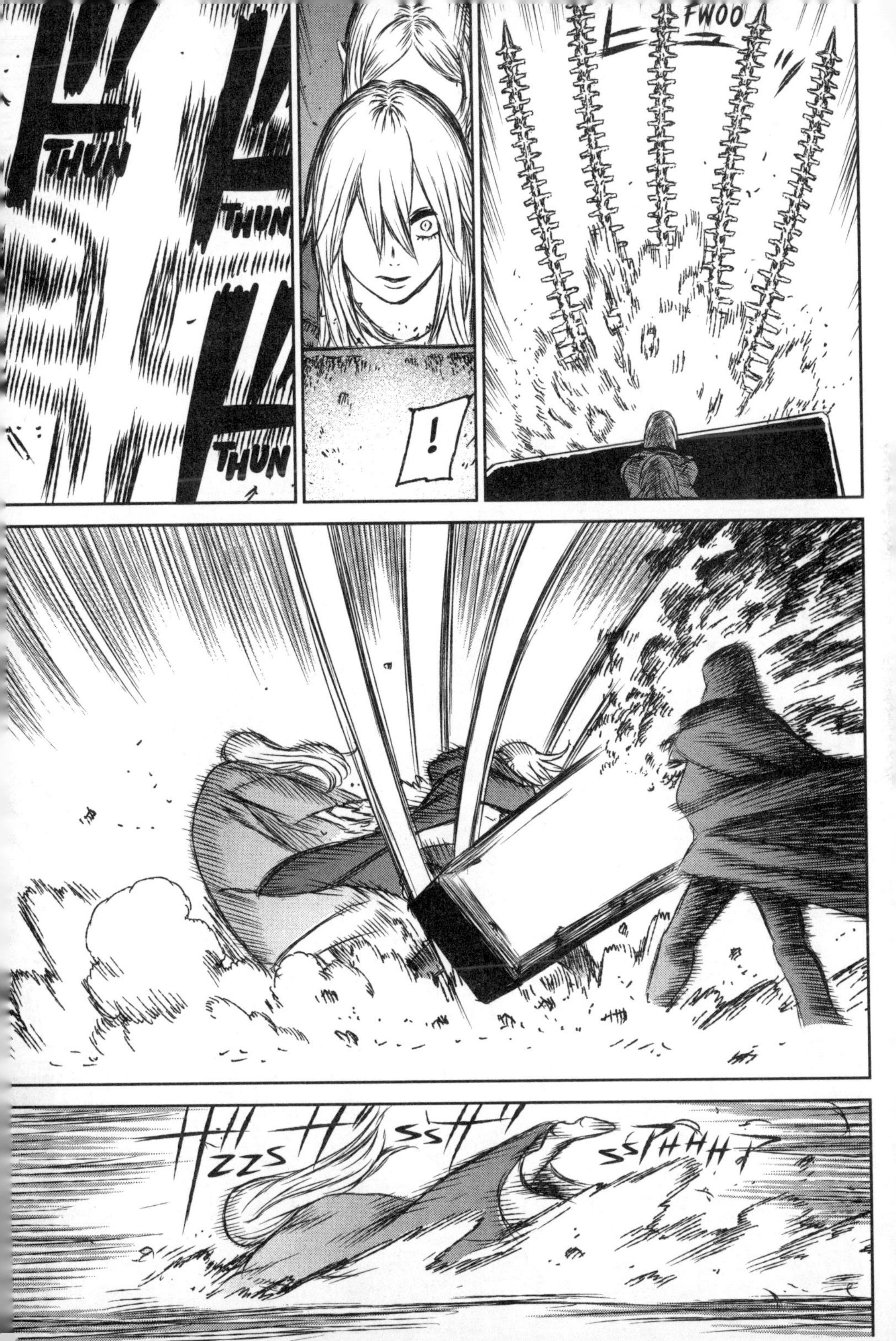
FWOO
!
THUN
THUN
THUN
SSPHHH
SS
ZZS

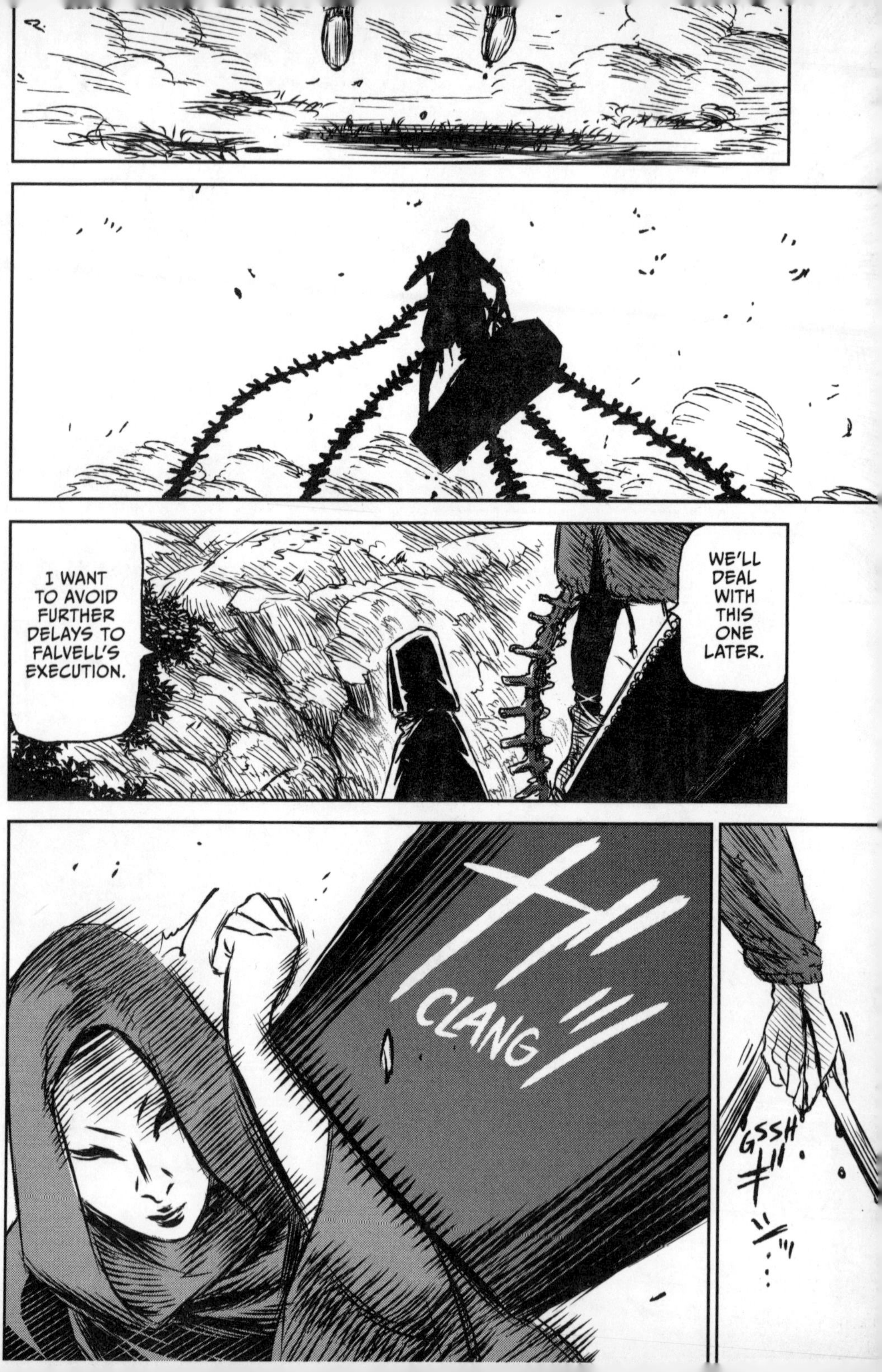
WE'LL DEAL WITH THIS ONE LATER.
I WANT TO AVOID FURTHER DELAYS TO FALVELL'S EXECUTION.
GSSH
CLANG

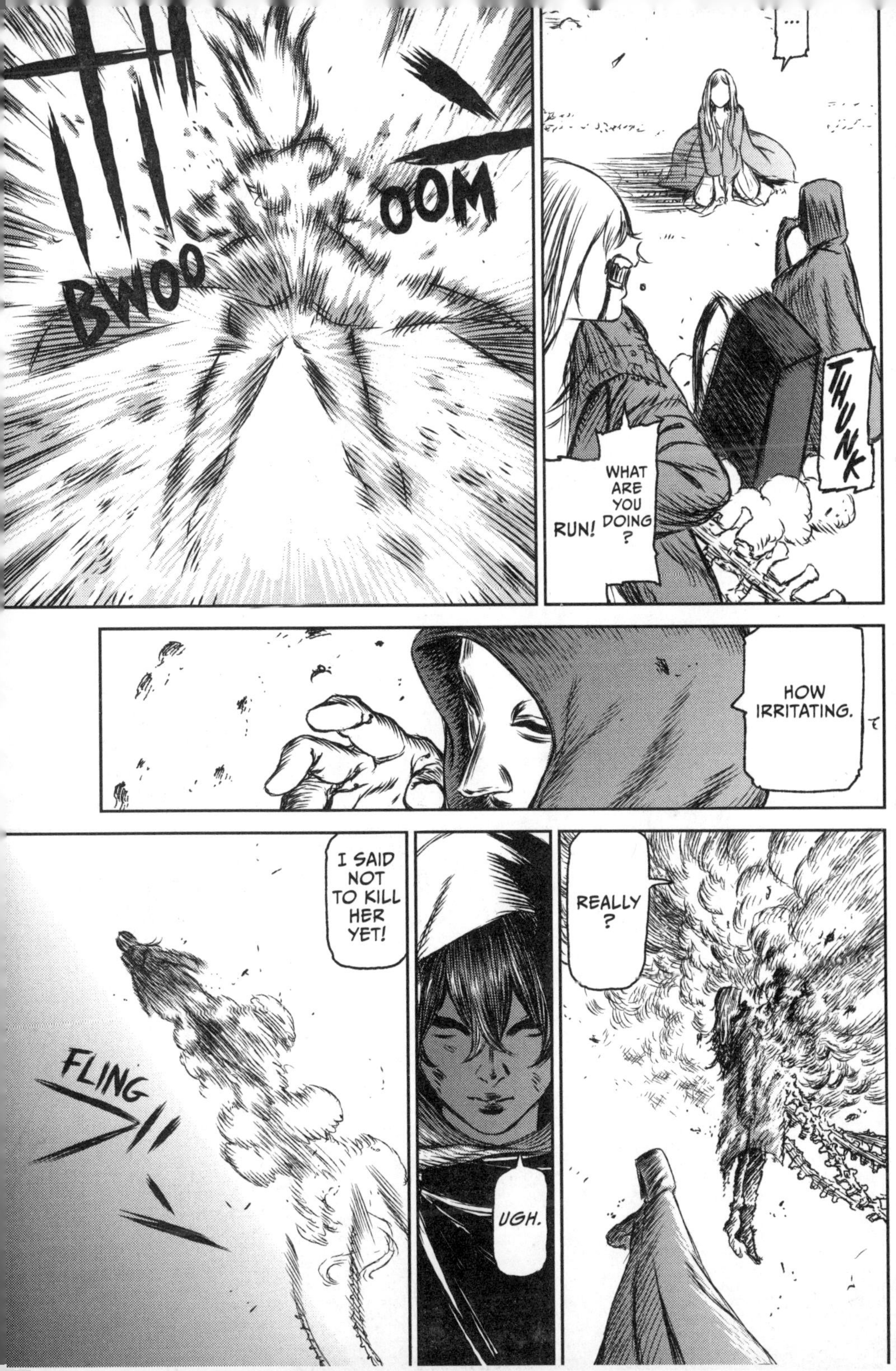
...
WHAT ARE YOU DOING?
RUN!
THUNK
BWOOOOM
HOW IRRITATING.
REALLY?
I SAID NOT TO KILL HER YET!
UGH.
FLING

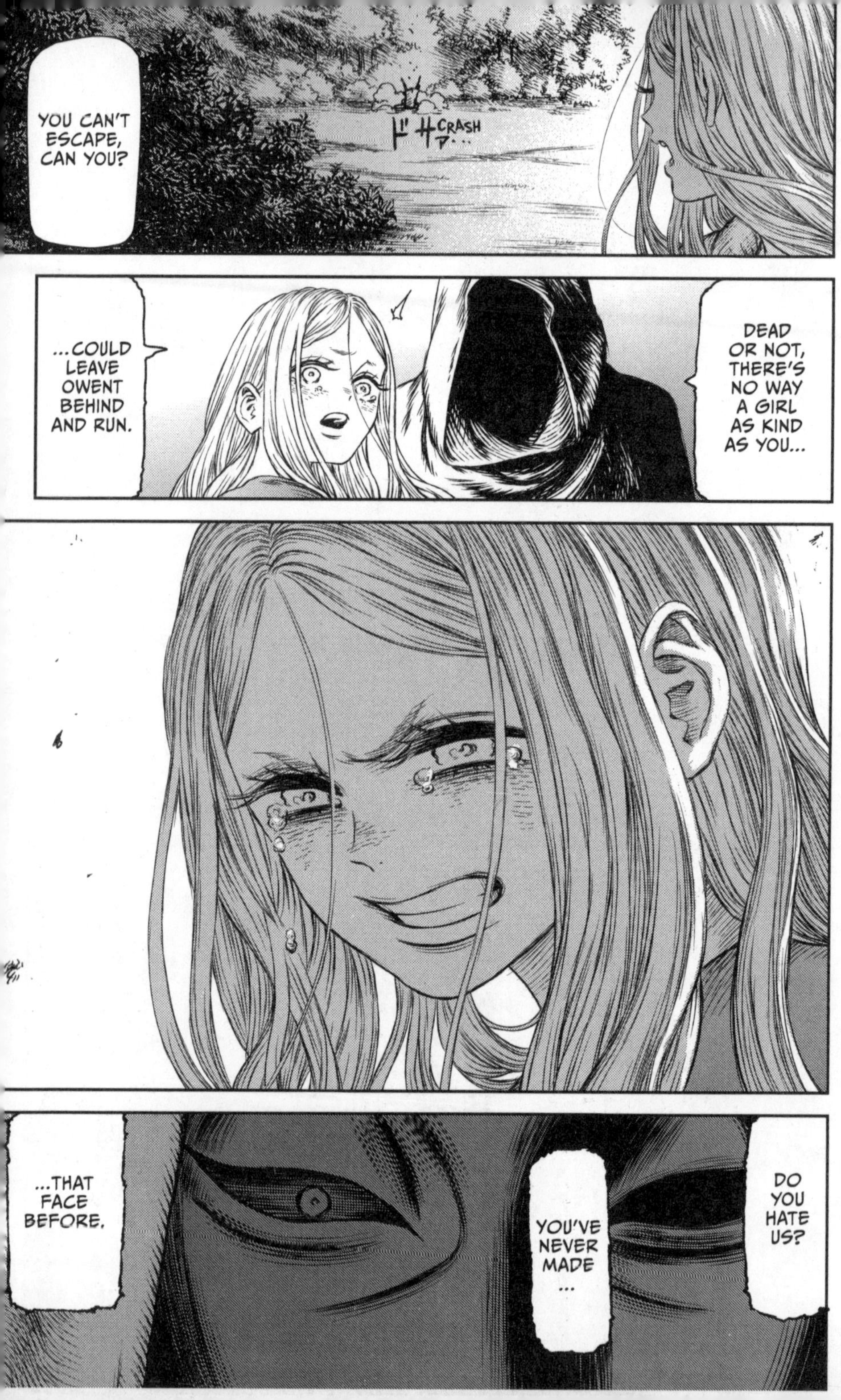
ドサァ…
CRASH
YOU CAN'T ESCAPE, CAN YOU?
DEAD OR NOT, THERE'S NO WAY A GIRL AS KIND AS YOU...
...COULD LEAVE OWENT BEHIND AND RUN.
DO YOU HATE US?
YOU'VE NEVER MADE ...
...THAT FACE BEFORE.

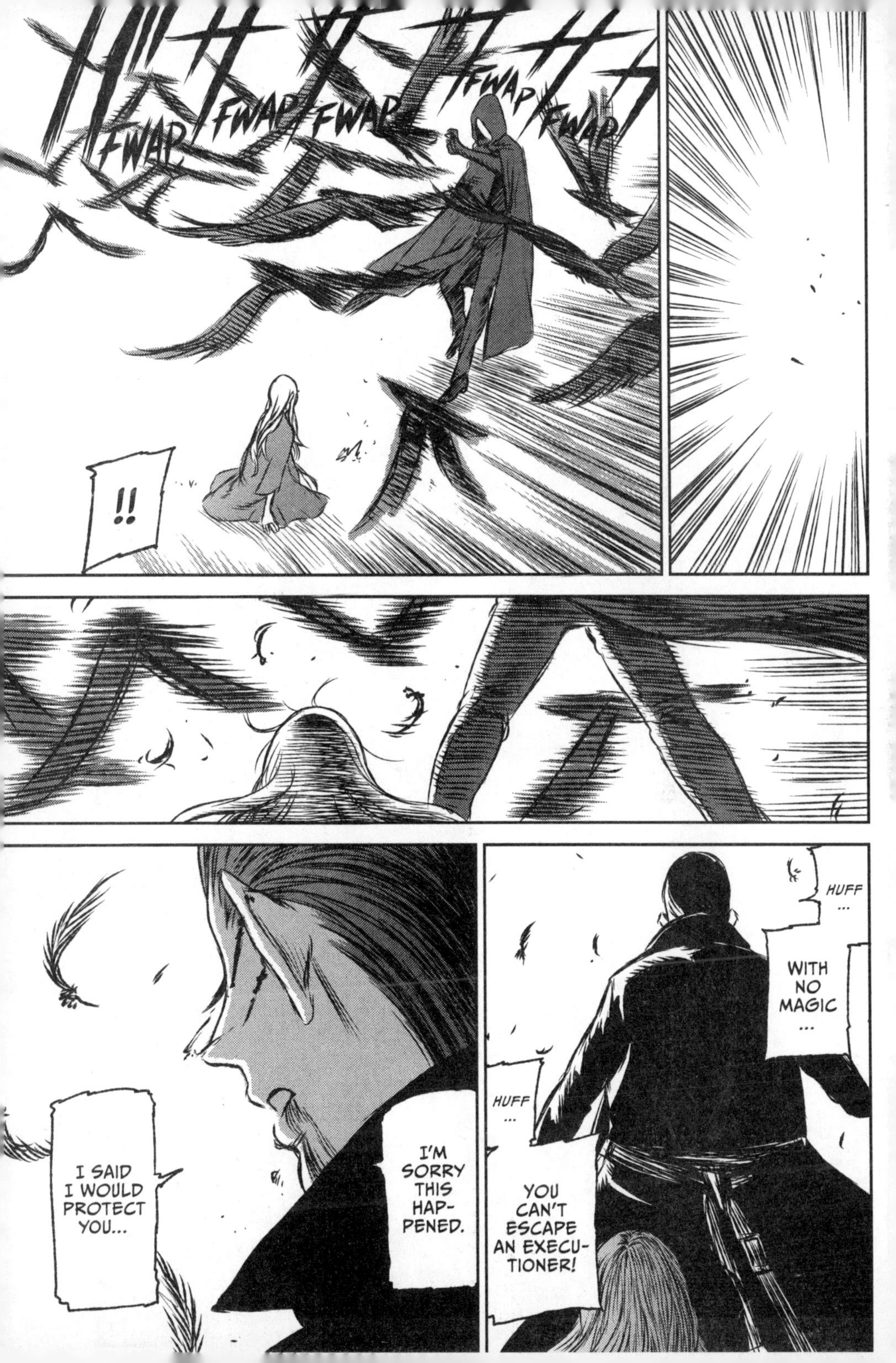
FWAP
FWAP
FWAP
FWAP
FWAP
!!
HUFF...
WITH NO MAGIC...
HUFF...
YOU CAN'T ESCAPE AN EXECU-TIONER!
I'M SORRY THIS HAP-PENED.
I SAID I WOULD PROTECT YOU...

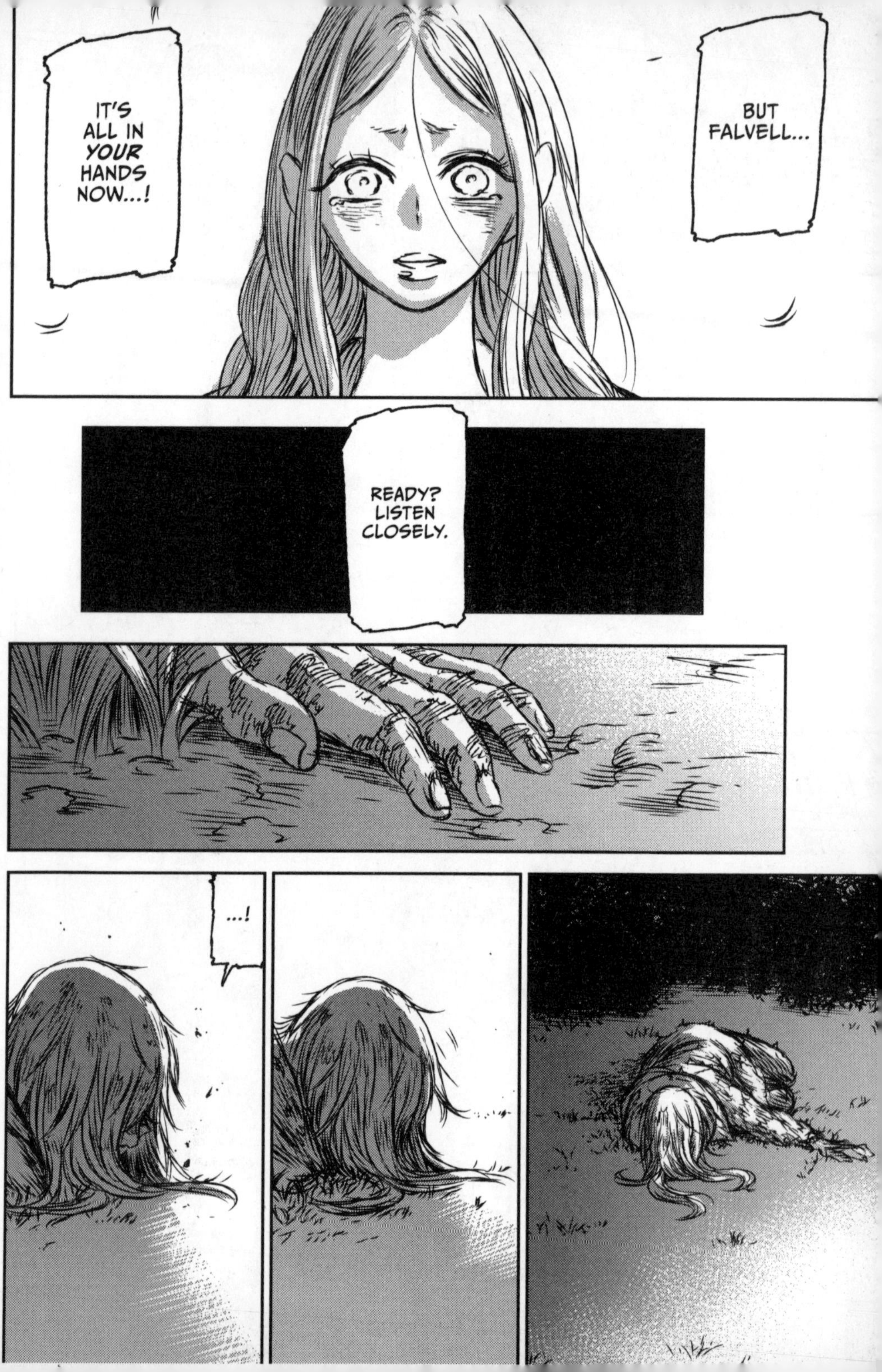
BUT FALVELL...
IT'S ALL IN *YOUR* HANDS NOW...!
READY? LISTEN CLOSELY.
...!

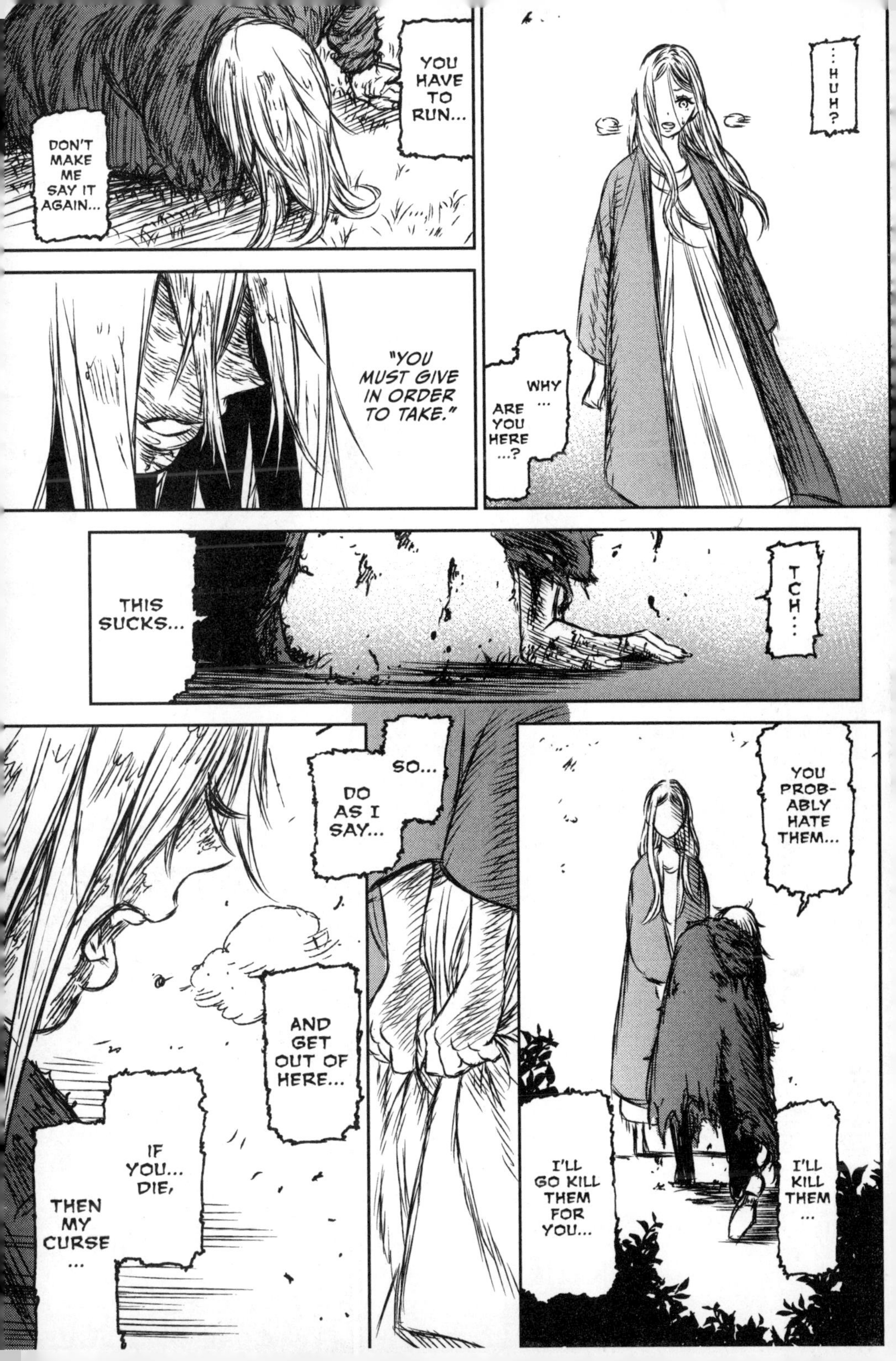
...HUH?
WHY ... ARE YOU HERE ...?
YOU HAVE TO RUN...
DON'T MAKE ME SAY IT AGAIN...
"YOU MUST GIVE IN ORDER TO TAKE."
TCH...
THIS SUCKS...
YOU PROBABLY HATE THEM...
I'LL KILL THEM ...
I'LL GO KILL THEM FOR YOU...
SO... DO AS I SAY...
AND GET OUT OF HERE...
IF YOU... DIE,
THEN MY CURSE ...

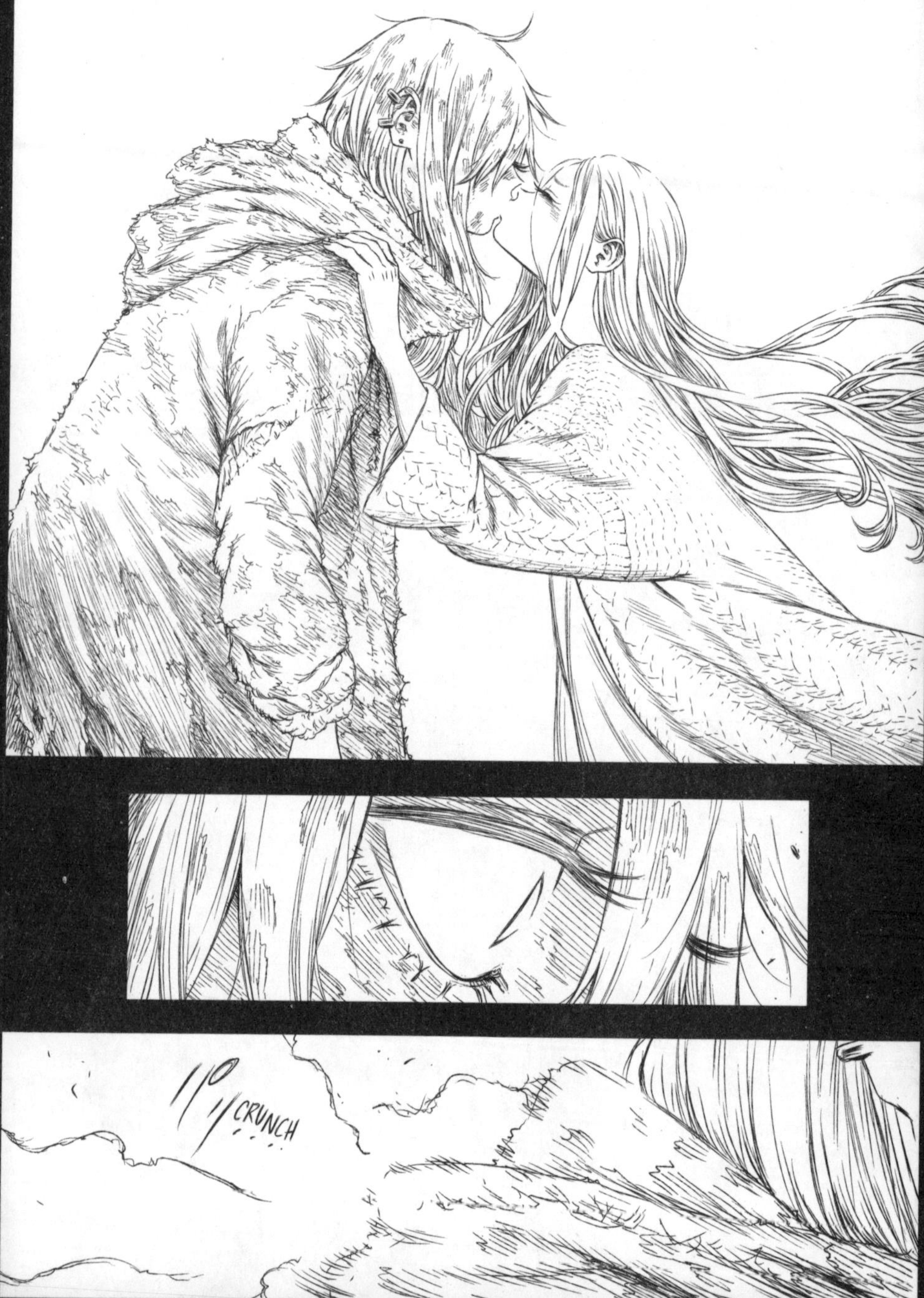
CRUNCH

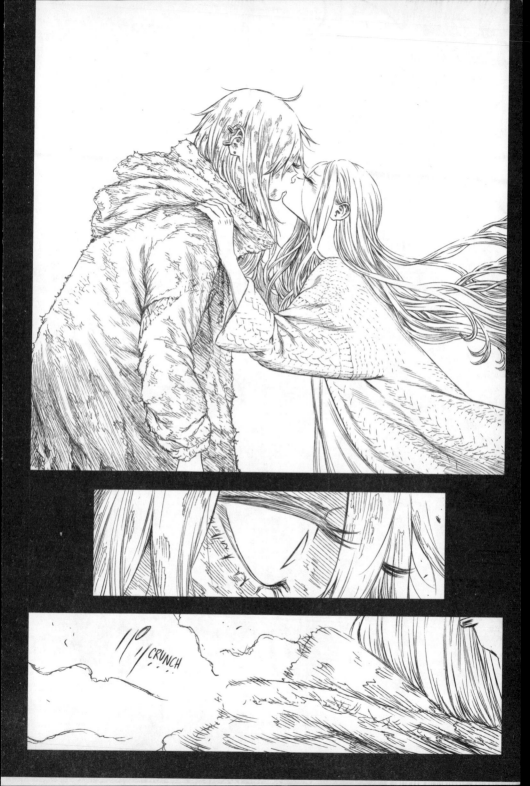

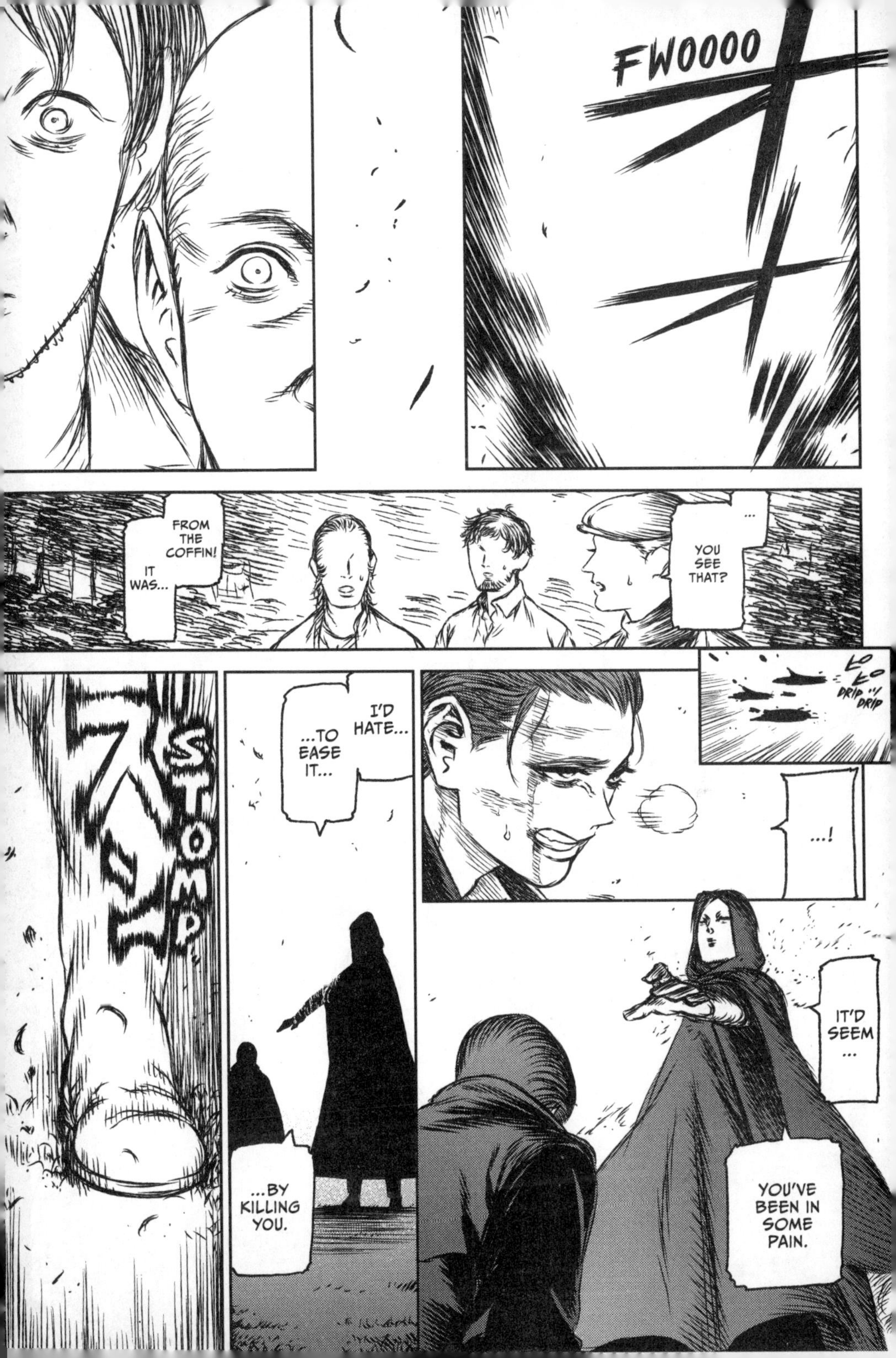
FWOOOO
...
YOU SEE THAT?
FROM THE COFFIN!
IT WAS...
DRIP DRIP
...!
IT'D SEEM ...
YOU'VE BEEN IN SOME PAIN.
I'D HATE...
...TO EASE IT...
...BY KILLING YOU.
STOMP

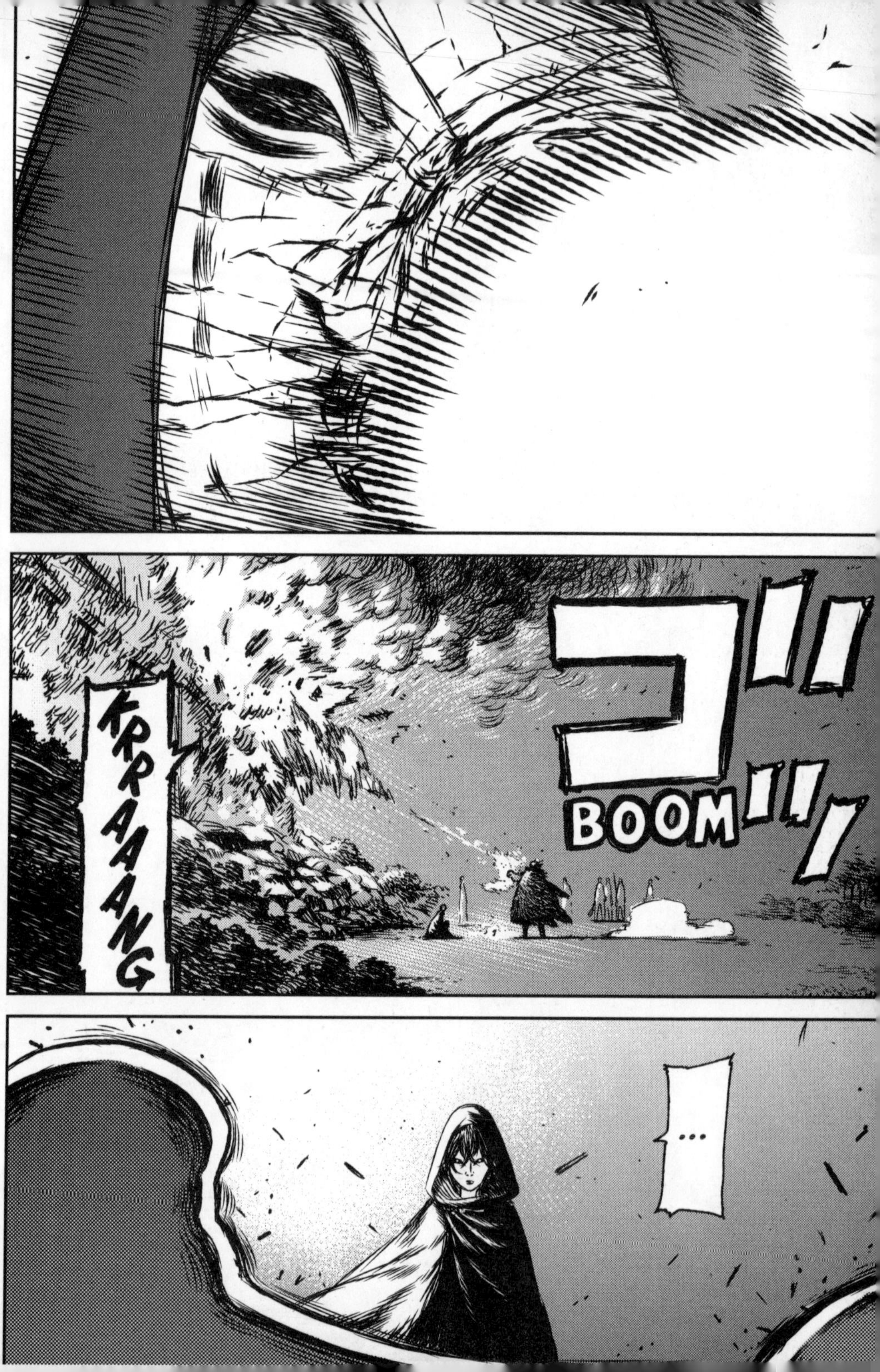

コ゛
BOOM
KRRAAAANG
...

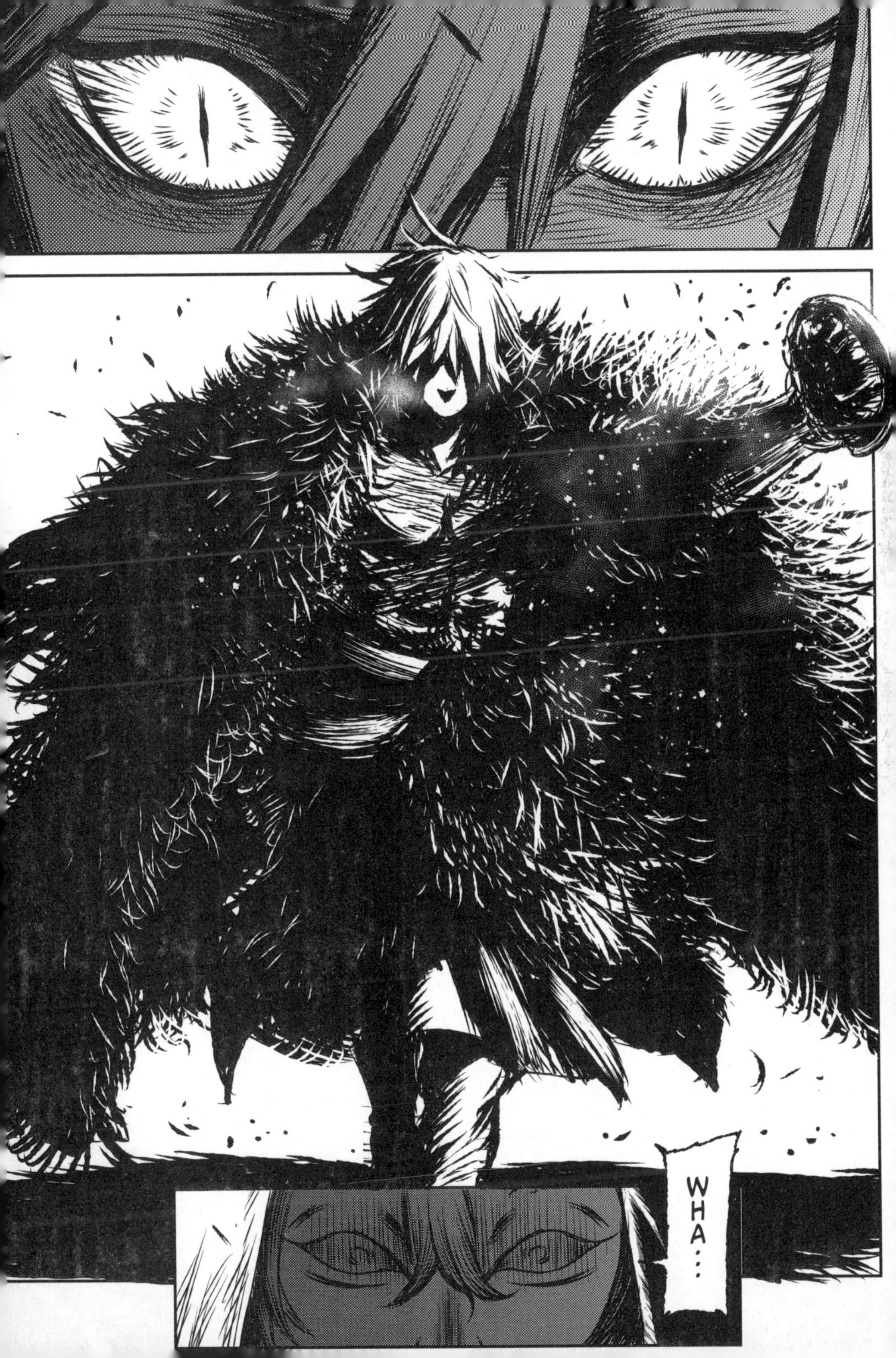
WHA...

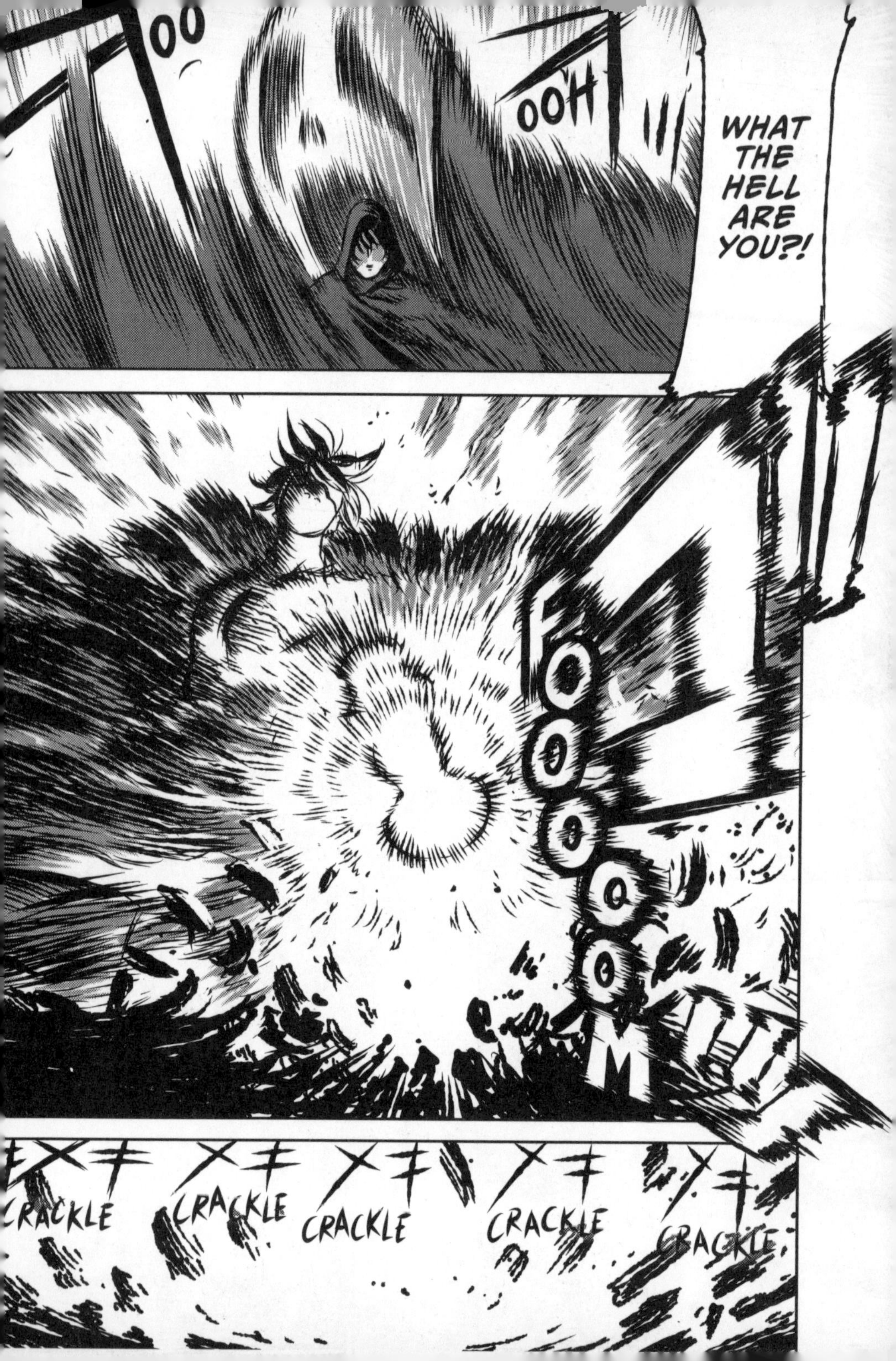
WHAT THE HELL ARE YOU?!
OOH
OO
FOOOOOOM
CRACKLE
CRACKLE
CRACKLE
CRACKLE
CRACKLE

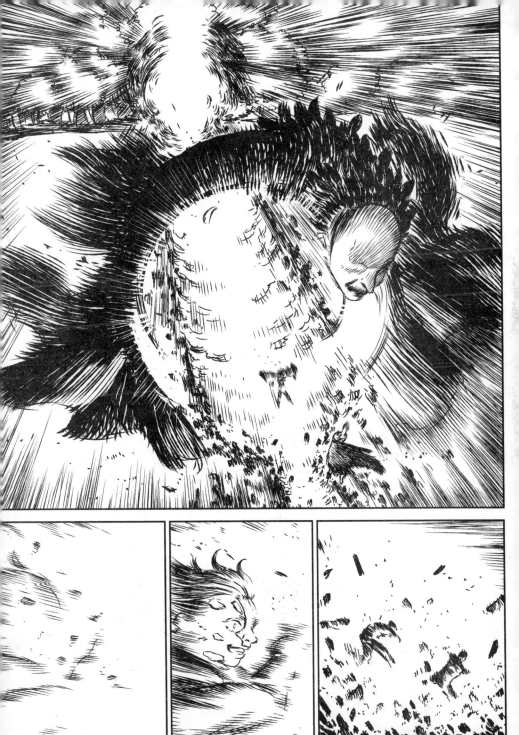

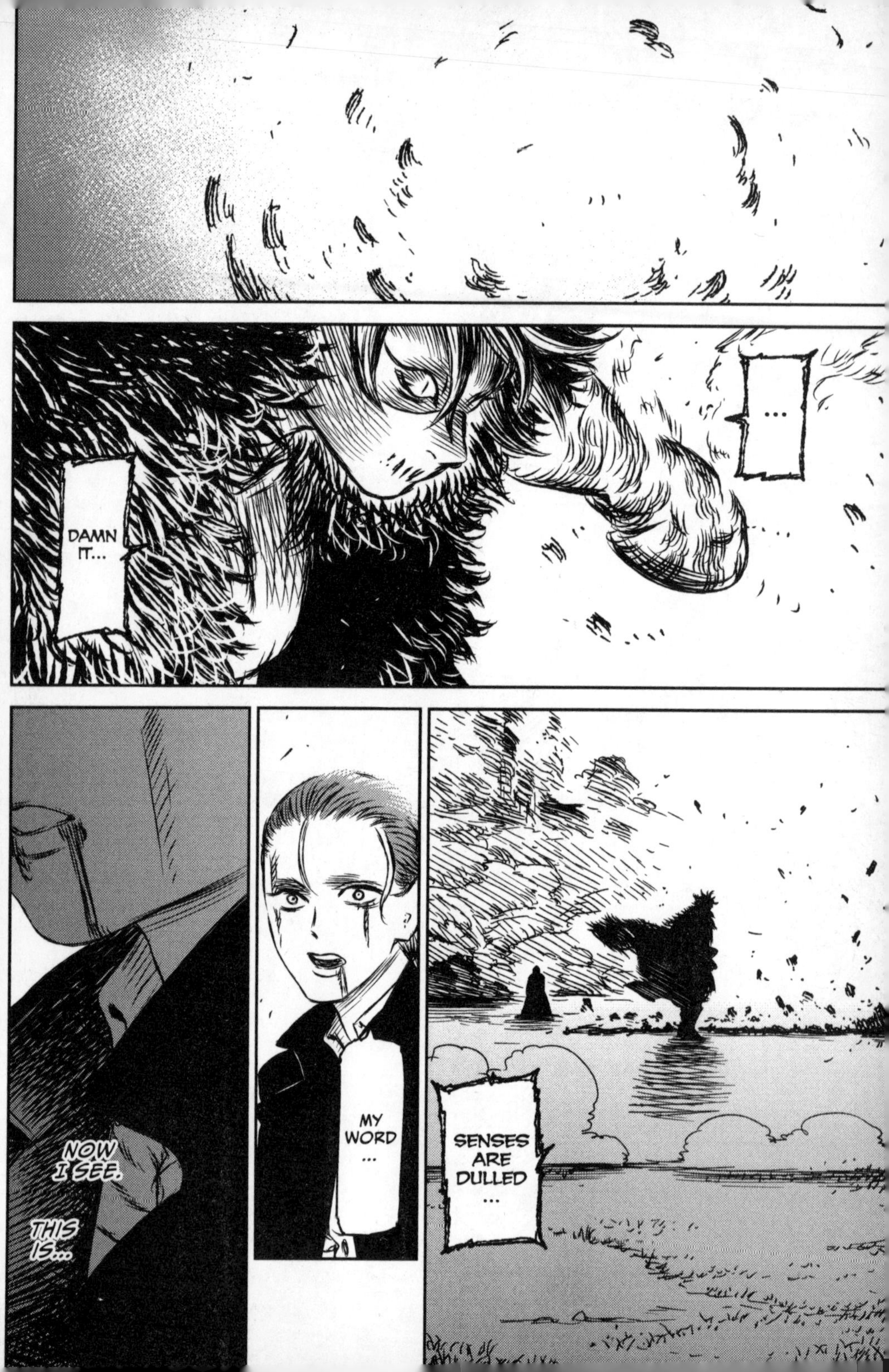
...
DAMN IT...
SENSES ARE DULLED ...
MY WORD ...
NOW I SEE.
THIS IS...

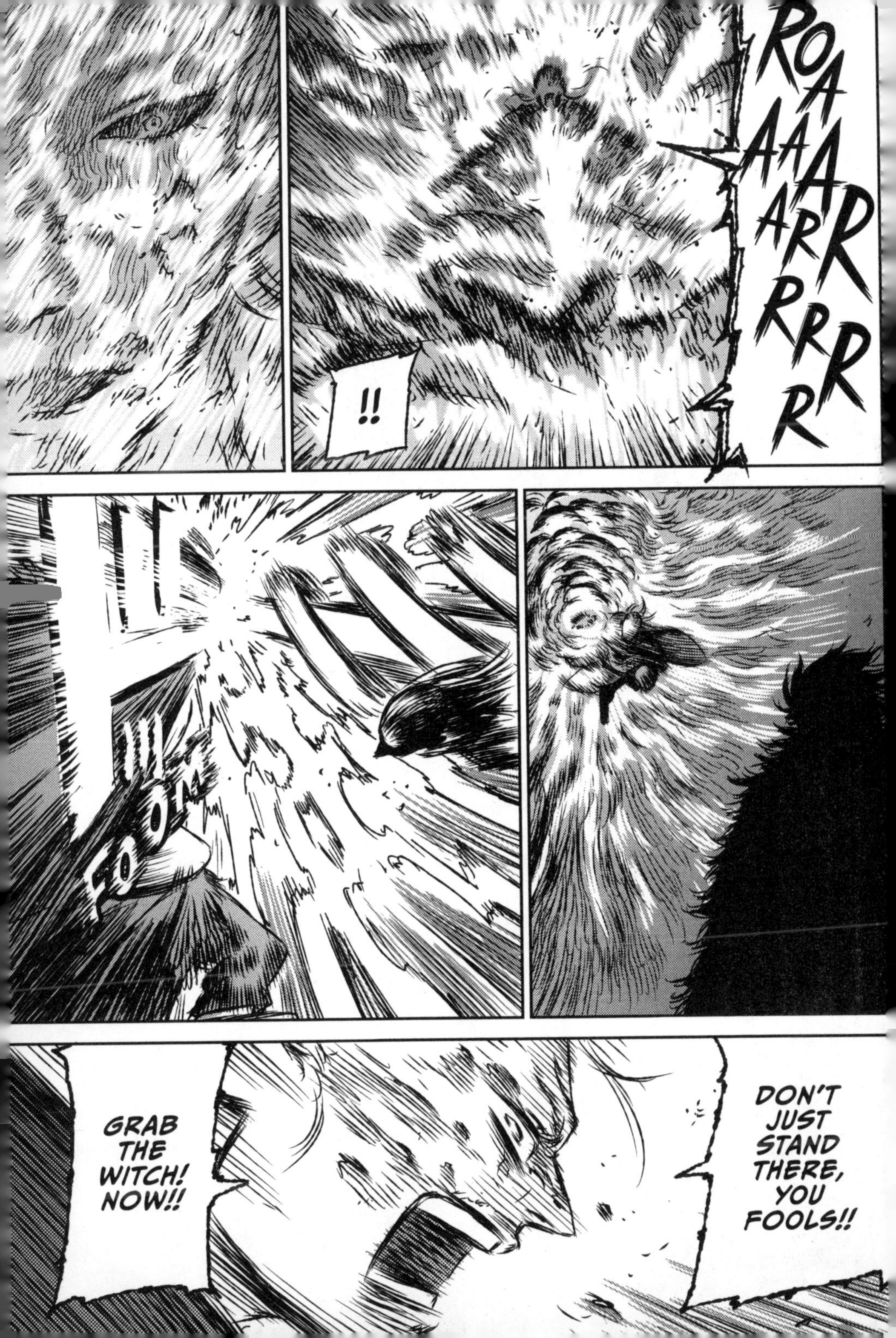
ROAAAAARRRRRR
!!
FOOM
DON'T JUST STAND THERE, YOU FOOLS!!
GRAB THE WITCH! NOW!!

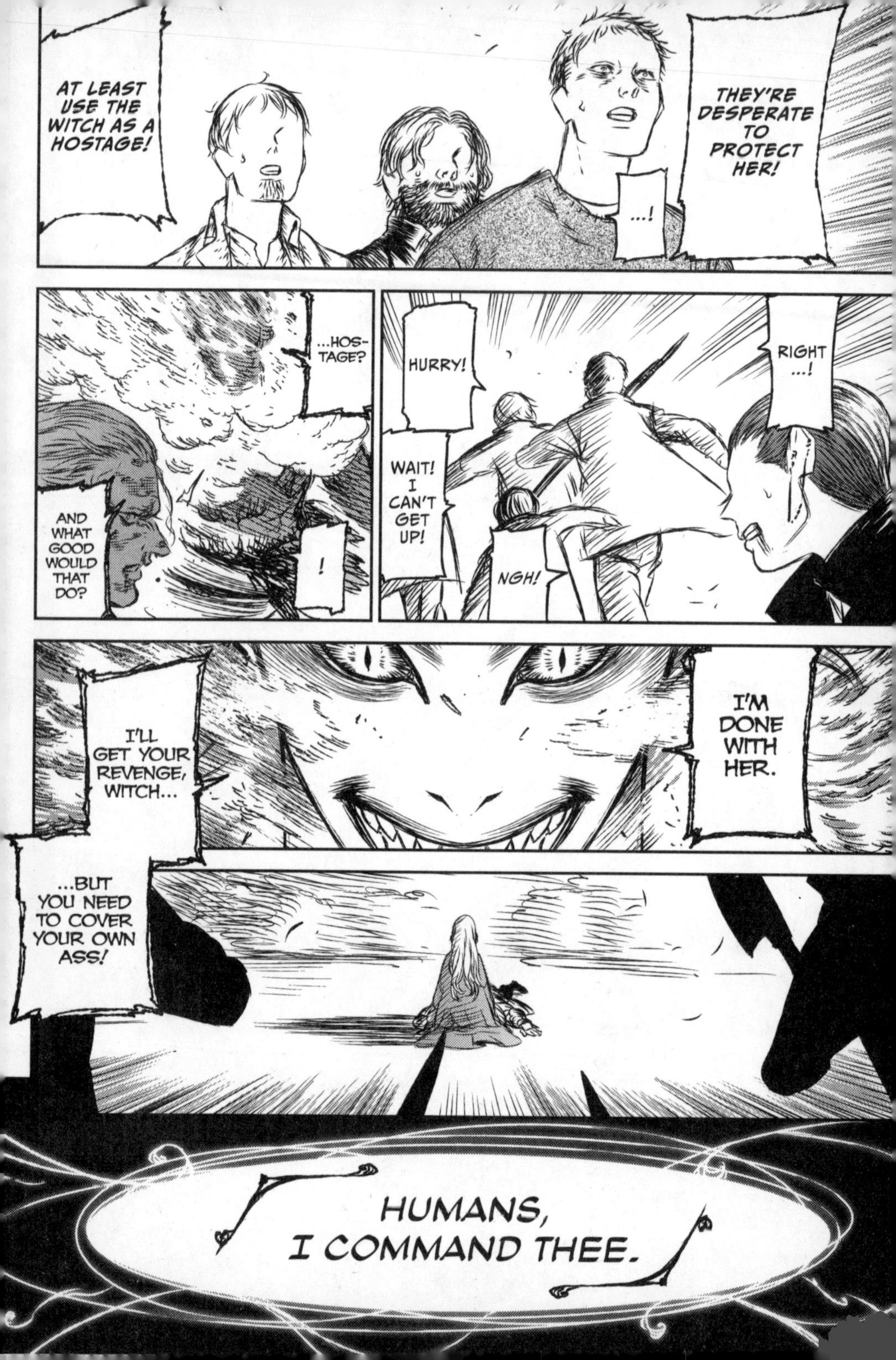
THEY'RE DESPERATE TO PROTECT HER!
...!
AT LEAST USE THE WITCH AS A HOSTAGE!
RIGHT ...!
HURRY!
WAIT! I CAN'T GET UP!
NGH!
...HOS-TAGE?
!
AND WHAT GOOD WOULD THAT DO?
I'M DONE WITH HER.
I'LL GET YOUR REVENGE, WITCH...
...BUT YOU NEED TO COVER YOUR OWN ASS!
HUMANS, I COMMAND THEE.

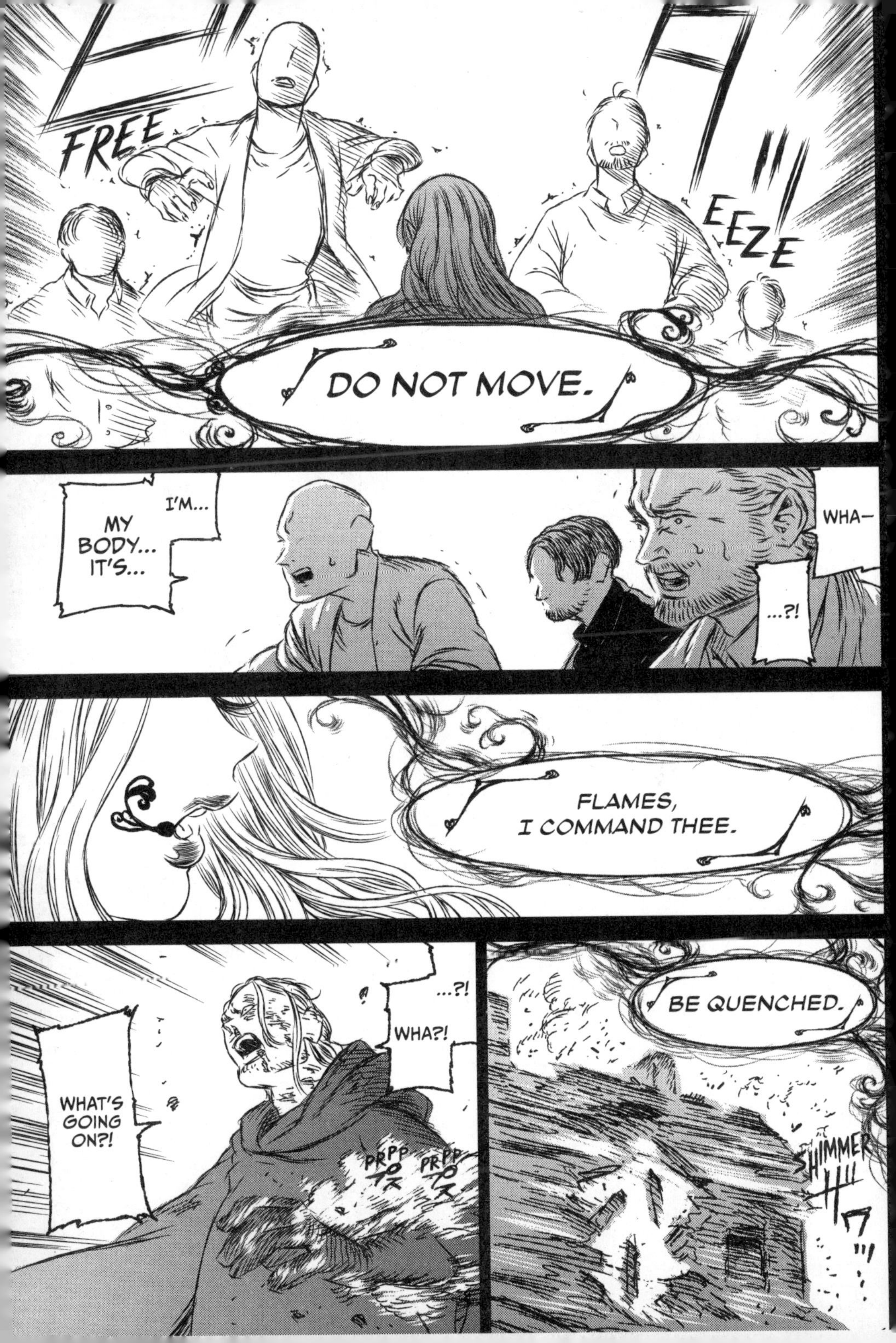
FREE
EEZE
DO NOT MOVE.
WHA—
...?!
I'M...
MY BODY... IT'S...
FLAMES, I COMMAND THEE.
BE QUENCHED.
SHIMMER
...?!
WHA?!
WHAT'S GOING ON?!
PRPP
PRPP

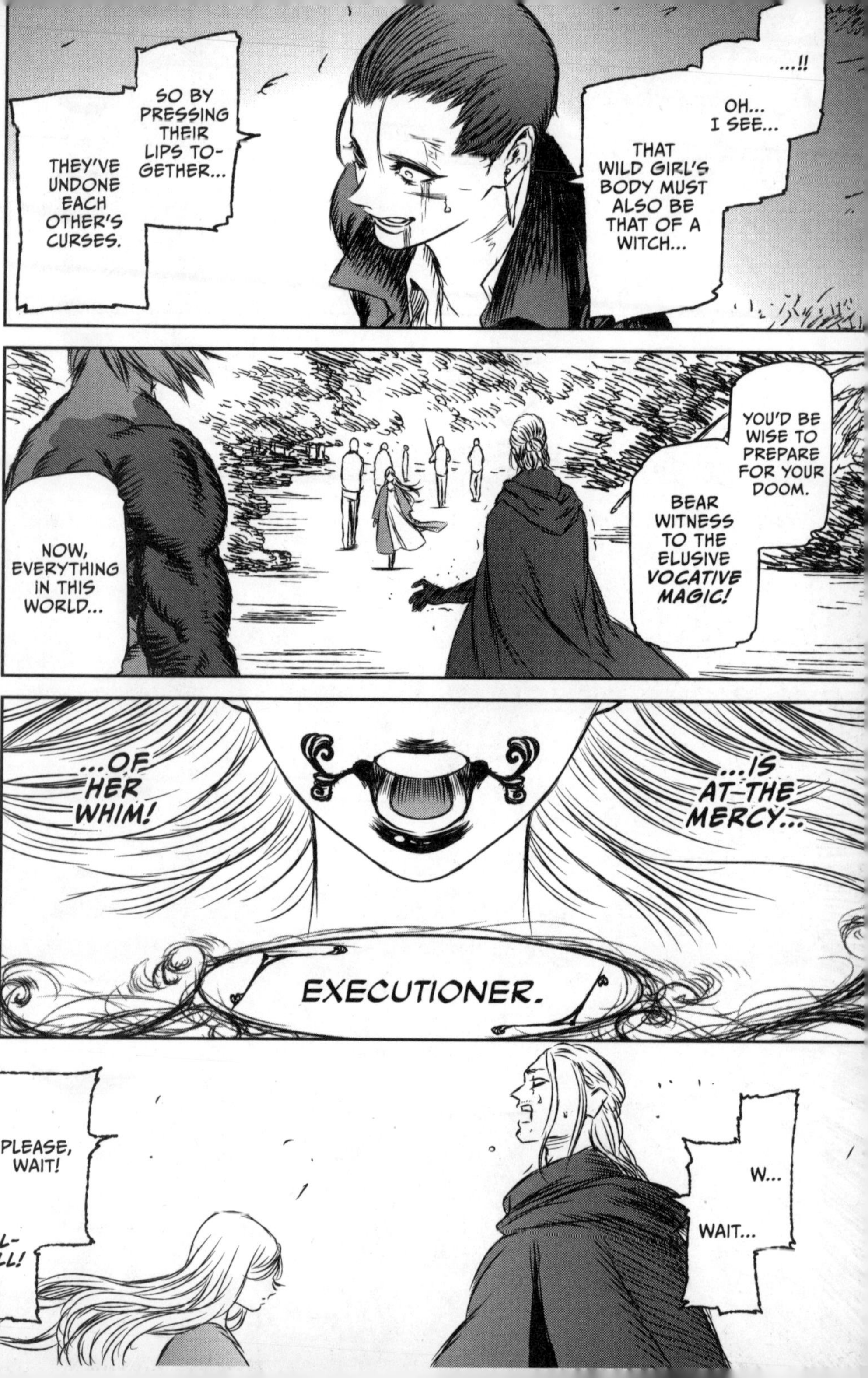
...!!
OH... I SEE...
THAT WILD GIRL'S BODY MUST ALSO BE THAT OF A WITCH...
SO BY PRESSING THEIR LIPS TOGETHER...
THEY'VE UNDONE EACH OTHER'S CURSES.
YOU'D BE WISE TO PREPARE FOR YOUR DOOM.
BEAR WITNESS TO THE ELUSIVE VOCATIVE MAGIC!
NOW, EVERYTHING IN THIS WORLD...
...IS AT THE MERCY...
...OF HER WHIM!
EXECUTIONER.
W...
WAIT...
PLEASE, WAIT!
FALVELL!

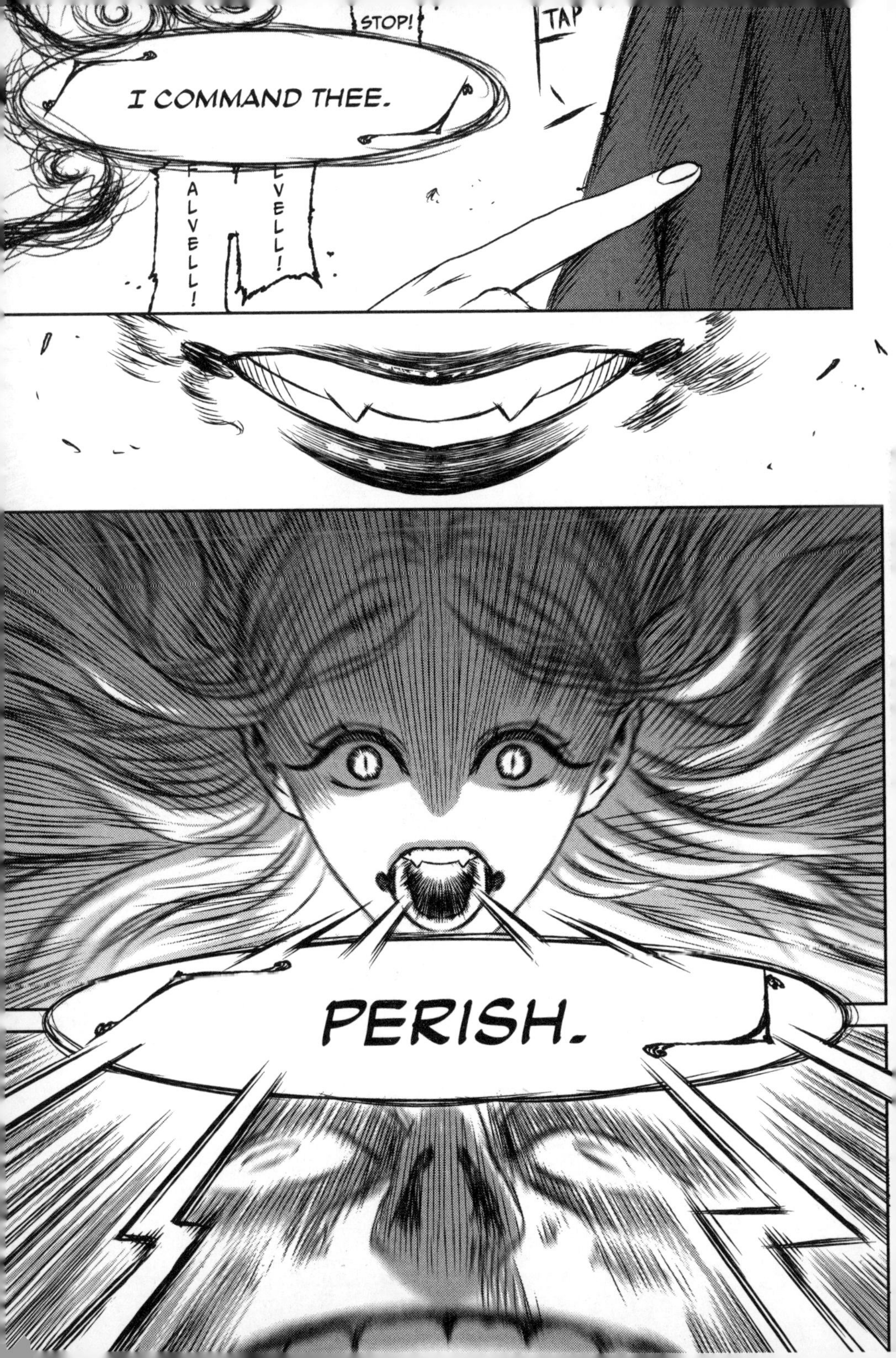
TAP
STOP!
I COMMAND THEE.
FALVELL!
LVELL!
PERISH.

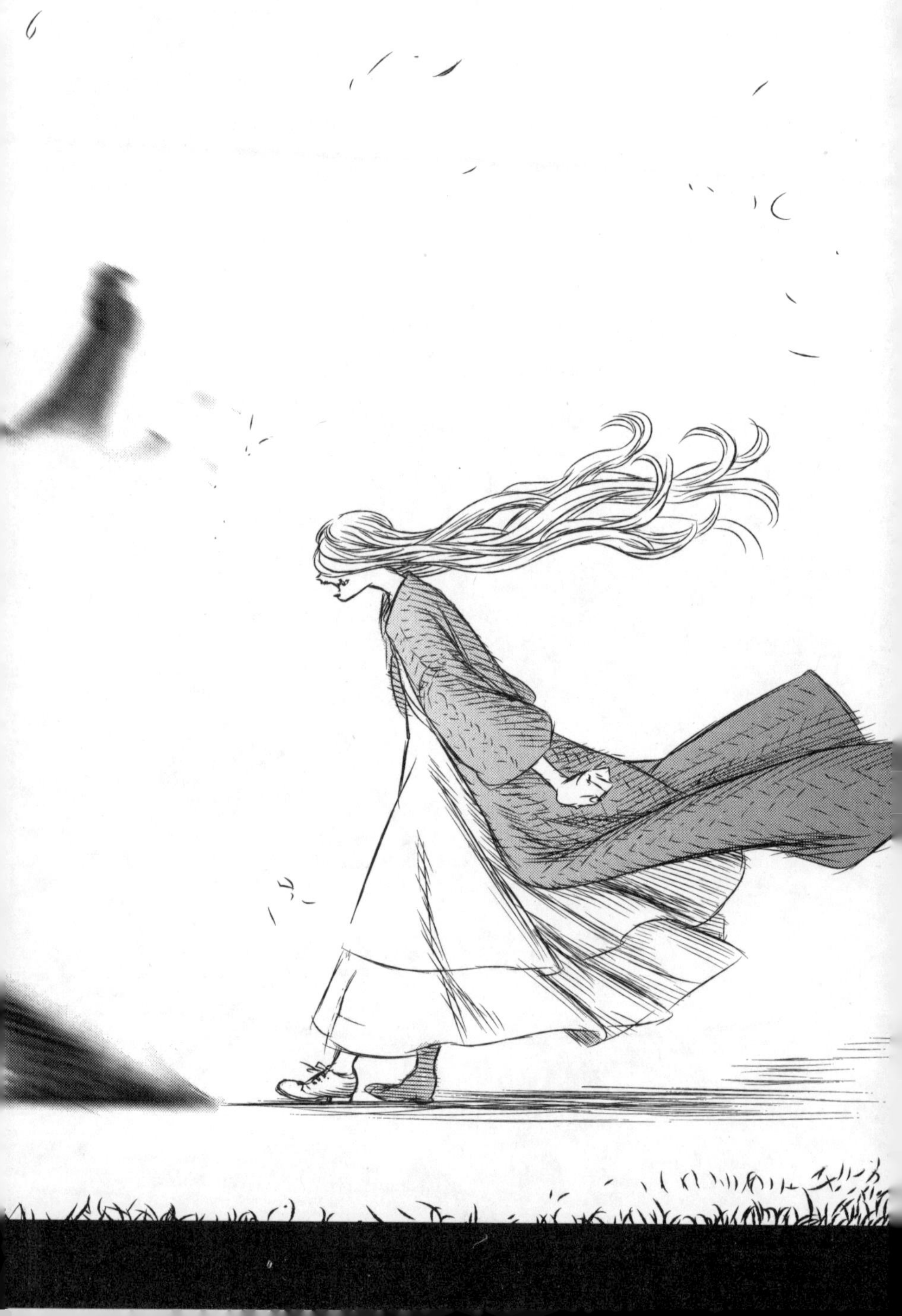

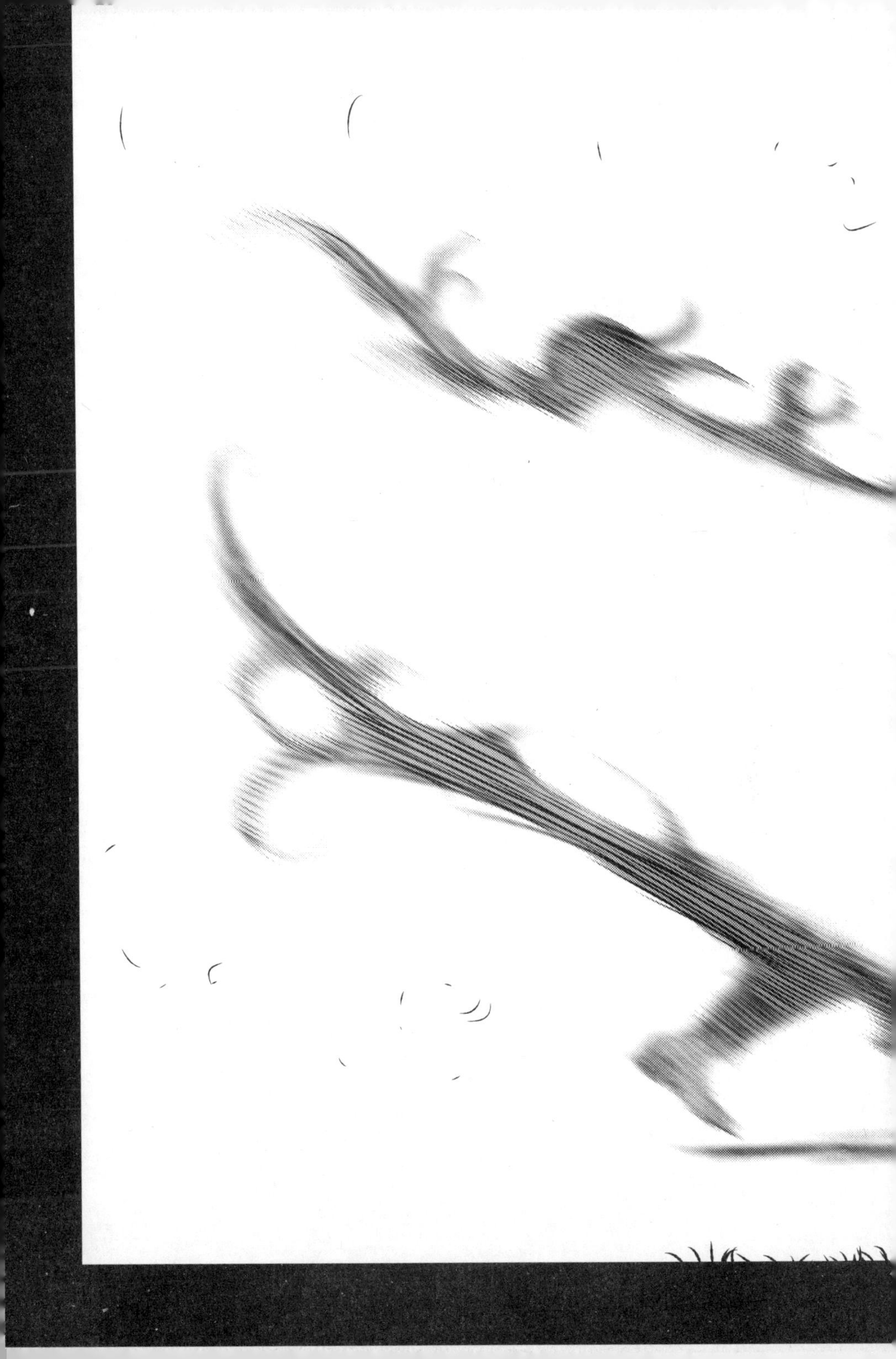

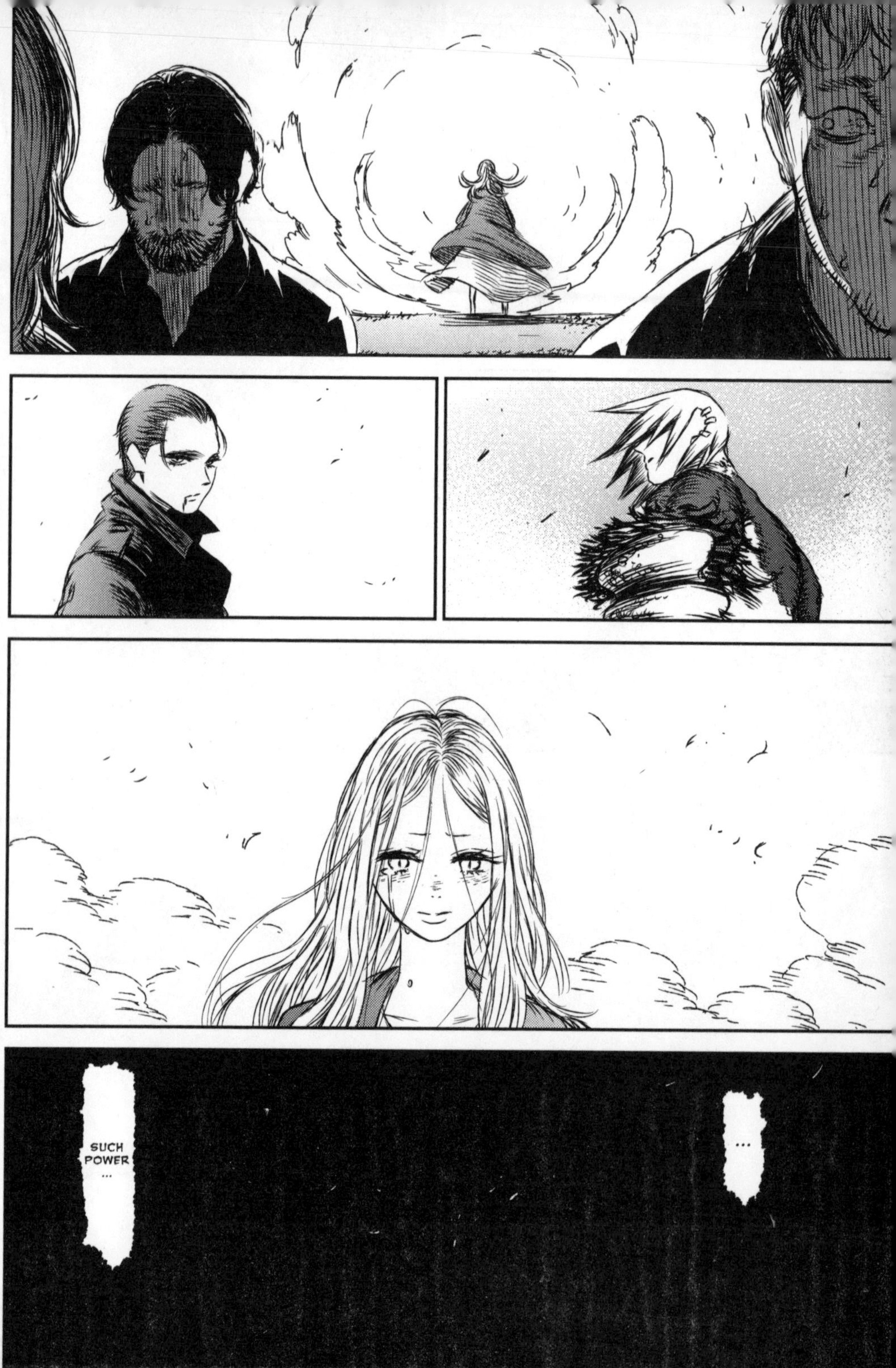
...
SUCH POWER ...

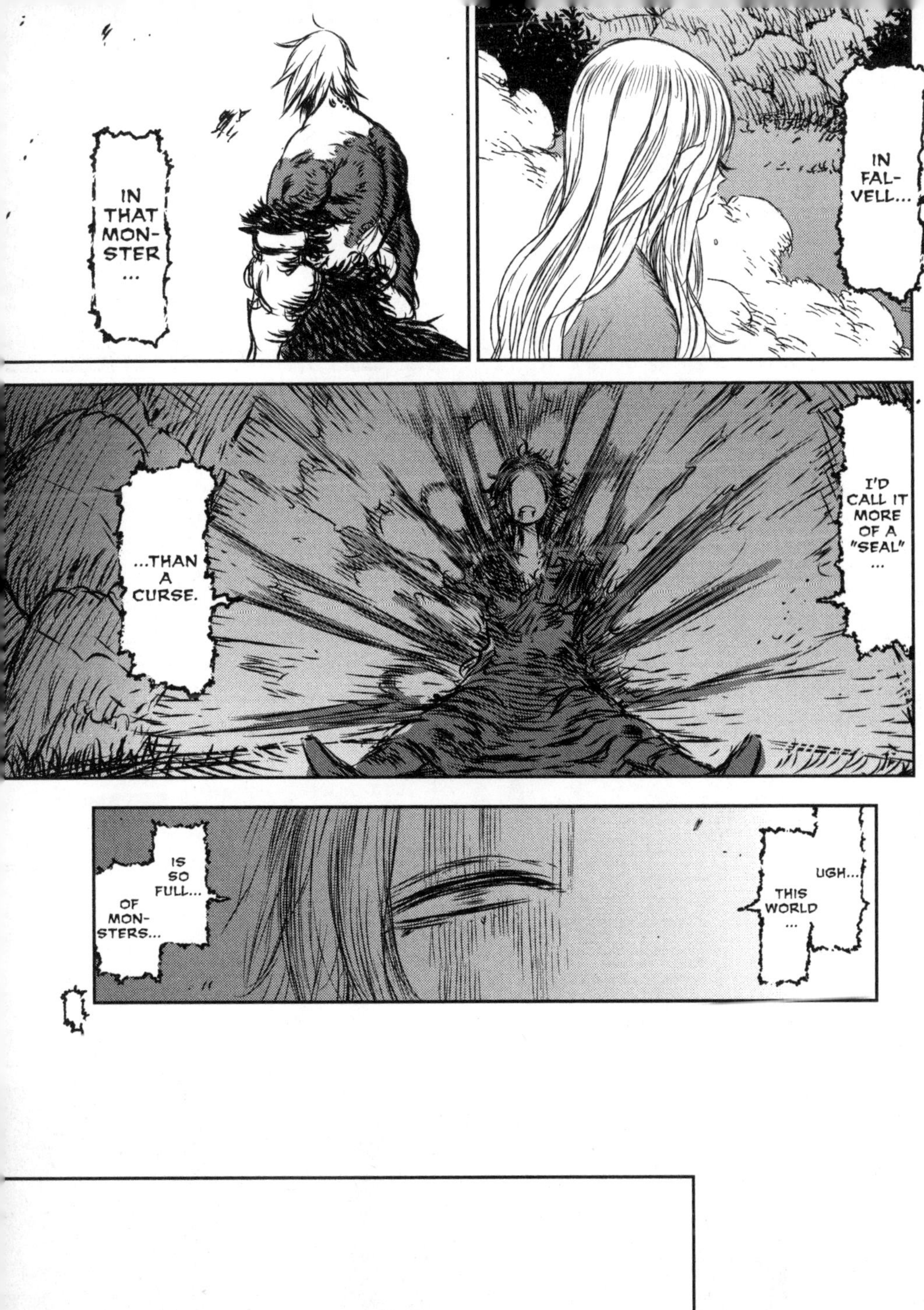
IN FAL-VELL...
IN THAT MON-STER...
I'D CALL IT MORE OF A "SEAL"...
...THAN A CURSE.
UGH...
THIS WORLD...
IS SO FULL...
OF MON-STERS...

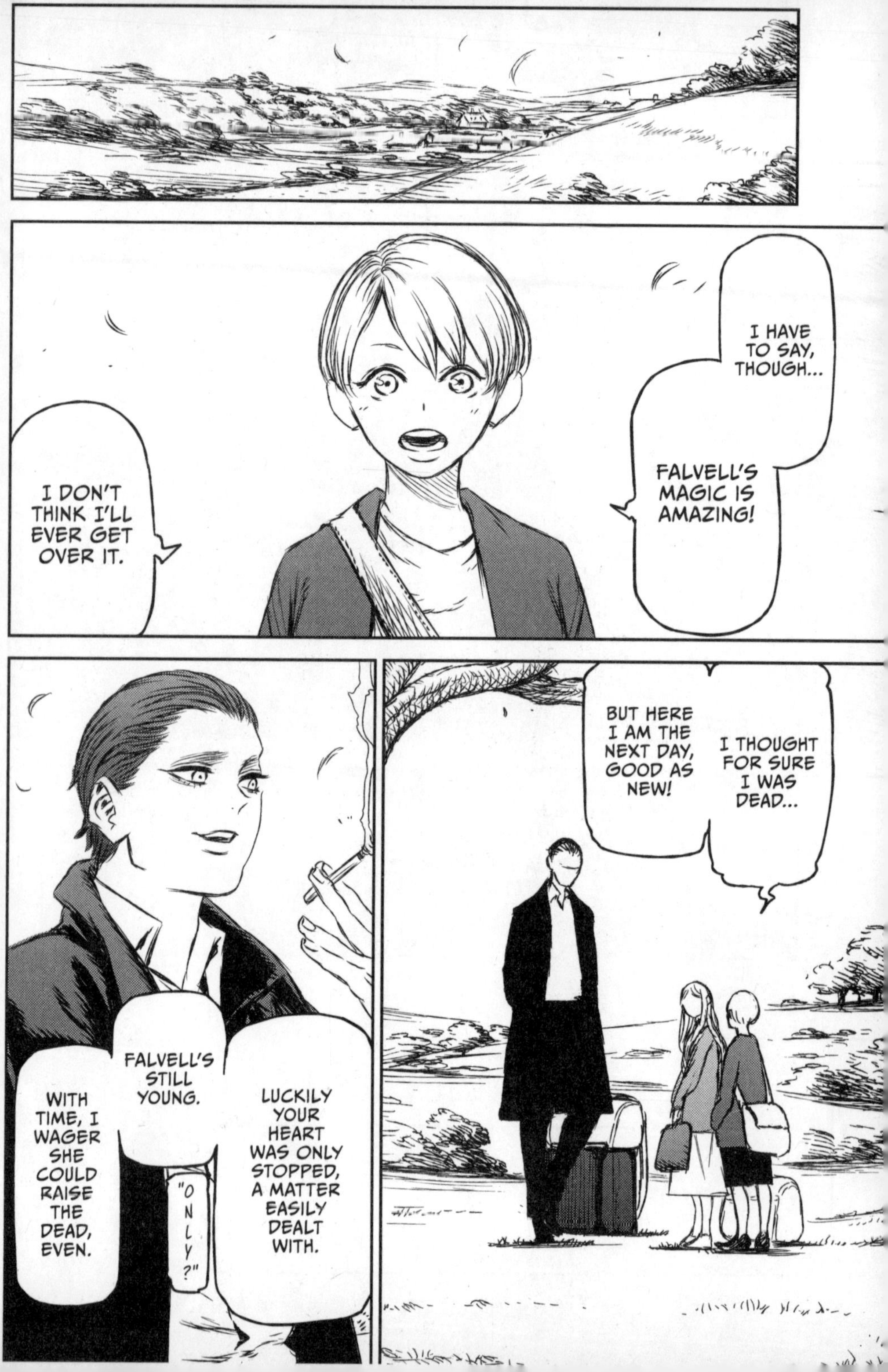
I HAVE TO SAY, THOUGH... FALVELL'S MAGIC IS AMAZING!
I DON'T THINK I'LL EVER GET OVER IT.
I THOUGHT FOR SURE I WAS DEAD...
BUT HERE I AM THE NEXT DAY, GOOD AS NEW!
LUCKILY YOUR HEART WAS ONLY STOPPED, A MATTER EASILY DEALT WITH.
"ONLY?"
FALVELL'S STILL YOUNG.
WITH TIME, I WAGER SHE COULD RAISE THE DEAD, EVEN.

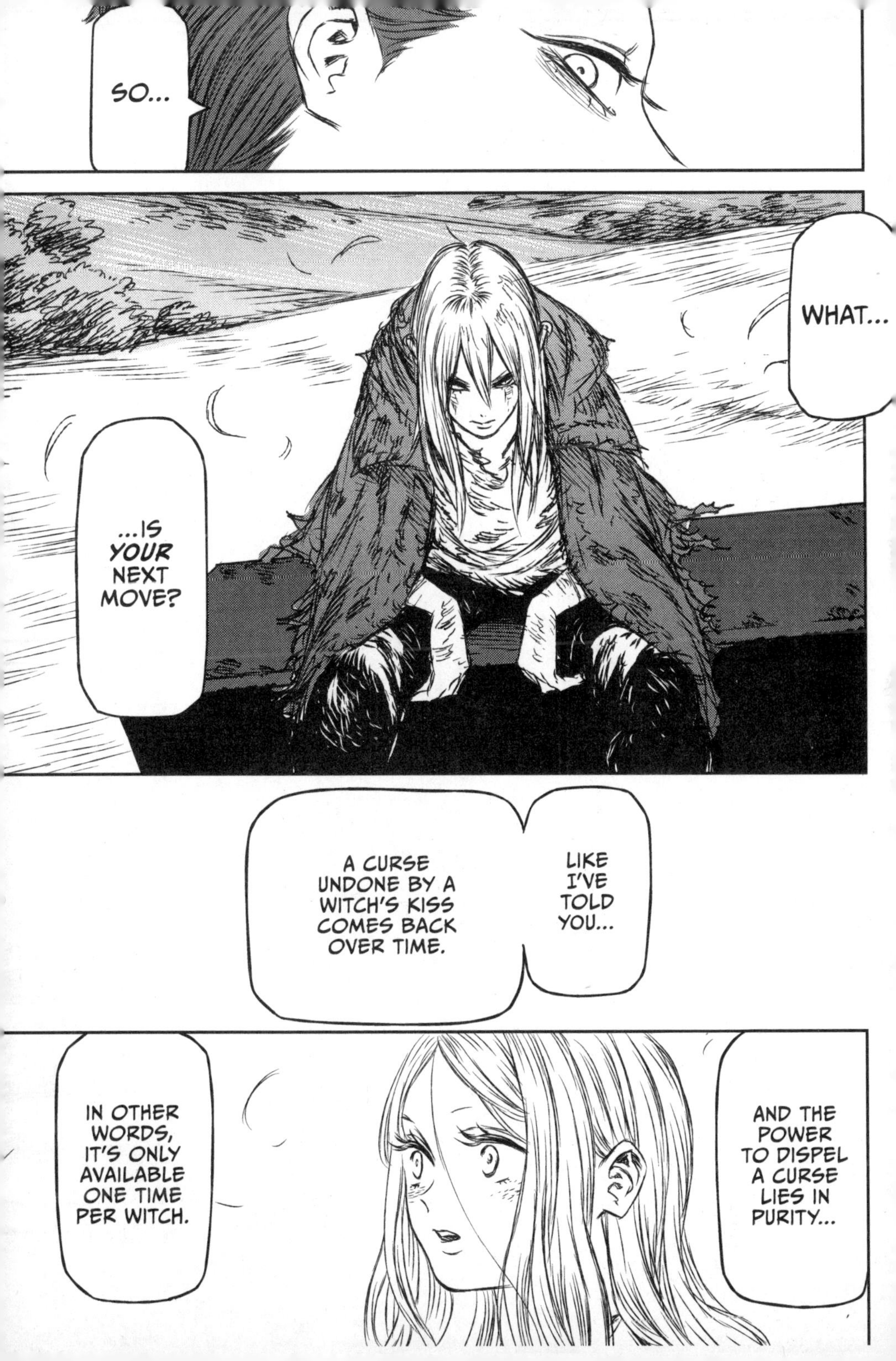
SO...
WHAT...
...IS *YOUR* NEXT MOVE?
LIKE I'VE TOLD YOU...
A CURSE UNDONE BY A WITCH'S KISS COMES BACK OVER TIME.
AND THE POWER TO DISPEL A CURSE LIES IN PURITY...
IN OTHER WORDS, IT'S ONLY AVAILABLE ONE TIME PER WITCH.

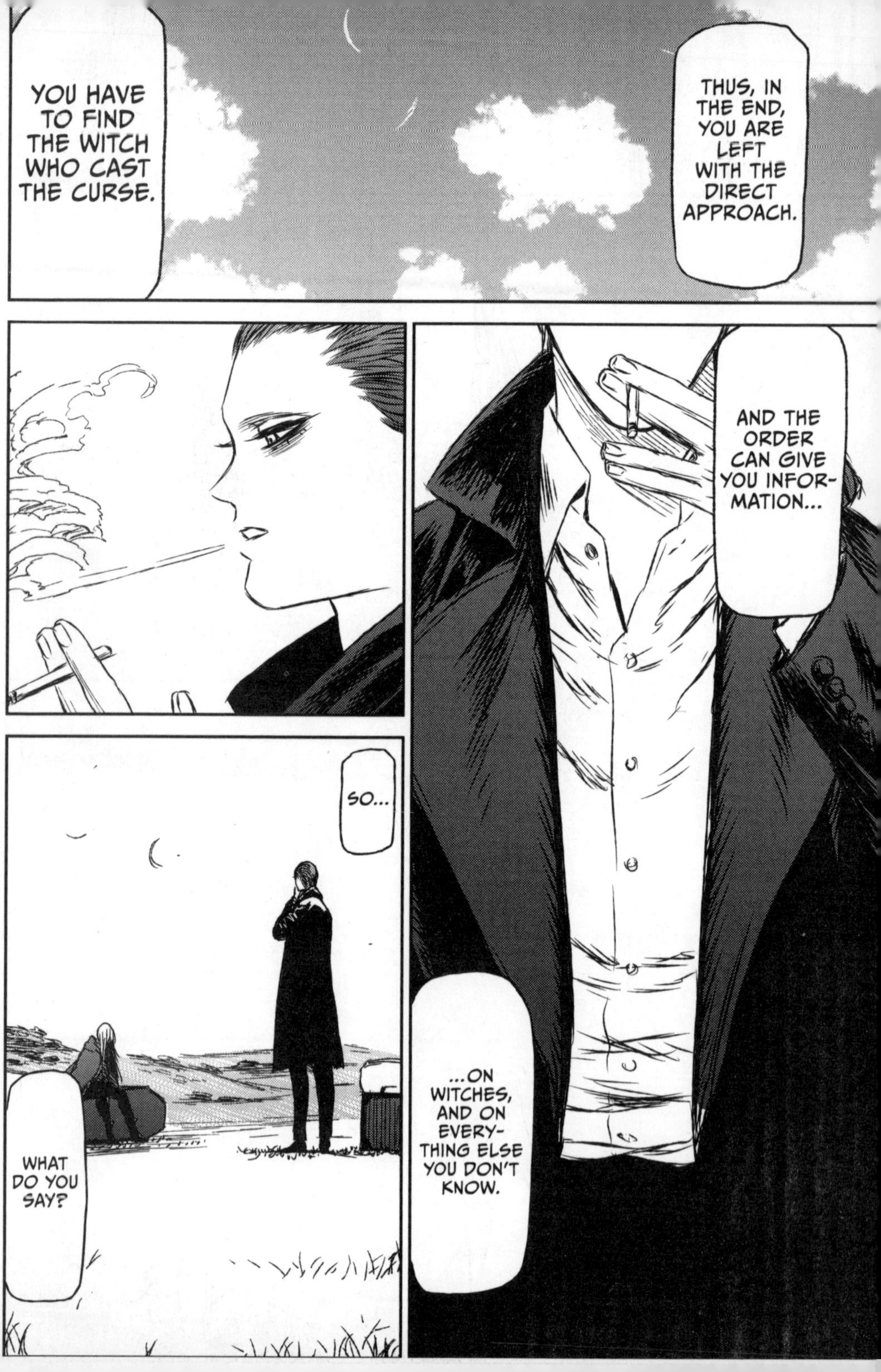
THUS, IN THE END, YOU ARE LEFT WITH THE DIRECT APPROACH.
YOU HAVE TO FIND THE WITCH WHO CAST THE CURSE.
AND THE ORDER CAN GIVE YOU INFOR-MATION...
...ON WITCHES, AND ON EVERY-THING ELSE YOU DON'T KNOW.
SO...
WHAT DO YOU SAY?

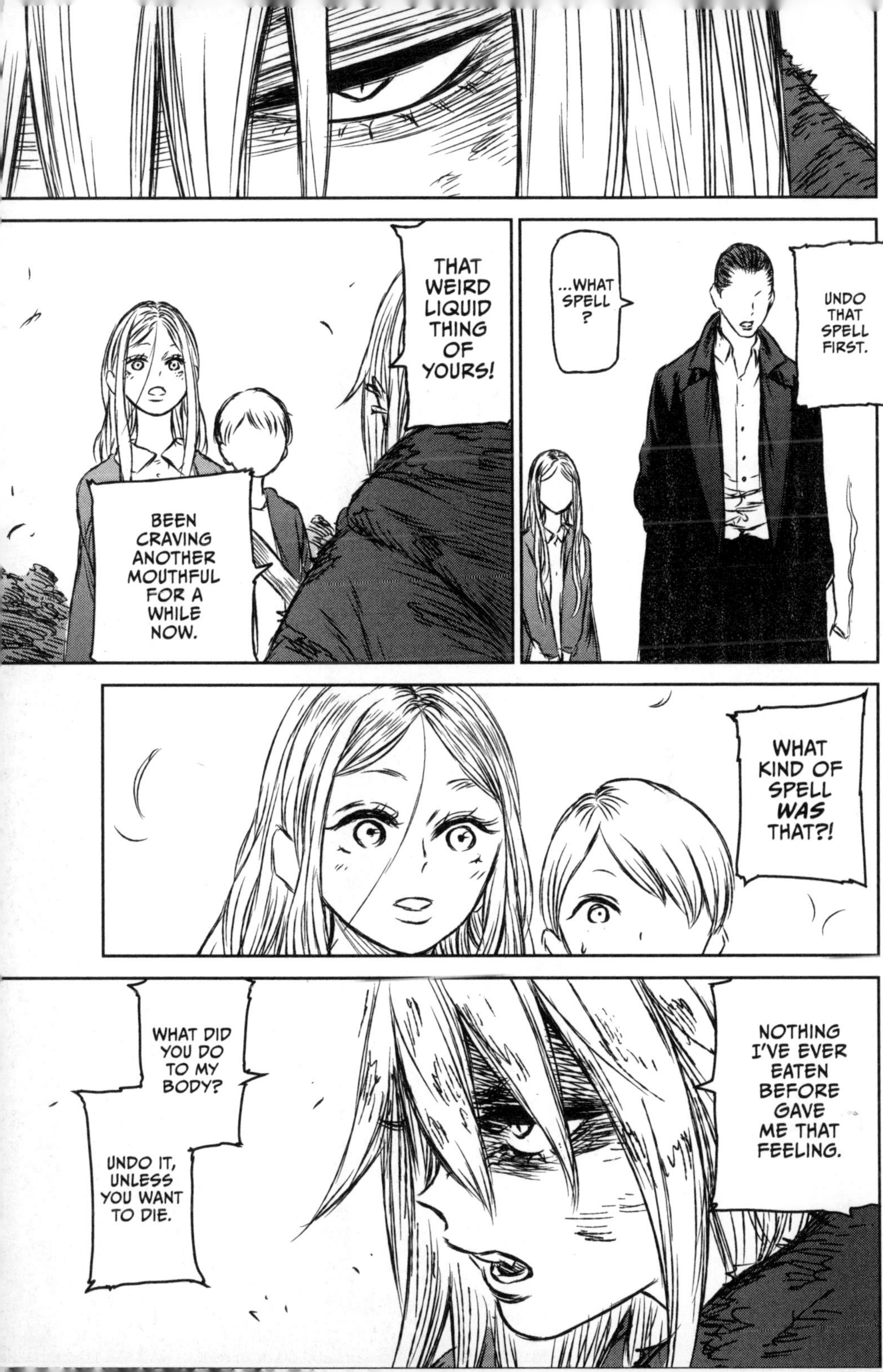
UNDO THAT SPELL FIRST.
...WHAT SPELL?
THAT WEIRD LIQUID THING OF YOURS!
BEEN CRAVING ANOTHER MOUTHFUL FOR A WHILE NOW.
WHAT KIND OF SPELL WAS THAT?!
NOTHING I'VE EVER EATEN BEFORE GAVE ME THAT FEELING.
WHAT DID YOU DO TO MY BODY?
UNDO IT, UNLESS YOU WANT TO DIE.

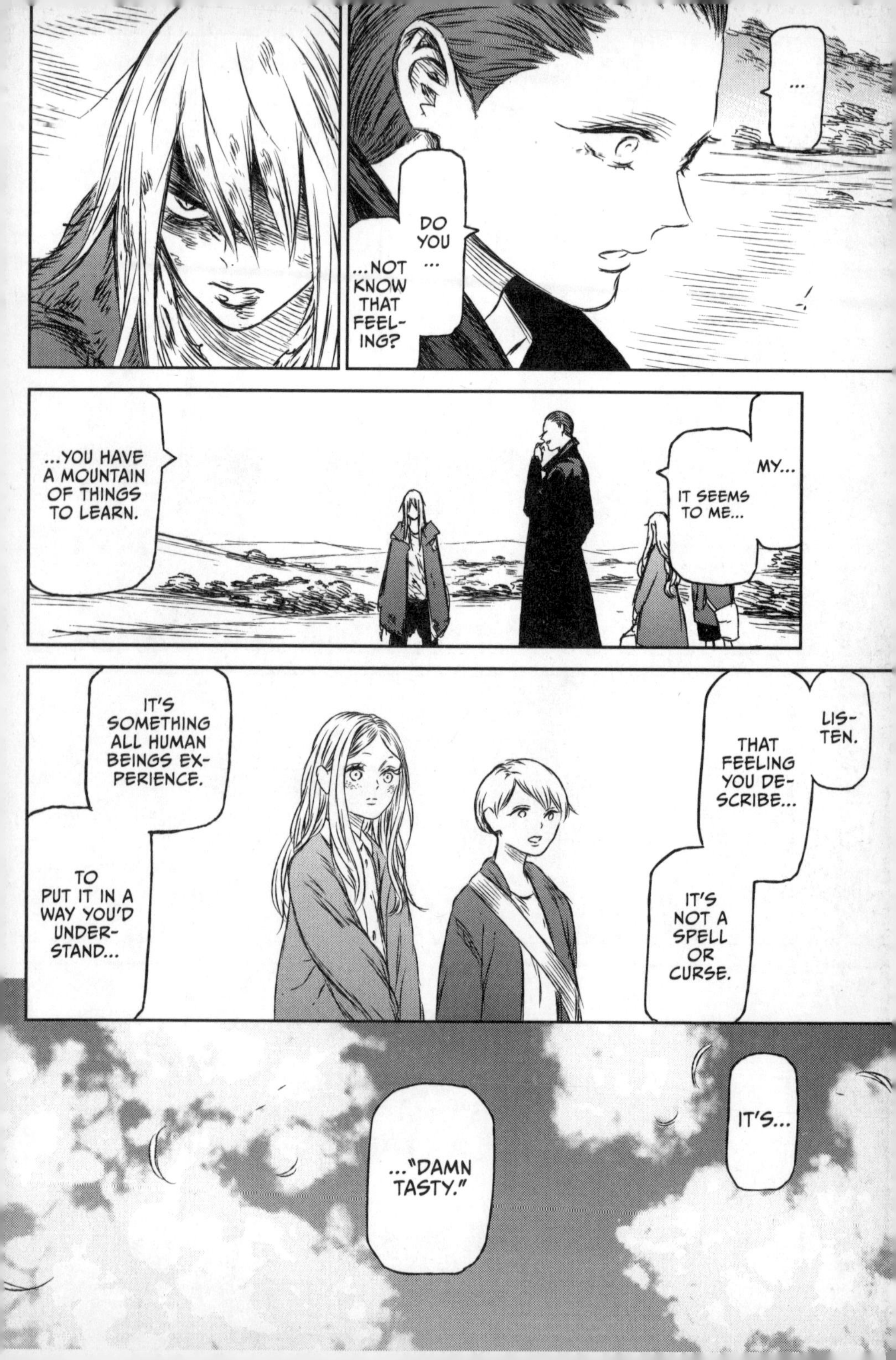
...
DO YOU ...
...NOT KNOW THAT FEELING?
MY...
IT SEEMS TO ME...
...YOU HAVE A MOUNTAIN OF THINGS TO LEARN.
LISTEN.
THAT FEELING YOU DESCRIBE...
IT'S NOT A SPELL OR CURSE.
IT'S SOMETHING ALL HUMAN BEINGS EXPERIENCE.
TO PUT IT IN A WAY YOU'D UNDERSTAND...
IT'S...
..."DAMN TASTY."

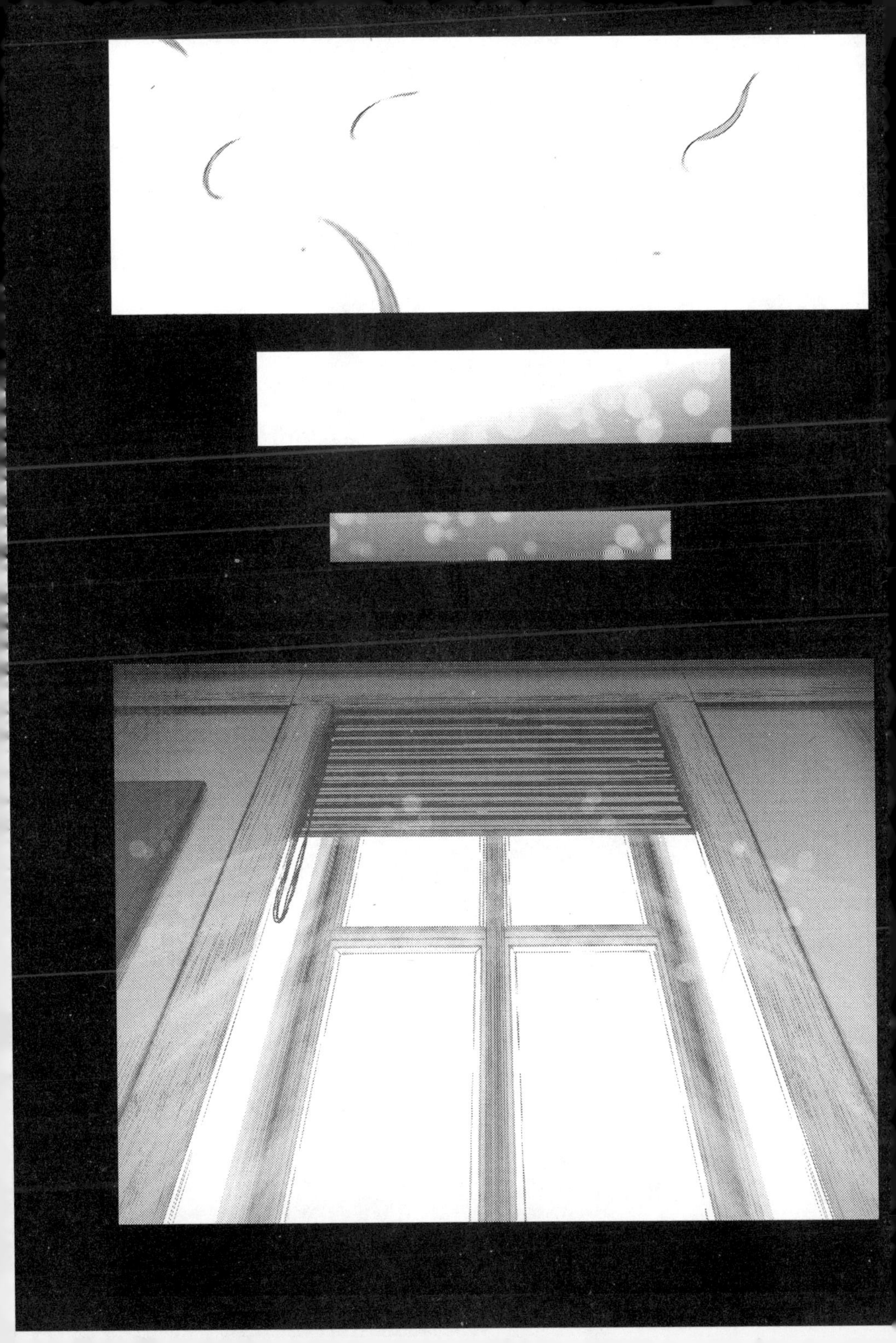

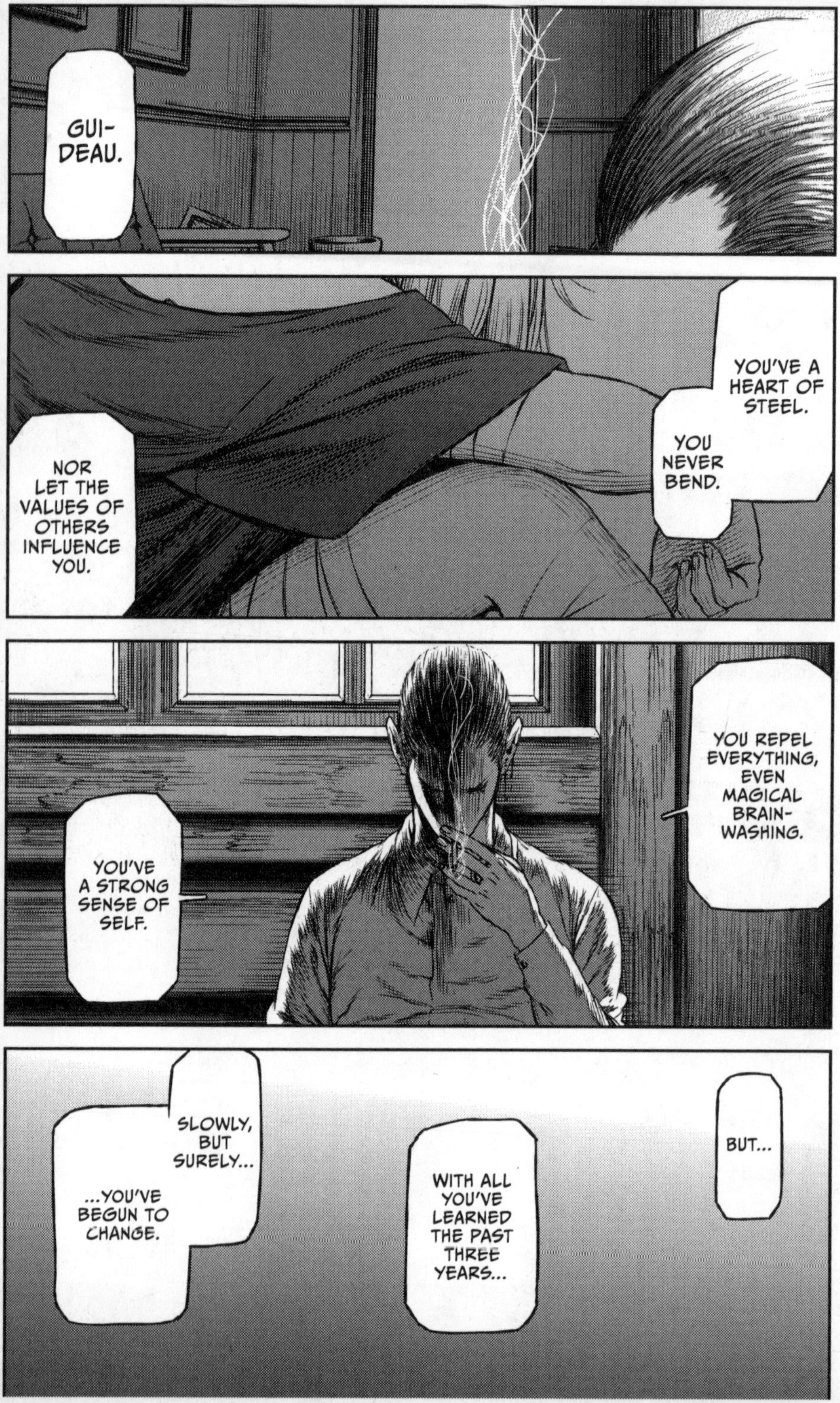
GUI-DEAU.
YOU'VE A HEART OF STEEL.
YOU NEVER BEND.
NOR LET THE VALUES OF OTHERS INFLUENCE YOU.
YOU REPEL EVERYTHING, EVEN MAGICAL BRAIN-WASHING.
YOU'VE A STRONG SENSE OF SELF.
BUT...
WITH ALL YOU'VE LEARNED THE PAST THREE YEARS...
SLOWLY, BUT SURELY...
...YOU'VE BEGUN TO CHANGE.

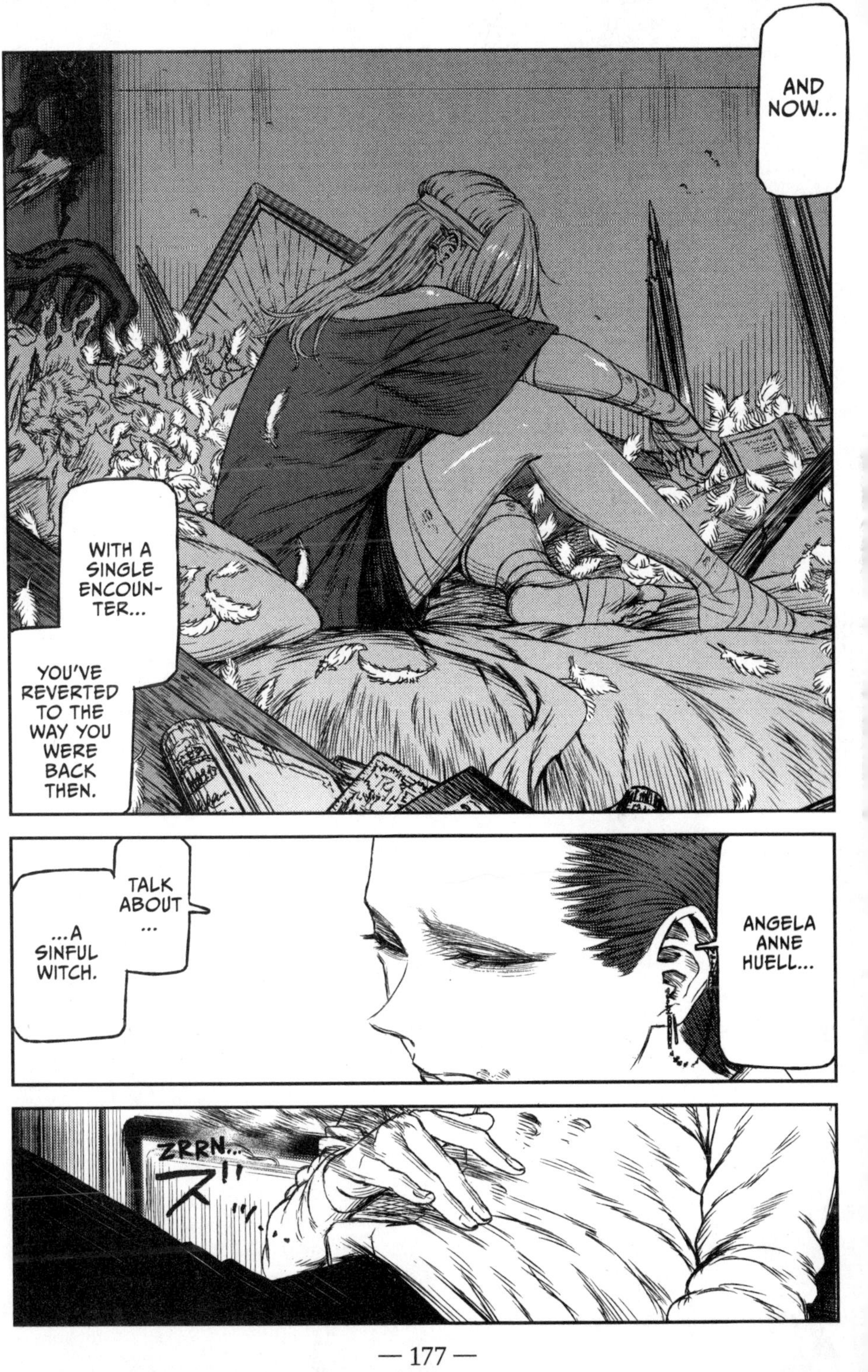
AND NOW...
WITH A SINGLE ENCOUNTER...
YOU'VE REVERTED TO THE WAY YOU WERE BACK THEN.
ANGELA ANNE HUELL...
TALK ABOUT ...
...A SINFUL WITCH.
ZRRN...
ス

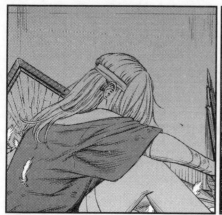

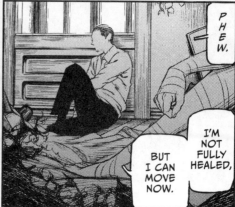

PHEW.
I'M NOT FULLY HEALED,
BUT I CAN MOVE NOW.
I'LL TRUST THIS ISN'T A COMPLETE REGRES-SION,
MERELY A FLARING OF THE TEMPER.
PLEASE CALM DOWN SOON.
THERE'S STILL A VERY IMPORTANT LESSON I WANT TO TEACH YOU.

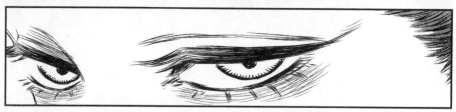

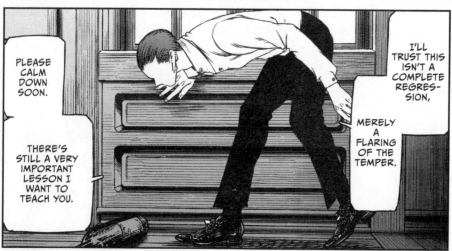

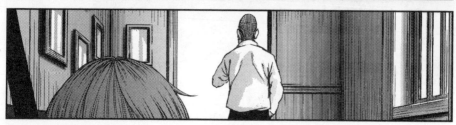

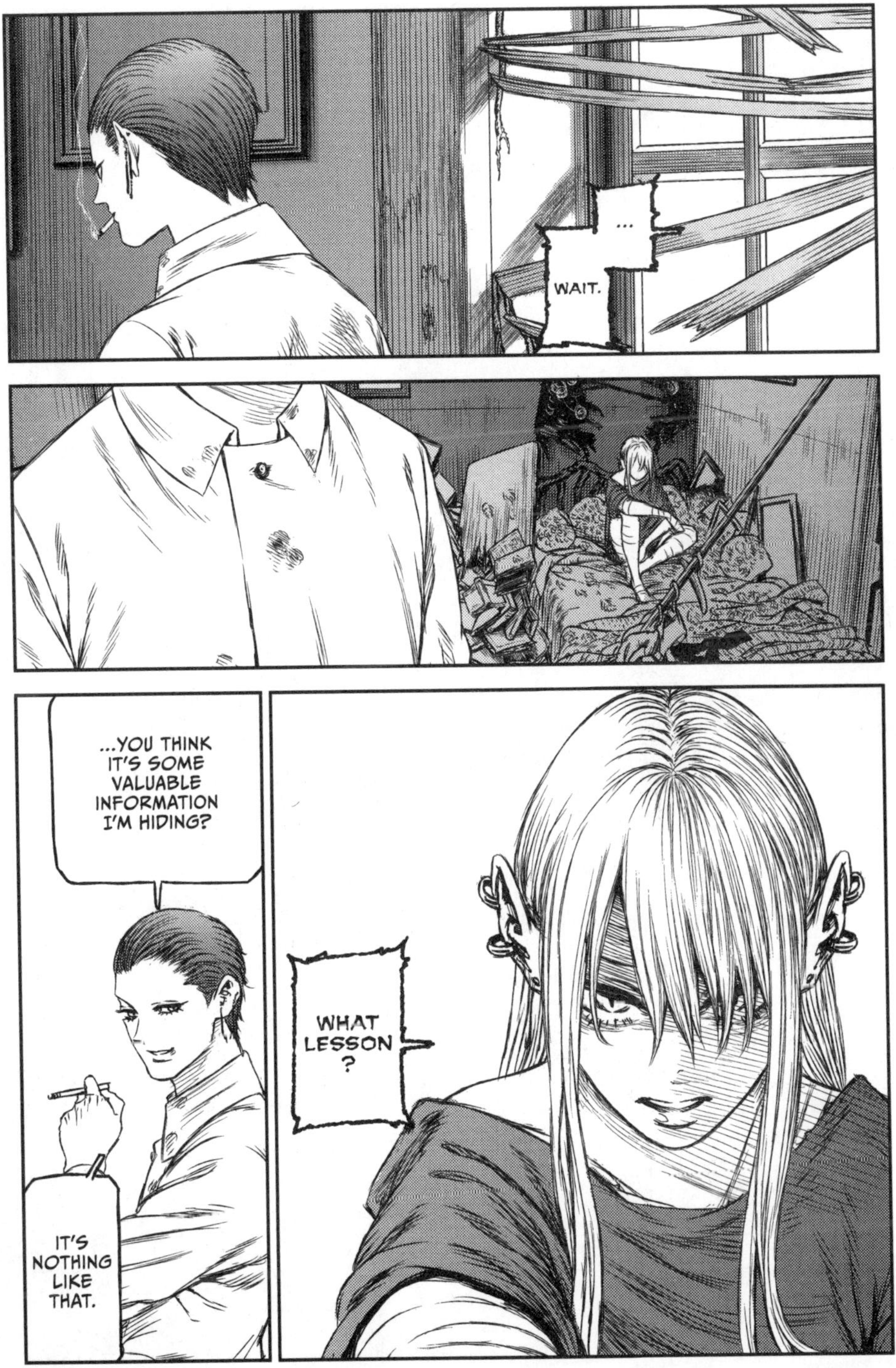
...
WAIT.
WHAT LESSON?
...YOU THINK IT'S SOME VALUABLE INFORMATION I'M HIDING?
IT'S NOTHING LIKE THAT.

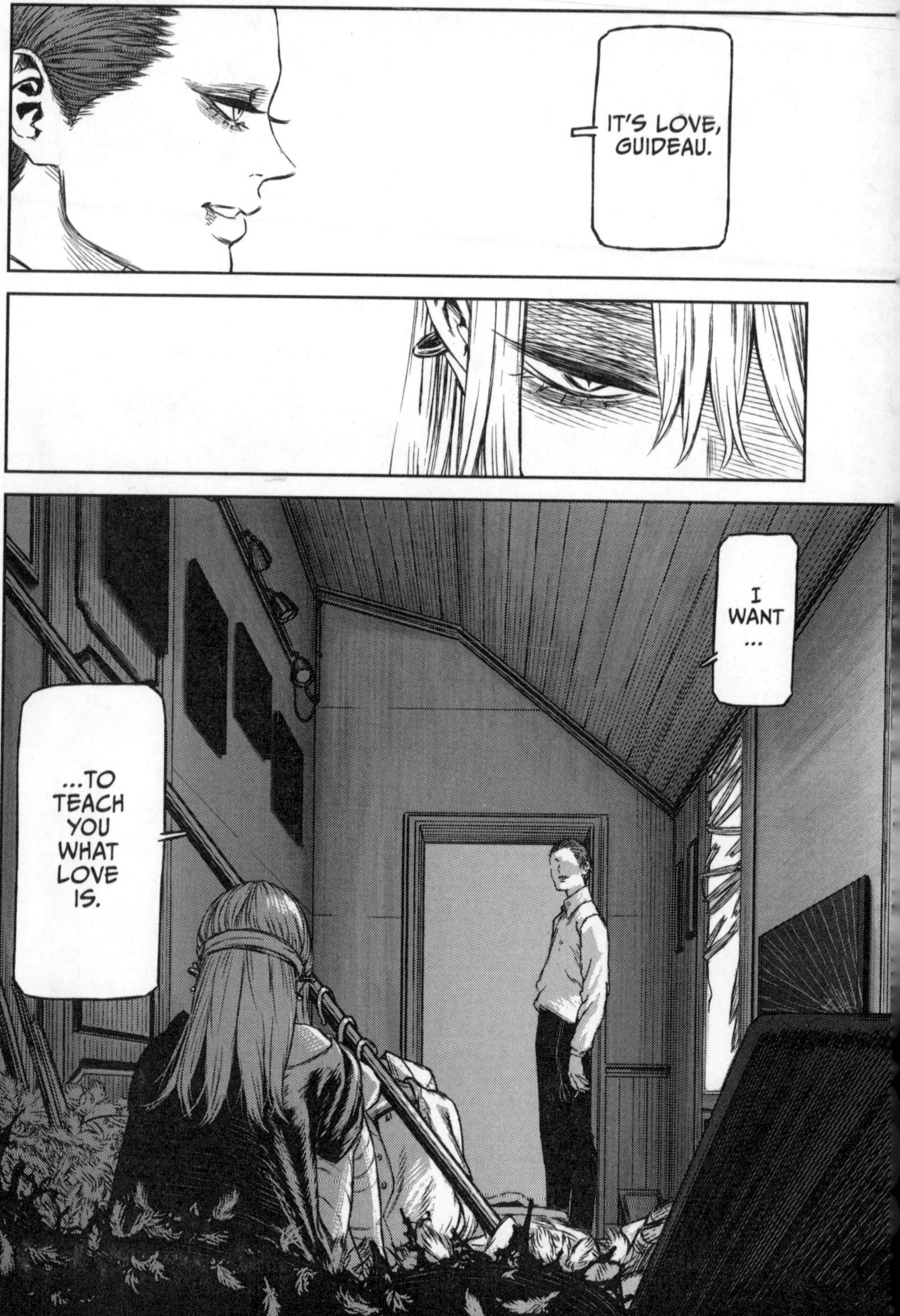
IT'S LOVE, GUIDEAU.
I WANT ...
...TO TEACH YOU WHAT LOVE IS.

THE WITCH AND THE BEAST

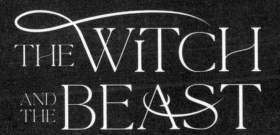

THE WITCH AND THE BEAST

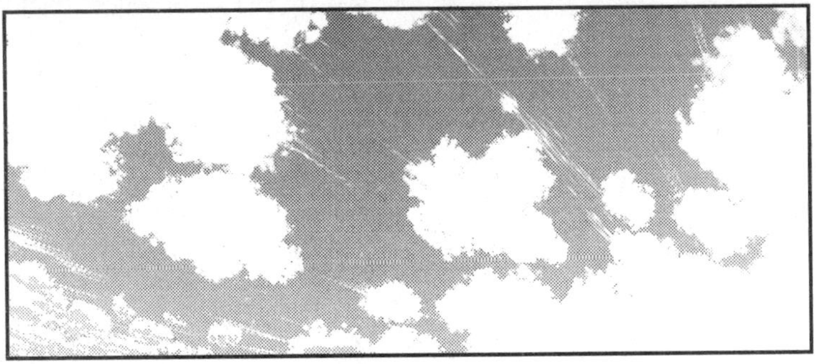

CHAPTER 28: FOUR LEVELS BELOW—PROLOGUE

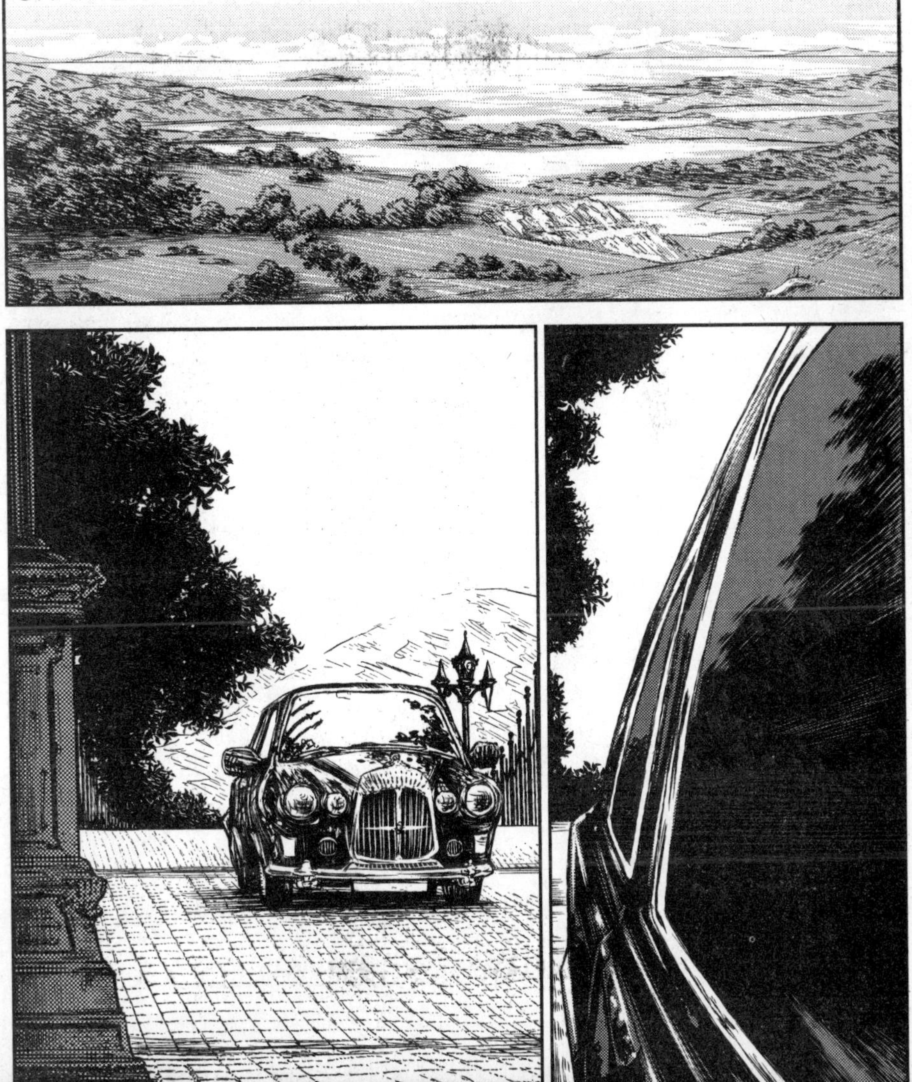

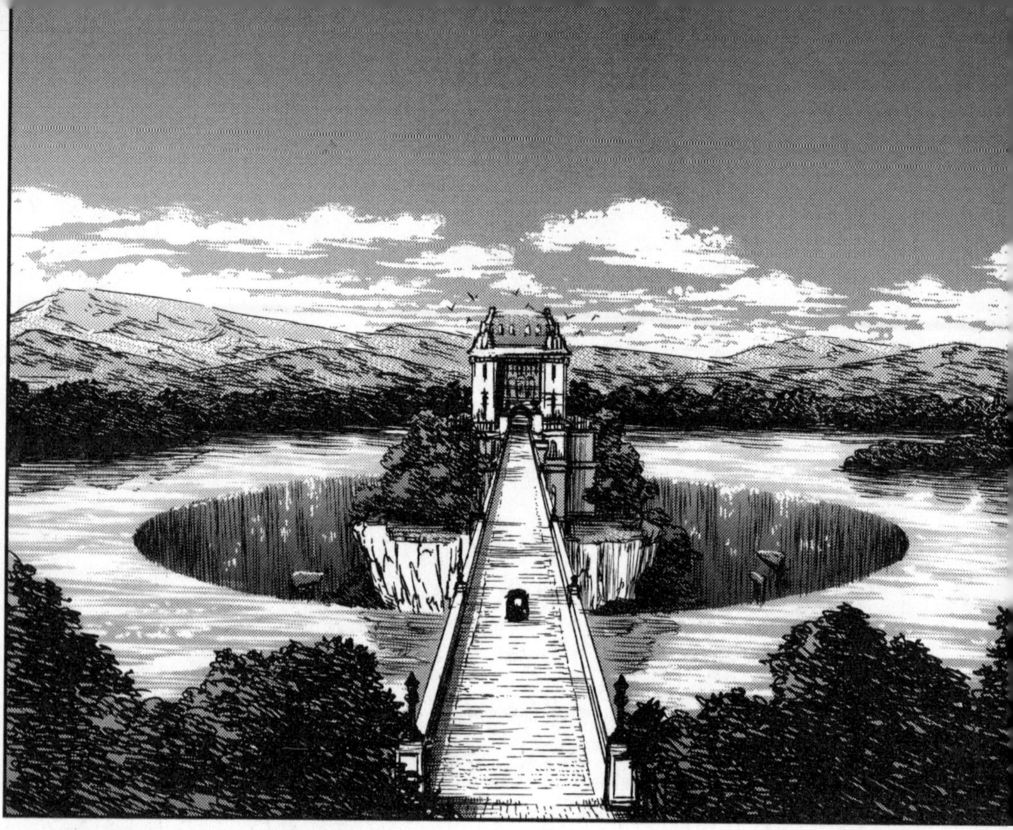

THE WORLD HAS EIGHT CONTINENTS.

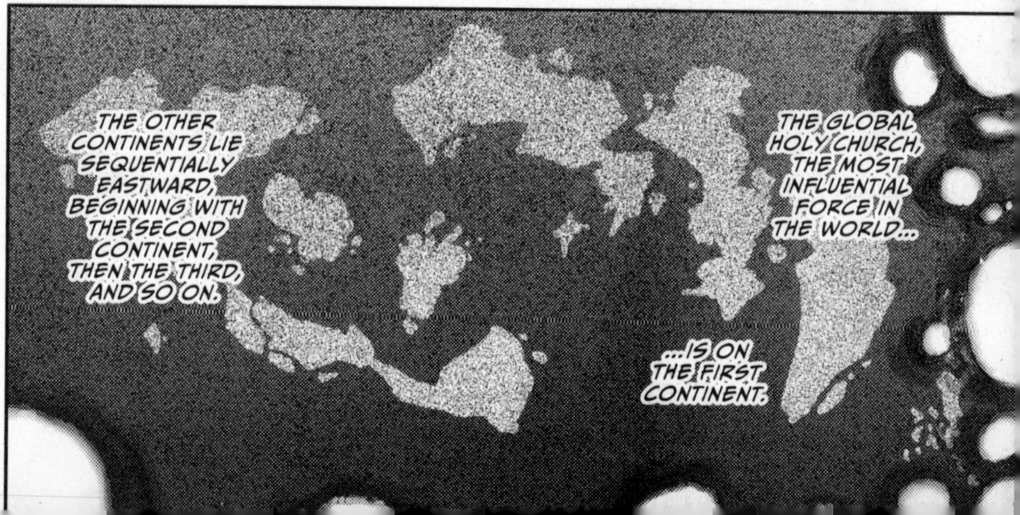
THE GLOBAL HOLY CHURCH, THE MOST INFLUENTIAL FORCE IN THE WORLD...
...IS ON THE FIRST CONTINENT.
THE OTHER CONTINENTS LIE SEQUENTIALLY EASTWARD, BEGINNING WITH THE SECOND CONTINENT, THEN THE THIRD, AND SO ON.

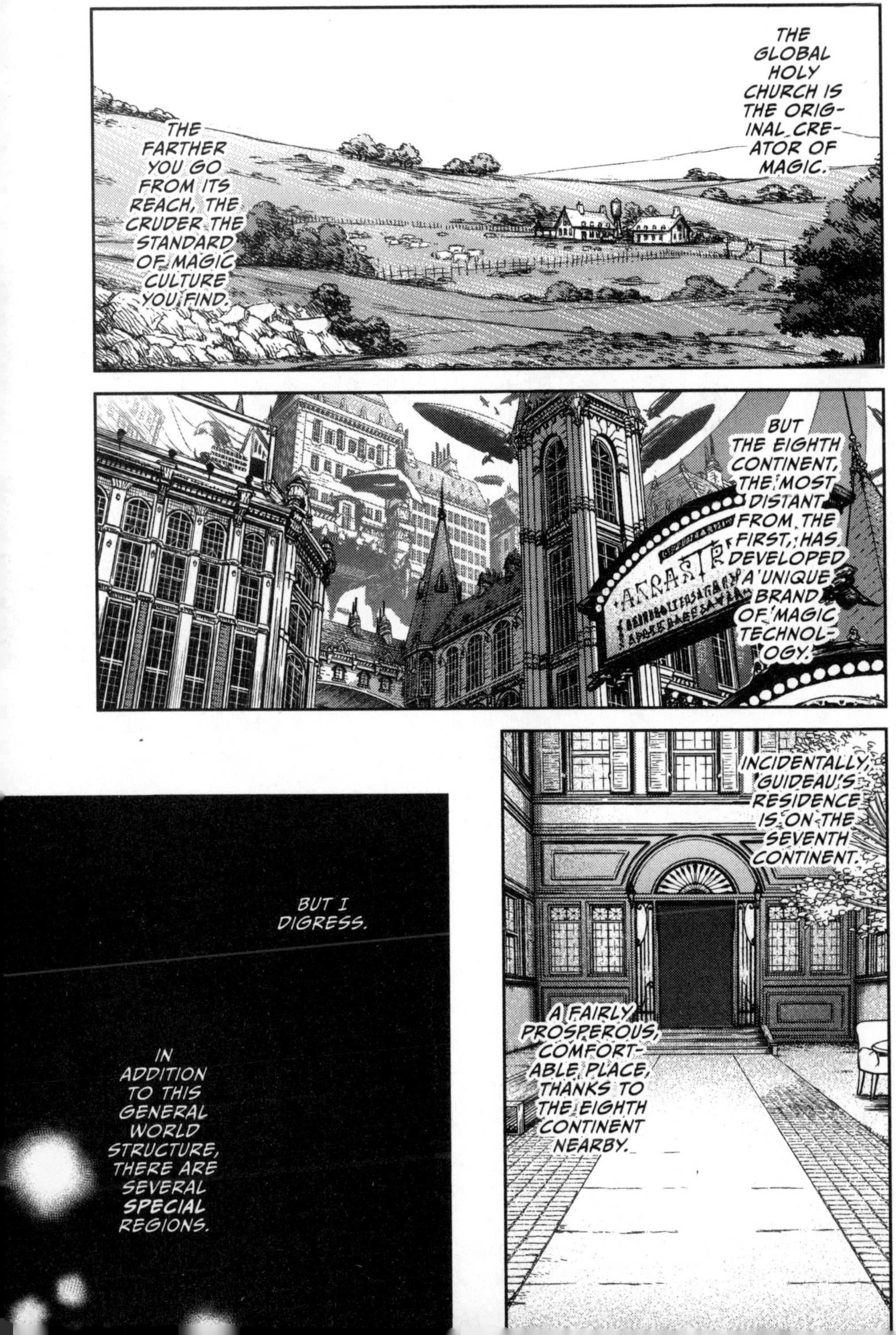
THE GLOBAL HOLY CHURCH IS THE ORIGINAL CREATOR OF MAGIC.
THE FARTHER YOU GO FROM ITS REACH, THE CRUDER THE STANDARD OF MAGIC CULTURE YOU FIND.
BUT THE EIGHTH CONTINENT, THE MOST DISTANT FROM THE FIRST, HAS DEVELOPED A UNIQUE BRAND OF MAGIC TECHNOLOGY.
INCIDENTALLY, GUIDEAU'S RESIDENCE IS ON THE SEVENTH CONTINENT.
A FAIRLY PROSPEROUS, COMFORTABLE PLACE, THANKS TO THE EIGHTH CONTINENT NEARBY.
BUT I DIGRESS.
IN ADDITION TO THIS GENERAL WORLD STRUCTURE, THERE ARE SEVERAL **SPECIAL** REGIONS.

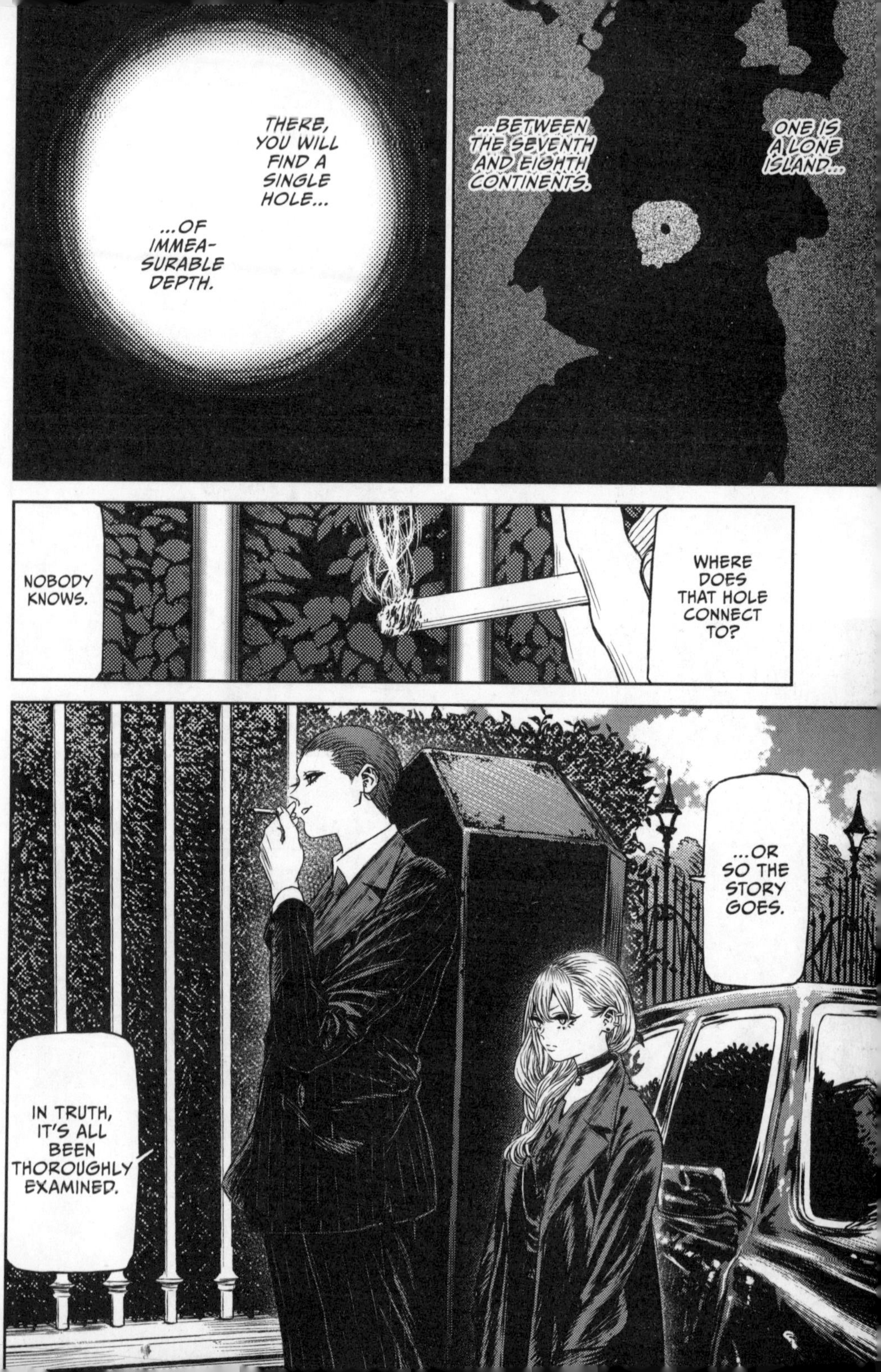
ONE IS A LONE ISLAND...
...BETWEEN THE SEVENTH AND EIGHTH CONTINENTS.
THERE, YOU WILL FIND A SINGLE HOLE...
...OF IMMEASURABLE DEPTH.
WHERE DOES THAT HOLE CONNECT TO?
NOBODY KNOWS.
...OR SO THE STORY GOES.
IN TRUTH, IT'S ALL BEEN THOROUGHLY EXAMINED.

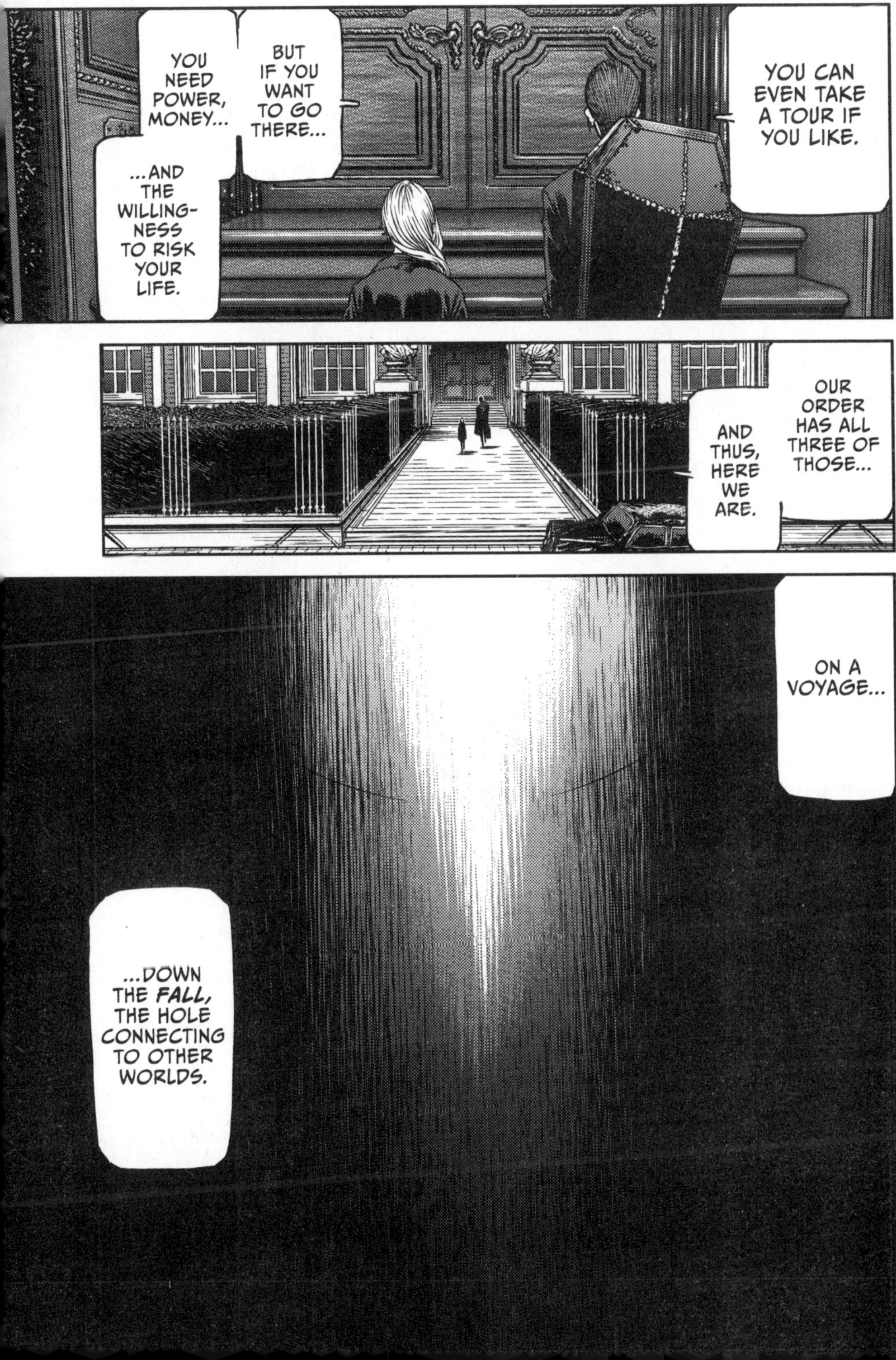
YOU CAN EVEN TAKE A TOUR IF YOU LIKE.
BUT IF YOU WANT TO GO THERE...
YOU NEED POWER, MONEY...
...AND THE WILLINGNESS TO RISK YOUR LIFE.
OUR ORDER HAS ALL THREE OF THOSE...
AND THUS, HERE WE ARE.
ON A VOYAGE...
...DOWN THE *FALL,* THE HOLE CONNECTING TO OTHER WORLDS.

...ASHAF, SIR.

THANK YOU VERY MUCH FOR COMING...

PLEASE PROCEED THROUGH THE RIGHT-HAND DOOR.

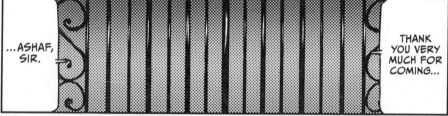

CREAK...

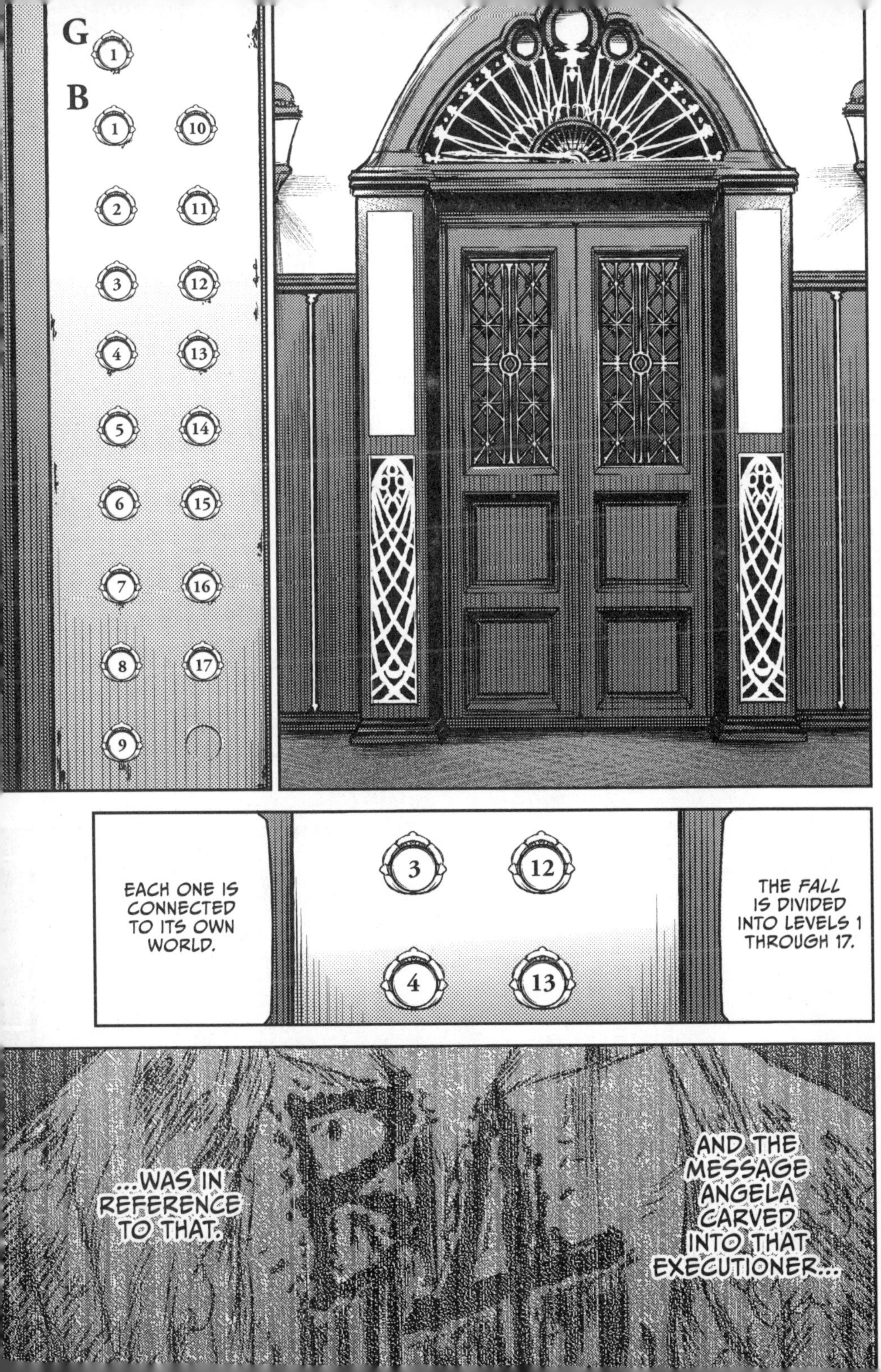
G
1
B
1 10
2 11
3 12
4 13
5 14
6 15
7 16
8 17
9
THE *FALL* IS DIVIDED INTO LEVELS 1 THROUGH 17.
3 12
4 13
EACH ONE IS CONNECTED TO ITS OWN WORLD.
AND THE MESSAGE ANGELA CARVED INTO THAT EXECUTIONER...
...WAS IN REFERENCE TO THAT.

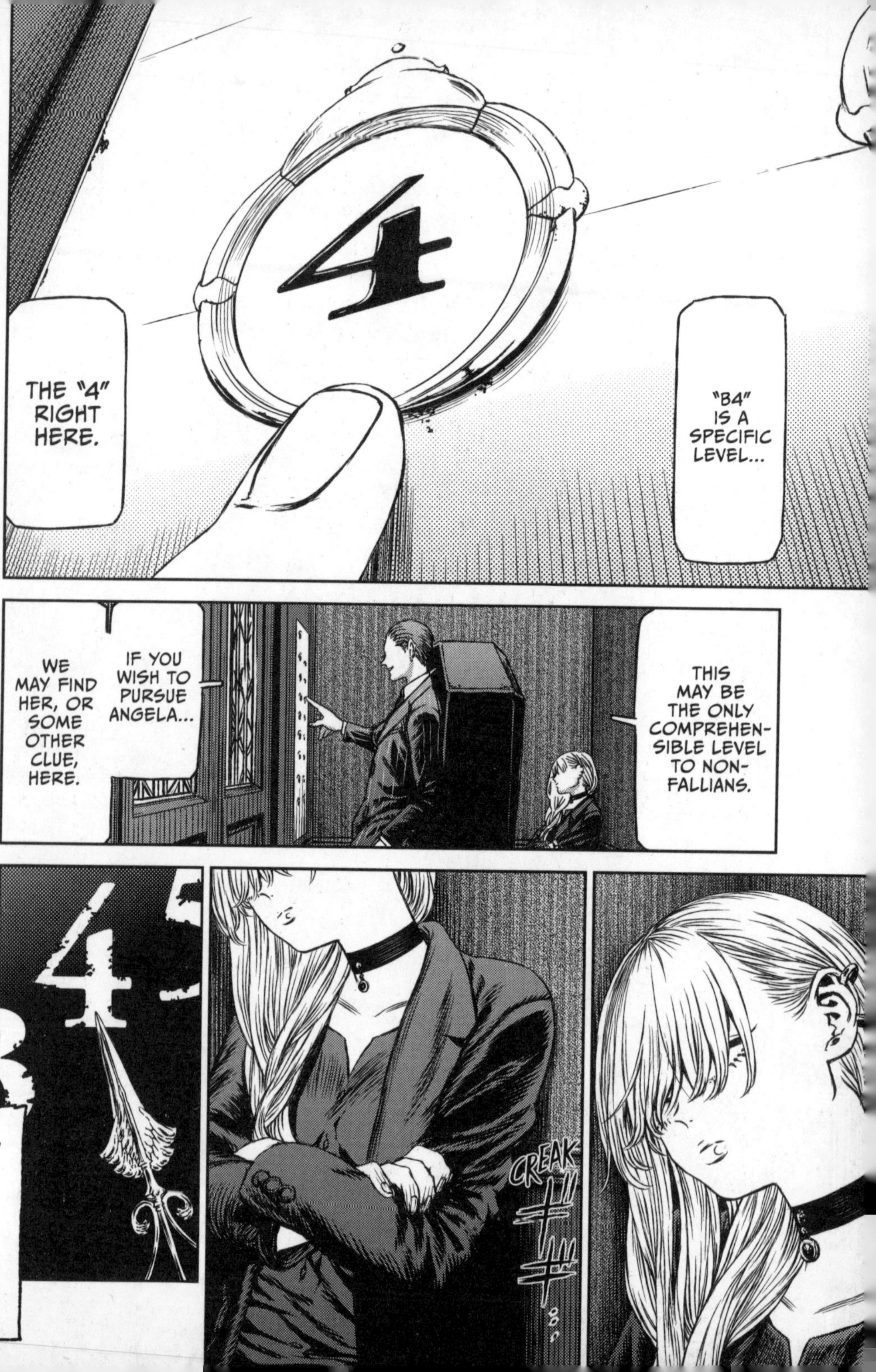
"B4" IS A SPECIFIC LEVEL...
THE "4" RIGHT HERE.
THIS MAY BE THE ONLY COMPREHEN-SIBLE LEVEL TO NON-FALLIANS.
IF YOU WISH TO PURSUE ANGELA...
WE MAY FIND HER, OR SOME OTHER CLUE, HERE.
CREAK
DIIIING

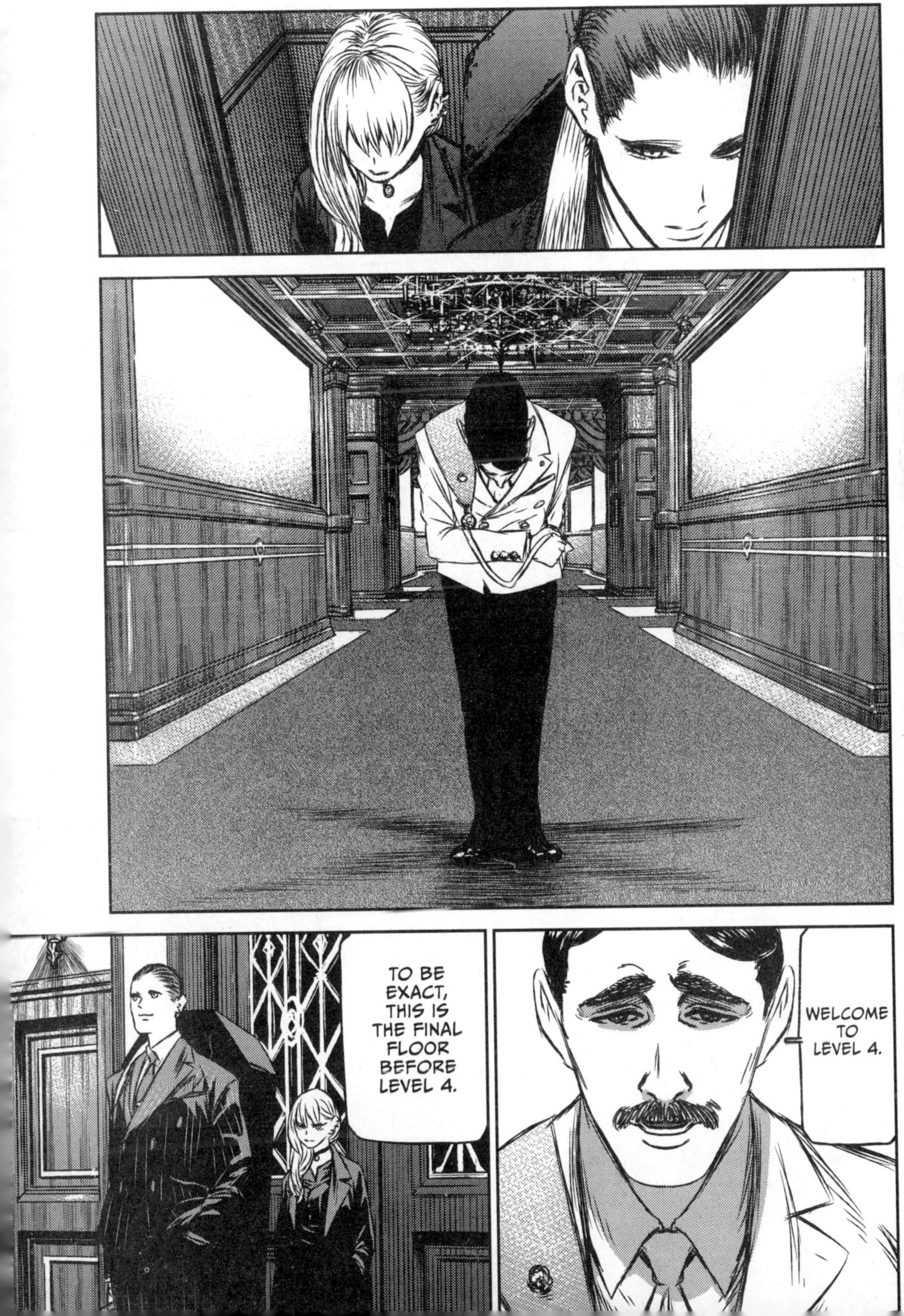
WELCOME TO LEVEL 4.
TO BE EXACT, THIS IS THE FINAL FLOOR BEFORE LEVEL 4.

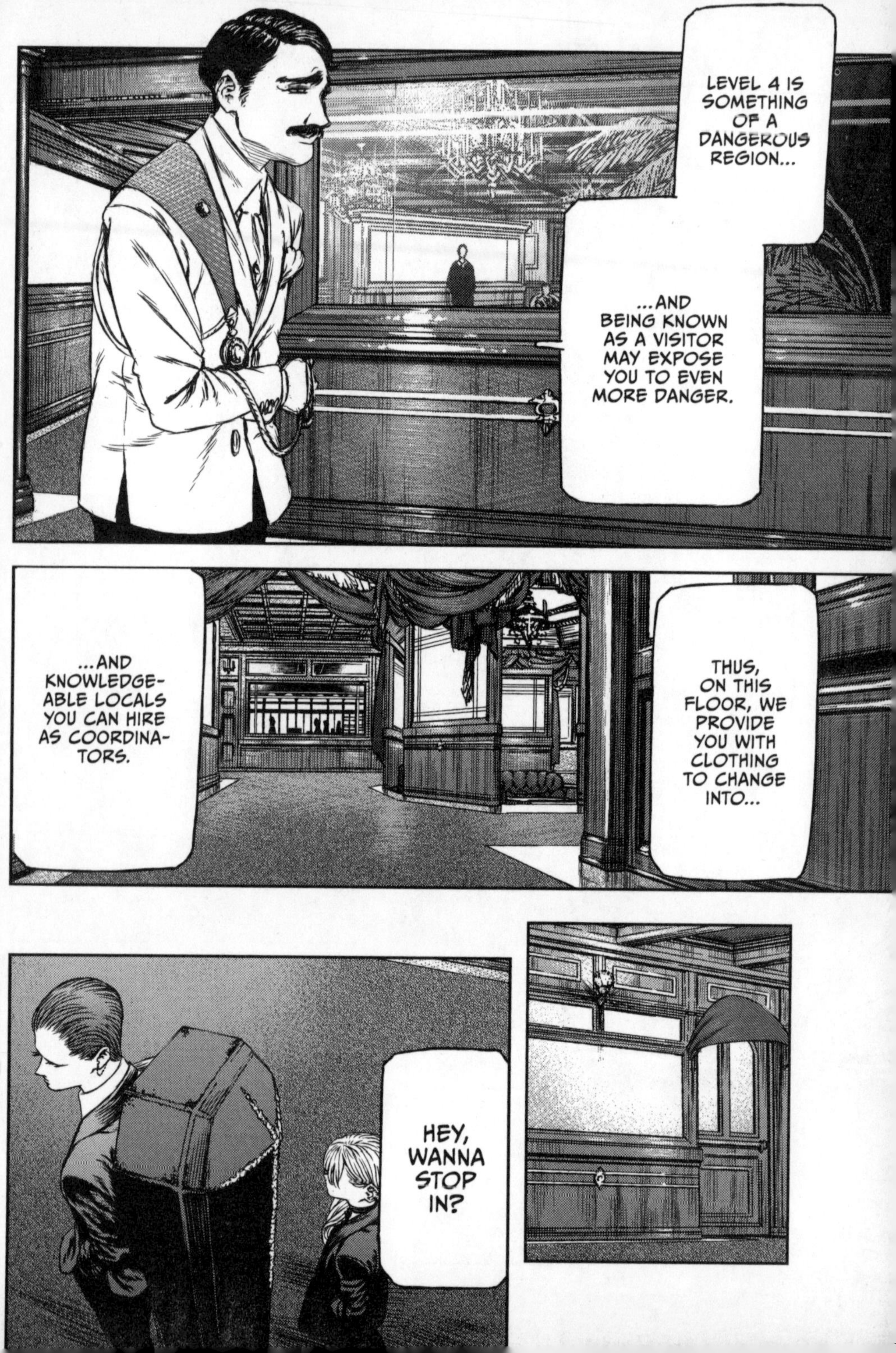
LEVEL 4 IS SOMETHING OF A DANGEROUS REGION...
...AND BEING KNOWN AS A VISITOR MAY EXPOSE YOU TO EVEN MORE DANGER.
THUS, ON THIS FLOOR, WE PROVIDE YOU WITH CLOTHING TO CHANGE INTO...
...AND KNOWLEDGE-ABLE LOCALS YOU CAN HIRE AS COORDINA-TORS.
HEY, WANNA STOP IN?

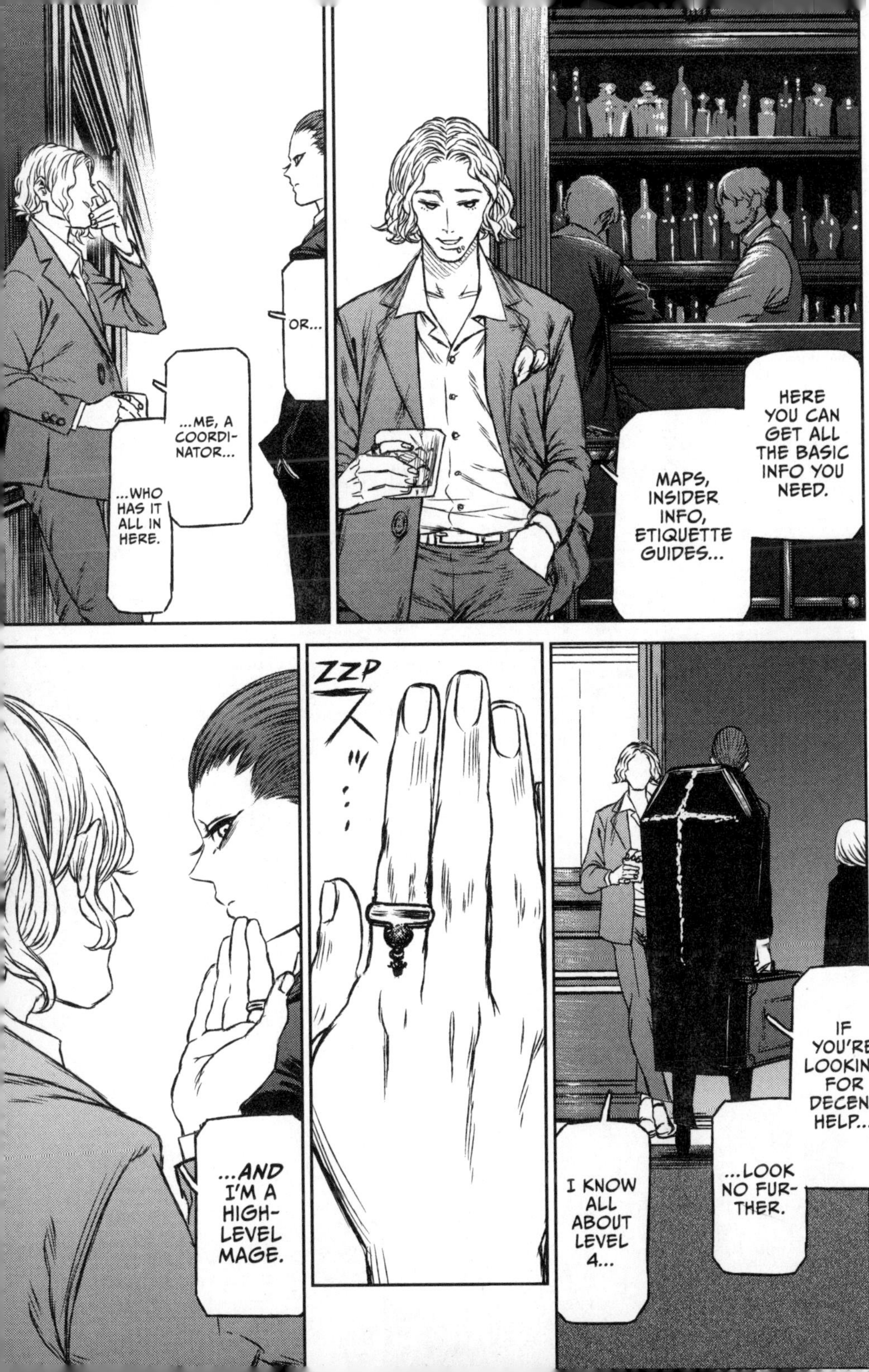
HERE YOU CAN GET ALL THE BASIC INFO YOU NEED.
MAPS, INSIDER INFO, ETIQUETTE GUIDES...
OR...
...ME, A COORDINATOR...
...WHO HAS IT ALL IN HERE.
IF YOU'RE LOOKING FOR DECENT HELP...
...LOOK NO FURTHER.
I KNOW ALL ABOUT LEVEL 4...
ZZP
...AND I'M A HIGH-LEVEL MAGE.

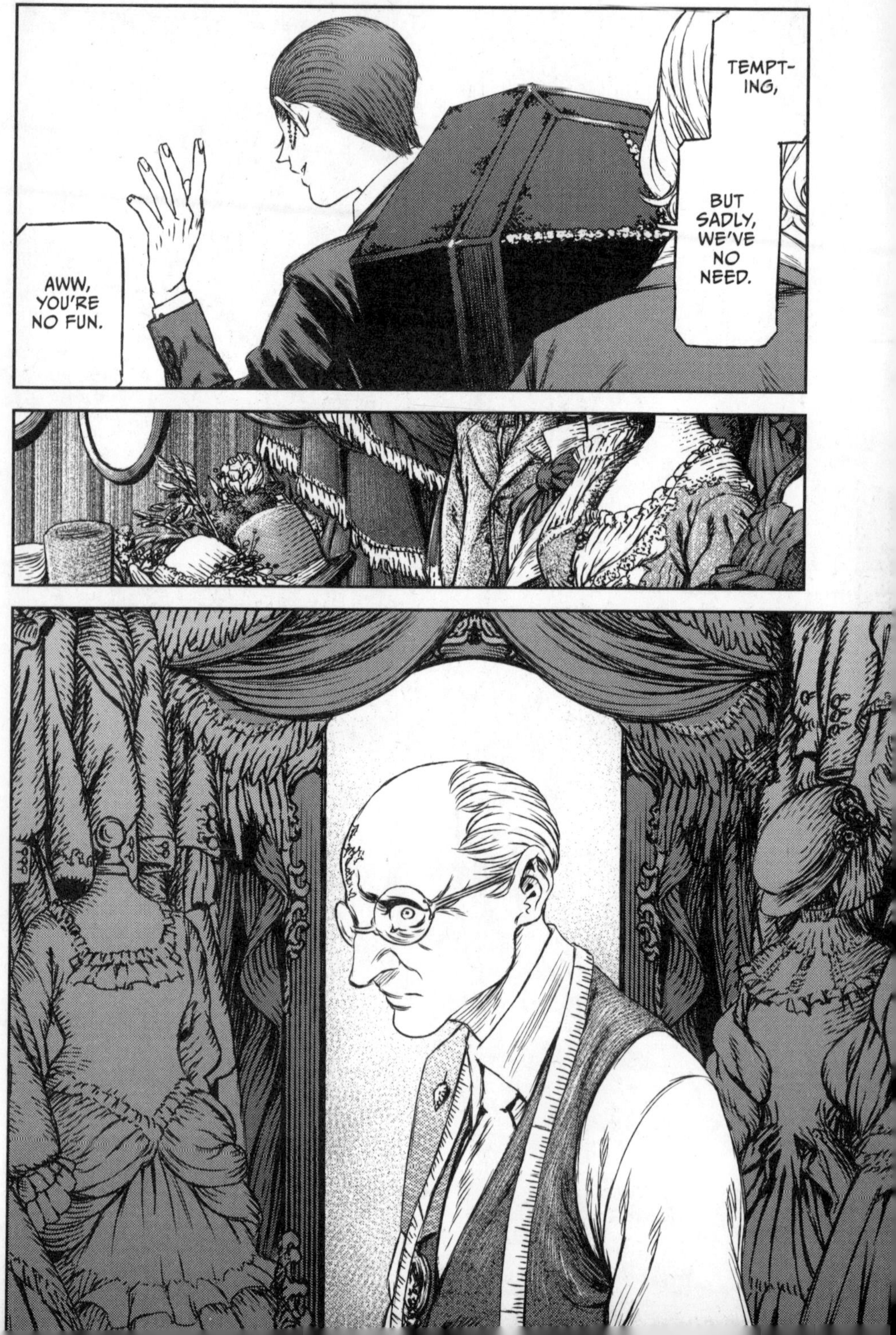
TEMPT-ING,
BUT SADLY, WE'VE NO NEED.
AWW, YOU'RE NO FUN.

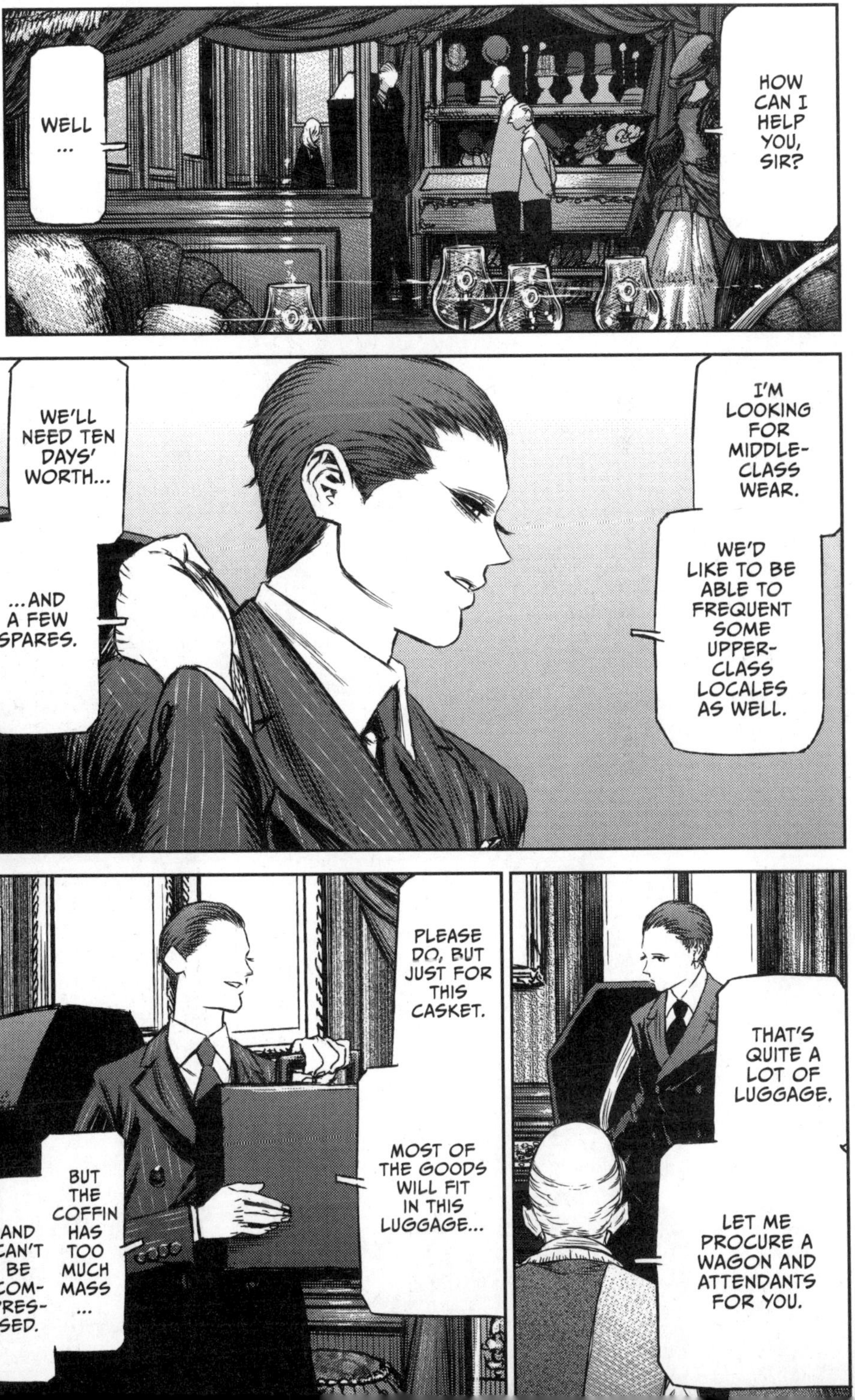
HOW CAN I HELP YOU, SIR?
WELL ...
I'M LOOKING FOR MIDDLE-CLASS WEAR.
WE'D LIKE TO BE ABLE TO FREQUENT SOME UPPER-CLASS LOCALES AS WELL.
WE'LL NEED TEN DAYS' WORTH...
...AND A FEW SPARES.
THAT'S QUITE A LOT OF LUGGAGE.
LET ME PROCURE A WAGON AND ATTENDANTS FOR YOU.
PLEASE DO, BUT JUST FOR THIS CASKET.
MOST OF THE GOODS WILL FIT IN THIS LUGGAGE...
BUT THE COFFIN HAS TOO MUCH MASS ...
AND CAN'T BE COM-PRES-SED.

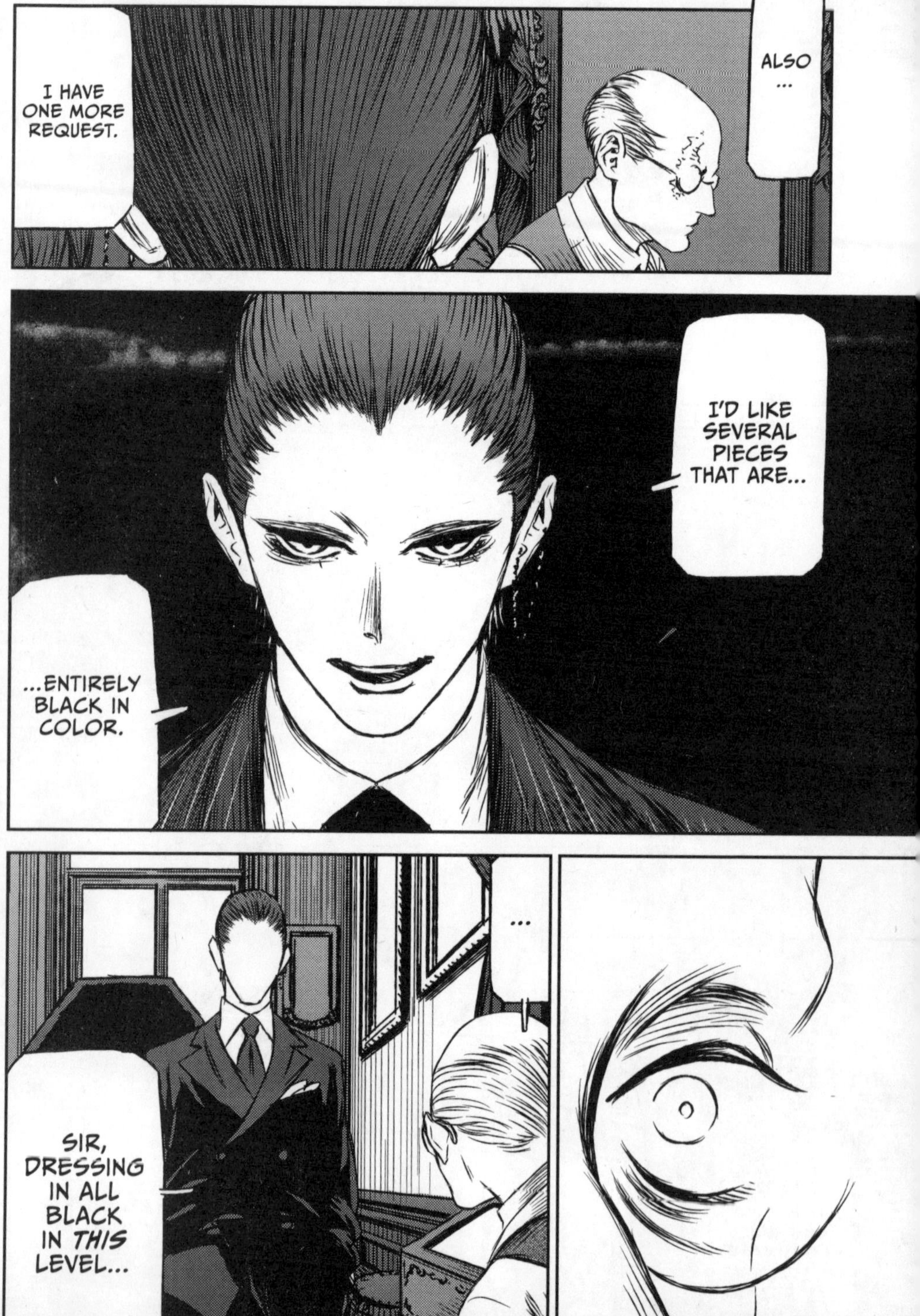
ALSO ...
I HAVE ONE MORE REQUEST.
I'D LIKE SEVERAL PIECES THAT ARE...
...ENTIRELY BLACK IN COLOR.
...
SIR, DRESSING IN ALL BLACK IN *THIS* LEVEL...

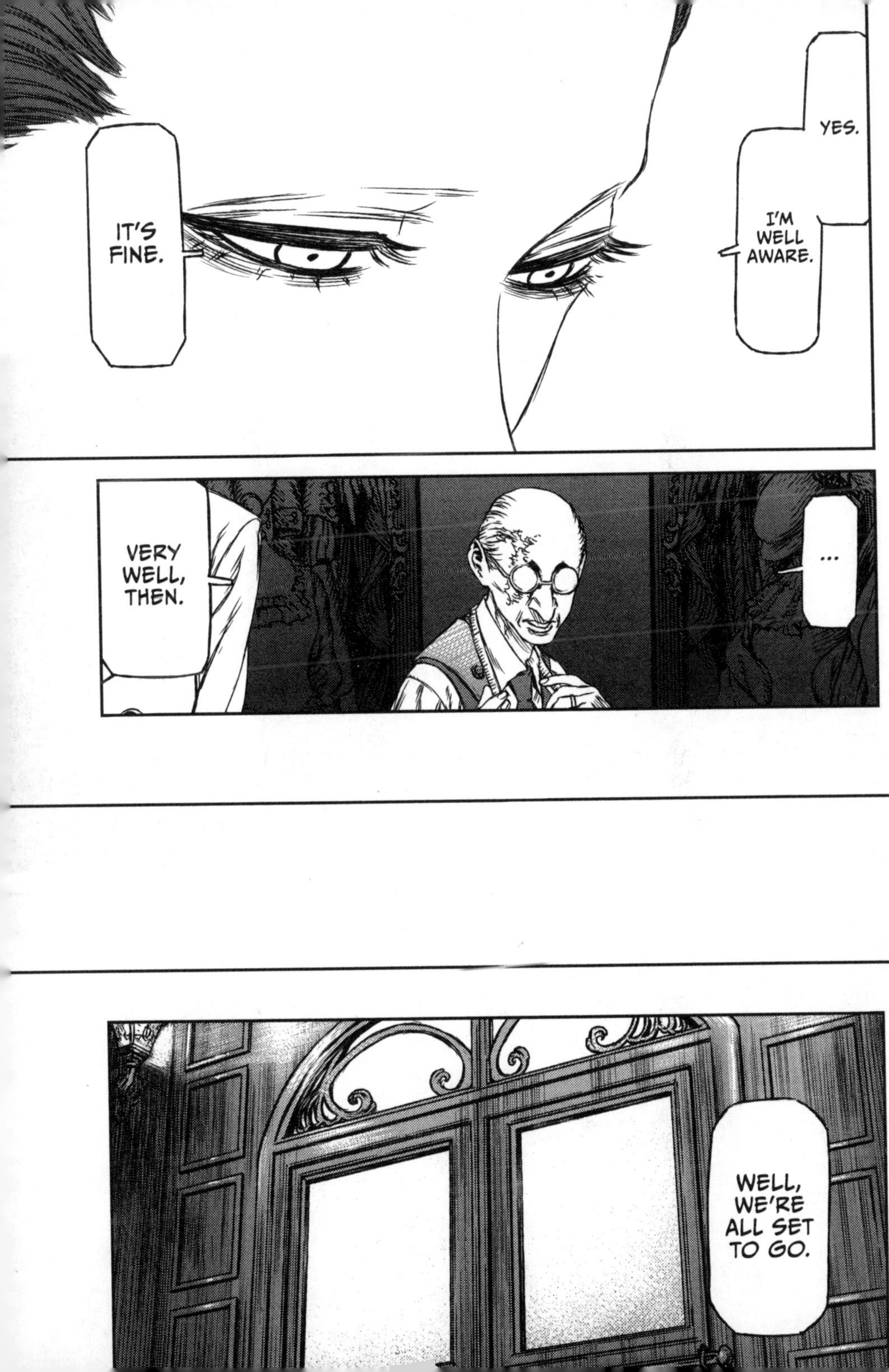
YES.
I'M WELL AWARE.
IT'S FINE.
...
VERY WELL, THEN.
WELL, WE'RE ALL SET TO GO.

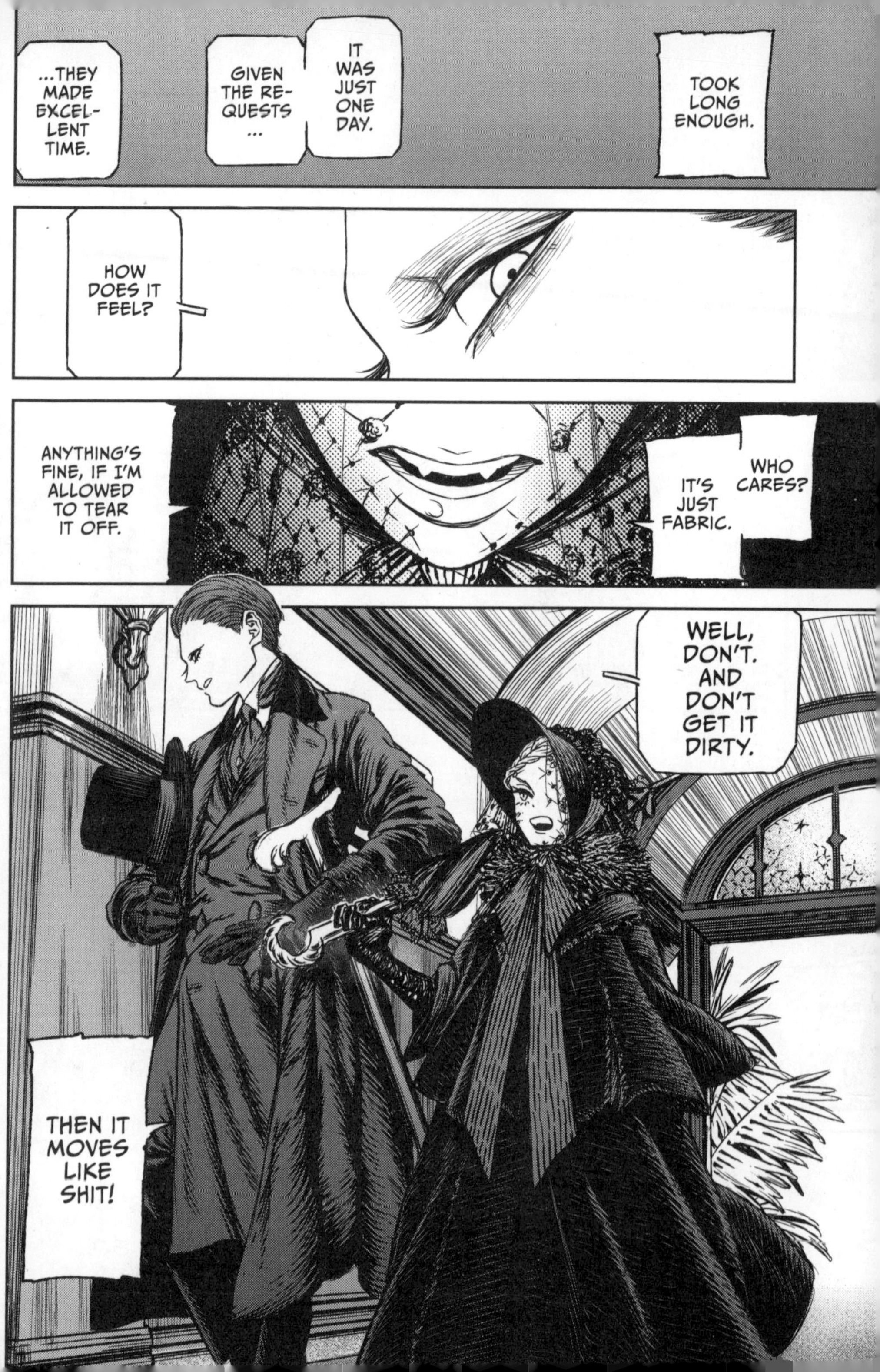
TOOK LONG ENOUGH.
IT WAS JUST ONE DAY.
GIVEN THE REQUESTS ...
...THEY MADE EXCELLENT TIME.
HOW DOES IT FEEL?
WHO CARES?
IT'S JUST FABRIC.
ANYTHING'S FINE, IF I'M ALLOWED TO TEAR IT OFF.
WELL, DON'T. AND DON'T GET IT DIRTY.
THEN IT MOVES LIKE SHIT!

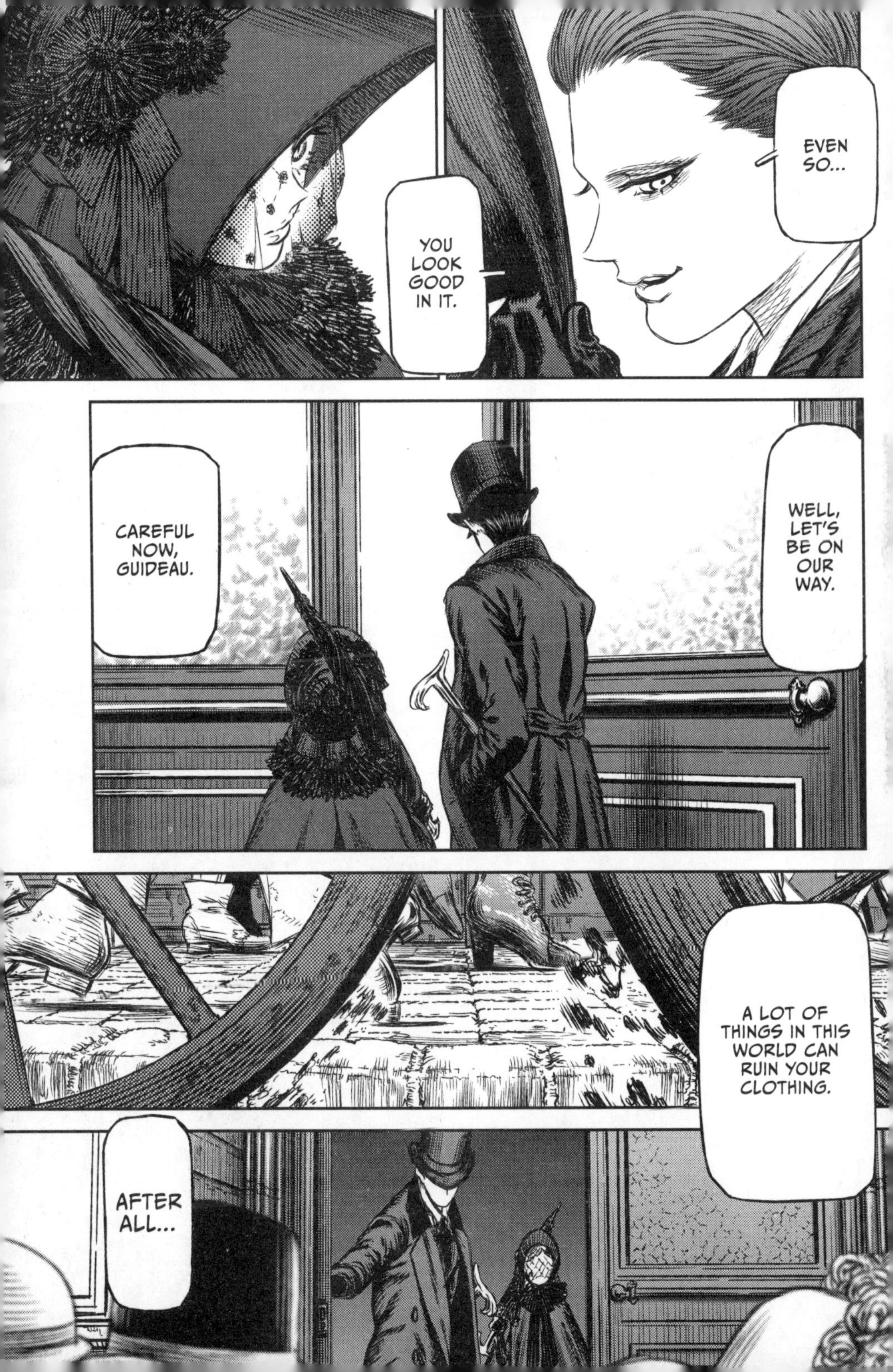
EVEN SO...
YOU LOOK GOOD IN IT.
WELL, LET'S BE ON OUR WAY.
CAREFUL NOW, GUIDEAU.
A LOT OF THINGS IN THIS WORLD CAN RUIN YOUR CLOTHING.
AFTER ALL...

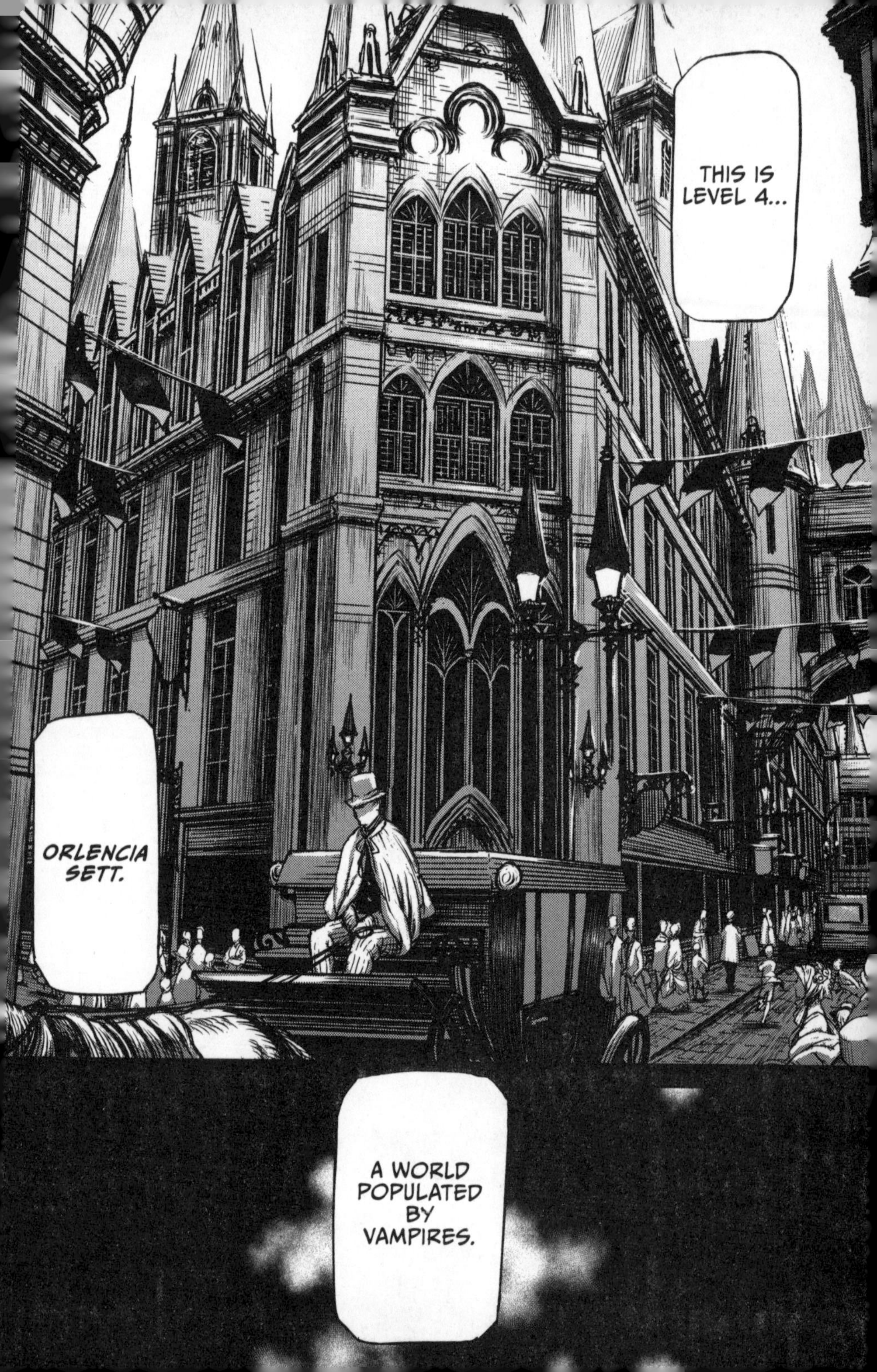
THIS IS LEVEL 4...
ORLENCIA SETT.
A WORLD POPULATED BY VAMPIRES.

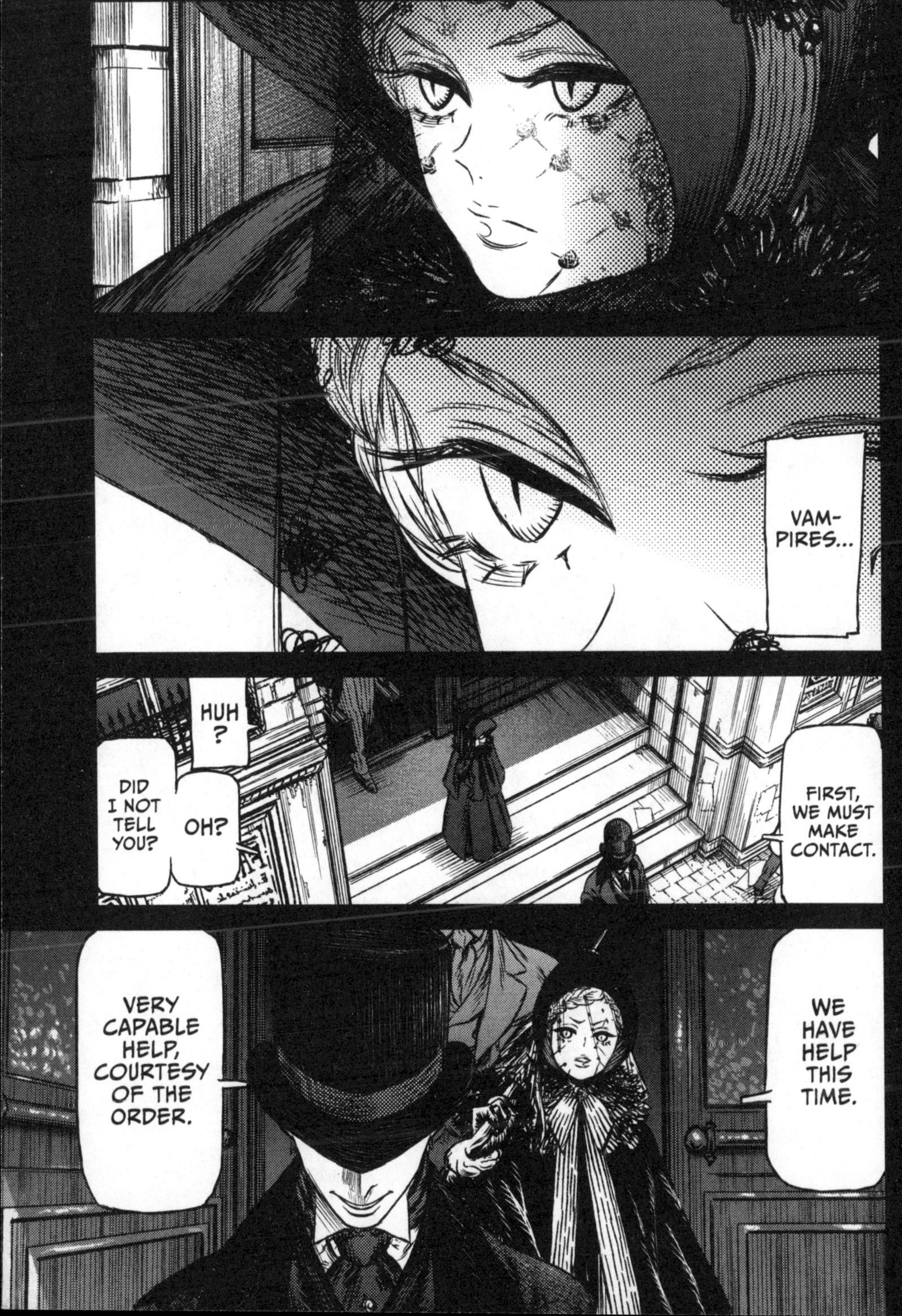
VAMPIRES...
FIRST, WE MUST MAKE CONTACT.
HUH?
OH?
DID I NOT TELL YOU?
WE HAVE HELP THIS TIME.
VERY CAPABLE HELP, COURTESY OF THE ORDER.

THE WITCH AND THE BEAST

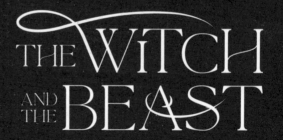

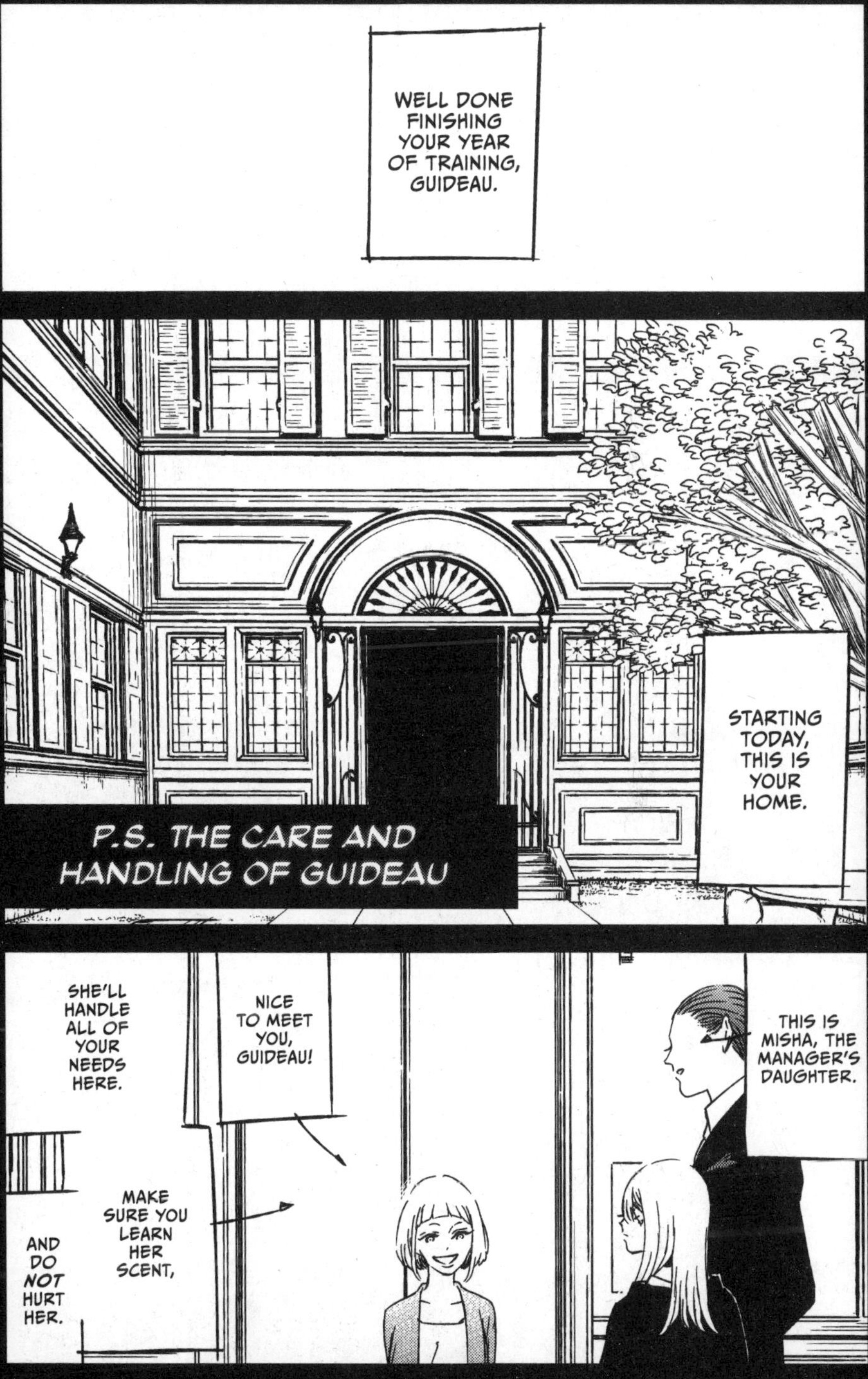
WELL DONE FINISHING YOUR YEAR OF TRAINING, GUIDEAU.
STARTING TODAY, THIS IS YOUR HOME.
P.S. THE CARE AND HANDLING OF GUIDEAU
THIS IS MISHA, THE MANAGER'S DAUGHTER.
NICE TO MEET YOU, GUIDEAU!
SHE'LL HANDLE ALL OF YOUR NEEDS HERE.
MAKE SURE YOU LEARN HER SCENT,
AND DO *NOT* HURT HER.

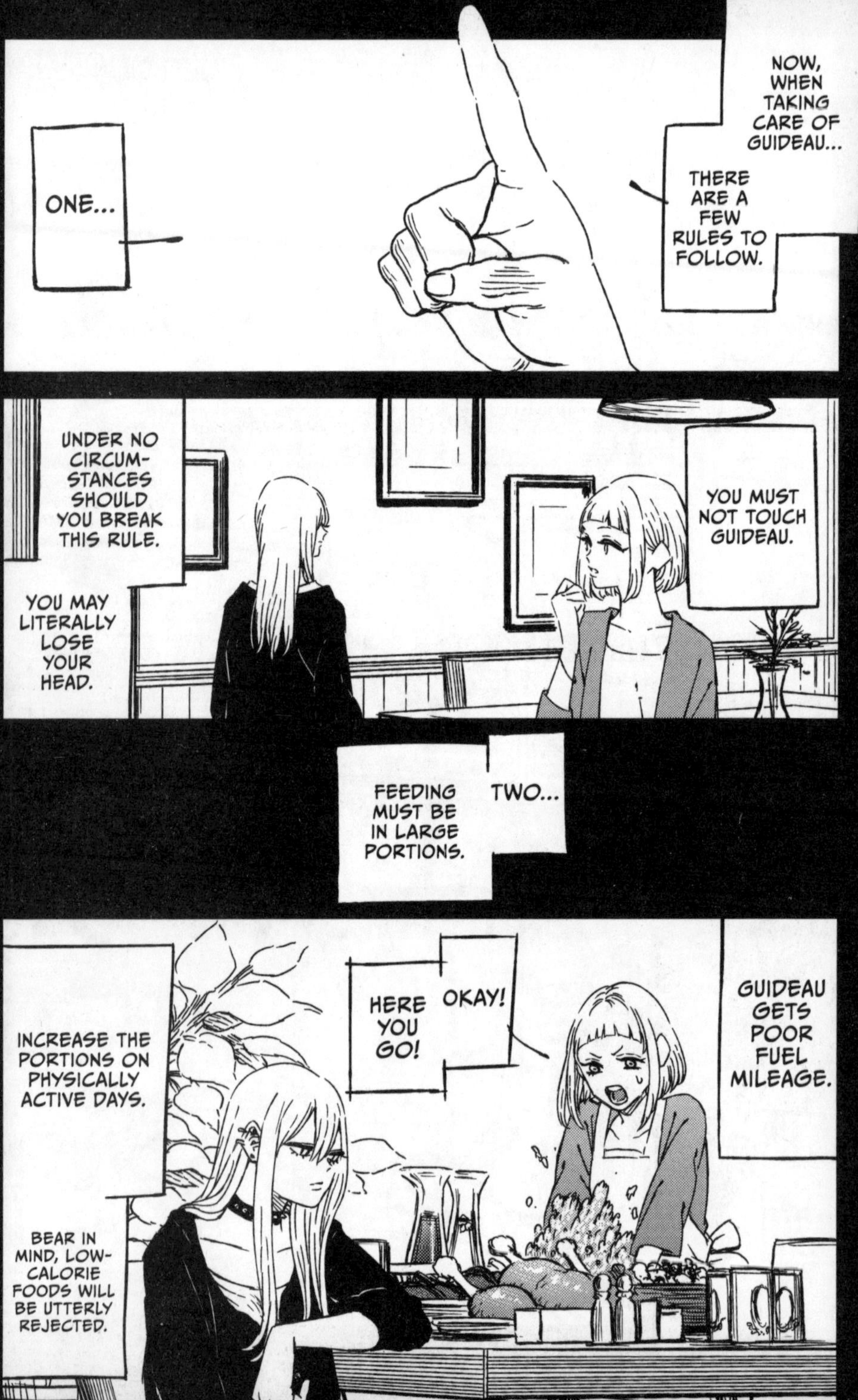
NOW, WHEN TAKING CARE OF GUIDEAU...
THERE ARE A FEW RULES TO FOLLOW.
ONE...
YOU MUST NOT TOUCH GUIDEAU.
UNDER NO CIRCUM-STANCES SHOULD YOU BREAK THIS RULE.
YOU MAY LITERALLY LOSE YOUR HEAD.
TWO...
FEEDING MUST BE IN LARGE PORTIONS.
GUIDEAU GETS POOR FUEL MILEAGE.
OKAY!
HERE YOU GO!
INCREASE THE PORTIONS ON PHYSICALLY ACTIVE DAYS.
BEAR IN MIND, LOW-CALORIE FOODS WILL BE UTTERLY REJECTED.

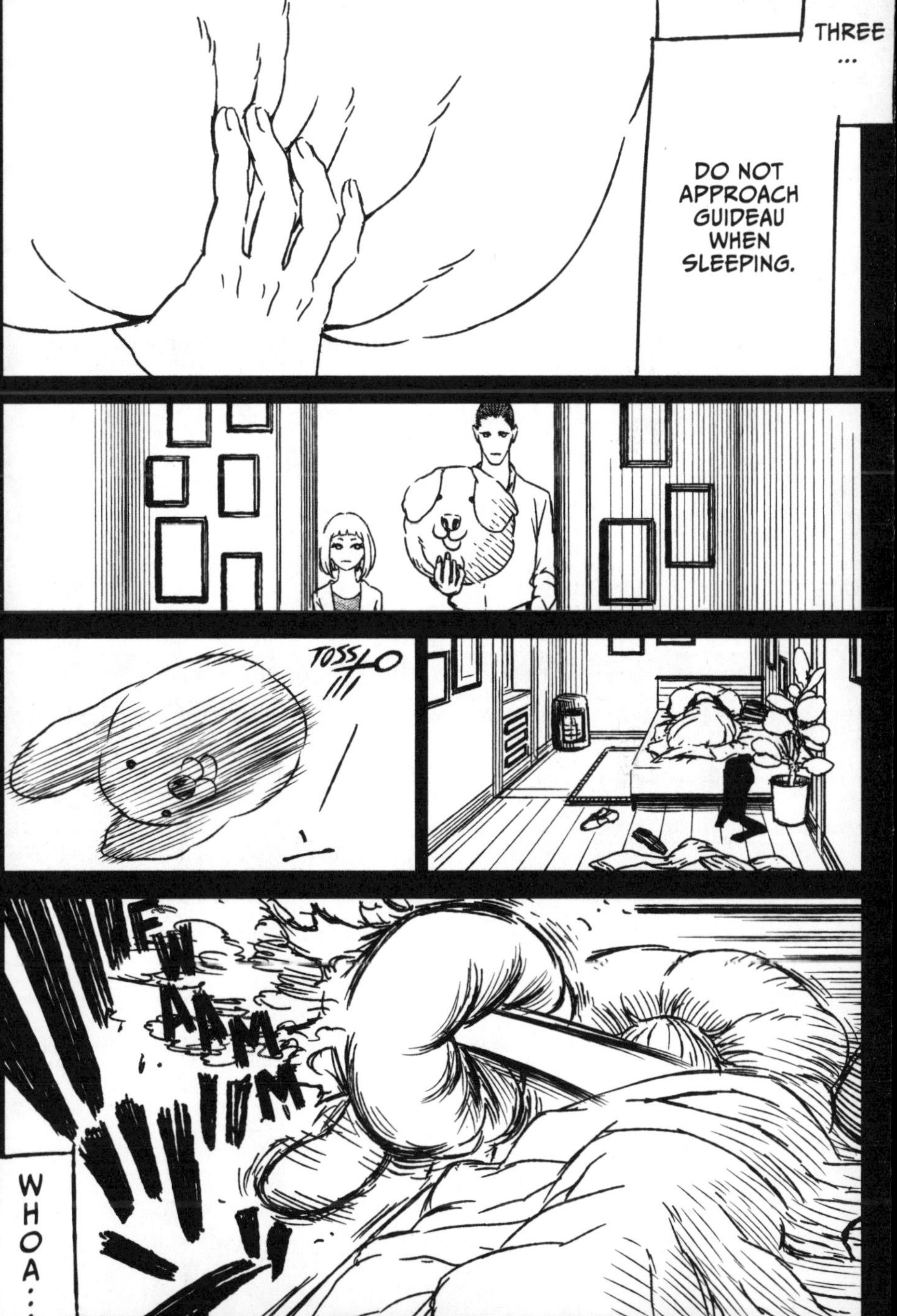
THREE ...
DO NOT APPROACH GUIDEAU WHEN SLEEPING.
TOSS
FWAAMMM
WHOA...

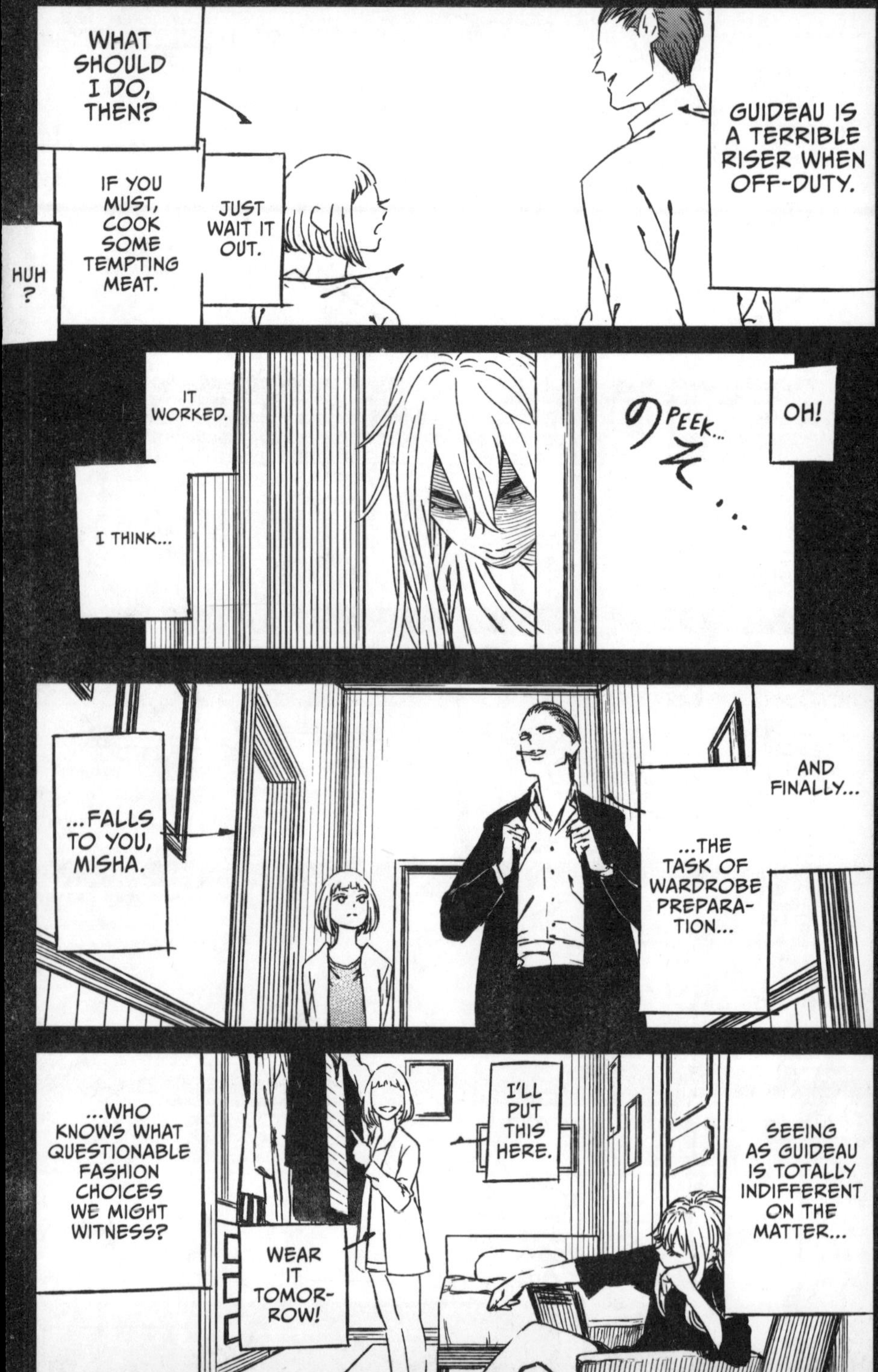
GUIDEAU IS A TERRIBLE RISER WHEN OFF-DUTY.
WHAT SHOULD I DO, THEN?
JUST WAIT IT OUT.
IF YOU MUST, COOK SOME TEMPTING MEAT.
HUH?
OH!
PEEK...
IT WORKED.
I THINK...
AND FINALLY...
...THE TASK OF WARDROBE PREPARATION...
...FALLS TO YOU, MISHA.
SEEING AS GUIDEAU IS TOTALLY INDIFFERENT ON THE MATTER...
I'LL PUT THIS HERE.
...WHO KNOWS WHAT QUESTIONABLE FASHION CHOICES WE MIGHT WITNESS?
WEAR IT TOMORROW!

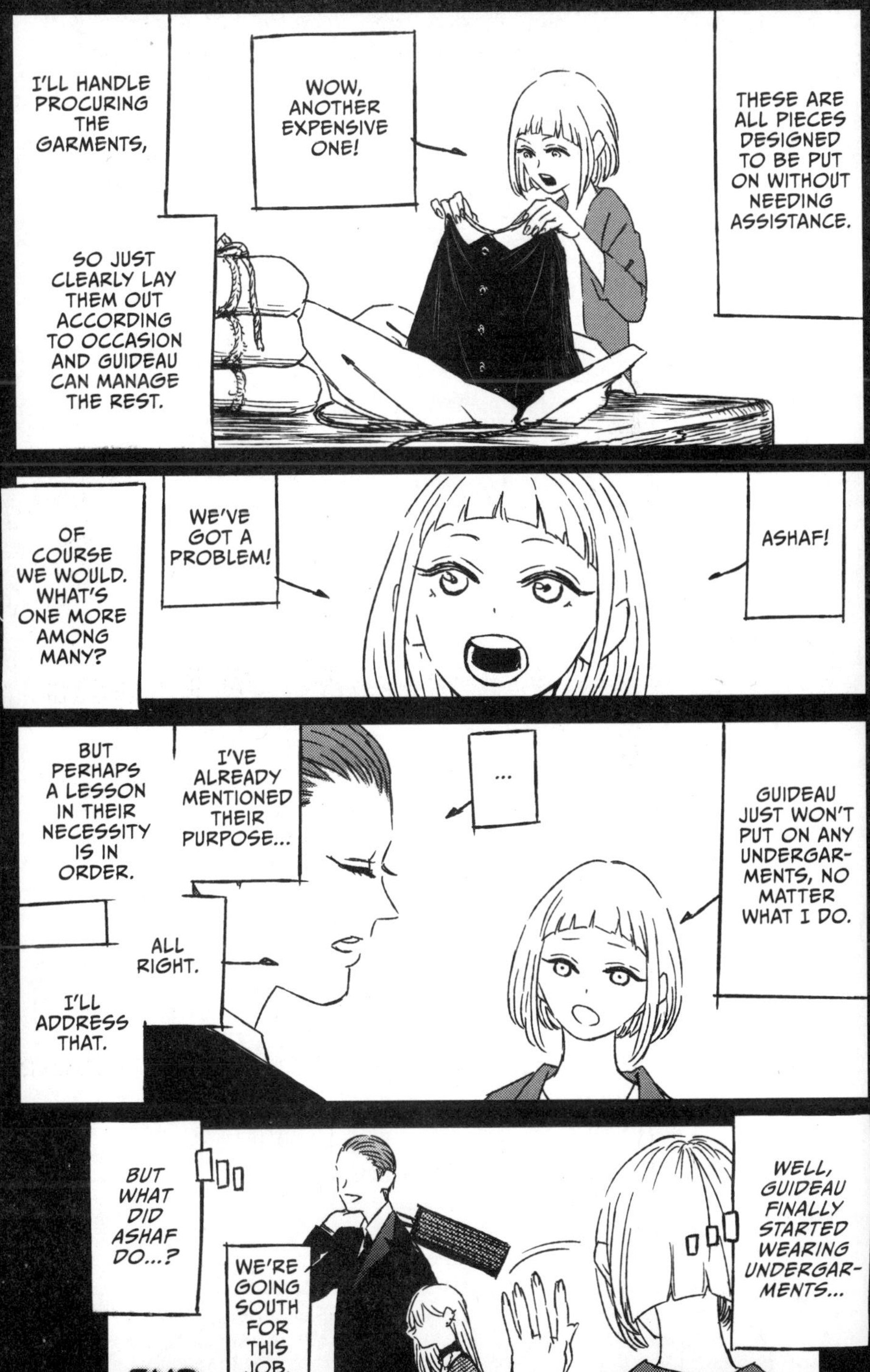
THESE ARE ALL PIECES DESIGNED TO BE PUT ON WITHOUT NEEDING ASSISTANCE.
WOW, ANOTHER EXPENSIVE ONE!
I'LL HANDLE PROCURING THE GARMENTS,
SO JUST CLEARLY LAY THEM OUT ACCORDING TO OCCASION AND GUIDEAU CAN MANAGE THE REST.
ASHAF!
WE'VE GOT A PROBLEM!
OF COURSE WE WOULD. WHAT'S ONE MORE AMONG MANY?
GUIDEAU JUST WON'T PUT ON ANY UNDERGAR-MENTS, NO MATTER WHAT I DO.
...
I'VE ALREADY MENTIONED THEIR PURPOSE...
BUT PERHAPS A LESSON IN THEIR NECESSITY IS IN ORDER.
ALL RIGHT.
I'LL ADDRESS THAT.
WELL, GUIDEAU FINALLY STARTED WEARING UNDERGAR-MENTS...
WE'RE GOING SOUTH FOR THIS JOB.
BUT WHAT DID ASHAF DO...?
END

A Kodansha Comics Trade Paperback Original
The Witch and the Beast 5 copyright © 2019 Kousuke Satake
English translation copyright © 2021 Kousuke Satake

Published in the United States by Kodansha Comics, an imprint of
Kodansha USA Publishing, LLC, New York.

Publication rights for this English edition arranged through
Kodansha Ltd., Tokyo.

First published in Japan in 2019 by Kodansha Ltd., Tokyo
as *Majo to yaju*, volume 5.

ISBN 978-1-64651-171-6

Original cover design by Yusuke Kurachi (Astrorb)

Printed in the United States of America.

www.kodanshacomics.com

9 8 7 6 5 4 3 2 1
Translation: Kevin Gifford
Lettering: Phil Christie
Editing: Vanessa Tenazas
Kodansha Comics edition cover design by My Truong

Publisher: Kiichiro Sugawara

Director of publishing services: Ben Applegate
Associate director of operations: Stephen Pakula
Publishing services managing editors: Alanna Ruse, Madison Salters
Assistant production managers: Emi Lotto, Angela Zurlo
Logo and character art ©Kodansha USA Publishing, LLC